LITERATURE OF

Africa

TRADITIONS IN WORLD LITERATURE

National Textbook Company
a division of NTC/CONTEMPORARY PUBLISHING GROUP
Lincolnwood, Illinois USA

Cover Illustration: Workman's Head, The Gareavi
Hermitage Museum, St. Petersburg, Russia
Leonid Bogdanov/SuperStock

ISBN (student edition): 0-8442-1201-6 (hardbound); 0-8442-1202-4 (softbound)
ISBN (teacher's edition): 0-8442-1328-4 (softbound)

Acknowledgments begin on page 279, which is to be considered an extension of this copy-right page.

Published by National Textbook Company,
a division of NTC/Contemporary Publishing Group, Inc.
4255 West Touhy Avenue,
Lincolnwood (Chicago), Illinois 60646-1975 U.S.A.
© 1999 NTC/Contemporary Publishing Group, Inc.

Library of Congress Cataloging-in-Publication Data

Literature of Africa.
    p. <tk> cm. <23> (Traditions in World Literature)
    Includes index.
    Summary: Presents writings from Ghana, Nigeria, Senegal, South Africa, and other
parts of Africa, with biographical information about the authors, discussion questions,
and writing prompts.
    ISBN 0-8442-1201-6 (hardbound). — ISBN 0-8442-1202-4 (softbound). —
ISBN 0-8442-1328-4 (teacher's edition)
    1. African literature —Translations into English. 2. African literature (English)
[1. African literature—Translations into English. 2. African Literature (English)
3. African literature—Translations into English—Collections. 4. African literature
(English)—collections.] I. Black African voices. II. Series.
PL8013.E5L57 1999
808.8'9896—dc21   98-31285
                                                                         CIP
                                                                          AC

90 QB 0987654321

Contents

INTRODUCTION

AFRICA OF MY GRANDMOTHER'S SINGING: CURVING RHYTHMS

Wilfred G. O. Cartey

We cannot pigeonhole the voices of the black continent of Africa, voices which recall the past, pulsate with the present, and are tremulous with the future. Mabel Segun of Nigeria wonders:

> . . . which part of me will be supreme—
> the old and tested one, the present
> or the future unknown.
> Sometimes all three have equal power
> and then
> how I long for a pigeon-hole.[1]

And like her, we may want to pigeonhole the various voices which speak in this anthology, but we dare not. For how can we pigeonhole a gourd full of wisdom scattered all over the earth of Africa? Each person must take his own bit of wisdom from the earth of Africa, wisdom scattered generously by a folk hero, Anansi:

> "My son, you are right: but your words show to me that it is better for many people to have wisdom rather than one. . . ." So speaking, he opened the gourd and scattered the wisdom all over the ground so that he who may want it can gather what he will.

Wisdom comes from many voices: from the folk voices of Africa where reside the oral traditions of the Continent, and from the voices of those who speak to us now from Senegal and Nigeria, from Ghana and Sierra Leone in the west of the continent, from across the Sudan to Ethiopia in the east and down through Tanzania to South Africa at the southern end of the continent.

So let us accept the call of one of these voices, Léopold Sédar Senghor of Senegal:

---

1. The authors and selections from which the quotations in this essay are taken, together with the pages on which the quotations may be found, are listed at the end of the essay in the order in which they are mentioned.

Let the rhythmic silence cradle us.
Let us listen to its song, let us listen to the beat of our dark blood,
    let us listen
To the deep pulse of Africa beating in the midst of forgotten
    villages.

But the villages of Africa are not forgotten, for their pulse beat is so strong that both animate and inanimate things are vital. The whole landscape through which we travel in these selections is animated. The spirit world is alive and gives life to the living: The essential ontology of Africa linking and curving through ancestor and offspring, man and nature, beast and trees, sea and fires . . . nothing is dead, no voice is still:

Hear the fire's voice,
Hear the voice of water.
In the wind hear the sobbing of the trees,
It is our forefathers breathing.

The dead are not gone forever. . . .
They are in the rustling tree,
In the murmuring wood,
In the still water,
In the flowing water,
In the lonely place, in the crowd. . . .
They are in a woman's breast,
A child's crying, a glowing ember. . . .

An essential continuity is preserved between mother and child—the mother whose breast provides sustenance and the child through whom life flows. In African belief, the child is close to the ancestors: thus, in Abioseh Nicol's short story "Life Is Sweet at Kumansenu," it is the child Asi who can communicate with the spirit of her father or with the spirit of her father's father. So it is that sometimes the past and present and future merge and "sometimes all three have equal power."

In Efua Sutherland's play *Edufa*, Ampoma, fated to die, bridging past, present, and future, wails to her mother a lament for her children:

. . . Children! My children! If I could cross this water, I would pluck you back from the mountainside. . . . Children! . . . And . . . Mother . . . Mother.

Edufa, the son, will turn back to Kankam, his father, for solace:

If you see my father, call him back that I may weep on his shoulder.

And Abena, Edufa's sister, grieves for the child of Ama, for Ampoma's dying:

O child of Ama,
Child of Ama in the night
Is wandering,
Crying, "Mm-m-m-m,
How my mother's pondering."
O child of Ama,
Why is she wandering,
Why wandering,
Why wandering in the night
Like the dying?
Meewuo!

So the play of daughter-father, daughter-mother, of son-father, of the African child, unfolds before us in many of these selections.

Camara Laye tells us of his early childhood in Guinea, of totemic traditions, of his father's craft wisdom, and of his father's creative genius inspired by the guardian spirit of the little black snake. He tells too of his mother's careful nurturing and of his grandmother's pampering. From all of these he garners his wisdom. He also gathers his wisdom from oral tradition, from the folk tales.

Like Camara Laye's mother, concerned about her husband's largess and his wasting his powers in the creating of gold trinkets, the wife in an anonymous Ethiopian folk tale is equally concerned about her husband's squandering his powers on other women and not on her. As in so many of the folk tales and selections, where mediation, counseling, and judgment play a large part, the woman here turns to a mediator for advice. His counsel is sage and natural—the cat is wild, sweeten him.

At times the mediator's judgment elicits a chuckle and wry commentary from the plaintiffs and the bystanders:

> "Ah, how good it is!" they said to each other. "How did we ever get along before justice was given to us?"

For here, in the humorously told folk tale "Justice" the judge is not only blind but deaf. The anonymous "Talking Skull," "Talk," and "Anansi's Fishing Expedition" are all humorously told. In "Talking Skull" the humor is macabre; in "Talk" the humor stems from the natural animation of landscape and matter; yams talk, dogs talk, trees talk, branches talk, stones talk, fish traps talk, cloths talk, and rivers talk. Using an incremental repetition, this folk tale comes full circle with the final parody of a pompous chief:

> The chief listened to them patiently, but he couldn't refrain from scowling. . . . So the men went away, and the chief shook his head and mumbled to himself, "Nonsense like that upsets the community."
>
> "Fantastic, isn't it?" his stool said. "Imagine, a talking yam!"

However, even when parodied, the general counseling and mediation by elders—chiefs, witch doctors, judges—represents the lore in action serving as a basis for morality, a directive to behavior, a carrier of traditional wisdom.

But the essence of the folk tale is its easy narrative element, its story-telling, yarn-spinning quality which makes of disbelief belief and wonder. Many African writers attempt to capture the fluidity of traditional tales in their stories, adding, of course, their own personal stamp to their creation.

There is an easy lyrical note singing through Fagunwa's "Forest of the Lord" where

> "... The birds there speak with human voices and the animals buy and sell with each other. Many of the trees there have no roots, yet their wood is fresh and their leaves are glossy and green. A mouse in the Forest of the Lord is bigger than an ordinary bush-rat and a snail is bigger than a tortoise. Powerful sprites and grim hobgoblins are in league there and all sorts of bold snakes cast fear on hunters, for it is there that the chief snake of all the world lives, whose name is 'Angry Python.'"

Peopling his forest with snakes and animals and sprites, this Nigerian writer evokes a whole spirit world which can be charmed by the sound of an ancestral flute played by a brave man, father to the storyteller:

> My father ... took this flute and began to blow it and the sound of this flute filled the whole place. ... and the songs were echoed throughout the forest. Now this flute was sweeter than a king's flute and as the song of the flute was a lament it could not fail to enter the recesses of the sprite's brain. ... The little creature ... spoke, saying ... "I thank you for the lament which you sang, a song full of wisdom. ..."

The ancestral flute had charmed the forest; in Ghana the traditional drums boom out to pay homage to the spirit of the sea, the whale, in Blay's essay "Funeral of a Whale" when

> ... bound by tradition, the fishermen must bear the unhappy tidings to the ruler of the town. ... The state drums boom out the warning of great calamity. ... The funeral ceremony being declared open, the women like minstrels tell the story of the whale in parables. ... The young men keep order and play native instruments, while the old correct any departure from the traditional funeral procedure.

And a single drum roll also heralds another death when Stanley meets Mutesa: [2]

---

2. **Stanley meets Mutesa**: Henry Morton Stanley, an American journalist, led an expedition to the court of King Mutesa of Buganda, a region northwest of Lake Victoria, in 1875.

Only a few silent nods from aged faces
And one rumbling drum roll
To summon Mutesa's court to parley
For the country was not sure.

The gate of reeds is flung open,
There is silence . . .
The tall black king steps forward,
He towers over the thin bearded white man
Then grabbing his lean white hand
Manages to whisper
"Mtu mweupe karibu"
White man you are welcome.
The gate of polished reed closes behind them
And the West is let in.

Many conflicts ensued from the opening of that gate to the West. The many traditions questioned and abused, the many doubts aroused, the many allegiances shaken trouble Mabel Segun to identify the world, the culture to which she really belongs:

poised between two civilizations. . . .
I'm tired of hanging in the middle way—
but where can I go?

The encounter of these two civilizations brought not only tiredness but also death to the people of the African continent, to the people so fertile in humanity that Bernard Dadié of the Ivory Coast sings:

I would sing to you
You who hold heaven within reach. . . .
You who like to hear a woman laugh,
You who like to watch a child play,
You who like to offer your hand
To form a chain

Bullets still behead the roses
in the mornings of dreams.

And now, Rui Nogar's conscripted warrior, thinking of his love and of his child, dies fighting to regain his land from Stanley and the West:

He went there
Involuntarily
He went there
And the courage was not his own
And the hate was not his own. . . .

There was his wife
There were his children his mother a letter
There was so much
But all crumbled away
All
In the treacherous cackling
Of the grenades
With yellow beaks
And red tails . . .

Yet even though others flee their homeland, going into exile like Peter Abrahams to tell freedom, or are jailed in South Africa without raising a hand of protest, the song to the African earth continues. The song to the earth which nourishes its children is told in many lyric and epic passages, like this in Richard Rive's "African Song."

And then everyone was standing and Muti watched fascinatedly as the people sang. . . . And already this one was led away because he had no pass. . . . one must not lift the hand in protest. And still the people sang. . . . God bless Africa. God bless the sun-scorched Karoo and the green of the Valley of a Thousand Hills. . . . the mountain streams that chatter impudently. . . . the mighty waters that hurl themselves against her shores. . . . the cataracts that taunt the solemn rocks, and the African sky that spits blood in the evening. . . . the timeless hills. . . . this Africa of heat and cold, and laughter and tears, and deep joy and bitter sorrow . . . . this Africa of blue skies and brown veld. . . .

The earth of Africa, sung of in many of these selections, is reassuring, revitalizing its children, promising new beginnings. Lenrie Peters of Gambia sings in "Parachute":

As the warm earth
Reaches out to you,
Reassures you
The vibrating interim is over . . .
Earth has nowhere to go:
You are at the starting point . . .
We are always at the starting point.

And David Diop of Senegal accepts the message of these beginnings, hears the singing of the rebirth of his continent:

Africa of my grandmother's singing
Along the banks of her far-off river . . .
Africa tell me Africa
Is it you . . .

Then gravely a voice answered me:
Impetuous son, that young and robust tree
That tree over there
Splendidly alone midst white faded flowers
It is Africa your Africa that springs up again
Springs up patiently obstinately
And whose fruits ripen with
The bitter flavor of freedom.

Now Soyinka's appeal for rain

O it must rain
These closures on the mind, binding us
In strange despairs, teaching
Purity of sadness

no longer goes unanswered. Now the fertilizing rain pounds through the
land and the continent bringing rest and freedom, and Clark says:

So let us roll over on our back
And again roll to the beat
Of drumming all over the land
And under its ample soothing hand
Joined to that of the sea
We will settle to sleep of the innocent and free.

Now the splendid vision opens out, the vision of freedom, liberation and
the regrouping of black comrades. The vision extends beyond the shores
of Africa, outwards, to the Americas. And as before, time—past, present,
and future—merged, so too here, distant geographies where the black
man lives flow together. Diop can exhort:

For there rings out higher than my sorrows
Purer than the morning where the wild beast wakes
The cry of a hundred people smashing their cells
And my blood long held in exile
The blood they hoped to snare in a circle of words
Rediscovers the fervor that scatters the mists
Listen comrades of the struggling centuries
To the keen clamor of the Negro from Africa to the Americas
It is the sign of the dawn
The sign of brotherhood which comes to nourish the dreams of men.

And with the awakening, with the rediscovery, with the vigilant returning, with the shedding of the foreigner's suit, the comrades can

Walk in peace, walk alone, walk tall,
walk free, walk naked

as the Ethiopian poet Tsegaye Gabre-Medhin sings out:

Let the roots of your motherland caress your body,
Let the naked skin absorb the home-sun and shine ebony.

Passages Quoted in the Essay
Mabel Segun, "The Pigeon-Hole," page 211
Anonymous, "The Gourd Full of Wisdom," page 12
Léopold Sédar Senghor, "Night of Sine," page 215
Birago Diop, "Forefathers," page 65
Abioseh Nicol, "Life Is Sweet at Kumansenu," page 174
Efua T. Sutherland, *Edufa,* page 221
Anonymous, "Justice," page 15
Anonymous, "Talk," page 16
D. O. Fagunwa, *The Forest of the Lord,* page 109
J. Benibengor Blay, "Funeral of a Whale," page 48
James D. Rubadiri, "Stanley Meets Mutesa," page 208
Mabel Segun, "Conflict," page 211
Bernard Dadié, "Men of All Continents," page 55
Rui Nogar, "Poem of the Conscripted Warrior"
Richard Rive, "African Song," page 193
Lenrie Peters, "Parachute," page 191
David Diop, "Africa," page 67
Wole Soyinka, "I Think It Rains," page 218
J. P. Clark, "Night Rain," page 52
David Diop, "Listen Comrades," page 67
Tsegaye Gabre-Medhin, "Home-Coming Son," page 267

PROVERBS

The number of different languages spoken by the peoples of Africa is enormous—estimates have placed it as high as 800. Nearly all of these languages and their literatures remained unwritten until the arrival of missionaries and later, linguists who studied and recorded them in the orthography of the European languages. Much of this oral tradition is in the form of proverbs. They represent a large and ever-growing body of literature. A sampling of proverbs from different parts of the continent is given below. As a general rule in the pronunciation of African languages, most syllables are open, i.e., they end in a vowel or diphthong; vowels are pronounced much as in Italian, i.e., *a* as in f*a*ther, *e* as *ay* in d*ay*, *i* as in mach*i*ne, *o* as in g*o*, *u* as in r*u*le; consonants are pronounced much as in English. In some East African languages, like Kikuyu or Swahili, *m* and *n* appear as syllables in themselves, pronounced as if they were preceded by a schwa (an unstressed vowel sound like the *a* in *a*lone).

Gutiri muthenya ukiaga ta ungi. (No day dawns like another.)

Kikuyu (Kenya)

Jalele sainou ane na sainou guissetil dara, tey mague dieki thy soufe guissa yope. (The child looks everywhere and often sees nought; but the old man, sitting on the ground, sees everything.)

Wolof (Senegal)

Julu life lisekana ifoso. (Two tortoises laughing at each other's shell.)

Mongo (Zaire)

Mbaara ti ucuru. (War is not porridge.)

Kikuyu

Akundlovu yasindwa umboko wayo. (No elephant ever found its trunk too heavy.)

Zulu (South Africa)

Mmea se, "Wo ho ye fe," a, ene ka. (When the women say to you, "You are a handsome fellow," that means you are going to run into debt.)

Twi (Ghana)

Akamo ekun o ni iyonnu. (It is difficult to encompass a leopard.)

Yoruba (Nigeria)

Msitukane wakunga na uzazi ungalipo. (Do not abuse midwives while child-bearing continues.)

Swahili (Tanzania)

Kwa mwendwo gutiri irima. (On the way to one's beloved there are no hills.)

Kikuyu

Aya yo ni ijokan, o ni ki aka on li ehin okankan. (The monkey, having one day eaten to the full, desires that his fore-teeth may be drawn.)

Yoruba

Didime na yi bronni nansin adi. (A feast uncovers a European's wooden leg.)

Oji (Ghana)

Ba don tsawo a kan ga wata ba. (Not through height does one see the moon.)

Hausa (Nigeria)

NEGRITUDE

One of the major forces shaping African culture in the 20th century was the Negritude movement, through which African artists and intellectuals attempted to resist European dominance by asserting the primacy of African cultural values. Considered as a literary movement, Negritude had its beginning in Paris in 1934 with the founding of the journal *L'Étudiant Noir* ("The Black Student"). The group of young students that founded it included Léopold Sédar Senghor (p. 214) from Senegal, Léon Damas from French Guiana, and Aimé Césaire from the island of Martinique in the French West Indies. These young men argued for a reappraisal of African culture, with the aim of rediscovering and developing its authentic content. The proponents of Negritude stressed the immediacy and universality of their approach to African culture. Césaire understood Negritude to be "the simple recognition of the fact of being a Negro and the acceptance of its cultural and historical consequences." Senghor defined it as "the sum total of all the cultural values of Africa." The principal themes employed by these poets and those writers that followed them, like David Diop (p. 67) from Senegal, include the slave trade, colonialism, the feelings of the African exile for his home, the sufferings of black people everywhere in the world.

English-speaking African writers like James D. Rubadiri (p. 208) from Malawi and Ezekiel Mphahlele (p. 165) from South Africa have been sharply critical of Negritude, feeling that its result would be to cramp the creative spirit. While not embracing it wholeheartedly, other English-speaking writers like the Nigerians John Pepper Clark (p. 52), Wole Soyinka (p. 218), and Amos Tutuola (p. 271) have employed many of the themes and adopted many of the outlooks of the French-speaking poets of the Negritude school.

Literature of Africa

FOLK TALES

In many parts of Africa, the art of story-telling is still very much alive. Storytellers go from village to village telling tales that have been handed down in the oral tradition from ancient times. The stories they tell represent a wide and colorful variety of folk tales that embody the African people's most cherished religious and social beliefs. Nature and the close bond that Africans share with the natural world are high-lighted in these tales, and the relationship between elements in nature and the spiritual world is emphasized in them. The almost mystical impor-tance of the forest, sometimes called the bush, is often featured. Africans have used these tales for generations to entertain, to teach, and to explain.

The following sampling of folk tales is orga-nized in four groups. The first group is Origin sto-ries, including a creation story ("How the World Changed") and a story explaining the origin of death ("The Eye of the Giant"). The second group is the Trickster Tale, an enormously popular type of folk tale. The best known African trickster figure is Anansi the Spider, both the hero and villain of a huge body of folk tales that spread from their West African origin to the Caribbean and other parts of the Western Hemisphere as a result of the slave trade. Three spider stories ("Anansi's Fishing Expedition," "The Singing Cloak," and "The Gourd Full of Wisdom") are included here. The third group is Moral Stories, which attempt to teach a lesson. Three examples of this type ("How Hawk Learned of the Shallow Hearts of Men," "The Hunter Who Hunts No More," and "The Talking Skull") are included here. The last group is Humorous Stories ("Justice" and "Talk"), stories whose primary purpose is to amuse. These ten tales offer a small sample of the extraordinary richness and variety of the African folk tale tradition. ∎

ORIGIN STORIES

HOW THE WORLD CHANGED

Meleka (God) made the world and the moon and the sun. The sun shone all the time, for Meleka considered that constant light would benefit men and beasts. Therefore, there was no night. For every man there was a woman. There were no white or brown or yellow people, there was only a single race of noble and pure-black men. In those days men and animals were friends and wandered freely in the forest eating fruit and nuts and green foods. Caves and houses were not needed, for when a man or a beast was tired he simply lay down to sleep where he was. Men possessed no spears and animals had no claws.

Little children left their parents whenever they pleased, wandering for months and years in foreign places. This was a source of worry and grief to men and animals, for they loved their children well. Sometimes children wandered away and were never seen again. The mothers and fathers wept in sorrow and appealed to Meleka for aid.

Meleka then took away the sun. All the men and animals were alarmed as they could not understand what the darkness was. Families grouped together in defense against unknown terrors; children roaming far away called pitifully for their parents.

After a time, Meleka caused the sun to shine again. Everyone was happy again; children who had been returning home began to wander about again. Meleka decided to divide time into nights and days to encourage the little ones to go back home and not to stray too far from their parents. In common protection against the night, men and animals united in a single friendly clan and lived together under a giant cotton tree. This tree was the only shelter they could find. They took good care of the tree for it was the only home they had. All of the animals and men loved one another and it was a happy home.

One day the son of a man discovered a piece of fire discarded by Lightning Bug. He played with it. Being a normal child with mischief in his head, he waited until no one was watching, then carried fire to the foot of the cotton tree. The giant tree had already been badly burned before the animals and men saw and smelled the smoke.

A great cry of despair rose up from the animals. They stood about in fear, helplessly watching fire consume their home in a roaring, smoking blaze. After many hours the tree groaned, cracked and came crashing down to earth amid a shower of bright red sparks. The men and animals fled in all directions.

"It is finished!" cried the animals. "We have been betrayed by man. We agreed to live in peace beneath the cotton tree, but man is wicked. We will not stay any longer. There is war between us!"

Most of the animals fled far into the forest where they made their homes in caves and thickets. Men built houses of mud and thatch and their tribe multiplied. A few brave or foolish animals, such as dogs, goats or cows, decided to live with them.

On the other side of a mountain there was a certain pond which Meleka had used as a painting bowl. His colors had settled to the bottom of the pond, leaving the water looking clear and sweet. A group of naughty children bathed there. Their swimming and splashing stirred up Meleka's colors and the children were astonished to see their skins change color from lustrous black to white, brown and yellow. In great alarm they rushed from the pond and washed themselves in a stream, but the colors were fixed and would not be washed off.

THE EYE OF THE GIANT

Long, long ago there was a great famine in the world, and a certain young man whilst wandering in search of food strayed into a part of the bush where he had never been before. Presently he perceived a strange mass lying on the ground. He approached and saw that it was the body of a giant whose hair resembled that of white men in that it was silky rather than woolly. It was of an incredible length and stretched as far as from Krachi to Salaga.[1] The young man was properly awed at the spectacle, and wished to withdraw, but the giant noticing him asked what he wanted.

The young man explained and begged the giant to give him some food. The latter agreed on condition that the youth would serve him for a while. This matter having been arranged, the giant said his name was Owuo or Death, and then gave the boy some meat.

Never before had the latter tasted such fine food, and he was well pleased with his bargain. He served his master for a long time and received plenty of meat, but one day he grew homesick, and begged his master to give him a short holiday. The latter agreed if the youth would promise to bring another boy in his place. So the youth returned to his village and there persuaded his brother to go with him into the bush and gave him to Owuo.

In course of time the youth got hungry again and longed for the meat which Owuo had taught him to like so much. So one day he made up his mind to return to his master, and leaving the village made his way back to the giant's abode. The latter asked him what he wanted, and when the youth told him that he wanted to taste once more of the good meat, the giant told him to enter the hut and take as much as he liked, but he would have to work for him again.

The youth agreed and entered the hut. He ate as much as he could, and set to at the task his master set him. The work continued for a long time and the boy ate his fill every day. But to his surprise he never saw anything of his brother, and whenever he asked about him the giant told him that the lad was away on his business.

Once more the youth grew homesick and asked for leave to return to his village. The giant agreed on condition that he would bring a girl for him, Owuo, to wed. So the youth went home and there persuaded his sister to go into the bush and marry the giant. The girl agreed, and took with her a slave companion, and they all repaired to the giant's abode. There the youth left the two girls and went back to the village.

It was not very long after that he again grew hungry and longed for the taste of the meat. So he made his way once more into the bush and found the giant. The giant did not seem overpleased to see the boy and grumbled at being bothered a fourth time. However, he told the boy to go into the inner chamber of his hut and take what he wanted. The youth did so and took up a bone which he began to devour. To his horror he recognized it at once as being the bone of his sister. He looked around at all the rest of the meat and saw that it was that of his sister and her slave girl.

Thoroughly frightened he escaped from the house and ran back into the village. There he told the elders what he had done and the awful thing

---

1. **from Krachi to Salaga:** about sixty miles. Krachi and Salaga are two towns in what is now Ghana.

he had seen. At once the alarm was sounded and all the people went out into the bush to see for themselves the dread thing they had heard about. When they drew near to the giant, they grew afraid at the sight of so evil a monster. They went back to the village and consulted among themselves what best they should do. At last it was agreed to go to Salaga where the giant's hair finished and set light to it. This was done, and when the hair was burning well, they returned to the bush and watched the giant.

Presently the latter began to toss about and sweat. It was quite evident that he was beginning to feel the heat. The nearer the flames advanced the more he tossed and grumbled. At last the fire reached his head, and for the moment the giant was dead.

The villagers approached him cautiously, and the young man noticed "medicine" which had been concealed in the roots of the giant's hair. He took it and called the others to come and see what he had found. No one could say what power this medicine might have, but an old man suggested that no harm would be done if they took some and sprinkled it on the bones and meat in the hut. This idea was carried out, and to the surprise of everyone, the girls and the boy returned to life at once.

The youth who had still some of the medicine left proposed to put it on the giant. But at this there was a great uproar, as the people feared Owuo might come to life again. The boy therefore by way of compromise sprinkled it into the eye of the dead giant. At once the eye opened and the people all fled away in terror. But it is from that eye that death comes; for every time that Owuo shuts that eye a man dies, and unfortunately for us he is forever blinking and winking.

TRICKSTER STORIES

ANANSI'S FISHING EXPEDITION

In the country of Ashanti,[1] not far from the edge of the great West African forest, there was a man named Anansi, who was known to all the people for miles around. Anansi was not a great hunter, or a great worker, or a great warrior. His specialty was being clever. He liked to outwit people. He liked to live well, and to have other people do things for him. But because all the people of the country knew about Anansi and had had trouble with him, he had to keep thinking of new ways to get something for nothing.

One day Anansi was sitting in the village when a man named Osansa came along.

"I have an idea," Anansi said. "Why don't we go and set fish traps together? Then we shall sell the fish and be quite rich."

---

1. **Ashanti:** a region in the northern part of Ghana.

But Osansa knew Anansi's reputation very well, and so he said: "No, I have as much food as I can eat or sell. I am rich enough. Why don't you set your fish traps by yourself?"

"Ha! Fish alone? Then I'd have to do all the work!" Anansi said. "What I need is a fool for a partner."

Osansa went away, and after a while another man named Anene came along. "I have an idea," Anansi said. "Why don't the two of us go and set fish traps together? Then we shall sell the fish and be quite rich."

Anene knew Anansi very well too, but he seemed to listen thoughtfully. "That sounds like a fine idea," he said. "Two people can catch more fish than one. Yes, I'll do it."

The news went rapidly around the village that Anansi and Anene were going on a fishing expedition together. Osansa met Anene in the market and said: "We hear you are going to trap fish with Anansi. Don't you know he is trying to make a fool of you? He has told every one that he needs a fool to go fishing with him. He wants someone to set the fish traps and do all the work, while he gets all the money for the fish."

"Don't worry, friend Osansa, I won't be Anansi's fool," Anene said.

Early the next morning Anansi and Anene went into the woods to cut palm branches to make their fish traps.

Anansi was busy thinking how he could make Anene do most of the work. But when they came to the place where the palm trees grew, Anene said to Anansi: "Give me the knife, Anansi. I shall cut the branches for the traps. We are partners. We share everything. My part of the work will be to cut branches, your part of the work will be to get tired for me."

"Just a minute, let me think," Anansi said. "Why should I be the one to get tired?"

"Well, when there's work to be done someone must get tired," Anene said. "That's the way it is. So if I cut the branches, the least you can do is to get tired for me."

"Hah, you take me for a fool?" Anansi said. "Give me the knife. I shall cut the branches and you get tired for me!"

So Anansi took the knife and began cutting the branches from the trees. Every time he chopped, Anene grunted. Anene sat down in the shade and groaned from weariness, while Anansi chopped and hacked and sweated. Finally the wood for the fish traps was cut. Anansi tied it up into a big bundle. Anene got up from the ground, holding his back and moaning.

"Anansi, let me carry the bundle of wood now, and you can get tired for me," Anene said.

"Oh, no, my friend Anene," Anansi said, "I am not that simple-minded. I'll carry the wood myself, and you can take the weariness for me."

So he hoisted the bundle to the top of his head and the two of them started back to the village. Anene groaned all the way.

"Oh, oh!" he moaned. "Take it easy, Anansi! Oh, oh!"

When they came to the village Anene said: "Let me make the fish traps, Anansi, and you just sit down and get tired for me."

"Oh, no," Anansi said. "You just keep on as you are." And he made the fish traps while Anene lay on his back in the shade with his eyes closed, moaning and groaning.

And while he was making the traps, working in the heat with perspiration running down his face and chest, Anansi looked at Anene lying there taking all his weariness and sore muscles for him, and he shook his head and clucked his tongue. "Anene thinks he is intelligent," he said to himself. "Yet look at him moaning and groaning there, practically dying from weariness!"

When the fish traps were done Anene climbed to his feet and said, "Anansi, my friend, now let me carry the fish traps to the water, and you can get tired for me."

"Oh, no," Anansi said. "You just come along and do your share. I'll do the carrying, you do the getting tired."

So they went down to the water, Anansi carrying and Anene moaning. When they arrived, Anene said to Anansi: "Now wait a minute, Anansi, we ought to think things over here. There are sharks in this water. Some one is apt to get hurt. So let me go in and set the traps, and should a shark bite me, then you can die for me."

"Wah!" Anansi howled. "Listen to that! What do you take me for? I'll go in the water and set the traps myself, and if I am bitten, then you can die for me!" So he took the fish traps out into the water and set them and then the two of them went back to the village.

The next morning when they went down to inspect the traps they found just four fish. Anene spoke first.

"Anansi, there are only four fish here. You take them. Tomorrow there will probably be more, and then I'll take my turn."

"Now, what do you take me for?" Anansi said indignantly. "Do you think I am simple-minded? Oh, no, Anene, you take the four fish and I'll take my turn tomorrow."

So Anene took the four fish and carried them to town and sold them.

Next day when they came down to the fish traps, Anene said: "Look, there are only eight fish here. I'm glad it's your turn, because tomorrow there doubtless will be more."

"Just a minute," Anansi said. "You want me to take today's fish so that tomorrow you get a bigger catch? Oh, no, these are all yours, partner; tomorrow I'll take my share."

So Anene took the eight fish and carried them to town and sold them.

Next day when they came to look in the traps they found sixteen fish. "Anansi," Anene said, "take the sixteen fish. Little ones, too. I'll take my turn tomorrow."

"Of course you'll take your turn tomorrow, it's my turn today," Anansi said. He stopped to think. "Well, now, you are trying to make a fool out of me again! You want me to take these sixteen miserable little fish so that you can get the big catch tomorrow, don't you? Well, it's a good thing I'm alert! You take the sixteen today and I'll take the big catch tomorrow!"

So Anene carried the sixteen fish to the market and sold them.

Next day they came to the traps and took the fish out. But by this time the traps had rotted in the water.

"Well, it's certainly your turn today," Anene said. "And I'm very glad of that. Look, the fish traps are rotten and worn out. We can't use them any more. I'll tell you what—you take the fish to town and sell them, and I'll take the rotten fish traps and sell them. The fish traps will bring an excellent price. What a wonderful idea!"

"Hm," Anansi said. "Just a moment, don't be in such a hurry. I'll take the fish traps and sell them myself. If there's such a good price to be had, why shouldn't I get it instead of you? Oh, no, you take the fish, my friend."

Anansi hoisted the rotten fish traps up on his head and started off for town. Anene followed him, carrying the fish. When they arrived in the town Anene sold his fish in the market, while Anansi walked back and forth singing loudly: "I am selling rotten fish traps! I am selling wonderful rotten fish traps!"

But no one wanted rotten fish traps, and the townspeople were angry that Anansi thought they were so stupid they would buy them. All day long Anansi wandered through the town singing: "Get your rotten fish traps here! I am selling wonderful rotten fish traps!"

Finally the head man of the town heard about the affair. He, too, became very angry, and he sent messengers for Anansi. When they brought Anansi to him he asked indignantly: "What do you think you are doing, anyway? What kind of nonsense is this you are trying to put over the people of the town?"

"I'm selling rotten fish traps," Anansi said, "very excellent rotten fish traps."

"Now what do you take us for?" the chief of the town said. "Do you think we are ignorant people? Your friend Anene came and sold good fish, which the people want, but you come trying to sell something that isn't good for anything and just smell the town up with your rotten fish traps. It's an outrage. You insult us."

The head man turned to the townspeople who stood near by, listening.

"Take him away and whip him," he said.

The men took Anansi out to the town gate and beat him with sticks. Anansi shouted and yelled and made a great noise. When at last they turned him loose, Anene said to him: "Anansi, this ought to be a lesson to you. You wanted a fool to go fishing with you, but you didn't have to look so hard to find one. You were a fool yourself."

Anansi nodded his head.

"Yes," he said thoughtfully, rubbing his back and his legs where they had beaten him. And he looked reproachfully at Anene. "But what kind of partner are you? At least you could have taken the pain while I took the beating."

THE SINGING CLOAK

Anansi[1] and the Chameleon used to live in the same town. Anansi was a rich man and had plenty of children to help him with his farming, but the Chameleon was only a poor man and alone had to till his farm. Now it chanced that one year the rain fell only on the Chameleon's farm, and on Anansi's there was a complete drought. Thus the spider's farm did not come up at all, and the Chameleon's was already well up and a good harvest promised.

This annoyed Anansi, and one day he called on the Chameleon and asked him if he would sell him his farm, but the Chameleon said he would not, because if he did he would not be able to get any food during the dry season. Then Anansi was even angrier than before, and swore he would have revenge on the Chameleon.

Now it happens that chameleons do not make any roads as others do. They like to walk over the grass and bushes. Thus there was no path leading from the Chameleon's house to his farm. So that night, Anansi called all his children together and told them to clean and make a good path from his compound to the Chameleon's farm. At first, they begged their father not to do this, but as he insisted they obeyed him, and in the morning there was finished a clean road and a well-used one leading from Anansi's house to the farm.

Anansi at once went to the farm and began to pull up some cassava. Presently the Chameleon came along and saw Anansi taking his cassava and called out: "Hi! Anansi, what are you doing in my farm?" Anansi at once replied: "Go away and do not vex me. Can you not see that I am busy working in my farm?"

"Your farm," cried the Chameleon, "why, it is my farm, and everyone knows that." "Do not be silly; go away," answered the Spider, "or I shall get angry and kill you."

So the Chameleon went away and laid a complaint before the chief. Anansi was sent for, and when both had told him how the farm was theirs, the chief asked for proofs. Then Anansi said: "That is easy. I have a path from my house straight to the farm, which the Chameleon is falsely claiming. He has no path."

The chief saw that if Anansi was speaking true then verily the farm must be his. So he sent his messenger to see and the man came back and said that it was so. Then the Chameleon was asked what he had to say, and he said that he did not know anything about the path, that he always used to go there over the bushes and grass. This made the chief laugh, and he at once gave the farm to Anansi, who took all his children with him and gathered the crops.

The Chameleon did not know what to do. He was very poor and had

---

1. **Anansi:** See the introduction to these folk tales on page 3 for more information on Anansi the Spider.

but little food left to keep him alive. So he went to his house and shut the door and refused to see anyone.

For many days he remained thus thinking over his wrongs and wondering how to get revenge. Then he began to dig a hole. He dug and dug and dug and made an immense well. It went far down. No man had ever seen such a well. When the Chameleon thought he had made it large enough he made some mud and began to roof the well so that soon only a very small hole was left.

Then the Chameleon went out to see Anansi. He came to the latter's house and greeted him: "Master, I am only a poor man. May I go to your farm and glean what you have left there?" And Anansi was pleased at the Chameleon's humility and told him he could. But there was little in the farm to gather. Then the Chameleon, who had deceived the spider into thinking that he was properly humbled, again sat alone in his house. This time he amused himself in catching hundreds and hundreds of that great fly which makes so big a buzzing noise. These he tied to some dried yam vines which he had brought back from the farm.

One day, the chief sent messengers to all the land to call his people together, and from every place people came into town. Then the Chameleon arose and covered himself with the dried yam vines and walked slowly like a proud and rich man to the chief's compound, and as he went he kept swinging his strange costume and the flies, being shaken, buzzed. This was wonderful, and as he drew near the chief, swinging his dress, which buzzed more and more, every one admired it and the chief himself asked to buy it. But the Chameleon refused and went home. Now Anansi was late for the meeting, and when he did arrive everyone was talking about this wonderful costume. The chief told Anansi that the Chameleon had refused to sell it, and Anansi said that was nothing, and that he would buy it and would bring it to the chief.

He went and called on the Chameleon. "Friend," he said, "I hear you have a most wonderful cloak, which wherever you walk sings to you. Is this so?" The Chameleon answered that it was so, and then Anansi asked him if he would sell it.

The Chameleon at first refused, but after a time did agree to sell it if Anansi would give him some food. Anansi asked how much food he would want, and the Chameleon said that he did not require a great deal, merely enough to fill the hole which Anansi himself could see. Then Anansi laughed and said that he would willingly do that, and to show that he bore him no grudge, would give him twice as much.

Then Anansi went to his own house and called his children and told them to come with him and each to carry a little food. They all went to the Chameleon's house and began to fill the hole with food they had brought. But that hole could not be filled. All the family of Anansi worked, and for many days they carried the corn and other food to fill that hole and always the Chameleon reminded Anansi that he had promised twice the amount.

Anansi did not know what to do. He had finished all the food that there had been stored in his own bins and granaries and he had sent out in all directions to buy food. But still the hole was not filled. He sold his sheep and his cows and everything that he had, for he knew that when he did get the cloak the chief would repay him. But he could not fill the hole.

Then when the Chameleon saw that Anansi was no longer a rich man and that he had no food left for himself, he called him and said: "Friend, you have not paid me the agreed price. But I am not a hard man and I will now forgive you the rest of the debt. Here is the cloak."

Saying this he took out the cloak from its box and put it over the shoulders of Anansi.

But the cloak had been a long time in the box and the strings which held the flies were all rotted. This Anansi did not know, and when he went outside and began to swing the robe the flies all buzzed, but suddenly there came a strong blast of wind and shook the cloak too much. All the flies were released and flew away and left Anansi dressed only in the dried vine stalks of the yams.

Then all the town laughed, and Anansi grew so ashamed that he began to hide himself from that day away from the sight of man, and does not walk in the streets.

THE GOURD FULL OF WISDOM

The spider noticed one day how other people than himself were beginning to use wisdom. This did not suit him at all, as he wanted to keep all the wisdom for himself. So he collected it all and put it into a large gourd that he had hollowed out for the purpose. He then hung the gourd up on the wall of his house. But his fears were not allayed and he decided to hide it right away in the bush where no man could find it. Therefore on the following morning he took down the gourd from the wall, and accompanied by his son went forth into the bush. Presently they came to a tall palm tree, and it seemed to the spider that if he put the gourd at the top among the foliage it would be quite safe. So he began to climb the palm tree. But the gourd was a large one and the spider had slung it in front of him. So he could not make any progress. Always the gourd got in his way. Now the son of the spider had been watching his father's efforts and at last cried out: "Father, why not sling the gourd over your back?"

And Anansi the spider answered: "My son, you are right: but your words show to me that it is better for many people to have wisdom rather than one. For alone I should not have thought of that." So speaking, he opened the gourd and scattered the wisdom all over the ground so that he who may want it can gather what he will.

MORAL STORIES

HOW HAWK LEARNED OF THE SHALLOW HEARTS OF MEN

Chameleon has his home in a certain tree called the palmolin tree. Men plant these trees, in which the palm birds live, in the center of their villages. Thus it was that Chameleon lived in a tree by a village marketplace. People feared this animal, for although it was quite small, it possessed surprising strength. It would spring on the backs of passing men and could not be removed until it had been frightened by lightning and thunder. Then it would fall to the ground and run back to the palmolin tree.

One day when Hawk was flying above the town he saw Chameleon on the ground and swooping down he seized the little animal in his beak and carried him into the air. The people in the village below rejoiced and sang the praises of clever Hawk.

"O Hawk!" they cried, "O greatest of all birds! You have captured the awful Chameleon, that wicked animal who has lived among us causing fear and trouble. O clever Hawk, with all our hearts we thank you!"

The people were very happy. Meanwhile, up in the air Chameleon confided to Hawk, "Brother, let me go back to my tree. Long have I lived among men and I know they have two tongues. Today they praise a man and tomorrow they speak against him, for their hearts are shallow and their minds are weak. Let me return, O brother, to my tree."

But Hawk was proud of the praises of the villagers. "The people praise and love me," he declared. "I have found great favor with them. I will eat you and they may make me Chief!"

"Unhappy bird!" Chameleon said. "Tomorrow men will curse you. Their memories are brief. Men only love themselves, as you will see."

Suddenly he grasped Hawk by the throat. So powerful was his hold that Hawk began to choke. He fell and dropped breathless in the marketplace. The people quickly gathered and saw that Chameleon had overpowered Hawk.

"Noble Chameleon!" they cried. "O good and clever animal! You have defeated wicked Hawk, the thief who steals our chickens. With all our hearts we thank you for ridding us of that evil bird!"

They heaped praise on Chameleon and rejoiced. The Chameleon whispered in Hawk's ear, "You see now, brother? Now do you realize how shallow are the hearts of men? They have double tongues. How short their memories are! A little time ago they praised you and cursed me! Now they curse you and heap honor on me!"

"I understand," Hawk murmured. "Forgive me, Chameleon. Let us always be friends, for I know that Man will always be our common enemy!"

Then Hawk flew up into the air and Chameleon went back to his palmolin tree. These two today are still allied in friendship against the treachery of Man.

THE HUNTER WHO HUNTS NO MORE

As you know, I have killed many animals. Do you not see the heads of all I have killed at my door? But I do not go into the bush now to hunt, for I have seen a fearsome thing. All men who hunt learn strange things, but this is more fearful than any other I have seen or heard.

I had killed a large roan.[1] When I shot it, it ran away and I followed the blood trail. This led me to a great baobab tree and there the trail finished and I could see no more marks. I looked and looked everywhere, but I could see nothing. I grew tired and I sat down by a tree to rest, and as I was sitting there I saw an old man coming along.

He was carrying on his head a part of a white ants' nest for his fowls. When he came up he asked me what I was doing, and I told him how I had shot the large roan and how the trail had finished at the large baobab. He told me that was what one might have expected, and that if I followed him he would show me things.

He told me to leave my gun behind against the tree and then took me into the tree through a long dark hole. We came out into a wonderful village which I knew at once to be the village of the Kulparga.[2] It was a very rich place and the houses were much larger than ours and cleaner, and the people had rich clothes. But as we drew near, we heard the noise of much weeping, and we learned that the eldest son of the chief was dying.

We went to the house of the chief and there saw the young man. He was a very fine man to look at, but he had been wounded in the chest and his life was certainly near its end. I asked how the accident had occurred and I was told that there was a certain hunter in my own village who was always killing the young men of this fairy township and that they were very much afraid of him. They told me that they did not understand why he was always doing this as they had never done him any ill thing. I knew then that they spoke of me.

At last the young man died and my friend the old man told me to come away. We went back the road we had come and passed through the baobab tree. Then the old man left me. And as I came out, there at the foot of the tree lay my roan shot through the chest.

From that day to this I have never hunted. And you will hear that many other hunters have seen the same thing which I have just told you.

THE TALKING SKULL

A hunter goes into the bush. He finds an old human skull. The hunter says: "What brought you here?" The skull answers: "Talking brought me here." The hunter runs off. He runs to the king. He tells the king: "I found a dry human skull in the bush. It asks you how its father and mother are."

------

1. roan: a horse with a reddish brown color.

2. the Kulparga: a race of dwarfs who appear in Togoland folk tales.

The king says: "Never since my mother bore me have I heard that a dead skull can speak." The king summons the Alkali, the Saba, and the Degi and asks them if they have ever heard the like. None of the wise men has heard the like and they decide to send a guard out with the hunter into the bush to find out if his story is true and, if so, to learn the reason for it. The guard accompany the hunter into the bush with the order to kill him on the spot should he have lied. The guard and the hunter come to the skull. The hunter addresses the skull: "Skull, speak." The skull is silent. The hunter asks as before: "What brought you here?" The skull does not answer. The whole day long the hunter begs the skull to speak, but it does not answer. In the evening the guard tell the hunter to make the skull speak, and when he cannot they kill him in accordance with the king's command. When the guard are gone the skull opens its jaws and asks the dead hunter's head: "What brought you here?" The dead hunter's head replies: "Talking brought me here!"

HUMOROUS STORIES

JUSTICE

A woman one day went out to look for her goats that had wandered away from the herd. She walked back and forth over the field for a long time without finding them. She came at last to a place by the side of the road where a deaf man sat before a fire brewing himself a cup of coffee. Not realizing he was deaf, the woman asked:

"Have you seen my herd of goats come this way?"

The deaf man thought she was asking for the water hole, so he pointed vaguely toward the river.

The woman thanked him and went to the river. And there, by coincidence, she found the goats. But a young kid had fallen among the rocks and broken its foot.

She picked it up to carry it home. As she passed the place where the deaf man sat drinking his coffee, she stopped to thank him for his help. And in gratitude she offered him the kid.

But the deaf man didn't understand a word she was saying. When she held the kid toward him he thought she was accusing him of the animal's misfortune, and he became very angry.

"I had nothing to do with it!" he shouted.

"But you pointed the way," the woman said.

"It happens all the time with goats!" the man shouted.

"I found them right where you said they would be," the woman replied.

"Go away and leave me alone, I never saw him before in my life!" the man shouted.

People who came along the road stopped to hear the argument.

The woman explained to them:

"I was looking for the goats and he pointed toward the river. Now I wish to give him this kid."

"Do not insult me in this way!" the man shouted loudly. "I am not a leg breaker!" And in his anger he struck the woman with his hand.

"Ah, did you see? He struck me with his hand!" the woman said to the people. "I will take him before the judge!"

So the woman with the kid in her arms, the deaf man, and the spectators went to the house of the judge. The judge came out before his house to listen to their complaint. First, the woman talked, then the man talked, then people in the crowd talked. The judge sat nodding his head. But that meant very little, for the judge, like the man before him, was very deaf. Moreover, he was also very nearsighted.

At last, he put up his hand and the talking stopped. He gave them his judgment.

"Such family rows are a disgrace to the Emperor and an affront to the Church," he said solemnly. He turned to the man.

"From this time forward, stop mistreating your wife," he said.

He turned to the woman with the young goat in her arms.

"As for you, do not be so lazy. Hereafter do not be late with your husband's meals."

He looked at the baby goat tenderly.

"And as for the beautiful infant, may she have a long life and grow to be a joy to you both!"

The crowd broke up and the people went their various ways.

"Ah, how good it is!" they said to each other. "How did we ever get along before justice was given to us?"

TALK

Once, not far from the city of Accra on the Gulf of Guinea, a countryman went out to his garden to dig up some yams to take to market. While he was digging, one of the yams said to him:

"Well, at last you're here. You never weeded me, but now you come around with your digging stick. Go away and leave me alone!"

The farmer turned around and looked at his cow in amazement. The cow was chewing her cud and looking at him.

"Did you say something?" he asked.

The cow kept on chewing and said nothing, but the man's dog spoke up.

"It wasn't the cow who spoke to you," the dog said. "It was the yam. The yam says leave him alone."

The man became angry because his dog had never talked before, and he didn't like his tone, besides. So he took his knife and cut a branch from a palm tree to whip his dog. Just then the palm tree said:

"Put that branch down!"

The man was getting very upset about the way things were going, and he started to throw the palm branch away, but the palm branch said:

"Man, put me down softly!"

He put the branch down gently on a stone, and the stone said:

"Hey, take that thing off me."

This was enough, and the frightened farmer started to run for his village. On the way he met a fisherman going the other way with a fish trap on his head.

"What's the hurry?" the fisherman asked.

"My yam said, 'Leave me alone!' Then the dog said, 'Listen to what the yam says!' When I went to whip the dog with a palm branch the tree said, 'Put that branch down!' Then the palm branch said, 'Do it softly!' Then the stone said, 'Take that thing off me!' "

"Is that all?" the man with the fish trap asked. "Is that so frightening?"

"Well," the man's fish trap said, "did he take it off the stone?"

"Wah!" the fisherman shouted. He threw the fish trap on the ground and began to run with the farmer, and on the trail they met a weaver with a bundle of cloth on his head.

"Where are you going in such a rush?" he asked them.

"My yam said, 'Leave me alone!' " the farmer said. "The dog said, 'Listen to what the yam says!' The tree said, 'Put that branch down!' The branch said, 'Do it softly!' And the stone said, 'Take that thing off me!' "

"And then," the fisherman continued, "the fish trap said, 'Did he take it off?' "

"That's nothing to get excited about," the weaver said, "no reason at all."

"Oh yes it is," his bundle of cloth said. "If it happened to you you'd run too!"

"Wah!" the weaver shouted. He threw his bundle on the trail and started running with the other men.

They came panting to the ford in the river and found a man bathing.

"Are you chasing a gazelle?" he asked them.

The first man said breathlessly:

"My yam talked to me, and it said, 'Leave me alone!' And my dog said, 'Listen to your yam!' And when I cut myself a branch the tree said, 'Put that branch down!' And the branch said, 'Do it softly!' And the stone said, 'Take that thing off me!' "

The fisherman panted:

"And my trap said, 'Did he?' "

The weaver wheezed:

"And my bundle of cloth said, 'You'd run too!' "

"Is that why you're running?" the man in the river asked.

"Well, wouldn't you run if you were in their position?" the river said.

The man jumped out of the water and began to run with the others. They ran down the main street of the village to the house of the chief. The chief's servants brought his stool out, and he came and sat on it to listen to their complaints. The men began to recite their troubles.

"I went out to my garden to dig yams," the farmer said, waving his arms. "Then everything began to talk! My yam said 'Leave me alone!' My dog said, 'Pay attention to your yam!' The tree said, 'Put that branch down!' The branch said, 'Do it softly!' And the stone said, 'Take it off me!' "

"And my fish trap said, 'Well, did he take it off?' " the fisherman said.

"And my cloth said, 'You'd run too!' " the weaver said.

"And the river said the same," the bather said hoarsely, his eyes bulging.

The chief listened to them patiently, but he couldn't refrain from scowling.

"Now, this is really a wild story," he said at last. "You'd better all go back to your work before I punish you for disturbing the peace."

So the men went away, and the chief shook his head and mumbled to himself, "Nonsense like that upsets the community."

"Fantastic, isn't it?" his stool said. "Imagine, a talking yam!"

DISCUSSION QUESTIONS

Origin Stories

1. What details in "How the Word Changed" did you find most interesting? What fascinated you about these particular details?

2. Note the relationship of humans and animals in this tale. What point seems to be implied about how humans ought to relate to animals?

3. The young man in "The Eye of the Giant" is much too trustful of the giant. At what point in the proceedings should he have suspected that something was wrong?

4. This folk tale is an explanatory one because it explains why something happens or why something exists or where something came from. What is being explained in this tale?

Trickster Stories

1. In "Anansi's Fishing Expedition," what does Anansi plan to do, and how does Anene turn the tables on him?

2. Does Anansi's last comment to Anene in the tale indicate that he has learned the humor of how he has been tricked, or does it indicate that he is still in the dark?

3. If there is a lesson to be learned in this folk tale, what might it be?

4. In "The Singing Cloak," Anansi is clearly the villain. Is Chameleon the hero of the tale? Explain your answer.

5. You have no doubt heard the expressions "An eye for an eye, and a tooth for a tooth" and "Fight fire with fire." Explain how each of these expressions applies to "The Singing Cloak."

6. In "The Gourd Full of Wisdom," what does Anansi do that is consistent with his reputation as a trickster?

7. What other qualities does Anansi display in this tale that are consistent with the qualities of a hero?

Moral Stories

1. What simple point about human nature is made in "How Hawk Learned of the Shallow Hearts of Men"?

2. Do you think the portrayal of human nature in this tale is accurate? Explain your answer.

3. Supernatural fairy tales often use substitutions of identity—a frog turns into a prince, a hideous old hag turns into the most beautiful woman in the kingdom. Usually the substitution of identity is a reward for virtue. Is this true in "The Hunter Who Hunts No More"? Explain.

4. What message might be contained in this tale? Think back to the attitudes about humans and animals presented in the creation myth "How the World Changed." Do they shed any light on the message contained in this tale?

5. An *exemplum* is a brief tale or anecdote told to teach a lesson or moral. *Exempla* were especially common in Medieval sermons and are still popular with preachers around the world today. Explain how "The Talking Skull" serves as an exemplum.

6. Why do you think the skull refuses to speak until after the hunter has been killed?

Humorous Stories

1. The comedy of misunderstanding in "Justice" eventually reaches absurd proportions. How could the misunderstanding have been corrected at various points in the story?

2. This folk tale is a satire—pointed ridicule of human folly. What is being satirized? Do you think the satire is gentle or sharp?

3. Does it matter that the human characters in "Talk" are not fully developed individuals, but rather are types—the country man, the fisherman, and so on? Why or why not?

4. What elements contribute to the humor of this tale?

SUGGESTIONS FOR WRITING

1. The folk tale "Talk" is about a yam who feels mistreated and speaks out. It is also about a man who is astonished by the fact that a yam can talk. If you wanted to interpret this simple tale very generally as an allegory, what would the situation presented in this tale symbolically represent? Write a short essay in which you discuss possible symbolic interpretations of "Talk."

2. Three of the tales grouped together here feature Anansi the Spider, the famous trickster character of West African folklore. Find these three tales and compare them. In a short essay, discuss the character of Anansi in each. How does Anansi differ from one story to the next? What lesson or moral (if any) is illustrated in each tale? Study the tone of each tale. What do you think is the attitude of the "authors" and listeners or readers of these tales toward Anansi? Use evidence from each tale to support your ideas.

3. Using what you've learned about the qualities of folk tales, write a short tale that focuses on one important trait. For length, match "The Talking Skull" or "The Gourd Full of Wisdom." Keep your tale simple. Write a story about a trickster *or* a story explaining how something came about *or* a story with a moral *or* a story with supernatural elements. Don't try to do all of these things. If time permits, share your final product with the class.

PETER ABRAHAMS

(born 1919)

Peter Abrahams is considered the first black South African author to become internationally known. He is said to have influenced several founders of modern African fiction in English, including Cyprian Ekwensi, whose works are also included in this anthology.

He was born at Vrededorp, a slum of Johannesburg, South Africa, to a South African mother and an Ethiopian nobleman who had traveled to South Africa to work in the gold mines. Abrahams describes his early life in his autobiography, *Tell Freedom,* which was published in 1954. While he lived in South Africa, Abrahams was a victim of apartheid, the policy of white supremacy and racial segregation pursued by the white government of South Africa from just after World War II until 1994. Abrahams left South Africa in the late 1940s. He lived for a time in England before moving to Jamaica.

As a young man, Abrahams was attracted to communism and worked briefly on the staff of the Communist *Daily Worker,* but he soon became disillusioned. Much later in his career, Abrahams embraced the teachings of Christianity, which is evident in his latest novel, *The View from Coyaba* (1985). In it Abrahams remains committed to the struggle for the liberation of the black world from white domination—a consistent theme throughout his writing—but he emphasizes that there is no freedom without recognition and acceptance of human unity.

Abrahams is the author of several other novels, including *Mine Boy* (1946), *A Wreath for Udomo* (1956), and *Dark Testament* (1942), a collection of short stories. ∎

THE BLACKS

It was a hot, humid, oppressive August day in Accra, capital of the Gold Coast that was to become Ghana.[1] The air had the stillness of death. I walked down toward the sea front. Perhaps there would be the hint of a breeze there. As I neared the sea front I was assailed by a potent stench of the sea with strong overtones of rotting fish.

The houses were drab, run-down wooden structures or made of corrugated iron, put together any way you please. The streets were wide and tarred, and each street had an open drainage system. . . . I have seen women empty chamber pots into these drains in the early morning. The fierce sun takes care of the germs, but God help you if smells make you sick.

---

1. **the Gold Coast . . . Ghana:** The Gold Coast, upon gaining its independence from Britain in 1957, took the name of the ancient West African kingdom of Ghana.

In about eight minutes of walking, some fifteen "taxis" pulled up beside me: "Hi, massa! Taxi, massa! Me go anywhere you go cheap!" They are all private taxis with no meters and driven by strapping young men with flashing teeth. The place is full of taxi drivers willing to go anywhere and do anything cheap.

The street traders here are women. "Mammy traders," they are called. They trade in everything. They sell cigarettes, one at a time; round loaves of bread and hunks of cooked meat on which the big West African flies make sport. They love bargaining and haggling. They are a powerful economic factor in the life of the country. The more prosperous ones own their own trucks, some own fleets of trucks. These "mammy trucks" are the principal carriers of the country. They carry passengers as well as produce and go hurtling across the countryside with little regard for life or limb. Each truck has its own distinctive slogan, such as: *Repent for Death is Round the Corner,* or *Enter Without Hope,* or *The Last Ride* or *If It Must It Will.* My own favorite—and I traveled in this particular truck—pleaded *Not Today O Lord Not Today.*

I passed many mammy traders, many mammy trucks, before I reached the sea front. I crossed a street, jumped over an open drain, and there was the sea. But there was no breeze, and no shade from the terrible sun. In the end I gave in to the idea of "taxi, massa, taxi" and looked about for one. But now there was no taxi in sight. Instead, I saw suddenly a long procession of many women and a few men. The procession swung round a corner and came into full view, twenty or thirty yards long. The women wore white flowing robes and white kerchiefs on their heads. Their faces were painted into grotesque masks made with thick streaks of black, red, white and yellow paints. The heavy thud of bare feet rose above the hum of the sea.

Then, all at once, the drums burst forth and there was no other sound about me. The marching women began to jig, then dance. As the tail of the procession passed me the drums reached a frenzy. A thin, pure note from a reed rose above the drums. The whole procession became a shivering, shaking mass. The reed note held longer than seemed human. And then, dramatically, there was silence. The thudding feet faded away out of sight and sound. There was silence and a slight racing of my heartbeat and the hum of the sea, and, of course, the overpowering fishy stench.

I thought of Richard Wright,[2] with whom I had had breakfast that morning. This was his first visit to any part of Africa and he seemed to find it bewildering. Countee Cullen, the late American Negro poet, had speculated:

One three centuries removed
From the scenes his fathers loved,
Spicy grove, cinnamon tree,
What is Africa to me?

---

2. Richard Wright: (1908–1960), prominent black American novelist.

Wright was finding the answers and finding them disconcerting. . . . He expressed to me that morning what he later summed up in his book on the Gold Coast: "I was black and they were black but it did not help me."

What Wright did not understand, what his whole background and training had made difficult for him to understand, was that being black did not of itself qualify one for acceptance in tribal Africa. But how could he, when there are thousands of urbanized Africans up and down the vast continent who do not themselves understand this? The more perceptive of the urban Africans are only now beginning to comprehend, but slowly.

Being black is a small matter in tribal Africa because the attitude toward color is healthy and normal. Color does not matter. Color is an act of God that neither confers privileges nor imposes handicaps on a man. A man's skin is like the day: the day is either clear or dark. There is nothing more to it until external agencies come in and invest it with special meaning and importance.

What does matter to the tribal African, what is important, is the complex pattern of his position within his own group and his relations with the other members of the group. He is no Pan-African dreaming of a greater African glory when the white man is driven into the sea. The acute race consciousness of the American Negro, or of the black South African at the receiving end of apartheid,[3] is alien to him. The important things in his life are anything but race and color—until they are forced on him. And "Mother Africa" is much too vast to inspire big continental dreams in him. She is a land of huge mountains, dark jungles, and vast deserts. In her rivers and in her jungles and in her grasslands lurk creatures that are the enemies of man: the leopard and the lion, the snake and crocodile. All this makes travel, by the old African methods, extremely difficult and makes for isolation between one group of people and another. The African who is in Britain is likely to be a deal better informed on what is happening all over the continent than would be his fellow African in any of the main centers of both tribal and nontribal Africa. In terms of communications the man in the tribe lives in the Dark Ages.

Richard Wright was surprised that even educated Africans, racially conscious literate people, had not heard of him and were skeptical of a grown man earning his living by writing. They could not understand what kind of writing brought a man enough money to support a family. Wright really wanted to understand the African, but—"I found the African an oblique, a hard-to-know man."

My sympathies were all with Wright.

The heat and salty rancid fish smell had made me desperately thirsty. Across the way a mammy trader squatted beside her pile of merchandise: cooked meats, sweet potatoes—a whole host of edibles—and some bottles of opaque white liquid that could be either coconut milk or palm juice as well as the inevitable little pile of cigarettes priced at a penny

---

3. **apartheid** (ə pär′ tīt): the policy of white supremacy and racial segregation pursued by the white government of South Africa starting just after World War II. Apartheid ended in 1994.

apiece. I had been warned of the risks involved in eating anything sold by the street traders. But to hell with it. I was thirsty and not exactly a stranger to African germs. I crossed the street, felt the bottles and chose the one that seemed coolest and looked the least opaque.

"How much?"

"One shilling." The carved ebony face looked at me with dead eyes.

I pulled the screwed-up newspaper stopper from the bottle, wiped its mouth and took a swig. I could not decide whether it was coconut milk or palm juice. It had been heavily watered down and sweetened. But it was wet and thirst-quenching. I drank half the bottle, firmly ignoring the little foreign bodies that floated in the liquid. Then I paid her and drank the rest. I put down the empty and began to move away.

"You African?" she asked in her harsh, cold, masculine voice.

I stopped, turned and looked at her face. It was as deadly cold and impersonal as before: not a flicker of feeling in her eyes. Like an African mask, I thought. But unlike Wright, I did not try to penetrate it; I knew the futility of trying. She would show feeling if and when she decided, not before.

"Yes," I said, and added, "from the south. Far, far south."

She paused for so long that I began to move again.

"You like here?" Nationalism had obviously touched her.

I turned back to her. "No," I said.

"Why you don't like?"

"I don't say I don't like."

"But you don't like?"

I showed her my teeth, African-wise, which is neither smile nor grimace but a blending of the two. "*You* like Africa?" I asked.

Now it was her turn to show me her teeth. There was a flicker of feeling in her eyes, then they went dead again. She nodded. I had established my claim. Only outsiders—white people or the Richard Wrights—liked or disliked Africa.

I left the mammy trader and carried on up the smelly and hot street. Much and little had passed between us. Out to sea some fishing boats appeared on the sky line. About me were the citizens of Accra. Some wore the cloth of the country—the men looking like pint-sized citizens of ancient Rome painted black and the women looking extraordinarily masculine—and others wore western dress.

My thoughts shifted to my forthcoming meeting with Kwame Nkrumah,[4] Ghana's first prime minister. It was well over seven years since I had last seen him, in London. Then he was a poor struggling student; now he was the head of a state and the spokesman for the great Pan-African dream of freedom and independence.

I remembered our past friendship and wondered what changes I would

---

4. **Kwame Nkrumah** (ən krü′mə): (1909–1972), Ghanian nationalist who became the first president of the new Republic of Ghana in 1960. He was deposed by the army and the police in 1966.

find in him. Anyway, it was now 9 A.M. and my date with him was for 9:30. I would soon know.

A few minutes later I flagged a taxi and simply said, "Kwame's office."

A pale-brown West Indian miss was the prime minister's secretary. She welcomed me as though I was a V.I.P. The prime minister had not come back from a conference yet. The tribal business was taking up a lot of his attention. She told me with indignation how members of the Ashanti tribe had to crawl on their bellies for some twenty yards into the presence of their king, the Asantehene, and how tribalism had to give way or there would be no progress. If she was any indication, then Nkrumah was very worried about the opposition the tribesmen were offering his western-style Convention Peoples Party.

A number of officials came in. The lady stopped assailing the tribes. Then there was some bustle and the prime minister arrived. In something just over five minutes he had seen and dealt with these officials and I was ushered into his office. It was a big, pleasant, cool room.

Nkrumah came round his big official desk, took my hand and led me to a settee near the window. The now famous smile lit up his face. As we exchanged greetings, felt each other out with small talk in an attempt to bridge the gap of years, my mind went back to our London days. This poised, relaxed man, with the hint of guarded reserve about him, was a far cry from the friend I had last seen nearly eight years earlier.

For me, the most striking change of all was in his eyes. They reflected an inner tranquillity which was the one thing the Nkrumah in Europe never had.

Even his name had been subtly different then. He had been our friend Francis Nkrumah, an African student recently arrived from the United States, and he had not seen Africa for a decade and more. He had quickly become a part of our African colony in London and had joined our little group, the Pan-African Federation, in our protests against colonialism.

He was much less relaxed than most of us. His eyes mirrored a burning inner conflict and tension. He seemed consumed by a restlessness that led him to evolve some of the most fantastic schemes.

The president of our federation was an East African named Johnstone Kenyatta,[5] the most relaxed, sophisticated and "westernized" of the lot of us. Kenyatta enjoyed the personal friendship of some of the most distinguished people in English political and intellectual society. He was subtle, subtle enough to attack one's principles bitterly and retain one's friendship. He fought the British as imperialists but was affectionate toward them as friends.

It was to this balanced and extremely cultured man that Francis Nkrumah proposed that we form a secret society called The Circle, and that each of us spill a few drops of our blood into a bowl and so take a blood oath of secrecy and dedication to the emancipation of Africa.

---

5. **Johnstone Kenyatta:** (1893–1978), called *Jomo,* Kenyan nationalist. He became the first president of the new Republic of Kenya in 1964.

Johnstone Kenyatta laughed at the idea; he scoffed at it as childish juju.[6] He conceived our struggle in modern, twentieth-century terms with no ritualistic blood nonsense. In the end Francis Nkrumah drifted away from us and started his own little West African group in London. We were too tame and slow for him. He was an angry man in a hurry.

Then he went back to his part of Africa, and Francis Nkrumah became Kwame Nkrumah. He set himself at the head of the largely tribal populace and dabbled in blood ritual. There was some violence, a spell in prison, and finally Nkrumah emerged as the first African prime minister in a self-governing British African territory.

Tribal myths grew up around him. He could make himself invisible at will. He could go without food and sleep and drink longer than ordinary mortals. He was, in fact, the reincarnation of some of the most powerful ancestral spirits. He allowed his feet to be bathed in blood.

By the time I visited the Gold Coast the uneasy alliance between Nkrumah and the tribal chiefs had begun to crack. A week or so before my arrival he had threatened that, unless they co-operated with his government in turning the Gold Coast into an efficient twentieth-century state, he would make them run so hard that they would leave their sandals behind them. This was a calculated insult to the tribal concept that a chief's bare feet must never touch the earth.

That was the beginning of the secret war. Nkrumah thought he would win it easily. He was wrong.

And the chiefs have, negatively, scored their victories too. They have pushed him to a point where his regime is, today, intolerant of opposition. The tribal society brooks no opposition. Nkrumah's government banishes its most active opponents. As a modern socialist leading a western-style government, he justifies this as a temporary expedient. But his less sophisticated ministers frankly talk the tribal language of strength, frankly express the tribal impulse to destroy those who are out of step.

There was an air of delicacy about our conversation and we were both aware of this. We touched on local politics. He let off at full blast against the tribalist. I told him I had heard that the Accra Club was still exclusively European. His eyes lit up. "You wait and see," he said. Then, in relation to nothing either of us had said, he leaned toward me and exclaimed, "This place is rich! God, man, there's so much riches here!"—as though the revelation had just been made to him.

But always, throughout our talk, I sensed a new reserve, a new caution that had not been there in the young student I had known in Europe.

As we talked in Nkrumah's cool office that hot August day in Accra, my mind kept slipping back to our mutual friend Jomo or Johnstone Kenyatta, now imprisoned in his native Kenya for leading the Mau-Mau

---

6. juju: West African belief in the magical powers of certain ornamental charms.

movement.[7] Significantly, though we mentioned many friends, both Nkrumah and I avoided Kenyatta. I had decided not to mention him first. I had hoped Nkrumah would. He did not.

A year earlier, I had flown up to Kenya from South Africa and visited Kenyatta. I felt terribly depressed as I got off the plane. Things had grown so much uglier in the Union. The barricades were up in the ugly war of color. When I had left South Africa in the dim-and-distant past, there were isolated islands where black and white could meet in neutral territory. When I went back in 1952, the islands were submerged under the rising tide of color hatreds, and I was glad to quit that dark, unhappy land which yet compelled my love.

It was in this mood that I got off the plane. I had not seen my friend Jomo for years. Now there he was, just outside the airport terminal building, leaning on a heavy cane, bigger than I remembered him in Europe, paunchy, his face looking puffy. And behind him was a huge crowd of Africans.

I began to move toward him when a lean-faced, lean-hipped white colonial-administrator type suddenly appeared beside me and said: "Mr. Abrahams."

I stopped and thought, "Oh, Lord."

Kenyatta also came forward. The two men ignored each other. Lean-face introduced himself and said the Colonial Office had alerted them that I was coming to do some writing for the London *Observer* and they had drawn up a provisional schedule for me. Had I done anything about accommodations?

Before I could answer, Kenyatta said, "You are staying with me, of course." The old detachment was back in his eyes. They seemed to say, "You've got to choose, pal. Let's see how you choose."

Lean-face said, "We've got something set up for you for tomorrow and—"

"I live in the bush," Kenyatta added.

It dawned on me that I had become, for the moment, the battlefield of that horrible animal, the racial struggle. I made up my mind, resenting both sides and yet conscious of the crowd of Africans in the background. A question of face was involved.

"I've promised to spend this weekend with Mr. Kenyatta," I said.

Lean-face was graceful about it. I promised to call the Secretariat first thing on Monday morning. He gave me a copy of the schedule that had been prepared for me and wondered, *sotto voce,*[8] whether I knew what I was letting myself in for. Kenyatta assured me that I would be perfectly

---

7. **the Mau-Mau movement:** The Mau-Mau rebellion in the early 1950s primarily involved Kikuyu (kē kü´yü) tribesmen who wanted to drive European settlers from the fertile highlands of Kenya. A state of emergency was declared by the British government, and troops were brought in to crush the revolt. Most of the rebels had been driven into remote areas by 1956, but order was not completely restored until the end of the decade.

8. *sotto voce:* in an undertone or very softly. [Italian]

safe, that nobody was going to cut my throat. I was aware that they were talking to each other through me. I was aware that they knew I was aware, and that made me bad-tempered.

"Then I'll say good night, Mr. Abrahams," Lean-face said pointedly.

As soon as he was out of hearing Kenyatta began to curse.

"It's good to see you again, Johnstone," I gripped his hand.

"Jomo," he replied. The hint of ironic speculation was back in his eyes. A slightly sardonic, slightly bitter smile played on his lips.

"Welcome to Kenya, Peter," he said. Then, abruptly: "Come meet the leaders of my people. They've been waiting long."

We moved forward and the crowd gathered about us. Jomo made a little speech in Kikuyu,[9] then translated it for my benefit. A little old man, ancient as the hills, with huge holes in his ears, then welcomed me on behalf of the land and its people. Again Jomo translated.

After this we all bundled into the fleet of rattling old cars and set off for the Kikuyu reserve in the heart of the African bush. Kenyatta became silent and strangely remote during the journey.

We stopped at the old chief's compound, where other members of the tribe waited to welcome me. By this time the reception committee had grown to a few hundred. About me, pervading the air, was the stench of burning flesh; a young cow was being roasted in my honor. Before I entered the house a drink was handed to me. Another was handed to the old chief and a third to Kenyatta. The old man muttered a brief incantation and spilled half his drink on the earth as a libation. Jomo and I followed suit. Then the three of us downed our drinks and entered the house.

A general feasting and drinking then commenced, both inside and outside the house. I was getting a full ceremonial tribal welcome. The important dignitaries of the tribe slipped into the room in twos and threes, spoke to me through Kenyatta for a few moments, and then went away, making room for others.

"Africa doesn't seem to change," Kenyatta murmured between dignitaries. There was a terrible undercurrent of bitterness behind the softly murmured words. I was startled by it and looked at his face. For a fleeting moment he looked like a trapped, caged animal.

He saw me looking at him and quickly composed his face into a slightly sardonic, humorous mask. "Don't look too closely," he said.

And still the dignitaries filed in, had a drink, spoke their welcome and went out.

The ceremonial welcome reached its high point about midnight. Huge chunks of the roasted cow were brought in to us, and we gnawed at the almost raw meat between swigs of liquor. Outside, there was muted drumming. Voices were growing louder and louder.

Suddenly, in the midst of a long-winded speech by an immensely

---

9. **Kikuyu:** the language of the principal people of Kenya.

dignified Masai[10] chief from a neighboring and friendly tribe, Kenyatta jumped up, grabbed his heavy cane and half staggered through the door.

"Come, Peter," he called.

Everybody was startled. I hesitated. He raised his cane and beckoned to me with it. I knew that this would be a dreadful breach of tribal etiquette.

"Come, man!" he snapped.

I got up, aware of the sudden silence that had descended on the huge gathering. By some strange magic everybody seemed to know that something had gone wrong.

"Jomo," I said.

"I can't stand any more," he snapped. "Come!"

I followed him to the door. I knew the discourtesy we were inflicting on the tribe. I also knew that my friend was at the breaking point. We walked through the crowd of people, got into Kenyatta's car and drove off into the night. The African moon was big and yellow, bathing the land in a soft light that almost achieved the clarity of daylight.

He took me to his home. It was a big, sprawling, empty place on the brow of a hill. Inside, it had nothing to make for comfort. There were hard wooden chairs, a few tables and only the bed in the bedroom. There were no books, none of the normal amenities of western civilization. When we arrived two women emerged from somewhere in the back and hovered about in the shadows. They brought in liquor, but I never got a clear glimpse of either of them. My friend's anguish of spirit was such that I did not want to ask questions. We sat on the veranda and drank steadily and in silence until we were both miserably, depressingly drunk.

And then Kenyatta began to speak in a low, bitter voice of his frustration and of the isolated position in which he found himself. He had no friends. There was no one in the tribe who could give him the intellectual companionship that had become so important to him in his years in Europe. The things that were important to him—consequential conversation, the drink that represented a social activity rather than the intention to get drunk, the concept of individualism, the inviolability of privacy—all these were alien to the tribesmen in whose midst he lived. So Kenyatta, the western man, was driven in on himself and was forced to assert himself in tribal terms. Only thus would the tribesmen follow him and so give him his position of power and importance as a leader.

To live without roots is to live in hell, and no man chooses voluntarily to live in hell. The people who could answer his needs as a western man had erected a barrier of color against him in spite of the fact that the taproots of their culture had become the taproots of his culture too. By denying him access to those things which complete the life of western man, they had forced him back into the tribalism from which he had so painfully freed himself over the years.

---

10. **Masai** (mə sī′): a nomadic people of East Africa.

None of this was stated explicitly by either Kenyatta or myself. But it was there in his brooding bitter commentary on both the tribes and the white settlers of the land. For me, Kenyatta became that night a man who in his own life personified the terrible tragedy of Africa and the terrible secret war that rages in it. He was the victim both of tribalism and of westernism gone sick. His heart and mind and body were the battlefield of the ugly violence known as the Mau-Mau revolt long before it broke out in that beautiful land. The tragedy is that he was so rarely gifted, that he could have made such a magnificent contribution in other circumstances.

What then is tribal man? Perhaps his most important single characteristic is that he is not an individual in the western sense. Psychologically and emotionally he is the present living personification of a number of forces, among the most important of which are the ancestral dead. The dead have a powerful hold on the living. They control and regulate the lives and activities of the living from the grave. They hand out the rules and codes by which the living conduct their daily affairs. If there is a drought, if there is a famine, it is a sign that the ancestors are angry because someone has broken a rule of the tribe, a law laid down by the dead. There will be no peace, no order, no prosperity in the tribe until the ancestors are appeased.

So the chief calls the whole tribe to a meeting in which the guilty ones will be "smelled out." The procedure begins with the drums—a key factor in African life. Their insistent throbs call the people to the gathering on a placid, almost monotonous key at first, but working on the emotions. Everyone in the village will be present; no man, woman or child would think of not obeying the summons. They form a circle, with the witch doctor or medicine man and the drummers to the fore. When all the people are assembled the throbbing of the drums increases. They beat in tune to the heartbeats of the human circle.

The witch doctor is dressed in lion or leopard skin, sometimes in monkey skin. His face is painted in bold streaks of color: white, black, red. There are crisscrossing lines on his body too. He wanders about the center of the circle, almost idly at first. Every now and then he pauses and looks straight into someone's eyes and keeps on looking. For the person looked at, this is an encounter with fate. Few stare back. Their eyes slide past his face or go glazed. They fear but are not supposed to fear. They know the ancestors are just, that the innocent are never punished. To experience fear, therefore, is an acknowledgment of guilt. It is not necessary to know the nature of your guilt; if you were not guilty, there would be no fear in your mind.

The tempo of the drums increases. The witch doctor begins to dance, slowly at first. He begins to talk in a high-pitched nasal voice; spirits always talk through their noses. The drums and the incantations go on and on, getting faster and wilder, dominating the hearts and minds of all the circle. People begin to tremble and shiver. Some drop down in a trance and lie moaning on the ground. Everyone is possessed by the frenzy of the drums. The spirits of the ancestors are abroad.

Suddenly the drums stop. The witch doctor stands fixed for a dreadful moment that seems without end. Then he pounces. He grabs his victim and drags him or her into the center of the circle. The victim does not resist, does not protest. The ancestors are always just.

There may be one, there may be many victims. But once the victim or victims are "smelled out," the hypnotic spell of the drums is broken. People relax. Their hearts beat normally once more. Now the ancestors will be propitiated and the living freed of the evil which beset them. Now the famine or the drought or the plague or whatever had beset the land will depart from it. And so, while the victim or victims are put to death, the rest of the tribe celebrates the passing of the great evil.

Another key characteristic of tribal man is that his society is exclusive and not, like western society, inclusive. The lines are drawn very clearly, very sharply. Anybody not an "insider" is an enemy, actually or potentially—someone to distrust, someone to fear, someone to keep at bay. There is no choice, no volition about this. It is something ordained by the ancestral dead. The tribal society is therefore possibly the most exclusive society in the twentieth-century world. If you are not in the tribe, there is no way into it. If you are in it, there is no way out of it except death. Dissent is not recognized. To break the rules of the tribe is to court death.

Even the family, the foundation of the tribal in-group, is no simple affair. It is often a cluster of four generations. A man's family can be made up of his father, his father's first, second and third wives—there may be more—and the children of these. A man inherits the wives and children of his brothers who die before him. The wives then become his wives, the children of his brother become brothers and sisters to his own children by his own wife. Then there are the children's children. These and the old people, the grandparents, make up the immediate family, the heart of the in-group. Then there are the families related to one's family by blood ties—the families of uncles and cousins. These have the same complex structure of many wives and brothers and sisters, many of whom are inherited. A group of such blood-related families makes the clan. Clans have been known to be big enough to fill whole villages.

Another and most vital factor in the life of tribal man is his attitude to life and death. Neither life nor death is ever wholly accidental. Disease is never natural. These are brought about by the good and evil spirits all around us. The evil spirits are preoccupied with bringing disaster on the tribe, the good with protecting the tribe. To achieve their malign ends, evil spirits enter the bodies of ordinary human beings. To fight the evil spirits, good spirits enter the bodies of witch doctors. Life and death are thus out of the hands of mortal men.

The world of tribal man is so dominated by the spirits that some tribes will not eat birds because of the spirits that dwell in them, some will not eat fish, some are vegetarians and some eat meat only.

Tribal man is hemmed in, imprisoned by his ancestors. His horizons are only as wide as they permit. He is also protected by them. The rules are such that there are no orphans in the tribe, no misfits, no neurotics. And of course, the ancestral dead are hostile to change.

This, then, is the "oblique, the hard-to-know man" whom Richard Wright encountered on his first visit to Africa. He is the man who raised Nkrumah to power. He is the man whose pressures led Jomo Kenyatta to the Mau Mau and then to his lonely prison-exile in a barren and isolated spot. He, tribal man, will have a crucial say in the future of Africa.

The ancestral dead notwithstanding, change is being imposed on him. How he reacts to the change will have a powerful bearing on tomorrow's Africa.

If the men inaugurating the new ways have the sense and the patience to preserve the finer qualities of the old ways and fuse these with the new, then we can expect something magnificently new out of Africa.

DISCUSSION QUESTIONS

1. In the first few pages of his essay, Abrahams paints a vivid picture of the street life of Accra. List examples of sense imagery in his description that you found most memorable.

2. Abrahams describes Nkrumah and Kenyatta as he knew them in London and then again when he meets each of them in Africa. How did Nkrumah and Kenyatta change after returning to Africa?

3. What does Abrahams mean by saying that "being black is a small matter in tribal Africa"? How does this statement contrast with Abrahams's own experience as a black South African?

4. What is of greatest importance to the tribal African?

5. In the last paragraph of the essay Abrahams voices a hope that in the Africa of the future "the finer qualities of the old ways" may be fused with the new. What might be considered among the best qualities of the old ways? What is good about the new ways?

SUGGESTION FOR WRITING

Imagine that you are given the opportunity to abandon your western way of life and become a member of a tribal African group. Write two paragraphs. In the first, explain what adjustments to tribal life would be the easiest for you to make. In the second, explain what adjustments would be the hardest. Base your opinions on the description of tribal Africans that Abrahams provides.

from TELL FREEDOM

*"And judgment is turned away backward,
and justice standeth afar off: for truth is
fallen in the street, and equity cannot enter."*
ISAIAH

Wednesday was crackling day. On that day the children of the location[1] made the long trek to Elsburg siding for the squares of pig's rind that passed for our daily meat. We collected a double lot of cow dung[2] during the day before; a double lot of *moeroga*.[3]

I finished my breakfast and washed up. Aunt Liza was at her wash-tub in the yard. A misty, sickly sun was just showing. And on the open veld[4] the frost lay thick and white on the grass.

"Ready?" Aunt Liza called.

I went out to her. She shook the soapsuds off her swollen hands and wiped them on her apron. She lifted the apron and put her hand through the slits of the many thin cotton dresses she wore. The dress nearest the skin was the one with the pocket. From this she pulled a sixpenny piece. She tied it in a knot in the corner of a bit of colored cloth.

"Take care of that. . . . Take the smaller piece of bread in the bin but don't eat it till you start back. You can have a small piece of crackling with it. Only a small piece, understand?"

"Yes, Aunt Liza."

"All right."

I got the bread and tucked it into the little canvas bag in which I would carry the crackling.

"Bye, Aunt Liza." I trotted off, one hand in my pocket, feeling the cloth where the money was. I paused at Andries's home.

"Andries!" I danced up and down while I waited. The cold was not so terrible on bare feet if one did not keep still.

Andries came trotting out of their yard. His mother's voice followed; desperate and plaintive: "I'll skin you if you lose the money!"

"Women!" Andries said bitterly.

I glimpsed the dark, skinny woman at her wash-tub as we trotted across the veld. Behind, and in front of us, other children trotted in twos and threes.

There was a sharp bite to the morning air I sucked in; it stung my nose so that tears came to my eyes; it went down my throat like an icy draft; my nose ran. I tried breathing through my mouth but this was worse. The

---

1. **location:** the district in which nonwhites were required to live in South Africa under the apartheid system.

2. **cow dung:** Cow dung is used for fuel in treeless areas.

3. ***moeroga:*** a type of wild spinach.

4. **veld:** a grassland with scattered trees.

cold went through my shirt and shorts; my skin went pimply and chilled; my fingers went numb and began to ache; my feet felt like frozen lumps that did not belong to me, yet jarred and hurt each time I put them down. I began to feel sick and desperate.

"Jesus God in heaven!" Andries cried suddenly.

I looked at him. His eyes were rimmed in red. Tears ran down his cheeks. His face was drawn and purple, a sick look on it.

"Faster," I said.

"Think it'll help?"

I nodded. We went faster. We passed two children, sobbing and moaning as they ran. We were all in the same desperate situation. We were creatures haunted and hounded by the cold. It was a cruel enemy who gave no quarter. And our means of fighting it were pitifully inadequate. In all the mornings and evenings of the winter months, young and old, big and small, were helpless victims of the bitter cold. Only towards noon and the early afternoon, when the sun sat high in the sky, was there a brief respite. For us, the children, the cold, especially the morning cold, assumed an awful and malevolent personality. We talked of "It." "It" was a half-human monster with evil thoughts, evil intentions, bent on destroying us. "It" was happiest when we were most miserable. Andries had told me how "It" had, last winter, caught and killed a boy.

Hunger was an enemy too, but one with whom we could come to terms, who had many virtues and values. Hunger gave our *pap*,[5] *moeroga*, and crackling a feast-like quality. We could, when it was not with us, think and talk kindly about it. Its memory could even give moments of laughter. But the cold of winter was with us all the time. "It" never really eased up. There were only more bearable degrees of "It" at high noon and on mild days. "It" was the real enemy. And on this Wednesday morning, as we ran across the veld, winter was more bitterly, bitingly, freezingly real than ever.

The sun climbed. The frozen earth thawed, leaving the short grass looking wet and weary. Painfully, our feet and legs came alive. The aching numbness slowly left our fingers. We ran more slowly in the more bearable cold.

In climbing, the sun lost some of its damp look and seemed a real, if cold, sun. When it was right overhead, we struck the sandy road which meant we were nearing the siding. None of the others were in sight. Andries and I were alone on the sandy road on the open veld. We slowed down to a brisk walk. We were sufficiently thawed to want to talk.

"How far?" I said.

"A few minutes," he said.

"I've got a piece of bread," I said.

"Me too," he said. "Let's eat it now."

"On the way back," I said. "With a bit of crackling."

"Good idea. . . . Race to the fork."

---

5. **pap:** a porridge made with coarsely ground corn.

"All right."

"Go!" he said.

We shot off together, legs working like pistons. He soon pulled away from me. He reached the fork in the road some fifty yards ahead.

"I win!" he shouted gleefully, though his teeth still chattered.

We pitched stones down the road, each trying to pitch further than the other. I won and wanted to go on doing it. But Andries soon grew weary with pitching. We raced again. Again he won. He wanted another race but I refused. I wanted pitching, but he refused. So, sulking with each other, we reached the pig farm.

We followed a fenced-off pathway round sprawling white buildings. Everywhere about us was the grunt of pigs. As we passed an open doorway, a huge dog came bounding out, snarling and barking at us. In our terror, we forgot it was fenced in and streaked away. Surprised, I found myself a good distance ahead of Andries. We looked back and saw a young white woman call the dog to heel.

"Damn Boer[6] dog," Andries said.

"Matter with it?" I asked.

"They teach them to go for us. Never get caught by one. My old man's got a hole in his bottom where a Boer dog got him."

I remembered I had outstripped him.

"I won!" I said.

"Only because you were frightened," he said.

"I still won."

"Scare arse," he jeered.

"Scare arse, yourself!"

"I'll knock you!"

"I'll knock you back!"

A couple of white men came down the path and ended our possible fight. We hurried past them to the distant shed where a queue[7] had already formed. There were grown-ups and children. All the grown-ups, and some of the children, were from places other than our location.

The line moved slowly. The young white man who served us did it in leisurely fashion, with long pauses for a smoke. Occasionally he turned his back.

At last, after what seemed hours, my turn came. Andries was behind me. I took the sixpenny piece from the square of cloth and offered it to the man.

"Well?" he said.

"Sixpence crackling, please."

Andries nudged me in the back. The man's stare suddenly became cold and hard. Andries whispered into my ear.

"Well?" the man repeated coldly.

---

6. **Boer:** a South African of Dutch descent.

7. **queue:** a line of people.

"Please, *baas*,[8] I said.

"What d'you want?"

"Sixpence crackling, please."

"What?"

Andries dug me in the ribs.

"Sixpence crackling, please, *baas*."

"What?"

"Sixpence crackling, please, *baas*."

"You new here?"

"Yes, *baas*." I looked at his feet while he stared at me.

At last he took the sixpenny piece from me. I held my bag open while he filled it with crackling from a huge pile on a large canvas sheet on the ground. Turning away, I stole a fleeting glance at his face. His eyes met mine, and there was amused, challenging mockery in them. I waited for Andries at the back of the queue, out of the reach of the white man's mocking eyes.

The cold day was at its mildest as we walked home along the sandy road. I took out my piece of bread and, with a small piece of greasy crackling, still warm, on it, I munched as we went along. We had not yet made our peace so Andries munched his bread and crackling on the other side of the road.

"Dumb fool!" he mocked at me for not knowing how to address the white man.

"Scare arse!" I shouted back.

Thus, hurling curses at each other, we reached the fork. Andries saw them first and moved over to my side of the road.

"White boys," he said.

There were three of them. Two of about our own size and one slightly bigger. They had school bags and were coming toward us up the road from the siding.

"Better run for it," Andries said.

"Why?"

"No, that'll draw them. Let's just walk along, but quickly."

"Why?" I repeated.

"Shut up," he said.

Some of his anxiety touched me. Our own scrap was forgotten. We marched side by side as fast as we could. The white boys saw us and hurried up the road. We passed the fork. Perhaps they would take the turning away from us. We dared not look back.

"Hear them?" Andries asked.

"No."

I looked over my shoulder.

"They're coming," I said.

"Walk faster," Andries said. "If they come closer, run."

---

8. **baas** (bäs): master. [Afrikaans]

"Hey, *Klipkop!*"[9]

"Don't look back," Andries said.

"Hottentot!"

We walked as fast as we could.

"Bloody kaffir!"[10]

Ahead was a bend in the road. Behind the bend were bushes. Once there, we could run without them knowing it till it was too late.

"Faster," Andries said.

They began pelting us with stones.

"Run when we get to the bushes," Andries said.

The bend and the bushes were near. We would soon be there.

A clear young voice carried to us:

"Your fathers are dirty black bastards of baboons!"

"Run!" Andries called.

A violent, unreasoning anger suddenly possessed me. I stopped and turned.

"You're a liar!" I screamed it.

The foremost boy pointed at me: "An ugly black baboon!"

In a fog of rage I went towards him.

"Liar!" I shouted. "My father was better than your father!"

I neared them. The bigger boy stepped between me and the one I was after.

"My father was better than your father! Liar!"

The big boy struck me a mighty clout on the side of the face. I staggered, righted myself, and leaped at the boy who had insulted my father. I struck him on the face, hard. A heavy blow on the back of my head nearly stunned me. I grabbed at the boy in front of me. We went down together.

"Liar!" I said through clenched teeth, hitting him with all my might.

Blows rained on me, on my head, my neck, the side of my face, my mouth, but my enemy was under me and I pounded him fiercely, all the time repeating: "Liar! Liar! Liar!"

Suddenly, stars exploded in my head. Then there was darkness.

I emerged from the darkness to find Andries kneeling beside me.

"God, man! I thought they'd killed you."

I sat up. The white boys were nowhere to be seen. Like Andries, they'd probably thought me dead and run off in panic. The inside of my mouth felt sore and swollen. My nose was tender to the touch. The back of my head ached. A trickle of blood dripped from my nose. I stemmed it with the square of colored cloth. The greatest damage was to my shirt. It was ripped in many places. I remembered the crackling. I looked anxiously about. It was safe, a little off the road on the grass. I relaxed. I got up and brushed my clothes. I picked up the crackling.

---

9. **Klipkop:** literally, stone-head. [Afrikaans]

10. **Hottentot . . . kaffir:** abusive terms for a black South African.

Peter Abrahams   37

"God, you're dumb!" Andries said. "You're going to get it! Dumb arse!"

I was too depressed to retort. Besides, I knew he was right. I was dumb. I should have run when he told me to.

"Come on," I said.

One of many small groups of children, each child carrying his little bag of crackling, we trod the long road home in the cold winter afternoon.

There was tension in the house that night. When I got back Aunt Liza had listened to the story in silence. The beating or scolding I expected did not come. But Aunt Liza changed while she listened, became remote and withdrawn. When Uncle Sam came home she told him what had happened. He, too, just looked at me and became more remote and withdrawn than usual. They were waiting for something; their tension reached out to me, and I waited with them, anxious, apprehensive.

The thing we waited for came while we were having our supper. We heard a trap[11] pull up outside.

"Here it is," Uncle Sam said and got up.

Aunt Liza leaned back from the table and put her hands in her lap, fingers intertwined, a cold, unseeing look in her eyes.

Before Uncle Sam reached it, the door burst open. A tall, broad, white man strode in. Behind him came the three boys. The one I had attacked had swollen lips and a puffy left eye.

"Evening, *baas!*" Uncle Sam murmured.

"That's him," the bigger boy said, pointing at me.

The white man stared till I lowered my eyes.

"Well?" he said.

"He's sorry, *baas,*" Uncle Sam said quickly. "I've given him a hiding he won't forget soon. You know how it is, *baas.* He's new here, the child of a relative in Johannesburg and they don't all know how to behave there. You know how it is in the big towns, *baas.*" The plea in Uncle Sam's voice had grown more pronounced as he went on. He turned to me. "Tell the *baas* and young *basies* how sorry you are, Lee."

I looked at Aunt Liza and something in her lifelessness made me stubborn in spite of my fear.

"He insulted my father," I said.

The white man smiled.

"See, Sam, your hiding couldn't have been good."

There was a flicker of life in Aunt Liza's eyes. For a brief moment she saw me, looked at me, warmly, lovingly, then her eyes went dead again.

"He's only a child, *baas,*" Uncle Sam murmured.

"You stubborn too, Sam?"

"No, *baas.*"

"Good. . . . Then teach him, Sam. If you and he are to live here, you must teach him. Well. . . . ?"

"Yes, *baas.*"

---

11. **trap:** a light, one-horse carriage.

Uncle Sam went into the other room and returned with a thick leather thong. He wound it once round his hand and advanced on me. The man and boys leaned against the door, watching. I looked at Aunt Liza's face. Though there was no sign of life or feeling on it, I knew suddenly, instinctively, that she wanted me not to cry.

Bitterly, Uncle Sam said: "You must never lift your hand to a white person. No matter what happens, you must never lift your hand to a white person . . ."

He lifted the strap and brought it down on my back. I clenched my teeth and stared at Aunt Liza. I did not cry with the first three strokes. Then, suddenly, Aunt Liza went limp. Tears showed in her eyes. The thong came down on my back, again and again. I screamed and begged for mercy. I grovelled at Uncle Sam's feet, begging him to stop, promising never to lift my hand to any white person. . . .

At last, the white man's voice said: "All right, Sam."

Uncle Sam stopped. I lay whimpering on the floor. Aunt Liza sat like one in a trance.

"Is he still stubborn, Sam?"

"Tell the *baas* and *basies* you are sorry."

"I'm sorry," I said.

"Bet his father is one of those who believe in equality."

"His father is dead," Aunt Liza said.

"Good night, Sam."

"Good night, *baas*. Sorry about this."

"All right, Sam." He opened the door. The boys went out first, then he followed. "Good night, Liza."

Aunt Liza did not answer. The door shut behind the white folk, and soon we heard their trap moving away. Uncle Sam flung the thong viciously against the door, slumped down on the bench, folded his arms on the table, and buried his head on his arms. Aunt Liza moved away from him, came on the floor beside me and lifted me into her large lap. She sat rocking my body. Uncle Sam began to sob softly. After some time, he raised his head and looked at us.

"Explain to the child, Liza," he said.

"You explain," Aunt Liza said bitterly. "You are the man. You did the beating. You are the head of the family. This is a man's world. You do the explaining."

"Please, Liza. . . ."

"You should be happy. The whites are satisfied. We can go on now."

With me in her arms, Aunt Liza got up. She carried me into the other room. The food on the table remained half eaten. She laid me on the bed on my stomach, smeared fat on my back, then covered me with the blankets. She undressed and got into bed beside me. She cuddled me close, warmed me with her own body. With her big hand on my cheek, she rocked me, first to silence, then to sleep.

For the only time of my stay there, I slept on a bed in Elsburg.

When I woke next morning Uncle Sam had gone. Aunt Liza only once referred to the beating he had given me. It was in the late afternoon, when I returned with the day's cow dung.

"It hurt him," she said. "You'll understand one day."

That night, Uncle Sam brought me an orange, a bag of boiled sweets, and a dirty old picture book. He smiled as he gave them to me, rather anxiously. When I smiled back at him, he seemed to relax. He put his hand on my head, started to say something, then changed his mind and took his seat by the fire.

Aunt Liza looked up from the floor where she dished out the food.

"It's all right, old man," she murmured.

"One day. . . ." Uncle Sam said.

"It's all right," Aunt Liza repeated insistently.

The long winter passed. Slowly, day by day, the world of Elsburg became a warmer place. The cracks in my feet began to heal. The spells of bearable, noonday cold gave way to warmth. The noise of the veld at night became a din. The freezing nights changed, became bearable; changed again, became warm. Warm nights and hot days!

Summer had come, and with its coming the world became a softer, kindlier, more beautiful place. Sunflowers began blooming in people's yards. And people themselves began to relax and laugh. When, one evening, as I came in with some washing from the line, I heard Uncle Sam's voice raised in laughter, and saw him and Aunt Liza playing, I knew the summer had really come. Later that same evening he went into the other room and returned with a guitar. Aunt Liza beamed.

"Open the door?"

Uncle Sam nodded. He played. Soon people from the other houses came, in ones and twos, till our little room was crowded. Someone sang with his arms on his wife's shoulders, a love song:

I'll be your sweetheart,
If you will be mine . . . .

Summer had come indeed.

In the long summer afternoons, after my day's work, I went down to the river. Sometimes Andries and some of the other children went with me. Often I went alone.

Often, with others, or alone, I climbed the short willows with their long drooping branches. The touch of willow leaf on the cheek gives a feeling of cool wonder. Often I jumped from stone to stone on the broad bed of the shallow, clear, fast-flowing river. Sometimes I found little pools of idle water, walled off by stones from the flow. I tickled long-tailed tadpoles in these. The sun on the water touched their bodies with myriad colors. Sometimes I watched the *springhaas*—the wild rabbit of the veld—go leaping across the land, almost faster than my eye could follow. And sometimes I lay on my back, on the green grass, on the bank of the river, and looked up at the distant sky, watching thin fleecy white clouds form and re-form and trying to associate the shapes with people and things I knew. I loved being alone by the river. It became my special world.

Each day I explored a little more of the river, going further up or downstream, extending the frontiers of my world. One day, going further downstream than I had been before, I came upon a boy. He was on the bank on the other side from me. We saw each other at the same time and stared. He was completely naked. He carried two finely carved sticks of equal size and shape, both about his own height. He was not light brown, like the other children of our location, but dark brown, almost black. I moved almost to the edge of the river. He called out in a strange language.

"Hello!" I shouted.

He called out again, and again I could not understand. I searched for a place with stones, then bounded across. I approached him slowly. As I drew near, he gripped his sticks more firmly. I stopped.

He spoke harshly, flung one stick on the ground at my feet, and held the other ready as though to fight.

"Don't want to fight," I said.

I reached down to pick up the stick and return it to him. He took a step forward and raised the one in his hand. I moved back quickly. He stepped back and pointed at the stick on the ground. I shook my head.

"Don't want to fight."

I pushed the stick towards him with my foot, ready to run at the first sign of attack. I showed my new, stubby teeth in a tentative smile. He said something that sounded less aggressive. I nodded, smiling more broadly. He relaxed, picked up the stick, and transferred both to his left hand. He smacked his chest.

"Joseph! Zulu!"[12]

I smacked my own chest.

"Lee. . . ." But I didn't know what I was apart from that.

He held out his hand. We shook. His face lit up in a sunny smile. He said something and pointed downstream. Then he took my arm and led me down.

Far downstream, where the river skirted a hillside, hidden by a cluster of willows, we came on a large clear pool. Joseph flung his sticks on the ground and dived in. He shot through the water like a tadpole. He went down and came up. He shouted and beckoned me to come in. I undressed and went in more tentatively. Laughing, he pulled me under. I came up gasping and spluttering, my belly filled with water. He smacked me on the back and the water shot out of my mouth in a rush. When he realized I could not swim he became more careful. We spent the afternoon with Joseph teaching me to swim. At home, that evening, I stood beside Aunt Liza's wash-tub.

___

12. **Zulu:** a Bantu-speaking people of South Africa, who in the first half of the 1800s conquered all of Natal province in southeastern South Africa.

"Aunt Liza. . . ."

"Yes?"

"What am I?"

"What are you talking about?"

"I met a boy at the river. He said he was Zulu."

She laughed.

"You are Colored. There are three kinds of people: white people, Colored people and black people. The white people come first, then the Colored people, then the black people."

"Why?"

"Because it is so."

Next day, when I met Joseph, I smacked my chest and said: "Lee Colored!"

He clapped his hands and laughed.

Joseph and I spent most of the long summer afternoons together. He learned some Afrikaans[13] from me; I learned some Zulu from him. Our days were full.

There was the river to explore.

There were my swimming lessons, and others.

I learned to fight with sticks; to weave a green hat of young willow wands and leaves; to catch frogs and tadpoles with my hands; to set a trap for the springhaas; to make the sounds of the river birds.

There was the hot sun to comfort us. . . .

There was the green grass to dry our bodies. . . .

There was the soft clay with which to build. . . .

There was the fine sand with which to fight. . . .

There were our giant grasshoppers to race. . . .

There were the locust swarms when the skies turned black and we caught them by the hundreds. . . .

There was the rare taste of crisp, brown-baked, salted locusts. . . .

There was the voice of the wind in the willows. . . .

There was the voice of the heaven in the thunderstorms. . . .

There were the voices of two children in laughter, ours. . . .

There were Joseph's tales of black kings who lived in days before the white man. . . .

At home, I said: "Aunt Liza. . . ."

"Yes?"

"Did we have Colored kings before the white man?"

"No."

"Then where did we come from? Joseph and his mother come from the black kings who were before the white man."

And laughing, and ruffling my head, she said: "You talk too much. . . . Go'n wash up."

---

13. Afrikaans: the Dutch dialect spoken in South Africa.

And to Joseph, next day, I said: "We didn't have Colored kings before the white man."

And he comforted me and said: "It is of no moment. You are my brother. Now my kings will be your kings. Come: I have promised the mother to bring you home. She awaits you. I will race you to the hill."

From the top of the hill I looked into a long valley where cattle grazed. To the right, on the sloping land, nestled a cluster of mud huts. Round each hut was a wall built of mud.

"That is my home." Joseph pointed.

We veered right and went down to it. From a distance, we saw a woman at the gate of one of the huts.

"There is the mother!" He walked faster.

She was barefooted. She wore a slight skirt that came above her knees. A child was strapped to her back. The upper part of her body was naked except for the cloth across her chest that supported the child. Round her neck, arms, and legs were strings of white beads. As we drew near, I saw that she was young. And her broad, round face was beautiful. Her black eyes were liquid soft. She called out a greeting and smiled. Joseph pushed me forward.

"This is my brother, Lee of the Coloreds, little mother."

"Greetings, Mother," I said.

"I greet you, my son," she said softly, a twinkle in her eyes.

"As the man of my house has told you, food awaits. Come."

"See!" Joseph puffed out his chest. To his mother he said, "He would not believe when I told him I was the man in our house."

"He is indeed," she said.

Circling the hut was a raised platform. We sat on this while she brought us the food; salted fried locusts and corn on the cob. She sat nearby and watched us eating.

"Show the mother," Joseph said, and took another bite at the mielies[14] "Show the mother you are not circumcised yet."

I showed her.

"This is strange," she said. "Have you no initiation schools?"

"No!" Joseph said.

"Then when do you enter manhood?"

"He does not know."

"Is it true?" She looked at me.

I nodded.

"He's still a child!" Joseph cried. "So big and a child!"

Christmas came and it was a feast of eating and laughter. I spent half my time at home with Aunt Liza and Uncle Sam and the other half with Joseph and the little mother.

My sixth birthday came. Joseph and the little mother and I celebrated it by the river.

---

14. **mielies** (mē′ lēz): corn. [Afrikaans]

Then, early one morning, just as the first cold touches crept into the morning air, Joseph came to our location.

I was washing up when I heard young voices shouting: "Look at the naked kaffir! Lee's kaffir!"

I rushed out. Joseph came gravely to me.

"I come to take leave, my brother. My father has died in the mines so we go back to our land."

He stood straight and stern, not heeding the shouts of the children about. He was a man. This was the burden of his manhood. I had learned much from him, so I said equally coldly: "I must take leave of the little mother."

"She is a woman. She weeps."

We ran all the way there. . . .

When the little cart had taken them away, I climbed the hill and went down to the river. I carried Joseph's two sticks with me. These were his parting gift to his brother.

"Defend yourself," he had said. "I will make others."

I walked along the river that had been our kingdom. Now it was a desolate place. Joseph had been here with me; now Joseph had gone. Before I realized it, my tears flowed fast. There had been much between us.

So the summer passed. The autumn came. The leaves went brown on the willows by the river. They fluttered to the ground and turned to mold. The long days shortened suddenly. The cold came. Winter had come to torture us again.

DISCUSSION QUESTIONS

1. Which part of this selection did you enjoy more, part one about Abrahams' confrontation with the three white boys or part two about Abrahams' friendship with Joseph? Why?

2. A novel that describes the growth of a child to maturity is called a *bildungsroman*. Why might this term be a good one to apply to this selection from Abrahams' autobiography? In what ways does Abrahams grow in this selection?

3. Reread the quotation from Isaiah that appears at the beginning of the selection. In what ways is the content of the quotation relevant to the selection?

4. Discuss Abrahams' meeting with Joseph. In what ways might this be considered one of the most important events in Abrahams' life?

5. In this selection, Abrahams describes two events from his childhood that made a lasting impression on him. Think back to your own childhood. What event made a lasting impression on you? How did it affect you?

SUGGESTION FOR WRITING

Compare and contrast the first part of this selection (Abrahams' confrontation with the three white boys) with the second part (Abrahams' friendship with Joseph). You may do this by discussing both parts in one paragraph or by writing one paragraph in which you discuss part one and another paragraph in which you discuss part two. Whichever format you choose, note the weather, Abrahams' activities, and the attitudes of the people with whom Abrahams comes in contact. Also describe the difference in mood between the two parts.

R. E. G. ARMATTOE
(1913–1953)

Before his untimely death from pneumonia in Hamburg, Germany, in 1953, Raphael Ernest Grail Armattoe had nevertheless led a wide and varied life. Born in Denu in the Gold Coast (now Ghana), he worked as a poet, anthropologist, historian, and physician. Educated in Europe from the time he was 13, Dr. Armattoe practiced medicine during World War II in Northern Ireland. He spent ten years in Ireland except for a brief trip home in 1950 to enter politics. While in Ireland, Armattoe wrote two volumes of poetry, *Between the Forest and the Sea* (1950) and *Deep Down the Black Man's Mind,* published after his death (1959). While his poetry avoids bitterness and protest, Armattoe does proclaim the nobility of blackness, but he also recognizes the harsh realities of a life where dreams remain unfulfilled. ∎

THE LONELY SOUL

      I met an old woman
      Talking by herself
      Down a lonely road.
      Talking to herself,
5   Laughing all the time,
      Talking to herself
      Down a country road.
      Child, you cannot know
      Why folks talk alone.
10   If the road be long
      And travelers none,
      A man talks to himself.
      If showers of sorrows
      Fall down like arrows
15   The lone wayfarer
      May talk by himself.
      So an old woman
      On lone country roads,
      Laughing all the time,
20   May babble to herself
      To keep the tears away.
      Woman, you are sad!
      'Tis the same with me.

DISCUSSION QUESTIONS

1. Have you ever caught yourself talking out loud to yourself in private or in public? What were the reasons?

2. What event does the speaker in this poem describe? According to the speaker, why does the woman laugh and talk to herself?

3. What does the speaker realize in the last two lines of the poem?

4. If you look below the surface meaning of the lines, what might the long road (line 10) represent? Who might the travelers (line 11) be? What might the showers (line 13) be? Who do you think the child (line 8) is that the speaker addresses?

SUGGESTION FOR WRITING

Is the title "The Lonely Soul" an appropriate one for this poem? Write a paragraph in which you discuss this question. Consider the identity of the lonely soul. Also consider the words and phrases and the stylistic devices the speaker uses to get across his point.

J. BENIBENGOR BLAY

(born 1925)

J. Benibengor Blay has written novelettes, short stories, radio scripts, and poems. Though critics have called his writing derivative and uninspired, Blay's numerous short stories and radio scripts are highly popular in his native Ghana. He has published three collections of poetry in one volume entitled *Thoughts of* *Youth* (1967). His poetry often tackles the problems of a changing Africa during pre-independence. Blay owns his own publishing company and has published many of his works himself. He has traveled extensively in both Europe and the United States and has served as a member of parliament in Ghana. ∎

FUNERAL OF A WHALE

There is great excitement in the ancient town of Missibi in Ghana.

The previous night had been wet and stormy and one which the fishermen were not likely to forget. Caught in the storm, their canoes had been dashed to pieces on the rocks and their nets swept away on the swift current. Only the fact that they were all strong swimmers had saved the men from drowning.

The sun is not yet up when they collect again on the shore to watch for their nets. The moon is still shining and little waves dance merrily on the strand, while the sea crabs scuttle among the scattered shells. But these things do not interest the fishermen, and even the search for nets is forgotten as they catch sight of a huge object, surrounded by a shoal of fish, tossing on the rolling sea. Their slow, questing advance is halted as a nauseating stench greets them. Fingers to their noses, they crane and peer. It is a whale—and judging by the smell, it has been dead for some days.

Now, such a sight is no mere spectacle to the people of Missibi. As descendants of a strong and virile race which long ago came by sea in great barge-like ships to settle in these parts, they hold to the tradition that the sea is their home and they worship it to this day. In any crisis—whatever its nature, whether drought or famine or war—they call upon the sea for help. The whale is the king of their sea. And it has been the custom, throughout their long history, to accord a ceremonial funeral to any whale that comes rolling ashore dead.

So, bound by tradition, the fishermen must bear the unhappy tidings to the ruler of the town. Their waists girdled with palm leaves and fingers to lips as signs that their news is urgent, and as yet secret, they go on their errand.

The chief's advisers are called together by the court messenger for a palaver.[1] Now the fishermen are permitted to tell their news. Only after the chief's bodyguards have visited the beach to confirm this statement may the townsfolk be told. It is now past eight o'clock in the morning. The state drums boom out the warning of great calamity. The people from the busy market place, the farmers, coconut breakers and rice growers who have risen at cockcrow and gone to the farms, all come trooping to the palace yard, agog with excitement.

The chief comes to the courtyard with his advisers and sits on the landing of the dais. His face betokens sadness. His attendants bow and leave the palace. The drums are still booming. Outside are packed lorries[2] and cars from up country bringing loads of hawkers and buyers to the market while the occupants move in with the still surging crowd.

The court messenger comes into the yard, bows to the chief and courtiers, commands silence and after giving a brief survey of the history of Missibi and her connection with the sea, makes his announcement to the assembled throng.

"The State is in mourning. A whale is dead and has been washed ashore. The funeral will be held at two o'clock at Aposika where the king of the sea now lies."

There is no whisper nor laughter nor cough as the great crowd moves from distant parts, out of the palace. The market day is postponed. The school bell's tolling stopped. All is sad silence. Yet it is a great day for the hawkers from distant parts, for now they will see something of which so far they have only heard. To the aged of the town it is history repeating itself, and the announcement seems to bring back pictures of half-forgotten times.

By order of a committee appointed by the chief's advisers, funeral preparations are put in hand at once. Cases of gin, beer, kola and palm wine are brought from the stores and cellars. A body of young men is engaged in the erection of bamboo huts, and the bush around the area is cleared, while musicians polish their instruments in readiness. Word is passed to neighboring places and more people arrive to swell the numbers.

At two o'clock the procession leaves for the scene of the funeral, guns booming, state guns rumbling, ivory horn blaring. The chief and his counselors are dressed in red. The womenfolk, besmeared with red clay and wearing pieces of red calico tied around their hair, are in front with the children. The men bring up the rear.

The tail of the column is as yet only at the outskirts of the town when its head reaches the place where, a little off the beach, lies the great shapeless mass of the whale. Gallons of disinfectant have already been sprinkled around to kill the smell.

---

1. palaver: conference; discussion.

2. lorries: trucks.

Now the chief's messenger calls for silence and orders the crowd to be seated. The chief steps forward followed by his advisers. Dropping the red cloth from his shoulder and gathering the folds in his left arm, with a glass of rum held in his right hand, he first raises his eyes to heaven then looks to the ground as he pours out a libation with these words: "Tradition binds us to the sea and the whale is king of the elements there. My people and I pay you homage and lament your death. How it happened we do not know. Whether it was in combat with your fellow kings, or whether it was inflicted by those who delight in making sport of you, or whether it was a natural death, we are afflicted all the same with a great sense of personal loss. We reaffirm our traditional ties with your descendants, will look to them in anxious days for help, and beg of you, who now belong to the ages, to release this land from starvation and sickness; leave in their place health and plenty. Rest in peace."

The funeral ceremony being declared open, the women like minstrels tell the story of the whale in parables; its connection with the state is recounted and the dead one praised. The chief and his advisers are head mourners and make themselves responsible for the fair distribution of drinks, providing food for those who have come from afar and recording donations received.

The young men keep order and play native instruments, while the old correct any departure from the traditional funeral procedure. Boys and girls play "Hunt the Slipper" and "Ampay." Hunters fire off guns and firecrackers at intervals in honor of the majesty of the dead. Fishermen fish in the waves and cast their nets on the beach; farmers sow their seeds on the strand, fetish priests play tom-toms and perform their feats of walking barefoot on broken bottles and gashing their stomachs with sharp knives. Everybody, in fact, is doing something. And all the men are partly or completely drunk.

As the celebration continues, weeping becomes the order of the day; there is competition among the womenfolk in pitch, tone, and rendering of phrases, and prizes are offered to those who maintain the high standard of wailing set by their ancestors.

Further away from the crowds a great number of seagulls gather. Some are twittering, others are flying around the whale. The tide begins to rise and the waves are swelling high. Deep clouds overshadow the clear blue sky, and for a while the heavens are pouring rain. It seems that nature, too, is paying tribute to the king of the sea.

At six o'clock, as the sun is setting behind the clouds, the celebrations reach their climax—the solemn spreading of a long white sheet over the whale. Now each mourner takes a pebble, a shell, a stick, a coin or anything handy and, whispering a few words, whirls it around his head and throws it in the direction of the whale. Then without a further glance, all return to town.

The funeral of the king of the sea is over.

DISCUSSION QUESTIONS

1. The immense and expensive effort put forth to honor the death of a whale must tax the Missibi community heavily. In what ways do you think it is worth it to the people of Missibi to go to this trouble?

2. What is the color of mourning in the Missibi community? How do you know?

3. At the funeral everyone seems to have some responsibility. What are the responsibilities of the old men? the young men? the women? What do the hunters, fishermen, farmers, and priests do?

4. Although the funeral for the whale is a time for mourning, in what ways is it also a time for celebration for the people of Missibi?

SUGGESTION FOR WRITING

In one or two paragraphs, compare the funeral ceremony for the whale with funeral ceremonies you are familiar with. What obvious differences can you identify? What similarities can you identify? In your paragraph(s), discuss both the differences and the similarities.

J. P. CLARK
(born 1935)

John Pepper Clark was born in Kiagbodo, Nigeria, to an Ijo chief and an Urhobo princess. Clark pursued an education at University College, Ibadan, and also at Princeton University. Clark is considered one of the foremost writers in Africa. He has written literary and dramatic theory and criticism, but is best known as a poet and a playwright. Clark's second collection of poetry, *A Reed in the Tide* (1965), was the first volume of verse by an African poet to be published internationally. *A Decade of Tongues* (1981) is a collection of ten years of Clark's poetry. For a time Clark taught at the University of Lagos, retiring from that position in 1980. In 1982 he and his wife founded a repertory theatre in Lagos where he still serves as artistic director. ∎

POEMS

NIGHT RAIN

What time of night it is
I do not know
Except that like some fish
Doped out of the deep[1]
5   I have bobbed up bellywise
From stream of sleep
And no cocks crow.

It is drumming hard here
And I suppose everywhere
10   Droning with insistent ardor upon
Our roof-thatch and shed
And through sheaves slit open
To lightning and rafters
I cannot quite make out overhead
15   Great water drops are dribbling
Falling like orange or mango
Fruits showered forth in the wind

---

1. Doped out of the deep: Fishermen in central Africa often drop drugs into the water and then gather the fish which float paralyzed to the surface.

Or perhaps I should say so
Much like beads I could in prayer tell
20 Them on string as they break
In wooden bowls and earthenware
Mother is busy now deploying
About our roomlet and floor.
Although it is so dark
25 I know her practiced step as
She moves her bins, bags, and vats
Out of the run of water
That like ants filing out of the wood
Will scatter and gain possession
30 Of the floor. Do not tremble then,
But turn, brothers, turn upon your side
Of the loosening mats
To where the others lie.
We have drunk tonight of a spell
35 Deeper than the owl's or bat's
That wet of wings may not fly.
Bedraggled upon the *iroko*,[2] they stand
Emptied of hearts, and
Therefore will not stir, no, not
40 Even at dawn for then
They must scurry in to hide.
So let us roll over on our back
And again roll to the beat
Of drumming all over the land
45 And under its ample soothing hand
Joined to that of the sea
We will settle to sleep of the innocent and free.

GIRL BATHING

Her basket of cassava set away from reach
Of a log basking smooth on the beach,
She wades gingerly up to her high
Girdled hips, her underskirt lapping her thigh
5 Like calyces[3] a corn. And as she ducks
Under, with deft fingers plucks
Loose her hair, the sweat and dirt long dried in every pore
Fall off her back, and in their place once more

---

2. *iroko:* a very tall Central African tree.

3. calyces: the outer green leaves of a flower; here, the husks of corn.

The unguent[4] flow of limbs, the fresh
10 Warm smell of her flesh.
    O girl of erect and rearing breast,
    So ripe with joy for the blest,
    Splash, your teeth flashing pearls, in the whirlpool
    You have made, its lively cool
15 Waters lambent[5] through your veins,
    A tonic at the core of your bones.
    And striding back to land, neat
    On sands golden at your feet,
    How iridescent[6] breaks all
20 Your porcelain skin to tattoo beads of coral!

————

4. **unguent:** a soothing salve.

5. **lambent:** flickering; softly bright or radiant.

6. **iridescent:** displaying shifting, rainbow-like colors.

DISCUSSION QUESTIONS

1. To what does the speaker compare himself in lines 3–6 of "Night Rain"?

2. What is happening in lines 15–27, and what is the speaker's mother doing?

3. What does the speaker mean when he refers to the "ample soothing hand" of the drumming of the rain as being "joined to that of the sea"?

4. Often in poetry a storm is presented as threatening or violent, inspiring fear or awe. Is that an accurate description of the speaker's reaction to the storm in "Night Rain"? Use evidence from the poem to support your answer.

5. In the poem "Girl Bathing," describe the woman's physical actions. What does she do?

6. As part of their program of rediscovery of authentic African culture, the French-speaking Negritude poets (see Introduction, page xvii) often take as their theme the beauty of black women. In "Girl Bathing" the speaker celebrates the beauty of a black woman. Do you think the speaker celebrates something more than the woman's beauty? Explain your answer with evidence from the poem.

SUGGESTION FOR WRITING

Which of these two poems by J. P. Clark did you enjoy reading more? Choose one of the poems and write a paragraph in which you discuss your reasons for enjoying it. Consider the content of the poem, its imagery, and its theme.

BERNARD DADIÉ

(born 1916)

One critic has said that the work of Bernard Dadié deals very simply with Africa and the Africans' desire to proclaim its equality with other peoples. Dadié is one of the major African authors who writes in French. He has written in virtually every major genre, including novels, poetry, plays, short stories, essays, and criticism. Dadié's strong loyalty to Africa is evident in all of his work. Born in Assinie, Ivory Coast, he was educated in Dakar, Senegal, and worked for a time on the newspaper of the Nationalist party in the Ivory Coast. Later he entered government service and served in several positions, the latest being Minister of Culture and Information of the Ivory Coast. Dadié has traveled extensively and holds numerous honorary degrees from European and American universities. He has published several volumes of poetry, including *Afrique debout* (1950), *Ronde de jours* (1956), and *Hommes de tous les continents* (1967). ■

MEN OF ALL CONTINENTS

I emerge from blood-spattered nights.

Look at my flanks
Plowed by hunger and fire
I was an arable land
5   See my callused hand,
            black
from ever working the world.
My eyes burned by the fire of Love.

I was there when the angel drove out the ancestor
I was there when the waters consumed the mountains
10   Also there, when Jesus reconciled heaven and earth
Still there, when his smile above the ravines
Bound us together in the same destiny.

Men of all continents
Bullets still behead the roses
15   in the mornings of dreams.

Having left the night of artificial hopes
I would sing to you
You who hold heaven within reach
    We
who seek ourselves in the false dawn of the streetlamps.

20 I too know
Of cold in the bones, of hunger in the belly,
Of waking up startled by the clatter of carbines
But a star has always given a wink
On evenings of fires, in the hours drunk with gunpowder.

25 Men of all continents
Holding heaven within reach
You who like to hear a woman laugh,
You who like to watch a child play,
You who like to offer your hand
30 To form a chain

Bullets still behead the roses
in the mornings of dreams.

DISCUSSION QUESTIONS

1. Who is the speaker—the "I"—of the poem? Who is being addressed—the "you"—in the poem? Who might the "we" be in lines 18–19?

2. What is the speaker saying in lines 8–12?

3. What does the speaker mean by saying that "Bullets still behead the roses / in the mornings of dreams"?

SUGGESTION FOR WRITING

Do you think this is a poem of hope or despair? Write a paragraph in which you argue for one side or the other or perhaps both. Support your opinion with evidence from the poem.

BIRAGO DIOP

(born 1906)

The father of Birago Diop (dē´op) died when his son was an infant, and he grew up under the strong influence of his mother's family, including the family *griot* (grē´ō) or oral historian Amadou Koumba, who inspired Diop to write retellings of the African tales he learned as a child. Born in Dakar, Senegal, Diop was educated there and then later studied veterinary medicine in Paris. While in Paris he began writing poetry. After graduation Diop worked as a veterinary surgeon first in the Sudan and later in the Ivory Coast, Upper Volta, and Mauritania. From 1960 to 1965 Diop served as the Senegalese ambassador to Tunisia, after which he returned to his veterinary practice. Though not a prolific writer, Diop is highly regarded by critics, who consider him one of Africa's most accomplished and elegant prose stylists. His retellings of African tales from the oral tradition have been singled out for praise as being charming, exquisitely written, and profound. ■

TRUTH AND FALSEHOOD

Translated from the French by Dorothy S. Blair

Fene-Falsehood had grown big and had learned many things. But there were many things that he still did not know, notably that man—and woman even less—bears no resemblance to the good Lord. And so he took umbrage[1] and considered himself hard done by every time he heard anyone say: "The good Lord loves Truth!" and he heard it very often. Some certainly said that nothing looks more like the truth than a falsehood, but the majority stated that Truth and Falsehood were like night and day. That is why, when one day he set out on a journey with Deug-Truth, Fene-Falsehood said to his traveling companion:

"You are the one whom the Lord loves, you are the one whom people no doubt prefer, so it is you who must do the talking everywhere we go. For if I were recognized we should be very badly received."

They set out early in the morning and walked for a long time. At midday they entered the first house of the village which they reached. After they had exchanged greetings they had to ask before being given anything to drink. The mistress of the house gave them, in a calabash[2] of doubtful cleanliness, some lukewarm water which would have made an ostrich vomit. There was no question of giving them anything to eat, although a

---

1. **umbrage:** offense.

2. **calabash:** a gourd whose hard shell is used as a utensil like a bottle or a dipper.

pot full of rice was boiling at the entrance to the hut. The travelers lay down in the shade of a baobab in the middle of the courtyard and awaited the good Lord, that is to say, luck and the return of the master of the house. The latter came back at twilight and asked for food for himself and the strangers.

"I haven't got anything ready yet," said the woman, who could not have swallowed by herself the whole contents of the pot.

The husband flew into a great rage, not only on his own account, although he was famished after having spent the whole day working in the fields in the blazing sun, but because of his unknown guests, whom he was unable to honor (as every master of the house worthy of the name should do) and who had been left with empty bellies. He asked: "Is that the action of a good wife? Is that the action of a generous woman? Is that a good housewife?"

Fene-Falsehood, as agreed, prudently said nothing, but Deug-Truth could not keep silent. She answered sincerely that a woman worthy of the name of mistress of the house might have been more hospitable to strangers, and ought always to have something prepared for her husband's return.

Then the woman flew into a mad rage and, threatening to arouse the whole village, ordered her husband to throw out these impertinent strangers, who interfered in the way she ran her house and took it upon themselves to give her advice, otherwise she would return home to her parents on the spot. So the poor husband, who could not see himself managing without a wife (even a bad housekeeper) and without any cooking because of two strangers, two passers-by whom he had never seen and whom he would probably never see again in his life, was forced to tell the travelers to be on their way. Did they not remember, these ill-bred travelers, that life was not all *couscous*[3] but that it did need some softening, however? Did they have to say things so crudely?

So Deug and Fene continued their journey which had begun so ill. They walked on for a long time and reached a village in the entrance to which they found some children busy sharing out a fat bull which they had just slaughtered. On entering the house of the village chief, they saw some children who were saying to him: "Here is your share," and they gave him the head and the feet of the animal.

Now, since time immemorial, since n'Diadiane n'Diaye,[4] in every village inhabited by man, it is the chief who gives every one his share, and who chooses his own—the best.

"Who do you think commands here in this village?" the chief asked the travelers.

---

3. *couscous:* a highly seasoned dish made from coarsely ground meal mixed with saltwater, to which vegetables, meat, or fish are added. It is eaten in different forms throughout West Africa.

4. n'Diadiane n'Diaye: a traditional hero. His name is introduced to suggest the beginning of history.

Prudently Fene-Falsehood kept silent and did not open his mouth: Deug-Truth was obliged, as agreed, to give her opinion: "To all appearances," she said, "it is these children."

"You are insolent folk!" cried the old man in a rage. "Leave this village, go, go immediately, or else you will never leave it again! Begone, begone!"

And the unfortunate travelers continued on their way.

As they went, Fene said to Deug: "The results have not been very brilliant so far, and I am not sure if they will be any better if I go on any longer leaving you in charge of our affairs. So from now on I am going to look after both of us. I am beginning to think that even if the good Lord loves you, man doesn't appreciate you over much."

Not knowing how they would be received in the village they were approaching, and from whence came cries and lamentations, Deug and Fene stopped at the well before entering any dwelling, and were quenching their thirst, when a woman came along all in tears.

"What is the meaning of these cries and tears?" asked Deug-Truth.

"Alas!" said the woman (she was a slave) "our favorite queen, the youngest of the king's wives, died yesterday, and the king is so heart-sore that he wishes to kill himself, so that he may rejoin the woman who was the fairest and most gracious of his wives."

"And is that the sole cause of so much lamenting?" asked Fene-Falsehood. "Go tell the king that there is at the well a stranger who can bring back to life people who have even been dead for long."

The slave went off and returned a minute later accompanied by an old man who led the travelers into a fine hut, where they found a whole sheep roasted and two calabashes of *couscous*.

"My master brings you here," said the old man, "and bids you rest after your long journey. He bids you wait and he will send for you ere long."

The next day an even more copious repast was brought to the strangers, and the day after the same thing happened. But Fene pretended to be angry and impatient; he said to the messenger: "Go tell your king that I have no time to waste here, and that I shall continue on my way if he has no need of me."

The old man returned, telling him: "The king is asking for you." And Fene followed him, leaving Deug-Truth in the hut.

"First, what do you desire as a reward for what you are about to do?" asked the king, when he came before him.

"What can you offer me?" replied Fene-Falsehood.

"I will give you one hundred things from all that I possess in this land."

"That will not satisfy me," calculated Fene.

"Say then yourself what you desire," suggested the king.

"I desire the half of all that you possess."

"That is agreed," the king accepted.

Fene had a hut built above the grave of the favorite, and went in alone, armed with a hoe. He could be heard puffing and panting; then, after a very long time, he began to talk, softly at first, then in a very loud voice as if he were arguing with several persons; at length he came out of the hut and stood with his back firmly pressed against the door.

"Things are getting very complicated," he said to the king. "I have dug up the grave, I have woken your wife, but scarcely had she returned to life and was about to emerge from beneath the ground than your father woke up too and seized her by the feet, saying to me: 'Leave this woman alone. What can she give to you? Whereas if I return to earth, I will give you all the fortune of my son.' He had barely finished making me this proposition than his father emerged in his turn and offered me all his goods and half the property of his son. Your grandfather was elbowed out of the way by the grandfather of your father, who offered me your property, your father's property, his son's property and the half of his own fortune. Scarcely had he finished speaking than his father arrived, so that your ancestors and the forbears of their ancestors are all at the exit of your wife's grave."

The King Bour looked at his advisers, and the notables looked at the king. The stranger was quite right to say that things were in a mess. Bour gazed at Fene-Falsehood, and the old men gazed at him. What was to be done?

"To help you out of your dilemma, and to avoid too difficult a choice," said Fene-Falsehood, "just give me an idea which I should bring back, your wife or your father?"

"My wife!" said the king, who loved the favorite more than ever and who had always been afraid of the late king, whose death he had precipitated, with the assistance of the notables.

"Naturally, naturally!" replied Fene-Falsehood. "Only, you see, your father did offer me double what you promised me just now."

Bour turned towards his advisers, and the advisers gazed at him and gazed at the stranger. The price was high, and what good would it do the king to see his most beloved wife again, if he were deprived of all his goods? Would he still be king? Fene guessed the thoughts of the king and of his notables: "Unless," he said, "unless you give me, for leaving your wife where she is at present, what you promised me to bring her back."

"That is certainly the best and the most reasonable thing to do!" replied in chorus the old notables who had contributed to the disappearance of the old king.

"What do you say, Bour?" asked Fene-Falsehood.

"Oh, well, let my father, the father of my father and the fathers of their fathers remain where they are, and my wife likewise," said the king.

And so it was that Fene-Falsehood, for bringing no one back from the other world, received half the property of the king, who, moreover, soon forgot his favorite and took another wife.

DISCUSSION QUESTIONS

1. Were you able to predict the outcome of this tale? If so, at what point in the tale did you know what would happen?

2. Very often in fairy tales, events happen in threes—someone gets three wishes, there are three bears, or a knight goes on three missions. What are the three events that lead to the outcome of this tale?

3. The dictionary defines *paradox* as "a seemingly contradictory statement that expresses a possible truth." What is the paradox in this tale? Why is it a paradox?

SUGGESTION FOR WRITING

Can you think of a different ending for this tale? For example, what would happen if Fene-Falsehood were defeated? Think of ways to change the ending and write a new ending for this tale. Begin your new ending with the third event in this tale, and consider these questions: How will the king learn the truth about Fene-Falsehood's deception? What will happen to Fene-Falsehood in the end? What role, if any, will Deug-Truth play? Share your ending with your classmates. Which of the new endings did you like most? Explain.

THE WAGES OF GOOD

Translated from the French by Robert Baldick

Diassigue-the-Alligator, scraping the sand with his flaccid belly, was returning to the channel after sleeping all day long in the hot sun, when he heard the women coming back from drawing water, scouring calabashes, and washing linen. These women, who had undoubtedly done more work with their tongues than with their hands, were still talking and talking. They were saying sorrowfully that the king's daughter had fallen into the water and been drowned, and that it was very likely—indeed it was certain, according to a woman slave—that at dawn the next day Bour-the-King would have the channel drained in order to find his beloved daughter's body. Diassigue, whose hole in the channel bank was close to the village, turned back the way he had come and went far into the interior in the dark night. The next day, sure enough, the channel was drained and, what is more, all the alligators that lived in it were killed; in the hole of the oldest of them all, they found the body of the king's daughter.

In the middle of the day, a child who was gathering dead wood found Diassigue-the-Alligator in the scrub.

"What are you doing there, Diassigue?" asked the child.

"I have lost my way," answered the alligator. "Will you carry me home, Goné?"

"There isn't a channel any more," the child told him.

"Then carry me to the river," said Diassigue-the-Alligator.

Goné-the-Child went to fetch a mat and some creepers. He rolled Diassigue up in the mat, which he fastened with the creepers. Then he put it on his head and walked until the evening, when he reached the river. Arriving at the water's edge, he put down his bundle, cut the creepers, and unrolled the mat. Then Diassigue said to him: "Goné, my legs are all stiff from that long journey. Will you put me into the water, please?"

Goné-the-Child walked into the water until it came up to his knees, and he was about to put Diassigue down when the latter said to him: "Go on until the water comes up to your waist, for I would find it hard to swim here."

Goné did as he asked and walked on until the water encircled his waist.

"Go on until it comes up to your chest," the alligator begged him.

The child went on until the water reached his chest.

"You might as well go on now until it comes up to your shoulders."

Goné walked on until his shoulders were covered, and then Diassigue said to him: "Now put me down."

Goné obeyed. He was about to return to the river bank when the alligator gripped him by the arm.

"Wouye yayô! Oh, Mother," cried the child. "What are you doing? Let go of me!"

"I shan't let go of you, because I'm very hungry, Goné."

"Let go of me!"

"I shan't let go of you. I haven't had anything to eat for two days and I'm too hungry."

"Tell me, Diassigue, do you repay a kindness with another kindness or with a bad turn?"

"A good deed is repaid with a bad turn and not with another good deed."

"Now it's I who am in your power, but what you say isn't true, and you must be the only person in the whole world to say it."

"Oh! You really think so?"

"Well, let's ask a few people and we'll see what they say."

"All right," said Diassigue; "but if we find three people who share my opinion, then you'll end up in my stomach, I promise you."

He had scarcely finished uttering this threat when an old, old cow arrived to drink out of the river. When she had quenched her thirst, the alligator called her and asked her: "Nagy, you who are so old and possess all wisdom, can you tell us whether a good deed is repaid with a kindness or with a bad turn?"

"A good deed," declared Nagy-the-Cow, "is repaid with a bad turn, and believe me, I know what I'm talking about. In the days when I was young, strong, and vigorous, when I came back from the pasture I was given bran, millet and a lump of salt, I was washed and rubbed down, and if Poulo, the little shepherd, happened to raise his stick against me, he was sure to receive a beating in his turn from his master. At that time I gave a lot of milk, and all my master's cows and bulls are offspring of mine. Now I am old and no longer give any milk or calves, so nobody takes care of me any more or takes me out to graze. At dawn every day, a blow from a stick drives me out of the park, and I go off on my own to look for my food. That is why I say that a good deed is repaid with a bad turn."

"Goné, did you hear that?" asked Diassigue-the-Alligator.

"Yes," said the child, "I heard it all right."

With her thin, bony buttocks swaying like a couple of swordblades, Nagy-the-Cow went off, swinging her old tick-bitten tail, towards the sparse grass of the scrubland.

Then gaunt old Fass-the-Horse arrived on the scene. He was about to brush the water with his lips before drinking when the alligator called out to him: "Fass, you who are so old and wise, can you tell us, this child and me, whether a good deed is repaid with a kindness or with a bad turn?"

"I certainly can," declared the old horse. "A kindness is always repaid by an evil deed, and I know something about it. Listen to me, the two of you. In the days when I was young, strong and high-spirited, I had three grooms all to myself; I had my trough filled with millet morning and night, and bran mash often mixed with honey at all hours of the day. I was taken for a bath and a rub-down every morning. I had a bridle and a saddle made by a Moorish saddler and adorned by a Moorish jeweler. I used to go on the battlefields, and the five hundred prisoners my master took in the wars were brought back on my crupper.[1] For nine years I carried my master and his booty. Now that I have grown old, all that they do for me is hobble me at dawn, and then, with a blow from a stick, they send me into the scrubland to look for my food."

Having spoken, Fass-the-Horse brushed the scum from the surface of the water, took a long drink, and then went off, hampered by his hobble, with his jerky, limping walk.

"Goné," said the alligator, "did you hear that? Now I'm too hungry to wait any longer: I'm going to eat you."

"No, Uncle Diassigue," said the child. "You said yourself that you would ask three people. If the next person who comes along says the same as those two, then you can eat me, but not before."

"Very well," agreed the alligator, "but I warn you that we shan't go any further afield."

Then Leuk-the-Hare came running up, his hindquarters twitching. Diassigue called him:

"Uncle Leuk, you who are the oldest among us, can you tell us which of us two is right? I say that a good deed is repaid with a bad turn, and this child declares that the price of a good deed is a kindness."

---

1. **crupper:** portion of a horse's harness that passes over the animal's rump.

Leuk rubbed his chin, scratched his ear, and then asked in his turn: "Diassigue, my friend, do you ask a blind man to tell you whether cotton is white or whether a crow is really black?"

"Of course not," admitted the alligator.

"Can you tell me where a child whose family you don't know is going?"

"Certainly not."

"Then explain to me what has happened and I may be able to answer your question without much risk of making a mistake."

"Well, Uncle Leuk, this is the position: this child found me in the interior, rolled me up in a mat and carried me here. Now I'm feeling hungry, and seeing that I have to eat, because I don't want to die, it would be stupid of me to let him go, to run after a dubious prey."

"Indubitably," said Leuk, "but when words are sick, ears have to be healthy, and my ears, to the best of my knowledge, are perfectly well, thank God, for there are some of your words, Brother Diassigue, which don't strike me as being in very good health."

"Which words are those?" asked the alligator.

"It's when you say that this little boy carried you in a mat and brought you all the way here. I can't believe that."

"All the same, it's true," declared Goné-the-Child.

"You're a liar like the rest of your race," said the hare.

"He is telling the truth," confirmed Diassigue.

"I can't believe that unless I see it," said Leuk increduously. "Get out of the water, both of you."

The child and the alligator came out of the water.

"You claim to have carried this big alligator in that mat? How did you do it?"

"I rolled him up in it and then tied it up."

"Well, I want to see how."

Diassigue lay down on the mat, and the child rolled it up.

"And you say that you tied it up?"

"Yes."

"Tie it up to show me."

The child tied the mat up securely.

"And you carried him on your head?"

"Yes, I carried him on my head."

"Well, carry him on your head so that I can see."

When the child had lifted up mat and alligator and placed them on his head, Leuk-the-Hare asked him: "Goné, are your family blacksmiths?"

"No."

"So Diassigue isn't a relative of yours? He isn't your totem?"[2]

"No, certainly not."

"Then take your bundle home. Your father and your mother and all your relatives and their friends will thank you, since you can eat alligator at home. That is how to repay those who forget a good deed."

---

2. **your totem:** The totem of a family or clan was the species of animal or plant regarded by the group as having a blood relationship with it. It was considered the family's guardian spirit and was therefore never used as food.

DISCUSSION QUESTIONS

1. Do you agree with Diassigue-the-Alligator or with Goné-the-Child? In general, is a good deed repaid with a bad turn or with another good deed? Explain your answer.

2. In what way is the conflict between Goné and Diassigue a struggle between an idealist and a realist? Who is the idealist, the boy or the alligator? Who is the realist? Explain.

3. This tale illustrates the common plot device of the trickster tricked. Who is the trickster? How is the trickster tricked?

SUGGESTION FOR WRITING

Do you feel sorry for Diassigue's plight at the conclusion of the story, or do you think justice was served? Write a paragraph in which you argue either that Diassigue got what he deserved or that he should have been treated more humanely. Whichever position you take, support your opinion with reasons.

FOREFATHERS

Listen more often to things rather than beings.
Hear the fire's voice,
Hear the voice of water.
In the wind hear the sobbing of the trees,
5   It is our forefathers breathing.

The dead are not gone forever.
They are in the paling shadows
And in the darkening shadows.
The dead are not beneath the ground,
10   They are in the rustling tree,
In the murmuring wood,
In the still water,
In the flowing water,
In the lonely place, in the crowd;
15   The dead are not dead.

Listen more often to things rather than beings.
Hear the fire's voice.
Hear the voice of water.
In the wind hear the sobbing of the trees.

20   It is the breathing of our forefathers
Who are not gone, not beneath the ground,
Not dead.

The dead are not gone forever.
They are in a woman's breast,
25   A child's crying, a glowing ember.
The dead are not beneath the earth,
They are in the flickering fire,
In the weeping plant, the groaning rock,
The wooded place, the home.
30   The dead are not dead.

Listen more often to things rather than beings.
Hear the fire's voice,
Hear the voice of water.
In the wind hear the sobbing of the trees.
35   It is the breath of our forefathers.

DISCUSSION QUESTIONS

1. Do you think that things in nature are important to the speaker of this poem? Why or why not?

2. The speaker says that the dead are not gone forever, that the dead are not dead. What does he mean?

3. One critic has suggested that this poem gives us a sense of the timelessness and unhurried pace of Africa, of a person who pauses silently listening and feeling the continuity of life. How are these ideas illustrated in the poem?

SUGGESTION FOR WRITING

It is obvious in this poem that the speaker's ancestors are very important to him. Why do you think this is so? Reread pages 30–31 of Peter Abrahams' essay "The Blacks." What light does he shed on this subject, and how does it relate to the ideas in this poem? After reading Abrahams' essay, write a paragraph in which you explain why ancestors are so important in the lives of tribal Africans and also explain how this information relates to the ideas in Diop's poem.

DAVID DIOP

(1927–1960)

David Diop, no relation to Birago Diop, was born in Bordeaux, France. His mother was from Cameroon, his father from Senegal. Although Diop attended school briefly in Dakar, Senegal, he lived most of his life in France. He did, however, visit Africa and had a fervent pride in and devotion to his African heritage. Although he was in poor health and frequently hospitalized throughout his life, there is little indication of his physical weakness in his work. He strongly empathized with the African struggle against colonialism and the the African hope for independence. Diop published one volume of 22 poems, *Coup de pilon* (1956). In 1960 Diop and his wife were killed in a plane crash en route from Dakar to France. All of Diop's unpublished work was destroyed with him in the crash. ∎

AFRICA

Translated by Anne Atik

     Africa my Africa
     Africa of proud warriors in ancestral savannas[1]
     Africa of my grandmother's singing
     Along the banks of her far-off river
5   I have never known you
     But my gaze is charged with your blood
     Your beautiful black blood spread abroad over the fields
     The blood of your sweat
     The sweat of your labor
10   The labor of your slavery
     Slavery of your children.
     Africa tell me Africa
     Is it you, then, this back that bends
     And sinks under the weight of humility
15   This trembling red-striped back
     That says yes to the whip on the noonday roads?

     Then gravely a voice answered me:
     Impetuous son, that young and robust tree
     That tree over there
20   Splendidly alone midst white faded flowers

---

1. savannas: tropical or subtropical grasslands with scattered trees.

It is Africa your Africa that springs up again
Springs up patiently obstinately
And whose fruits ripen with
The bitter flavor of freedom.

LISTEN COMRADES

Listen comrades of the struggling centuries
To the keen clamor of the Negro from Africa to the Americas
They have killed Mamba
As they killed the seven of Martinsville
5   Or the Madagascan down there in the pale light on the prisons
He held in his look comrades
The warm faith of a heart without anguish
And his smile despite agony
Despite the wounds of his broken body
10   Kept the bright colors of a bouquet of hope
It is true that they have killed Mamba with his white hairs
Who ten times poured forth for us milk and light
I feel his mouth on my dreams
And the peaceful tremor of his breast
15   And I am lost again
Like a plant torn from the maternal bosom
But no
For there rings out higher than my sorrows
Purer than the morning where the wild beast wakes
20   The cry of a hundred people smashing their cells
And my blood long held in exile
The blood they hoped to snare in a circle of words
Rediscovers the fervor that scatters the mists
Listen comrades of the struggling centuries
25   To the keen clamor of the Negro from Africa to the Americas
It is the sign of the dawn
The sign of brotherhood which comes to nourish the dreams of men.

HE WHO HAS LOST ALL

Translated by Dorothy Blair

The sun shone brightly in my hut
And my women were fair and pliant
As the palm in the evening breeze.
My children glided through the great river's waters
5   With its deadly depths

And my canoes struggled with the crocodiles.
The maternal moon accompanied our dances
The frenzied heavy rhythm of the tom-tom,
Tom-tom of joy days, careless of the morrow
10   In the midst of the fires of liberty.

Then one day, silence . . .
The rays of the sun seemed to die
In my hut now empty of meaning.
My women crushed their painted mouths
15   On the thin hard lips of the steel-eyed conquerors
And my children quit their peaceful nakedness
Donning the uniform of iron and bloodshed.
Your voice too had died
The chains of slavery have rent my heart
20   Tom-toms of night, tom-toms of my fathers.

YOUR PRESENCE

In your presence I rediscovered my name
My name that was hidden under the pain of separation
I rediscovered the eyes no longer veiled with fever
And your laughter like a flame piercing the shadows
5   Has revealed Africa to me beyond the snows of yesterday
Ten years my love
With days of illusions and shattered ideas
And sleep made restless with alcohol
The suffering that burdens today with the taste of tomorrow
10   And that turns love into a boundless river
In your presence I have rediscovered the memory of my blood
And necklaces of laughter hung around our days
Days sparkling with ever new joys.

DEFIANCE AGAINST FORCE

You who bow you who mourn
You who die one day like that without knowing why
You who struggle, who sit up and watch so the Other[2] can rest
You who no longer look with laughter in your eyes
5   You my brother with the face of fear and anguish
        Rise up and shout: NO!

———
2. the Other: the white man.

DISCUSSION QUESTIONS

1. In "Africa" what question does the speaker ask in lines 12–16? What answer is the speaker given in lines 17–24?

2. Why do you think the voice that answers describes freedom as having a "bitter flavor"?

3. In line 2 of "Listen Comrades" what is the "keen clamor of the Negro"?

4. In line 12 the speaker says that Mamba "poured forth for us milk and light." What do you think this means?

5. In the last line of the poem, what are "the dreams of men"?

6. The two stanzas of "He Who Has Lost All" stand in stark contrast to each other. What word in the first stanza describes the condition of life depicted in that stanza? What word in the second stanza describes the direct opposite condition? What has happened to the people in the poem between stanza one and stanza two?

7. In "Your Presence" the speaker seems to be declaring his love for another person. One possible interpretation is that metaphorically the object of the speaker's love is Africa. Defend this idea using evidence from the poem. (Reread David Diop's biography for help in answering this question.)

8. In "Defiance Against Force" whom is the speaker addressing? What message does the speaker give to his audience?

SUGGESTION FOR WRITING

All five of these poems by David Diop have a common idea running through them, although that idea is only lightly touched on in the poem "Your Presence." What is that idea and how is it treated in each poem? Write a paragraph or two in which you answer these two questions. Support your opinion with evidence from each poem.

R. SARIF EASMON

(born 1913)

R. Sarif Easmon is half Creole and half Susu, the African people who are the subject of his novella "The Feud." Born in Sierra Leone, Dr. Easmon was educated in England and practiced medicine in Freetown, Sierra Leone. He was also active in politics in Sierra Leone. Dr. Easmon is a playwright, novelist, and short story writer. His work skill-fully blends the customs and locale of western Africa with larger-than-life characters and good old-fashioned adventure. Of "The Feud" one critic has said that "Easmon paints with unrelenting urgency and vividness the inhumanity of the slave trade in all its bloodcurdling ramifications." ∎

THE FEUD

I

Dreaming of her lover, Nenneh Touray smiled in her sleep. Even her slumbers were pervaded by a kind of awareness that hers was no mean case of happiness: those days were the heydey of the West Indian Sugar Plantations; of the dreaded *Middle Passage*[1] whose Nineteenth Century infamy was worldwide, and had even penetrated into native gossip so deep in the West African hinterland; of intertribal wars to supply the slaves that made the sinews of an industry wringing bitterness out of Africa to supply Europe with sweetmeats. In spite of all this, Nenneh was not only on the free, African side of the great Ocean, but had that very night been betrothed, in a style befitting an African princess, to the one man in the world she would have chosen for husband.

The luckiest girl in the tribe! Yes, she realized, she was that, so soon to be the wife of her cousin, her hero, Luseni Touray. Even in her dream Luseni stood out so royally, a head taller than any man in any tribal assembly, a warrior by necessity of the times, a leader born. Soon Nenneh's smile changed to one of coyness as, in the disconnected way of dreams, the scene shifted to her bridal night; to the morning after, when, with processional song and dance, with the rejoicing of the entire

---

1. the dreaded *Middle Passage:* the part of the Atlantic Ocean between West Africa and the West Indies. Many Africans, being transported to the slave markets of the New World, died during this part of the journey from disease and maltreatment.

tribe, her maidenhood would be published to the world. That was the red letter day of a Susu[2] woman's life, cause worthy of festivity. Hence it was not at all strange in her dream that all Nenneh Touray's friends and relatives were out in the town's square dancing, while the tribal musicians—the *Yalies*[3]—played their *balanyis*[4] so gloriously that even the houses came forward from their foundations to gambol with the crowd.

Nenneh clung hard and, as things turned out, would gladly have clung forever to her dream. But she felt a sensation of discomfort that was soon sharply defined into the pain of someone smacking her very hard across the face.

"Poreh, you accursed girl!" she cried in outrage, rubbing her cheek and sitting up in the bed. "How dare you!"

"Hurry, N'ga[5] Nenneh!" the slave-girl shrieked through the gloom. "Hurry! The house is on fire."

Nenneh rubbed her eyes and coughed. Wood smoke was billowing into the room. A tongue of flame flashed and licked up the side of the muslin net around the bed. Swiftly the bed was ringed in fire.

With a scream Nenneh leapt down on the mat on which her servant had been sleeping on the floor beside her bed.

High above their heads the conical grass roof was ablaze. One rafter after another came crashing down in a constellation of sparks. The front door of the house stood open. The other women had already fled. There was no time to lose.

The two girls grasped each other's hand. For the moment they were not mistress and slave but fellow-humans, friends in a tight situation—a friendship welded by fire and agony.

Nenneh Touray had been sleeping with one white lappa tied round her waist and reaching down to her calves. She would have tarried to find a garment to throw over her chest. But the slave-girl gripped her by the wrist, rushed her incontinently across the room, through the door and balcony to the great square of the town.

Not ten yards from the blazing house strong arms leapt out of the night, grabbed them both, pinning their arms to their sides.

"Let me go—you brute!" Nenneh yelped with pain.

For answer a stranger slapped her disrespectfully across the face.

Jolted as never before in her life, Nenneh Touray gaped and stared. Only then was she aware of the transformation around her. This was the festive square of her dream: only now every house around it was on fire.

"Allah!" she wailed, "I must be dreaming still!"

But the vise-like hold on her arm was not dreamlike. Side by side with

---

2. Susu: an African people dwelling between the Congo and the Upper Niger.

3. *Yalies:* a subordinate tribe within Susu society, filling various menial occupations.

4. *balanyis:* lutelike stringed instruments.

5. N'ga: Mother, a term of affection. With the diminutive it becomes *N'gadee,* Little Mother.

Poreh she was propelled without dignity towards the coconut palm which, tall and lonely, stood at the square's center.

Halfway there she stumbled across a corpse. A spear impaled the man's chest on to the ground. There was little blood from the wound. Still dazed from sleep, Nenneh recoiled at the object at her feet.

"Don't look, *N'gadee!*" Poreh shouted in horror.

Too late. Nenneh Touray had looked down—and recognized the murdered man as her father.

Stunned beyond feeling, she ceased to struggle or to wonder. She resigned herself to be corraled with the other women—and that with less gentleness than if they had been cattle—round the palm tree in the square. There she stood by Poreh, seeing horror enacted around her, but unable to comprehend anything. Most of the women were wailing and gibbering and calling on her father's name—and calling her name too, in an agony full of timelessness but empty of meaning. . . .

Nenneh saw, too, but without the sight registering emotionally, that scores of men dead or dying lay about the square; that the whole town was aflame, turning the night into a hot, ghastly, crimson day; that through the smoke overhead white egrets, black kites and swallows dashed ceaselessly: just as ceaselessly as the invading soldiery in the square—the dreaded "Warboys," naked but for loin cloths, with their swords and spears flashing in the firelight, completely uninhibited in murder, crazy with shedding human blood. If anything, the war-whoops of the soldiers added the final meaninglessness to everything around the girl. . . .

The rapine[6] and slaughter did not reach to Nenneh's consciousness. But something more personal did. Between the house from which she and Poreh had fled, and her father's great *kounkoumah* house, there was a gap of some yards fenced by low, wooden palings. In the backyard behind this gap was a mango tree. She could remember it back to the earliest of her sixteen years. She had played under its shade, eaten each year of its fruit. Above everything in the town, that tree for her signified home. Now, with a fatal fascination, she watched it brilliantly lit up by the blaze from all the houses around it; watched its leaves shrivel, curl up, blacken and crackle. Then in an instant the whole tree roared like a round of musketry and burst into flames. From time to time as the wind blew volleys of sparks flew from it. And as time dragged on without meaning, it stood there like a skeleton glowing slowly and fitfully into ashes.

Poreh, seeing her "little mother" so stricken, squeezed her hand and whispered in her ear:

"Take heart, *N'gadee!* . . . Allah's still in heaven . . ."

Nenneh Touray turned towards her.

When Poreh looked more closely into the young face, she knew her mistress's mind had gone blank: she hadn't understood a word Poreh had said to her.

Only then the slave-girl began to cry to herself.

---

6. rapine: pillage; plunder.

R. Sarif Easmon   73

Of the ghastly march into slavery—a night followed by a day and another night on the road—Nenneh Touray recalled nothing. Not a hair of her head was injured in the sacking of her father's town. Nevertheless, for a week after, Poreh had had to tend and feed her as though she were an infant.

On the eighth morning, Nenneh turned suddenly to the short, muscular girl beside her.

"Poreh," she cried in dismay, "these are not my clothes!"

Poreh's face was black and oval, and would have been pretty if the brow were not so low. Its normal cast of a silent sorrow deepened, and tears settled in her long, half-closed eyes.

Nenneh looked with apprehension at the native-woven *taimlay* over her chest, at the indigoe-dyed *lappa* around her waist, at the slippers on her feet. Her eyes flew from her garments to the objects and outhouses in the back yard. She clutched desperately at Poreh's arm.

"P—P—Poreh . . . this—isn't *home!*"

Very distressed, Nenneh surveyed the mudhouses, the kitchen behind them; the mortars and pestles for pounding rice; above all, the small bushes crowded with ripe Chile peppers to one side of the kitchen. Everything here was ugly compared with those at home. Last of all, her gaze, now very troubled, rested on the calabash tree with its shining, gourd-fruits each twelve inches across.

Only then she recalled how the mango tree in the backyard at home had exploded and burned. She threw her arms round Poreh's neck and began to sob, brokenheartedly.

Poreh held on to her, and began to cry with relief: "I thank Allah, N'ga Nenneh, you recognize me again."

As suddenly as Nenneh had begun to weep she stopped and braced herself for the worst.

"Recognize you, Poreh?" Now and then a sob escaped her. The fingers she raised to her forehead were long and slender. She pushed the head-kerchief back on her head—a gesture full of tiredness, to reveal a high, cleanly chiseled brow. Below her plaited hair the face was oval, nut-brown; and, though tear-stained, exquisitely, refinedly beautiful. Her lips, very dark pink, were very boldly, even passionately cut—the hallmark of the high-born Susu woman. "Poreh," she sighed, "I begin to remember things that'll kill me if they are true."

The slave-girl led her towards the calabash tree and made her sit down on a log in its shade.

"And I feel," Nenneh ended brokenly, "as if I've been crying for years."

"You've cried three times since we came here, *N'gadee.*"

Nenneh contracted her brows, but could remember nothing.

"You must remember, little mistress," Poreh urged, squeezing her hands between hers. "Three times this Daimba has sent for you—you know, Daimba Seisay. This is his principal town."

"You must be mistaken, girl," Nenneh corrected her—corrected her from habit, not because she recalled what had happened to her. "Why, he succeeded his father not six months ago, if my memory does not confuse me . . . And, and . . . the old man and Father were friends: even good friends, as kings go."

"Well," Poreh insisted with diffidence and pathos—as though it was a pain to her to contradict her mistress—"both old men are dead now. And the young king intends to marry you. . . ."

Nenneh Touray leapt off the log. Her eyes blazed with anger as she looked down on Poreh. Without pausing to think, she leaned forward and slapped the girl across the face.

"You're lying!" she cried hotly. "Not—not after he's murdered my father!"

For a moment Poreh looked as if she was going to cry. But, used all her life to this kind of treatment from the proprietors of her life and liberty, she did not complain. "It's true, N'gadee," she said, biting her lip. "Three times he's called you to his house to tell you so. Each time, unable to speak but understanding what people say to you, why—each time you've covered your face with your hands and burst into tears . . ."

Nenneh's pride collapsed at the information. Trembling, she sat down on the log, leaned over and buried her face in the slave-girl's lap.

"What shall I do, Poreh—what shall I do?"

Downtrodden from her birth, the slave-girl had no answer to her own problems—let alone to her mistress's. She shook her head—even though Nenneh couldn't see the gesture—and remained silent!

When after some minutes Nenneh sat up again, she had stopped crying. But, in spite of the sunshine, she felt horribly chilly and lost. Poreh guessed she was troubled; that a problem was weighing down on her mind; and that whatever the answer to that problem—or even if there were no answer at all—it was going to plague young Nenneh even more than the fact of her father's death. "P—P—Poreh," the question came at last in this guise, "what happened to our people?"

At this point a cockerel trumpeted a challenge at one end of the yard and, head down, sped towards a hen pecking the ground near the pepper bushes. A more powerful bird—the lord of the roost—rushed from the opposite end of the yard, beat his eager wings against Nenneh's legs, and summarily skirmished and routed the usurper of his rights.

"A few of the men kept as slaves"—Poreh spoke in a whisper. "Most of the women shared out among the warriors. The rest sent down to the Coast to be sold to the white men . . ."

Laconic and brutal as the information was, it was no worse than Nenneh had expected. It was the logic of the times. Her father had done the same thing to other tribes. Only she had never, never realized it had been so bad for the others as it was turning out for her . . . She cleared her throat several times before she was able to continue. Even then her voice shook to ask: "Luseni Touray: was he—among—the captives?"

"I can't say, *N'gadee*," Poreh told her as gently as she could. "But," with tenderness as the girl wilted, "no one saw him fall that dreadful night."

While Nenneh shivered at this reprieve, several young slave-girls came from behind the yard balancing on their heads bundles of faggots, gourds of drinking water, baskets of vegetables.

At the same time a young woman came from the back door of the house opposite the calabash tree, and made straight towards the girls on the log.

"Poreh," the newcomer asked with the greatest self-assurance, "is that half-witted mistress of yours still crying?"

Poreh jumped off the log, curtsied hastily to her, and retired behind the calabash tree.

Nenneh Touray surveyed the newcomer. Then, her anger rising slowly like a ferment, she rose from the log. From her own much greater height she looked down on the woman.

"Where I come from," she said to the other's great astonishment, "women of the Yalie tribe are only allowed to wag their tongues while we free-born dance."

"I may be a *Yalie*—but I'm proud of it," the small woman's voice cracked like a whiplash across the air. "But," she continued, incensed by the reference to the parasitic place of her tribe in Susu society, "I—this *I!*—am mistress here. Understand this once and for all: *here* it is *you* who are a slave—an insignificant one among many taken in war."

For seconds together they glared at one another without exchanging a word.

"And now, saucy one," the stranger continued, sure she had put the wench in her place, "I'm glad you've found your tongue at last. Your bubblings were becoming rather a bore. But unless you want to have your tongue cut out of your head, be careful how you wag it in front of my husband, Daimba. He's asked me to take you along. Poreh, you stay here. Now, then, *come along!*"

It was an order—and both knew it.

But the freeborn Susu girl was not bred to take orders—and most certainly *not* from a Yalie woman. She bristled up and, under the brown, her face went red with anger and chagrin. Yalie Woanday smiled with delight at her annoyance. *She,* too, was very beautiful—though in a very distinct way from Nenneh. She was small, and in her elegant native costume, as smart as a firefinch. Each ear was pierced in fifteen different places along the edge, and each hole sported a small gold earring. Her face was small and black, her nose long, slightly upturned and excessively impudent. Nenneh had disliked her at sight. At home, now, she would have had her shipped to the Coast to be sold into slavery—but now to have to take orders from *her!*

Nenneh bit her lip—and, a testimony to the weirdness of the new life in which she now found herself, turned for guidance to the slave-girl lurking behind the calabash tree.

Poreh understood. She shook her head sadly, held her finger to her lips to enjoin caution—and waved her towards the house from which the Yalie woman had come.

Nenneh Touray followed Yalie Woanday through the house, through the great square in front. Except that the *barri* or tribal meeting place stood in the middle of the place, the square looked much like the one Nenneh used to know at home. And the great *kounkoumah*—a large, oblong native-built house—may also have been her Father's house. Her heart began to beat fast as she approached it. She stooped slightly to pass under the eaves and enter the front balcony.

"And how is N'ga Nenneh today?" asked the man in the balcony.

He was sitting astride a raffia hammock strung from the rafters. His feet rested on a sheep-skin rug atop one of the eighteen-inch-high mounds—which served as seats—to each side of the passage leading to the door in the inner wall: a very typical Susu husband, served hand and foot at breakfast by all his wives, backed by a reserve of women slaves. . . .

While the Yalie woman climbed the single step up the mound, Nenneh Touray stood in the passage looking up with misgiving at the man who now held her destiny in his hands. She knew him as Daimba Seisay. And he, as he looked down at her, thought the whole campaign worthwhile that could have brought him such a prize. He was smiling at her. Yet though strong, beautiful white teeth showed behind the lips, the smile could not hide the sardonic, down-drooping at the corners of the mouth. The face was long and strong, a dark brown. It was not unhandsome. Nevertheless, neither the smile nor his good looks altered the impact the man made on the girl: Daimba Seisay's face revealed only too clearly a personality driven by boundless arrogance and ruthlessness, never doubting in the glory and rightness of its cause.

"He's smiling," Nenneh thought, in the bitterness of both bereavement and slavery, "though it was he who murdered my father." Confronted with murder and pleasantry so blandly united in the man's nature, the girl not inexcusably began to feel weak at the knees. Weak, and very helpless.

"Lost your tongue again, saucy one?" Woanday asked with a soft laugh of malice. She had moved to the far side of the balcony, and was leaning against the rope supporting that end of the hammock, looking sardonically over her husband's head at her enemy.

"Woanday," Daimba Seisay remonstrated in a deep and rather pleasant, playful voice, "you mustn't antagonize one who'll soon be sharing household duties with you."

"Daimba Seisay," Nenneh forced herself to speak, "my father . . ."

". . . died fairly and bravely in war—" the king finished her sentence for her. He had wiped the smile off his face, knowing it was not fitting in the circumstances. Talking of death, he could not but sound serious. All the same, the tone of his voice left the girl in no doubt that her father's death was a matter of indifference to him—though he was quite prepared to use it as a political lever. "No man could have died more bravely . . ."

"*Fair war!*" Nenneh burst out in anger. "Father was at war with no one. He was murdered without provocation."

The man in the hammock frowned. There was a Jovian grandeur about his face when he frowned and like Jove his displeasure promised thunder.

"Young woman," he said gravely, "murder is not a gracious word to level at a king. You must not forget your father's dead; and that I, yes *I* am all you have in the world for father or friend."

"*Or* master!" Woanday interpolated sweetly.

"Quiet, Woanday," Daimba ordered. He strove against it, but the smile leapt out of his eyes to play like ghostly cynicism around the corners of his lips, but without invading his features.

"Only Allah I know as Master!" Nenneh Touray cried with the desperation of freedom staring slavery in the face—at the same time darting Woanday a look intended to keep that loathsome Yalie in her place.

But Woanday only laughed at her.

"She keeps forgetting, my husband," she said, "that *she* is one of many slaves brought here with ropes round their necks."

"A rope round Daimba Seisay's neck wouldn't make a slave of him," Nenneh turned hotly on her tormentor. "If you were not such a baseborn, beggarly Yalie you'd see I'm at least as well-born as he . . ."

"For a slave," Woanday retorted, even more hotly, for she was offended at the taunts about her tribe. "For a slave you are. . . ."

"She's right, my dear Woanday," the man interrupted her. "I mean," turning from one to the other and trying to embrace both in a smile of affability, "in her claim to be as good as you or me. And that, N'ga Nenneh," turning again to the girl he had orphaned, "is why I propose to marry rather than to sell you."

"I'm already promised to . . ." Nenneh began, but stopped when Yalie Woanday tittered, and then proceeded to laugh sarcastically at her. Even Daimba, in his more sophisticated and cruel way, was amused at her. For a while Nenneh struggled to control her anger. She perceived that a man who had killed her father to gain physical possession of her would pay scant respect to a previous engagement. "Only if you think me a slave, Daimba Seisay," she blurted out—and the statement sounded weak and absurd to herself—"would you want to compel me to marry you."

"Indeed!" ejaculated Woanday, astounded at the woman's madness and conceit. "Ain't we cocky! Slavery to marry Daimba Seisay!"

That young man's face had gathered into an angry, threatening mask. For some moments he was so angry his lips seemed to swell and the veins in his throat throbbed with a violence that threatened to burst them. "Slavery, indeed!" He looked so truculent as he leaned forward in the hammock that the girl in the passage backed away from him. He shook his fist and shouted at her: he had absolute power of life and death over everyone in his pocket-handkerchief plot of Africa. Young though he was, both as man and as king, absolute power had corrupted him beyond redemption. "Young woman," he blazed at her, "we are all free-born till a sword stronger than ours strikes ours from our hands. You are my slave by conquest. And I honor you by wanting to marry you. . . . *Slavery!* Ha-ha-ha!"

He leaned back in the hammock and began to laugh in a way so darkly sardonic it frightened the girl more than his anger had.

"The trouble with freeborn Susu women," he wagged his finger at her, even the harsh merriment dying out of his features, "is that you're all pampered and spoiled. This very day, Nenneh Touray, I'll take you to see what slavery is. Then you can make your choice between it and *me*."

III

A large retinue followed the King.

The honey-colored grass-thatches of Daimba Seisay's town soon thinned out as the road meandered out into the fields of manioc. Within a mile they were winding their way along a narrow track, while the sharp, pale-brown leaves of elephant grasses swished and whispered against their clothes, and the West African sun blazed down on them out of a shimmering sky. They passed huts solitary in the bush, a great baobab tree in fruit, several oil palms drooping their leaves in the heat. The ubiquitous and hardy "Monkey Apple" trees and large termite nests in the landscape made the view so much like the countryside around her home, they brought a lump into Nenneh Touray's throat.

They walked in single file. Sandwiched between Daimba Seisay in front and Woanday behind, Nenneh was the only stranger in the outing.

"This," said Yalie Woanday, over and over again, laughing at her new enemy, "this should put my saucy one in her place." She was the one discordantly cheerful member of the party.

In another mile, sweating with the heat and the exertion, they came to the brow of a hill overlooking the biggest river in those parts.

Below them the river wound in many peaceful loops, vanishing far to their right in a silver-blue mist shining in the sun. Both banks were densely covered with mangroves—so that the loops of the river looked like disconnected lakes. The mangroves possessed the earth as far as their eyes could see. As they paused there, the wind blew up from the valley a stench of decaying vegetation.

"That," Daimba Seisay told his captive, pointing towards a spot in the near bank, "that, Nenneh Touray, is slavery."

Tears settled in Nenneh's eyes as they strained to make out whether it was men or women who, with bare bending backs, were toiling in the valley of despair below them. They were cutting mangroves, clearing the swamps against the rainy season, when paddy rice would be transplanted stalk by stalk into the mud. Now the mud was not oozy. Except in the depths of the swamps, or in treacherous places where one suddenly sank up to the waist or disappeared forever, the mud had dried and cracked into millions of hard cakes, between which human feet too often slid—to be pulled out with the soles ripped to shreds. Every mortal down there ran the risk hourly of being bitten by swamp snakes—among the most venomous of their kind—or being carried away by crocodiles.

Nenneh observed with a sinking of the heart that though there were scores upon scores of slaves, and they appeared to be toiling so hard, the surface they had cleared looked hardly longer than a handkerchief spread on the landscape to dry. . . .

"Ah, N'ga Nenneh," Daimba Seisay murmured, watching the play of emotions in the girl's face, "hold back your tears till you see their misery at close quarters."

At his command the party moved off down the hill.

They had not gone half a mile when the head of the column halted.

"Why aren't you working?" The question was shouted out, raspingly, by the man at the head of the line.

"I'm having to rest a little . . . My chest is bleeding again . . ."

The rest of the answer was just a blur in Nenneh's ears. She stumbled against Daimba's heel, and fell face-down in the grass by the wayside.

Very anxiously the King bent over her to help her up.

"I hope you're not hurt?"

"No—no," Nenneh returned, trying to control her voice. "You stopped so suddenly I—I didn't have time to pull up . . . Sorry . . ." she mumbled and turned her back to him.

Woanday noted that she was an unconscionably long time dusting her clothes.

"Fishing for Daimba's sympathy," she thought, cattily.

Meanwhile things were taking a course at the head of the line that threatened disaster.

The slave to whom the question was put was sitting on a boulder under a tamarind tree just off the path. A *machete* lay at his feet. The strip of cloth tied round his chest was freshly stained with blood in the left armpit. He leaned rather wearily with his head against the tree trunk.

As the people ahead made way for the king, and Nenneh and Woanday came up behind him, the slave leaped off the rock in great excitement and bounded to the path.

"Nenneh Touray—*you!*" he rushed towards her, not so much glad as crazy with joy to see her again.

Nenneh backed away from him.

"Is he crazy?" she asked Daimba Seisay, shrinking in timidity.

The slave stopped as though a spear had been jabbed into his stomach.

"Only wounded," said Daimba with indifference, wiping the sweat off his face. "He was taken in your father's town. So I suppose you may know him."

"*Know him!*" Nenneh cried with a haughty pride. "Am I supposed to know every one of my father's slaves?"

"*I* a slave! *I!! Slave*—this *I!!!*"

The young man, taller than any human she had ever seen, looked so pained and horrified Yalie Woanday was moved with pity for him.

"Misfortune comes to anyone in war, young man," she observed softly. "King today—slave tomorrow."

"But *I* her father's slave!" The words jerked out of the slave's throat. He looked first towards Woanday—then at Nenneh, who continued to regard him with a scorn that wounded him. He shook his head—clearly he couldn't make head or tail of anything.

Meanwhile, to have his two women drawn into conversation with a wretch of a slave had set Daimba Seisay's anger on the boil.

"Nobody cares who you were," he cut the man's talk short with a brutal arrogance. "But you must be more than a fool if you don't realize you are a slave *now.*"

The slave's chest heaved at this affront. A fresh drop of blood oozed out of the bandage over his wound, and crept like a crimson tear down his side. But he must have had the discipline of a soldier, and he held his peace.

It was at this point that, with the inconsequence that men always find so disconcerting in a woman, Nenneh said:

"I'm thirsty, Daimba Seisay. I saw some *Malombo* fruits up there by the path." She pointed back along the track. "Please order the slave to go and pick some for me."

At this the young man drew himself up fiercely. His discipline did not extend to his dealings with the fair sex. Indeed, he looked so dangerous in his wrath that some of the men backed away from him, badly wounded though he was.

"I will *not* do it for Allah himself!" he shouted back—even before Daimba Seisay gave the order.

Incensed at the affront to his authority, the King's face suffused with blood.

"*Sinneh*—" he shouted, "execute him."

Sinneh was a veteran "warboy"—and so inured to bloodshed he looked upon his appointment as the king's killer-in-chief as a badge of honor. He was a short man, his naked arms and chest superbly muscled. He advanced from the group, sword in hand, upon the slave.

In a flash the wounded man leaped back under the tamarind, snatched his *machete* off the ground—and turned to face Sinneh.

Sinneh neither increased nor slackened his pace.

Just when it seemed nothing could stop the bloodshed, Nenneh Touray rushed between the two men.

"No! No!! No!!!" she screamed in agony, pushing the two men away from each other. She fell back on the boulder and began to sob: "NO! . . . Allah knows—I've seen—too much bloodshed—already—Free-born or slave, young man—if you knew my Father—and saw him die—as I did— you'd not refuse his daughter—such a small request . . ."

Daimba Seisay could only grumble at this damnable unpredictableness of womankind. But, with good grace, he ordered Sinneh to desist.

The slave threw down his weapon. Without another word, he walked up the path to the spot Nenneh had indicated.

All breathed in peace again. Only Woanday was thinking Nenneh must be a very queer fish. She needed watching. Women who cried so easily could tie men into knots. Certainly, she was not prepared to yield such a right over Daimba to any woman yet born . . .

"I see no fruits here," the slave's voice broke in on Woanday's jealous thoughts.

Nenneh Touray ran up the track to show him.

She soon returned with half a dozen bunches of orange-red fruits the size of tangerines.

"They're lovely!" she laughed gratefully through her tears.

And so they moved down into the swamps.

IV

When all the world was abed that moonless night, the slave sat alone on the boulder under the tree. The barking of a dog in the slaves' hamlet lower down the valley sounded faintly through the night—so faintly that when the wind soughed through the leaves overhead the barking was inaudible. In the sky the Milky Way shone like a girdle of silver round the waist of the Universe. And, to the slave, the stars shone so brightly they appeared to be glow-worms just beyond the level of the tree-tops.

After midnight a gentle patting on the ground made the young man start. It was the sound of footsteps lightly running. He jumped off the rock and ran into the path.

"Nenneh Touray!" he gasped.

"Ah—my Luseni!"

She ran into his arms gasping and sobbing together. Their first moments of bliss were too rapturous and choking for words. Deep in their hearts, each had believed the other dead or, worse still, sold into slavery. But now—

"Are you alone, *N'gadee?*" Yes, he called her his "little mother," his Darling that Death had given him back again. He asked the question all solicitude, incredulous at the feat.

"Yes, my dear," her sighs blended with the whispering of the leaves overhead. "Tonight, I couldn't risk coming even with Poreh . . . Allah has been merciful to us, Luseni."

He understood. When he had picked the *Malombo* fruits for her that afternoon, she had made this tryst with him in a whisper upon which Death might have eavesdropped. His heart had beat so violently at his good fortune born of her constancy that it had set the blood flowing from his wound.

"But for you," he murmured, while a shiver ran through him and while he felt more grateful than he'd ever dreamed he could be to a woman, "they'd have murdered me in cold blood today."

He led her deep into the grasses on the far side of the tamarind tree, pulled her down among the foliage beside him.

"Yes," she sighed again, very simply. "Allah is merciful. He made me hear your voice before I saw you. Otherwise, I'd foolishly have rushed into your arms. And if Daimba Seisay were even to suspect you are my husband-to-be . . . Ugghh!" she trembled in his arms.

In their perilous position, only two considerations counted with them:

to escape; and, because they might fail in this, to crowd into those starry, dangerous moments together what happiness might have sufficed in normal times for a lifetime. Even in her dreams the girl had not been so happy in her innocence as she was now yielding herself to this man. Her maidenly shyness vanished with the fear that rude hands might pluck her from what was in fact her bridal bed and plunge a dagger straight into her heart. Thus she yielded herself almost with violence to his desires. At the same time she told herself that, at the worst, she had stolen a march on the enemy who would mock her by marrying her; that at the best she had assured Luseni of a rare affection by defying a tyrant to yield to his slave.

"Where shall we go from here?" asked Nenneh, now become a woman.

"To my twin-brother's: Lansannah's town is the nearest. It's very well fortified, too."

"How soon, my dear—how *soon?*"

"As soon as my side heals."

"Yes, yes," she stroked his face agitatedly. In that light she was only a shadow between him and the stars. "But how soon will that be, darling? Don't forget I have to cope with Daimba Seisay and that jealous, firefinch Yalie Woanday—I wish she didn't hate me so! . . ."

"A month at the latest," he promised.

During that month she came sometimes once, sometimes twice a week, to meet him, risking her neck every time she did so. She was never sure she'd reach him when she set out—or return to the town alive having kept her tryst. And yet it never entered her head she should not go.

The last night of all Poreh came with her.

Yes, Poreh came, carrying a bundle on her head—not a large bundle: but it was all they possessed between them—a few miserable wearing apparel. . . . But how little that counted now—now that they were to make their bid for freedom.

How high their hearts beat out there, under the stars! Nenneh Touray was trembling so with excitement she feared she'd let Luseni down by fainting. Here was freedom at last—freedom within reach! To live and breathe freely, without that uncanny feeling that she was being watched by eyes she could not see; that her body was at the absolute disposal of someone for whom her only emotion was fear; to live without the constant foreboding that some danger would befall Luseni in the valley of slaves. How strange this thing called freedom was! Born free, she had never dreamed what it meant till she woke up that night to find her home in flames—Allah! was it only five weeks ago? . . .

And then she heard Luseni's whisper, barely above the sound of the wind rushing through the leaves all around them.

"Yes, we're ready and here, dear Luseni!" Nenneh whispered back, scarcely daring to breathe.

At her answer he emerged out of the night's shadows to greet them.

And at once he led them down the track, destination—Liberty.

In the starlight they were only shadows. Three shadows moving in a line, moving with high purpose down into the valley. There, in a tiny creek of the river, Luseni had concealed a small dugout, just large enough to take them across the river.

Luseni in front, *machete* in hand; Poreh in the rear, bundle on head—softly, surely the three moved through the night.

They had taken not more than a hundred steps to liberty when a voice thundered through the night:

"HALT!"

Luseni's *machete* flew up in his strong right hand. A heavy club smashed down from some point in the night, caught Luseni on the wrist—the *machete* flew from his grasp to swish and clatter in the grasses.

In a twinkling the man and two women found themselves ringed in a circle of spears whose points pricked their throats and the backs of their necks.

"Sinneh, light the torches."

It was Daimba Seisay's voice. The captives recognized its doom in the night—knew their fates were sealed.

Nenneh Touray's heart contracted into a hard, painful knot in her chest. Death indeed had come to claim them. But how—*how? She* had been so careful; and Poreh, she was certain, could not have breathed a word of their plan to anyone: their lives and liberties conjointly depended on silence. O Allah—what had she brought upon Luseni? . . .

Meanwhile, while Eternity stood still, they heard the whir of wood being rubbed on wood. And soon, too soon, six palm-oil flambeaux were kindled and incarnadined[7] the scene.

They made a ghastly light indeed—the light in miniature that rose from Nenneh Touray's home, and shone on her father's body in the square that dreadful night. And twenty of the very men who had sacked her father's town were now here around her, to complete the circle of treachery and murder. *Murder!* Were she and Luseni to die after all their sufferings? Allah could not be so cruel! Why, their lives had hardly begun! Surely, Allah owed them something beside pain and violence and lost hopes and purpose. . . . Why—

"Bring them here," Daimba Seisay ordered.

Violent hands descended on the captives and hustled them to the shade of the tamarind—Nenneh's tree of reunion with her lover, her arbor of love, and now, she was sure, her place of death.

Alimamy Daimba stood to one side of the boulder, his back to the trunk of the tree. His face showed ghastly in the light: it looked not so much angered as insane—insane with jealousy, wounded pride, and hurt, despotic majesty. Looking into that face, Luseni would sooner have expected mercy from a hungry, wounded leopard.

"Woanday," said Daimba Seisay bitterly, "you were right."

The small woman stepped lightly out of the shadows. She was smiling in this her hour of triumph. Her comment was almost superfluous: "You see, Nenneh Touray, a Yalie woman can do something else besides sing and dance."

Nenneh started violently. Only then she understood. The Yalie woman

---

7. **incarnadined:** reddened.

was so embittered with jealousy and a sense of inferiority that she had spied on her and betrayed her to her enemy. Oh, the madness of humans! Betray her, she thought, betray her when she should have done her best to help her escape so as to leave Daimba to her Yalie wiles and charms! Oh, the utter pointless madness of it all!

"Ah, Yalie Woanday!" the words, overcharged with despair, burst out of Nenneh Touray's breaking heart. "Ah, Woanday! I did not want your husband. You could have let me go in peace with mine. . . ."

"*Your* husband!" Woanday's scream struck out eerily through the night. She recoiled and staggered so that one of the warboys had to hold her up. "*Your*—" she gasped and stared at Nenneh, the horror of what she had done breaking on her.

"Yes, Woanday . . . I was betrothed to Luseni the very night your husband sacked my father's town . . . and have indeed . . . been his wife . . . this last month . . . Ah Woanday! Ah Woanday! . . ."

Her words rang like a deathknell in the night.

No less stricken than the woman she had betrayed, Woanday came forward and took Nenneh's hand. She turned instinctively with a prayer on her lips to Daimba. But the prayer died within her, unuttered.

"You told us," said Daimba Seisay, struggling to sound calm, while his eyes blazed with madness and hatred at Nenneh, "you told us he was your father's slave. But you *knew* he is my slave—and that it was my intention to marry you. I cannot, therefore, forgive the disgrace you have brought upon my name. I shall punish you with life. As to *him,* the question is not whether he is to die—but how? . . ." He remained silent for a while, while the chimera of power drove him headlong into fiendishness. And then he smiled in a way that killed the young girl before him over and over again. "Sinneh," turning to his specialist in murder, "cut me a stout stake, and sharpen it very fine at one end. And you, Hamid, fetch the heaviest stone you can carry."

The women trembled at these strange orders.

"Bah Daimba," Woanday began timidly. Even in that light her face looked pinched, and she shivered involuntarily every now and then.

"Quiet, woman!"

He did not have to repeat the order.

Minutes of agony slipped by.

The sharp sound of steel on raw wood struck repeatedly through the night. The flambeaux burned. Doubled over a stone, Hamid came from the shadows and set his burden down at the king's feet.

Soon, too soon, Sinneh brought forth *his* offering: a stick a yard long, thick as a man's wrist. He knelt down on the ground at his master's feet, set one end of the stick on the stone. Then, with deft blows of his *machete,* he sharpened the stick to a point. How curiously sweet and fragrant the raw wood smelled in the night!

"Bring the man here." Daimba ordered at last.

Luseni struggled fearfully with the men who fell on him.

Nenneh and Poreh pushed aside, Luseni was dragged forward, thrown flat on his back—spread-eagled at the king's feet.

The six men with their flambeaux drew in. The night was warm, so still that the six flames burned straight up, the smoke rising thick and straight up like a tube over each torch, joining it to the blackness of the night.

Through the somber light Daimba Seisay looked across the group struggling at his feet to where Nenneh stood, dumb with terror, too dazed even to cry. Not knowing that he did so, Daimba laughed—laughed like a madman—before he ordered:

"Hamid, Sinneh—drive the stake through his heart."

At this terrible command Nenneh wrenched her arms free of the men who held her, ran across to fall at the tyrant's feet, weeping.

"Daimba—Daimba—a woman bore you . . . Have pity on me . . . My Father—O, I'm too young to suffer so! . . . For Allah's sake—let him go! . . . I promise I'll—I'll never see him again . . . Or—Or—kill me first! . . ." Screaming and wailing at the top of her voice, in truth she had no idea what she was saying.

"Allah be kind to you, Nenneh . . ." cried the man on the ground. "Daimba Seisay, we kill and we are killed, and mercy is only in heaven. I do not ask for mercy . . . But I do ask this of you as a Moslem: let your men kill me swiftly—with a sword."

At this, even the warboys looked as though they expected their king to change from brutality to the sword. But they looked to him in vain.

"Sinneh!" Daimba Seisay roared in a tone of finality and rising anger, ashamed that his soldiers should be so soft-spirited.

And then Hamid set the point of the stake over Luseni's heart, steadied the shaft with both hands.

With apparently little effort Sinneh's mighty hands closed over the stone on the ground and raised it up.

"Ah—AAAAHHHH!!!!!! . . ."

At the first blow of the stone on the stake, Luseni's yell of agony burst out and echoed through and through the night. He writhed so violently that he pulled the dozen men holding him down as though they were puppets. At the second blow he wrenched his right foot free. A savage, chance kick with the heel caught one of the men flush on chin and throat: immediately there was a sharp crunch of bone, and the soldier fell dead and twitching with a broken neck.

But the others grabbed the freed limb, and held their victim down.

Five times more Sinneh crashed the stone on the stake, while Luseni yelled and writhed in agony.

At the seventh blow the point of the stick ripped and tore through Luseni's chest. His cry ended in a gurgle. Blood gushed and foamed through his mouth. His limbs quivered violently—and soon were still.

At the last blow Sinneh struck so viciously that the stake ran clean through their victim's chest and was firmly driven into the ground.

Nenneh Touray had fainted at the ghastly sight. She lay limp at Daimba's feet. Woanday was leaning over her, lying on the ground by her, her whole body shaking as she sobbed hysterically.

Poreh was made of sterner stuff than the princesses and parasites of

Susu society. Born and bred in domestic slavery, she knew that, as a slave, she was just as doomed as Luseni for her part in the night's misadventure. Therefore, taking advantage of the general confusion, she sidled into the shadows and vanished into the night.

V

A gaunt woman came through the dusk and along the track to the brow of the hill overlooking the swamps. An indigoed *lappa* tied under her armpits and reaching down to her calves was her sole garment. Her arms and face were nut-brown, but the forearms up to the elbow were stained with native indigo or *garra* dye. Beneath her closely tied head her plaited locks peeped out, more grey than black. Her oval face was lined and would have been lovely still but for her eyes which, sunk deep in their sockets, were hard with an unfeminine luster.

She left the track and passed under the branches of a tree towering thirty feet above her. She trod the grass down around her and soon came upon an old tree stump, partly eaten by termites.

She sat down on the stump, very, very still, looking casually down into the valley. The river had spread into a lake—it was the rainy season—and the mangroves made a forest at sea. On the nearer bank there was a break in the wilderness of water and swamps, paddy rice standing prosperous and green in many a crowded acre. Except for the ants crawling ceaselessly up and down the tree above her, there was not one other living creature in sight.

The woman looked up into the branches of the tree. As she did so, her eyes glowed with terrible, inward fire. But no sound escaped her. She had clearly learned to control her feelings over the years, though her eyes now and again might betray her.

Rain-clouds were gathering. There was no real sunset. The grey light drained out of the sky. The storm broke, the rain came rushing down.

But still the woman, drenched and roared over by the elements, sat immobile on the tree stump, waiting, waiting. She sat there for hours while the night grew wilder and wilder. Neither lightning, nor thunder, nor the penetrating wetness had power to disturb her patience.

At last, through the continuous rush of rain, she heard voices:

"She could not possibly have come in this weather," said a man querulously in the dark.

"Bah Lansannah," retorted a woman's voice, "you don't know N'ga Nenneh."

"You're right, Poreh," called the woman at the tree stump. "I'm here."

"My friends," continued Nenneh Touray, going forward to meet them, "welcome! Lansannah," shaking hands with dead Luseni's twin-brother, "this tree above us is witness that I have kept faith with your brother. It has grown from the stake our enemy drove through Luseni's heart. Look well on it!" As if in answer to her command the heavens fulminated again. "And you, the son I've seen but twenty times in twenty years, yet never by Allah's daylight, what think you of it?"

"My father's heart was stronger than my mother's womb," said a deep, rich voice. "It has bred in twenty years a son five times as tall as I am!"

She embraced him to her chest, tenderly, briefly.

"Had it been your mother's heart," cried his uncle, "the stake could never have gone through it—*never,* not even if it was sheathed with iron! Woman, twenty years is a long time—can't you forgive?"

"Lansannah," the woman answered, "Poreh will tell you I was a soft and kindly girl that lost her senses to see her father dead. If they'd killed my Luseni with a sword or a spear—as he begged in his last hour—Allah! It wasn't much to beg for!—I'd have forgiven. But—and Allah have mercy upon my withered soul—I cannot forget his agony. I heard him—even last night—I heard—I hear him, daily, yelling. Day and night these twenty years his tortured voice has rung in my ears. . . . And all the love I had for him my enemy took away and left nothing but hate and mockery. Forgive, Lansannah? *Forgive!*" her voice quavered and cracked with emotion. "*Never!*"

"You have suffered much, my mother," the youth told her gently. "I've come to avenge the living more than the dead."

"Avenge me?" his mother cried in astonishment. "I never saw it in that light before, Son. Are you strong enough for this work, boy? Or shall we wait another year? . . . Time means nothing—Justice is everything. . . . Stand in the lightning; let me look at you . . ."

It was raining so heavily now that she had to shout to make herself heard. They stood silent for a minute. Then the lightning forked and hissed and swished down, lighting up the rain-filled heavens like a vast bowl of milk. The earth trembled to the thunder-clap that followed. In the glare Nenneh Touray saw the gleam of a spear-point above the head of a giant standing six foot six inches.

"Tall as his father was!" she murmured with pride and satisfaction. "Kind Poreh," she went on in louder tones, with a subtle and deeply affectionate expression in her voice, "my boy's foster-mother, my sister rather than slave! Tonight your work is done. I have treasured you more than my own blood over the years. And now I give you what I've found is more precious than life itself: your freedom. . . . Allah bless you, dear friend, for the way you stood by me in my troubles . . . Lansannah Touray, bless you, too . . ."

"Let me come with you, my sister," the man pleaded.

"No, Lansannah," her voice turned suddenly harsh, reflecting the hardness life had shown her for twenty years. "If young Luseni and I fail, let their vengeance fall on no more than our two heads. You could then avenge your brother's death and ours . . ."

"Yes, Uncle," the young man agreed. "We are quite willing to die. And now, Mother, I'm ready."

"Lansannah," Nenneh Touray could not help her voice trembling—no one can face death completely unmoved, "if we don't return by dawn, you'll know we have failed. You and Poreh must then return home."

"We shall not fail, Mother!" the youth cried with confidence.

When the lightning flashed again, only two figures remained under Luseni's tree.

VI

A hundred yards up the track a woman walked sure-footed through the storm. She held the neck of a spear whose butt rested in the hand of a tall man behind her. The man could not see where he was going, but he followed resolutely wherever the spear led.

An hour later, the lightning flashes revealed the man and the woman passing by the *barri* in Daimba Seisay's town.

"He sleeps there," said the woman, pointing to the king's house down the square, "every night. Tonight Woanday sleeps with him."

The young man drew the spear into the front balcony after him. Out of the storm the air smelled both close and of wood smoke. High above their heads the rafters were dimly visible in a pink glow from the top of the inner wall; they all converged towards the point of a cone truncated by the wall.

"The strongest rafters are here, my son," Nenneh Touray whispered. She felt for his hand in the dark and raised it to the roof.

Heavy though his sword was, young Luseni gripped it without effort between his teeth. The rafters groaned as he clung to them with his powerful hands and heaved himself up. Hand over hand, toes clawing and holding on to the purlings lower down, the man climbed to the space between the top of the inner wall and the roof.

After what seemed an age to the woman waiting outside, the front door softly opened. "Come in, Mother."

In dead silence Nenneh Touray drew the spear into the house after her. Very, very softly she closed the door.

A wood fire was burning in the middle of the round house. To the far side of this large, central room stood a four-poster bed.

The intruders tiptoed towards the bed. The woman with the spear peered through the fire-glow.

"Yes," she whispered, "it's they."

Near the bedhead was a low, wooden stool. A crude metal lamp stood on top of it.

"Light the lamp, Mother," the young man whispered.

The woman obeyed. The rain water dripping from her hair hissed in the fire as she bent over it.

The sleepers stirred uneasily as the oil-lamp spread a sudden, ochre brightness over the room.

Gripping the hilt of his sword in his left hand, the young giant bent over the bed. With his right hand he grabbed the man by his trousers-waist, lifted him right out of the bed—and threw him flat on his back on the mud floor.

Daimba Seisay opened his mouth to shout. The sword point pricked his throat, and a foot heavily stamped the breath out of his chest.

"*Silence!*" hissed the man with the sword.

"*Luseni!*" Daimba Seisay croaked, his eyes almost jumping out of his head. The name stuck in his murderer's throat, and his expression was so craven and fearful he must have been sure he was seeing ghosts.

"Luseni is my name," said Nenneh's son, coldly.

Woanday jumped up from the bed. She stared wildly about her. She was too terrified to scream. Time had not much changed her and her husband: they had prospered and grown fat, that was all.

"Sit on that stool, woman," Luseni ordered, pointing with his sword.

"Twenty years ago," Woanday gibbered, not moving from the bed, "I saw you die under the tree."

She trembled violently at the look Luseni directed at her—got up, and staggered to the stool.

"Do I kill them here, Mother?"

The prostrate man and his wife looked towards Nenneh. A terrible figure she made leaning on the spear. Never had Justice taken a more unrelenting form—nor ever did her proceedings promise to be so summary.

"The woman shall not die," said Nenneh Touray calmly. "She repented after Luseni's death, and has always been secretly kind to me since."

"Good!" said young Luseni, raising his sword above Daimba's head. "It goes against the grain of my manhood to kill a woman—even in a feud."

"This, surely, is a ghastly dream," muttered the man on the floor. Sweat was pouring out of his face, and all over his naked chest.

The storm was raging outside with increased fury. A thunderclap louder than any yet that night cracked like doom overhead.

Nenneh's eyes glowed like a coal fire.

"His spear pierced my father's heart." She looked and spoke like a sybil. "Before my eyes he drove a stake into my Luseni's heart. It is just that a spear should end his wicked life."

Luseni reached for the spear.

"No. Not here!" his mother uttered a weird, sepulchral whisper. Her eyes appeared to expand in their sockets and looked so terrible that even her own son was afraid to look into them. "This is Allah's own vengeance weather. Do you think we can take them to your father's tree?"

Luseni started at the suggestion. "Very just!" was his comment. "A spear to match Grandfather's, and the stake that killed your husband to witness his execution. Allah counsels you well, Mother! . . . But the woman. Should we leave her here she'll raise the alarm against us."

"We'll take her to your Uncle's town, Luseni. She may return here later if she likes."

Thereupon Luseni handed his sword to his mother. In a few instants he had torn the bedcloth into the strips from which it was made. He gagged their prisoners, tied their hands behind their backs.

Which done, he raised Daimba Seisay from the floor, passed the spear shaft between his arm and chest, bound the arm securely to the spear. He did the same with Woanday.

Nenneh Touray took the spear head, followed by Woanday and Daimba. Young Luseni carried the butt of the spear, walking in the rear of the cortège, sword in hand at the ready.

All four grimly silent or silenced, they walked out of the house.

VII

An hour before dawn they found Lansannah Touray and Poreh still patiently awaiting them under the tree.

Luseni ungagged their victims, unbound Daimba Seisay from the spear—and threw him on the sodden ground: near enough to the spot where his father had lain twenty years before.

It was still raining, raining.

Poreh held up the fainting Woanday.

"Daimba Seisay," said Lansannah in a voice that sounded gravely through the dark, "when kings do wrong, only Allah can punish them. He has designed that this weak, humble woman should bring you to justice and your just downfall. Are you prepared to die?"

Young Luseni felt his hair stand on end. Nor, indeed, was the occasion without solemnity. Three of those who had stood there twenty years before could bear testimony to the heinousness of the man's crime. That crime had blasted at least one young life. Yes, Justice was there all somber and sacred, and they all felt awed, knowing that what they were doing was not so much right as the rightest thing in the world.

"Tell me, my good man," said the man on the ground, "what is *justice?*"

"As a king," Lansannah grumbled, "you at least ought to know."

"But I do not know," said Daimba Seisay, calmly. "As a king, I've tried to be just. But I believe justice is such a godly concept that we men are presumptuous to think ourselves capable of understanding it, let alone administering it, inviolate."

"We did not come here to argue," said young Luseni coldly, not yet old enough to understand the wisdom of a king's whole lifetime. "The question is: are you ready to die?"

"It is so written." Daimba's voice rose from the ground imbued with the fatalistic calm of his Moslem religion. "A thousand times these twenty years I had it in my mind to put the woman to death. I just hadn't the will . . . Her first husband's death weighed much on my conscience . . . Still, I cannot bear to enter Eternity with this mystery unsolved in my mind. Who, *now*, is this Luseni? Nenneh had but one child, and I saw that child dead the day it was born . . . People always said Nenneh Touray was a witch."

"There's no mystery, no witchcraft," said the woman, her voice colder than the rain. In the hour of a triumph for which she had waited twenty years, she sounded curiously unelated. "Two weeks after she ran away from this spot that dreadful night, Poreh came back to me secretly in the night. She's here now. . . ."

"*Allah Akhbarr!*"[8] Daimba burst out in astonishment.

". . . yes, she's *here* now as she was here twenty years ago. When Poreh came, I already knew I was pregnant. I prayed for a son to avenge my Luseni's death. Only Allah knew how hard I prayed. And he was kind to me . . .

"In my hour of travail, I stole to the marshes. Poreh attended me.

"Well, Daimba Seisay, my belly wasn't big for nothing. I brought forth twins. Boys . . ."

"Allah Akhbarr!" Daimba exclaimed again, beginning to understand.

"Yes, twins. Luseni was big. Lansannah very small. He died the same day—and you, Daimba, were pleased to see the end of my husband's line—as you imagined! But I had made Poreh take Luseni back to his uncle. This Luseni is he you see here now—and his Uncle Lansannah too is here. And," she ended grimly, "you and I are here. There's no mystery, Daimba—only justice!"

"But woman, woman!" Daimba burst out. "For five years you were my wife . . ."

"Yes." The woman's voice chilled him like an icicle. There was a change in her. She suddenly sounded weary, infinitely old. "You'd have sold me into slavery if I had refused to be your wife. Only Allah knows how it hurt my woman's pride to yield my body to you. But I learned to steel myself to it, for dead Luseni's sake."

"Truly, you're Vengeance and not a woman!" the man cried in astonishment that had something of admiration in it. "I woke up one night when you slept with me. Through the dimness of the fire, I saw you looking at me when you thought I was asleep. Allah knows I'm no coward. But I knew then you hadn't a woman's spirit, that you had it in you to bring death. And since that night I'd not had you in my bed . . . And yet," disjointedly, "and yet I did not kill you!"

"Daimba Seisay," Luseni asked with that disdain mingled with cruelty possible only in youth, "are you by any chance begging us for mercy?"

"Beg a woman and child for mercy!" Daimba Seisay laughed sardonically. "I have killed—and now I'm killed. There's an end to all. Nenneh Touray, be merciful to my Woanday as you say she was merciful to you. And now, boy, have done with talk. Pooh, boy! Daimba Seisay can face death with spirit."

"Yes, Luseni," Nenneh Touray shouted hysterically, "avenge your father's death!"

The young man took the spear from her.

For a minute the sound of falling rain filled the countryside. Then, from under their feet, a deep sigh seemed to issue out of the very bowels of the Earth.

"He is dead!" said Luseni.

---

8. *Allah Akhbarr:* "God is great." [Arabic]

"It cannot be!" Yalie Woanday wailed. "Daimba! Daimba! Daimba! . . . Ah!" She rushed forward, stumbled over the corpse, threw herself over the rapidly cooling form. "Ah—Daimba!" she wailed harrowingly through the night.

The two men pulled Woanday up, Poreh held her sobbing against her faithful heart.

Feeling lost—not unnaturally, now that the prop of her life was knocked away by her enemy's death—Nenneh Touray came forward shakily and felt in the darkness for the shaft of the spear. As she followed it down to the spot over Daimba's chest, the lightning flashed.

In the glare she saw all too briefly the spear sticking out of her enemy's heart. But she saw most clearly that Daimba Seisay's face was smiling peacefully in death.

"It was not so Luseni died," she cried bitterly, rising from the ground. "Is he dead? Really dead? . . . Lansannah, Luseni—*he* made no noise . . ."

True, he had made no noise. He had been too proud even to cry out in the agony of death. And who could tell if, knowing that he was expiating a murder twenty years old, he had not gone with relief tantamount to ecstacy, to meet his Maker with the slate wiped clean?

"He was at least a man!" Luseni exclaimed in a tone of admiration. "Pity he had to be our enemy. And now, my Mother, come home with me—and complete the journey you started twenty years ago."

But his words had only added wormwood to his mother's bitterness.

Now that vengeance was achieved, Nenneh Touray was overcome by an overwhelming sense of failure. Even a sense of doubt. . . .

"Yes, Nenneh," cried her brother-in-law, who was by now heartily sick of the weather, "come home and relax after two whole decades."

Thus Nenneh and Poreh resumed their journey interrupted so long ago. True, a Luseni was with them again—but how different from that first journey of hope!

Such were Nenneh's thoughts as she went with her kith and kin. She took the first twenty, thirty, hundred paces home, to the very Lansannah's town the other Luseni would have had them journey. And then, very abruptly, she stopped and refused to budge a foot further.

"*He* made no noise, Luseni . . ." She spoke but faintly, so that they just only heard her in the rain.

"Don't distress yourself, dear Mother. Daimba Seisay is quite dead."

"N'ga Nenneh," urged Lansannah, damning the woman in his heart, "come, let's away. Even Allah can't kill a man twice!"

"*Wait!*" Nenneh Touray cried with a note of urgency. "My friends, my child, be patient with me. Twenty years is a long time to wait for this . . . I'll run back and make quite, *quite* sure . . ."

Before they could restrain her she had bolted away up the track and disappeared into the night.

And then, as the two men and women stood helpless and miserable in the wet waiting for her, the thunderstorm gathered its forces for a

Parthian shot.[9] After *that* the rain did perceptibly abate—but then they had ceased to care. A white ball of fire tore through the dome of the night, exploded into the branches of a colossal tree of fire—whose stem instantly leaped towards the earth. A tearing sound and a peculiar sulphurous smell seemed to hit the hillside around them. The thunderclap that followed reverberated with such violence the airwave tossed the four people into the grasses by the track as if they were all made of chaff.

Luseni got up first, considerably shaken.

"Uncle! N'ga Poreh!" he called, almost scared, "are you two all right?"

"Yes, my boy," Lansannah answered from several yards away, where the thunderblast had hurled him. "But I fear for your mother."

The men left Poreh to help the half-concussed Woanday, and ran up the valley to Nenneh Touray's help.

They found her under Luseni's tree.

The spear shaft sticking out of Daimba's chest guided them to the spot where she lay.

The lightning had cleft Luseni's tree from top to bottom. One of its branches lay over Nenneh Touray as it lay, impartially, over Daimba Seisay. For they found her at the bottom of the foliage, gripping tight to the spear in Daimba's heart, lying dead across his chest.

"Allah," Lansannah cried in awe, feeling the hairs rise at the back of his neck, "Allah has at last made peace between them."

------

9. **a Parthian shot:** a parting shot.

DISCUSSION QUESTIONS

1. Note the title of this novella. What feud is presented in this story?

2. What changes do you notice in Nenneh during the twenty years the story covers? What sort of man is Daimba Seisay? What is your final impression of each of these characters?

3. After Daimba Seisay's death the narrator comments that Nenneh was "feeling lost . . . now that the prop of her life was knocked away by her enemy's death." What does this statement mean? Do you think this is a tale of justice or revenge? Explain your answer.

4. Throughout the story the narrator comments on people and society in general. Note the following quotations. What picture of African tribal life do you get from these quotations?

- "Laconic and brutal as the information [of the raid] was, it was no worse than Nenneh had expected. It was the logic of the times. Her father had done the same thing to other tribes. Only she had never, never realized it had been so bad for others as it was turning out for her."

- "Young though [Daimba] was, both as man and as king, absolute power had corrupted him beyond redemption."

- "Poreh was made of sterner stuff than the princesses and parasites of Susu society."

SUGGESTION FOR WRITING

Do you think that Nenneh was fated to die at the end of this story, or was it just a tragic coincidence that she was crushed by the fallen tree? Write a paragraph in which you defend one of these opinions. Use evidence from the story and your understanding of tribal beliefs as best you can to support your position.

C. O. D. EKWENSI
(born 1921)

Cyprian Ekwensi, a pioneer of modern African literature, considers himself a popular writer in the tradition of Dickens, Dostoyevsky, and Hemingway—someone who writes about life and death, truth and fiction, justice and injustice, corruption and the virtues of life. He has published numerous novels, children's stories, and collections of folk tales and short stories. His short fiction is a favorite of anthologists, and it has appeared in many collections. A member of the Igbo tribe, Ekwensi was born in Minna, Nigeria. His background is varied: he has studied forestry and pharmacy, the latter both at home and in England. He has worked as a teacher, a pharmacist, a lecturer, and as Nigerian Director of Information. Throughout his career and in much of his work Ekwensi has expressed his faith in a national harmony that transcends ethnic rivalry among the three major ethnic groups in Nigeria—the Igbo, the Yoruba, and the Hausa. ■

RITUAL MURDER

The two black men were afraid. Kofi could read it in their eyes. They did not wish to leave him. They stood on the steps of the palace, stubbornly loyal.

"We will wait for you here," they said. "We are your bodyguard. Your wife said we must not lose sight of you."

"There's no need, brothers. I'm quite safe."

They came nearer, their arms gesturing wildly. "You make light of the danger, Kofi."

"Nothing can happen to me." Kofi slung the velvet robe over one shoulder. "Do not fear. A new paramount chief is in office, true. . . ."

"And he will wash the golden stool[1] with human blood. Maybe yours. . . ."

Kofi laughed.

They were uneasy. "But, Kofi . . . Look! . . . Can't you understand?"

It was useless. Kofi had mounted the steps, and the door of the palace had opened and shut.

"He's mad," said one, shrugging. The other one scowled at him for a while. "Yes . . . really mad."

---

1. **the golden stool:** the most sacred object in Ashanti, a region in the north of Ghana.

2. *Omanhene:* the paramount chief among the Ashanti, who is the custodian of the golden stool.

In the distance the West African sunshine blazed downwards. Two girls hawking biscuits[3] strolled past the palace, their cotton dresses a feast of color. They made eyes at the two men on the steps. Cars, lorries,[4] hand-trucks, horse-drawn carts, were moving along the street. A policeman was directing the traffic, and he paused to show a white man the right road. It was impossible to contemplate ancient evil beneath this façade of Western law and order. Surely no harm could come to Kofi.

Kofi followed the guide through a dark corridor.

"They're expecting you," the guide said. "You'll find them in the black room."

"The black room?"

"Yes. . . ."

The room where, away from the eyes of the law, gruesome rites were performed; wherein stood the golden stool waiting, always waiting for an old *Omanhene* to die, so that a new one might wash it with blood. In the dark days, a slave's blood was easy to come by. But not now. The white men frowned on the use of human blood. For years the blood of a dove, a sheep, had provided a legal substitute.

The guide said: "Knock on the door. I leave you."

Kofi looked at the massive door. He looked behind him at the dark corridor. He was alone. There was no turning back. He flung his shoulders back and breathed deeply. His knees were trembling. He knocked. No one answered; but the door gave when he pushed and he went in.

At a table in the center of the room, six men were playing cards. The air smelled strongly of spirits. They turned and looked at Kofi grimly, their hard bare torsos etched out by the smoky hurricane lamp.

"Shut the door and sit down, Kofi." They indicated an empty seat at the table. A whole bottle of raw gin was pushed across to him. "Drink some! . . . It isn't poisoned!"

He was uncomfortable. He held his breath in the stuffy atmosphere. The mystery, the suspense, the secrecy irritated him. He did not wish to be a party to anything furtive.

"I am here now," he said. "What did you want me for?"

Apiedu, the eldest of the half-brothers, waved aside Kofi's fears. "Have patience, my boy," he soothed. "You'll soon know."

"I haven't got all day . . . there's work to do. The old *Omanhene,* your father, is dead. His affairs are in disorder. It is my duty . . ."

"We know you were his secretary. And that is why we sent for you. With your intimate knowledge of his private affairs, you are going to be very useful. You will be well paid, of course, if you cooperate."

They passed the raw gin round, and each of them sucked from the bottle and handed it to the next man. Kofi glanced about him uneasily. In a corner of the room, he could barely see the golden stool. It was not so golden now, with the dark stains on it. On top of the stool was a wickedly

---

3. **biscuits:** cookies.

4. **lorries:** trucks.

sharp knife . . . the *saw-paw* of the ritual murders. It was the same knife that had buried itself in the hearts of many a slave some half a century ago.

"Kofi," said Apiedu. "We want to ask you a little favor."

"Go ahead."

"It's about that money," Apiedu said. "Come, Kofi! You know about it!"

Kofi swallowed. "I . . . I. . . ."

"Ten thousand pounds. . . . My father took it out of the treasury and founded Kofo and Co. Everybody in the smallest village in West Africa knows about it. Of course the business is doing very well. But the new *Omanhene* may not like it; just as he may not like to take over our father's wives. He'll make changes. He'll tell the Government what happened. Where will we be then?"

Kofi said nothing. Apiedu glanced round the table. His brothers were dealing out cards with half an ear on the discussion.

"Ten thousand pounds is a lot of money for the auditors to overlook. And now, Kofi, what are *you* going to do about it?"

"Me? I . . . I don't understand . . ."

"It's easy! You are the only man in Africa who has access to the fatal papers. You alone can dig up the evidence the new *Omanhene* might want if he decides to make trouble. Got that? Well, we're asking a very simple favor. We want you to go back and destroy every scrap of evidence pointing to the theft of that ten thousand."

"I . . . I can't. It isn't my business to audit accounts. I have nothing to do with the money of the state."

"That's right! . . . You have nothing to do with it, but you know where to find the rope that will hang us. Go and burn that rope." The brothers had stopped playing their game. "If you talk too much, Kofo and Co. will be given to the state. We will go to jail. There'll be hard work to do. . . ." He glanced at his soft hands. "We have never worked in our lives, and it is too late to start now. Why do you look so worried? This is but a little favor we have asked of you. And your reward is . . . two thousand pounds!"

Kofi looked at them helplessly. It was true he knew about that deal: every single man involved in it. And he knew many more things besides. He could make life completely intolerable for the late chief's sons. He looked up. The light threw dark shadows on their faces. Their eyes were hard, unforgiving. He saw them through the smoky haze of the lamp, and somehow tried to fight against the mad idea that this was unreal, a mere dream.

"Give me time," he begged. "I have not yet come to that business. When I come to it, I'll know how to fix things."

The brothers exchanged glances. No one spoke.

"I . . . I don't think there is anything more," Kofi said rising. "I must go now. Don't worry! Everything will be all right." Did they believe him? The room was so still that he wanted to shout at them. Slowly he backed towards the door.

"Where are you going, Kofi?" They were all standing now.

"Don't you trust me? I've told you . . . there's nothing to worry about. Let me go home to my wife and children."

Apiedu laughed. "He's going home. Ha! ha! . . . And we'll be here. . . waiting!"

Panic seized Kofi. He had sensed something sinister beneath it all. In a sudden burst of recklessness he sprang for the door. But he was too late. They were between him and the massive structure. And he knew then that they meant to murder him.

"What did you want to do?" Apiedu said softly. "To go out and betray us?"

"Go and sit down," said Lampey.

Kofi stood his ground. "You cannot frighten me," he bluffed. "I came to the palace gate with two men. Your own guide brought me to this door. My wife knows where I am. If you do anything to me, everybody will know. Go back to your drink and don't touch me. You'll only regret it. I've given you my word: everything will be all right."

"Nonsense!" said Apiedu.

Kofi did a very foolish thing. Perhaps he thought he was being brave. He pushed Lampey aside and seized the door handle. Almost at once, something hard struck him on the back of the head, and he fell against the door and slid downwards.

"Bring him over to this corner," said Apiedu.

"But he's not dead."

"That's just it . . . his blood will be still warm . . . for the stool."

"We'll all hang!" said Kwame, the youngest brother. "God knows I am innocent."

"You can't prove it," Apiedu said. "We've done this thing to help you. Nobody will ever suspect us. Why would we want to kill anyone? We have no motive. But the new *Omanhene,* he has . . . he wants to wash the stool . . . an age-old ritual. And he kills Kofi. He cannot tell the white men, because no one will believe him. His hands are tied. And remember this: he has been boasting that he will not use pigeon's blood, or sheep's blood . . . so we're all right!"

"He's dead," said Lampey, who had been holding him.

Silence fell in the room.

"Two of you go for a cart," Apiedu said. "Hide it somewhere. As soon as it is dark we'll take the body away."

Kwame paced up and down the little room.

"You're frightened, Kwame."

"I've never seen a man killed before!"

Apiedu smiled. "Yes! But there's a reason, Kwame! Either we put this new *Omanhene* into trouble, or he puts us. There's no other way. We must live!"

"I don't want to live in that way. Let me work till my hands peel rather than kill a man and . . . and use his blood."

"Shut up, Kwame!"

Kwame pulled up, sweating and trembling. The others did not move.

Under the palm trees, in the market places, men and women talked about the missing official. With lips scarcely open, they hissed out the terrible word: *murder.*

"The *Omanhene* has killed Kofi, now he wants us to help him look for the man he has killed and buried."

And away on the rolling grassland where the nomads grazed their cattle, Apiedu was amusing his brothers.

"The police are so stupid! Look what a fuss they made about those drops of blood in the black room: giving it to the Government pathologist to analyze and to prove it was human blood. What else could it be?" He laughed. "But there's no blood without a body! Where is Kofi?"

"They will catch us," Kwame said. "We are wasting time by hiding here." Fear and hunger had worn him down.

"We are safe here," Apiedu said.

"Yes," put in the others.

Kwame spat. "They will catch us. If not today, tomorrow. But they will surely hang all of us. . . ." He broke off suddenly.

"Look! . . ." he panted. "See him!"

The brothers looked, but there was nothing to see. Kwame was gazing at the door of the hut, his face working.

"He is going mad," Apiedu said uneasily. "Sometimes he hears the voice of our father . . . sometimes he sees the spirit of Kofi."

"Who knows?" said Lampey. "Perhaps he may be seeing something."

Apiedu looked startled. "You too? Are you getting the fever?"

That night, after they had retired to their grass beds, Lampey suddenly cried out. "He's lying on my bed. . . . He's here! . . ."

A light was fetched. "Where is he?" said Apiedu.

"He was here in the bed beside me. I swear! I wouldn't deceive you, would I, Apiedu?"

Apiedu looked at him scornfully. "You are even worse than the boy, Lampey! Who's next?"

"He . . . he was here," said Lampey. "He lay beside me on this bed!"

"Yes," Apiedu said, "but where is he now?"

Lampey looked foolish. He had scared the whole party and now they crowded together around the lantern, and kept vigil the whole night through.

Long before dawn, Apiedu went out into the grassland. It was chilly. A mist hung in the air. In this lonely part of the veld no one was about. Their only contact was the next village where Lampey sometimes went to buy food. It seemed that the hard life, the fear of the police, the contemplation of the future which held nothing for them, was troubling his brothers. Something had to be done, and soon too.

He paused and looked about him. Somewhere ahead of him, leaning against a tree, was a dark figure. It was a man. Who could it be, at this early hour and in so lonely a place? Apiedu walked on, and the figure detached itself from the tree and moved quickly towards him, forcing him to step out of the narrow footpath.

The black man in the dark cloth passed him like a flash and disappeared behind the bend. The mist hung thick. The air seemed to become more chilly. It could have been a dream, if he had not noted that bare bald head, those bulging eyes. Back in the little hut, he asked Lampey whether they had a visitor.

"No," said Lampey.

Apiedu described the encounter as lightly as he could and dismissed it. But Lampey returned to the subject.

"Apiedu, you may be a very brave man; but let us go to Koforidua . . . to the fetishman. We can consult him about this evil spirit."

"Yes," said Kwame. "I was about to say the same, but I was afraid you would laugh at me."

"It is the best thing," agreed the others.

The three brothers entered the hut of the fetishman stealthily.

"You wish to make a confession?" said the priest. "Sit down!"

"We are haunted," Apiedu said.

"We cannot sleep," Lampey added. "At night, the man we killed comes. Sometimes he sleeps beside one of us." He shivered.

"And you want something to drive off this evil spirit?"

"Yes."

"I shall give you a powder to burn. But the preparation of this powder requires one very special ingredient. It may be too late to get it. Then I can do nothing. Something from the dead man's body."

Apiedu looked uneasily round. "We buried him. . . ."

"Yes, I know. Long ago?"

"Three weeks. What do you want? Tell me, I'll get it for you . . ."

The old man smiled. "That would destroy everything. I have to get it myself. You will come with me, and you will bring with you digging implements. It will have to be at night. No one will see us."

Apiedu said: "I . . . I must consult my brothers first. I. . . ."

"If you are afraid, let things lie. In my business privacy comes first. You can be sure I shall not discuss your affairs with anyone."

When they had gone, the fetishman looked up his manuscripts. It was a long time since he had handled a case of haunting.

The door darkened. New clients? But these two, the white man in plain clothes and the black man in a black robe, were not clients.

"I am a police officer," said the white man. "May I come in?"

"This is the new *Omanhene*. We have reason to believe that the sons of the late *Omanhene* visited you not long ago."

"Yes," said the *Omanhene*. "What did they tell you?"

"Long may you reign, chief! They were having stomach trouble." The fetishman smiled.

The white man smiled. "Those six boys are murderers. They have framed your chief here. We have no evidence against them. If you do not say what you know I will take it that you are a party to the crime. And in that case, I must ask you to come with me to the station. The car is outside."

"What do you want to know?"

"Just what you know."

"It is against my practice . . . but those boys are haunted."

The white man tapped the *Omanhene* on the shoulder. "And this is the ghost who did all the haunting. For three weeks he has been watching the brothers."

The fetishman's mouth widened. Then he grinned. "I see. So he is the ghost? Now, these boys want my help, and I want something—from the body. If they agree, they will take me to the spot tonight. If not . . ."

"I'm sure they'll come," the white man said. "And we'll be there, too! They won't know, of course."

"I knew they couldn't stand it," the *Omanhene* said. "Kwame was the first to break; the last was Apiedu."

"The reward for their capture is three hundred pounds," the police officer said.

"I do not want your money."

In the night the brothers slipped into the hut. They were wearing long dark caps pulled low over their eyes. "It is chilly outside," said Apiedu. "We are here, now. Let us go quickly!"

The fetishman put on a cape woven from elephant grass. "You'll have to carry me," he said. "I'm lame."

The brothers took him into the valley where a stream trickled over the sands. Kwame was shivering.

"The body is there," Apiedu said, "under the stream. We stemmed the water, then dug a hole and buried him. After that, we let the water flow over him."

"You can do the same now," said the old man. "You've got your tools?"

"Yes, we have our tools."

"You will have to excuse me while you work."

The fetishman turned away. He limped up the valley. The white man was in police uniform now. And so was every man in the party behind him. He did not speak to them.

From a bag under his arm he drew out a little packet and poured a powder down his throat.

"Eighty years," he muttered, "and I have never betrayed anyone." He sank on his knees, waiting for the poison to act.

DISCUSSION QUESTIONS

1. At the beginning of this story did you suspect something bad would happen to Kofi? Why or why not? If so, at what point did you become convinced?

2. The first scene takes place in the bright sunlight on the steps of a palace in a modern city; the second scene is in a dark corridor and a back room (called the black room) of the palace. What is the symbolic significance of this contrast?

3. Between the old Africa and the new one stand certain men ready to use old traditions unscrupulously to advance their position in the new world. In this story, who are these men and what old traditions do they use unscrupulously?

4. Why do you think the fetishman poisons himself at the end of the story?

5. Think about the title: "Ritual Murder." Are the killings in the story ritual murders? In what way might this story be about the "murder" of the old Africa?

SUGGESTION FOR WRITING

Compare the ending of "Ritual Murder" with the ending of "The Feud." Consider these questions in your composition: What happens to Nenneh Touray at the end of "The Feud"? What happens to the three half-brothers at the end of "Ritual Murder"? What part does guilt play in either story? In what way are Nenneh and the three brothers responsible for their own demise? What part do the old traditions play in each story?

LAW OF THE GRAZING FIELDS

This is the law of the wandering cattlemen of the savanna: that a man may elope with the woman of his choice, maiden or matron, wife or spinster. But woe betide him if he is caught on the run. Yet all is well if he can but get his beloved home without being caught.

On the evening of our story a brother and sister were quarreling. Modio, the brother, had just pushed Amina, the sister, violently.

"Kai!" Amina shouted, springing deftly backward, "Take your hands off me." Her lips were parted, but not in a smile, and her full breasts heaved so that the necklaces of silver and fruit seemed to come to life. Amina just managed to retain her balance by clutching at the wall of the grass hut. "Don't you dare touch me again!"

"By Allah," Modio raged, "I'll teach you some sense."

She glared at him. He was crouching before her, his hands curved like the claws of a hawk about to strike, his muscles tense. "You'll go nowhere!"

"You lie!" she cried. "This night I will be with Yalla. He's the husband I've chosen."

"What of Jama, the husband our father chose for you? What of the cattle Jama's been paying?"

"That is your affair," she said. "Did you—Oh, let me go, you devil. Are you mad?"

She felt the stroke of his rough hand across her mouth. His arm tightened about her waist and she was struggling as he carried her out to his own hut. With his bare foot he kicked open the door; dust rose in a cloud. He thrust her in. She fell forward on her face in the dust and lay there, her body heaving with sobs. Amina was young and in the fullness of her bloom. Her long hair, unplaited, fell over her back and lay buried in the dust. Tears mingled with the red cream she had painted on her cheeks.

"You wretch," she heard her brother say from the other side of the door. He was fastening the door and presently she heard him stamp away, cursing her.

She let the tears flow freely as if tears alone could heal the ache in her heart, the desire for the man she had chosen. But there must be hope, she thought. No one, nothing could shut her away from Yalla forever. She must go to him, she must.

Hatred burned within her breast. Was it her fault that she did not like Jama? Her father had accepted the cattle first and told her about him later. He turned out to be a weak-kneed, effeminate man. A man who could not weave mats or take the cattle out to graze. A coward who had wept and begged as they flogged him at the *sharro*.[1] He had taken his flogging, it was true, but he had not taken it like a man and it would be humiliating to marry him. Her father might give her away to Jama, but he would not be present when the other maidens would taunt her with having married a coward: "And how's your husband? The one who stays in bed till sunrise, who must not be soaked by the rain? Ha, ha! A husband, indeed!"

The mistake had been Yalla's, for he had not honored the arrangement in full. It had been a simple arrangement. She and Yalla were to escape from the camp before Jama brought the bulls that were the final installment of the bride-price. Yalla was to have come to the hut at the hour when the hyenas began to howl over the grazing fields. He was to screech in the manner peculiar to the gray hawk that steals chickens and she would then know that he was waiting for her under the dorowa tree.

She had waited for Yalla's screech. In the early hours of the evening before the hyenas slunk out of the rocks, she had thought about her man—tall, wide-shouldered, with a copper ring in his plaited hair, a man who could break a stubborn bull or calm the wildest pony in her father's stables. Yet when he smiled or held her hand, his face was so gentle and so sweet. She liked to place her head against his deep wide chest and look

---

1. the *sharro:* an initiation ceremony.

up into the darkness of his brown eyes. He was fond of playing with her ears, and sometimes he irritated her and she would threaten to go to Jama. What a contrast Yalla was to Jama. Jama, the coward. Could Jama protect a home from the gales that swept the grazing fields? Could he outwit the wild dogs, and the hyenas, the leopard and the lion, when they came to raid the herd?

A husband indeed. She had been his "wife" ever since she could remember. Five hundred head of cattle was a good price, but she was no article for sale.

Early this evening Yalla had come up to her father's settlement. He had stood outside near the dorowa tree and had whistled to her. She had been very excited. To think she was leaving her home for good. There could be no good-byes, no tears. She was running away with a man they would gladly kill. There was dead silence over the veld. Amina had peeped out cautiously. There was the veld before her. It was all hers and Yalla's if only they would dare. The stunted trees, bowing in the cold wind, the rushing streams, the rocks, the thorn forests. They were all calling out to her and to Yalla to go forth and conquer them; to begin their own camp with a group of bulls and cows—their own. Yalla had screeched again, impatiently, and this time he did sound like the gray hawk. She had not hesitated.

She ran. She took nothing with her, not even one of the wooden ladles that her mother had given her for stirring the milk. And that was when her brother had intercepted her. She did not know that he had been hiding all the while in a nearby tree. He had a pack of wild cattle-dogs with him, and these he at once unleashed on Yalla. He had seized Amina and had laughed at her threats and clawings and curses. For Yalla and Amina the law of the grazing fields was broken.

Now she was a prisoner in the hut, but Amina found it impossible to imagine that Yalla never would be hers. There must still be a chance. If only he could somehow manage to free her from this prison and take her to his hut before Jama paid the full price of five hundred cattle, she could still be Yalla's by right of his might. No one could deny this law of the grazing fields. All cattlemen knew it and respected it. But how was Yalla to know where she was, or when Jama would be coming. Everything was over, Amina decided with a fresh burst of tears.

"Oh, Yalla, my Yalla! Come and save me, Yalla. I am yours and you are my man!"

She pushed and screamed and threatened until her brother warned her to be quiet. But how could she be quiet when her body itched from the dust and the thorns? Oh, death! It were better to die than to live as Jama's wife.

Already she could hear an argument about the saddling of the horses. Her other brothers had returned from the fields. One of them said she must wear a black veil, and the other said a white one was the custom. Such trifles! The eldest brother said he would ride behind the bride; he couldn't trust her for a moment after what she had been through with Modio. And all this because of five hundred head of cattle.

Quite suddenly she became conscious of silence. The chattering ceased and the coarse jokes. A fearful pause lay over the veld. She began to cough. The air in the little room hung heavy and thick. And then her brother's voice cut in hoarsely.

"Fire!" he shouted. "Fire! . . . Yes . . . whoo . . . fetch water . . . Fire!"

Amina started. Heavy fumes began to fill her little prison. She was coughing and gasping fearfully. Desperation gave her the strength of ten. She flung herself at the door. The fumes were now pouring in through every crack in the hut. The boys outside shouted and yelled, keeping the cows from panicking. Their shouts beat dimly against her ears. She was choking. Did they not even remember her? Could they be so cruel? Were their cows more valuable to them than her life?

A rough hand thrust open her door, and a man's gruff voice urged her, "Follow me. It's Yalla."

Her heart gladdened, but no words came to her choking lips. The man's arm circled her waist and swept her off her feet. The thatch caught her hair, and the man's hands detached the burrs tenderly. She must be dreaming. She felt the air rush into her throat. She saw the yellow sheets of flame shoot skyward in dazzling columns. And, as she raised her hand to shield her eyes from the glare, Amina saw her brothers dashing here, there and yonder, collecting sleeping mats, money purses, milk bowls. It was a dream no longer. That voice—it was real. "There she is! . . . Brothers, there's our sister. Catch her! . . ."

"Yalla," Amina sobbed, "what shall we do? They are coming."

"Let them try. My hut is five miles from here. It will be a good race." She felt herself carried across the encampment and saddled on to a horse.

"Away, now!" Yalla shouted. "Away. . . ."

Every forward leap of the horse jarred her bones. Her hair streamed in the wind. Behind them came her brothers. Relentless, cunning riders, angered beyond repair. Amina could clearly hear the clatter of the pursuing horses. By Allah! What could she do?

Twang.

That was an arrow. Best to give up now.

"Oh, Yalla, let us get down and go back home. It's useless running in this manner."

The man's laugh, big and thunderous, made her feel silly. Was he laughing at the poisoned arrow that might have stiffened his back and sent him coughing and clutching to his death? What a nerve! Their horse had begun to pant under the combined weight. They were now in a part of the scrub with few trees and many rocks and hills. This was where clever horsemanship would tell. This was where this thief would lose her or gain her forever. She held her breath. Her body prickled with a thousand pains but she knew the prize that lay ahead and it gave her courage.

The horse labored. Even Yalla, man that he was, ground his teeth in pain and weariness, urging his steed ahead with a slashing whip.

"Yee-whoo!" he shouted, the sweat running down his face and falling into Amina's eyes. "Yee-whoo! . . ."

She was the first to see the light in the distance.

"My hut," Yalla said. "My lonely hut!"

"Our hut, you mean."

He laughed again.

Twang! And Yalla moaned. "They've shot me! My back . . . Allah save me, I'm dying. . . ."

Before the words were out of his mouth, Yalla was sliding down the saddle, for an arrow's poison acts fast. Yet more arrows twanged past even as the distance between them and their pursuers narrowed.

"If I die, you go ahead. They can't touch you once you're in my hut. It is the—the . . ."

Terror, panic. Amina looked over her shoulder and saw her elder brother's figure looming out of the darkness. Yalla had barely enough strength to crawl. Amina dragged him on. She was a girl of the veld, fresh, strong and brave. His strength waned fast. Ahead of them, the cows in the gloom bolted out of their paths. Rams bleated anxiously. A cock cackled, waking all the rest which now set up a deafening crow. They were actually in Yalla's settlement, but not in the hut.

"You thief!"

A few yards behind the paddocks, just beyond the poultry yard, Amina bent down. With all her might, she seized Yalla and pushed him into the hut, falling in after him.

He breathed a sigh of relief.

"My wife!" he moaned. "Mine at last! . . . But first, this arrow. You can still save me. . . . The antidote . . ."

Amina's brothers drew up before Yalla's hut.

"You thief!" they raved. "Give us our sister."

"Thief?" he sneered. "You are the thieves. Have you not stolen the bridal horse?"

"Our father, Jama, will know no rest till you've compensated him his cattle."

"Leave that to me," Yalla said. To Amina he murmured, "Oh, my back. The antidote . . ."

The brothers wheeled their horses and cantered slowly back to their own camp. One of them said: "That lad, Yalla, he is a man. Setting fire to our camp, stealing our sister, and then calling us thieves for taking back our own horse which we saddled for another bridegroom! The law of the grazing fields. He's won."

DISCUSSION QUESTIONS

1. What is the law of the grazing fields?

2. In what sense is Amina a victim of the society in which she lives? In spite of this, in what ways does Amina show that she is a strong woman?

3. Do you think Yalla lives or dies at the end of the story? Explain your answer.

SUGGESTION FOR WRITING

In what ways does this story seem similar to a story set in the Wild West of the United States? Write a paragraph in which you compare the elements of this story—setting, plot, and characters—with the elements of a story about the Wild West.

D. O. FAGUNWA
(1910–1963)

Daniel Fagunwa, the most popular and most widely read of all Nigerian writers, produced numerous novels and a collection of short stories, all in his native Yoruba language. "The Forest of the Lord" is an extract taken from his second novel *Igbo Olodumare*. His novels, written in the traditional style and employing traditional Yoruba subject matter, have a fairy-tale atmosphere and usually point to a distinct moral. Fagunwa was educated and trained as a teacher and at one time worked for the Ministry of Education in Ibadan. Fagunwa was awarded the Margaret Wrong Memorial Prize "for an outstanding contribution to literature in Africa by a person of the African race." He died in an automobile crash in 1963. ■

THE FOREST OF THE LORD

Translated from the Yoruba by E. C. Rowlands

Akara-Ogun began his narrative saying, "My friend, when it was now the twenty-fifth year since my father had come into the world he made himself ready one morning and betook himself to hunt in a certain strange forest which lies near our town. Our townsfolk call this forest the 'Forest of the Lord,' because it is a place which is full of fear. The hunters indeed fear this 'Forest of the Lord' more than the 'Forest of Spirits' and it is a fixed law in our town that no hunter must go there to hunt until he has become an elephant-killer, because that place is a place of wonders. The birds there speak with human voices and the animals buy and sell with each other. Many of the trees there have no roots, yet their wood is fresh and their leaves are glossy and green. A mouse in the Forest of the Lord is bigger than an ordinary bush-rat and a snail is bigger than a tortoise. Powerful sprites and grim hobgoblins are in league there and all sorts of bold snakes cast fear on hunters, for it is there that the chief snake of all the world lives, whose name is 'Angry Python.'"

Before my father set out from his house he showed himself to be a hunter indeed, for many were the charms which he tied round his waist, while his fingers were covered with such rings as elders wear. No fewer than six oxen were killed as an offering in our house. My father summoned the medicine-men of our town together and provided them all with food. Ancestral medicines were stored in our house in profusion. Six whole months had he spent scurrying to and fro in preparation for this visit to the Forest of the Lord, because those who used to go there did not return—they used to fall into the hands of one sprite after another. My father was indeed a man of energy. Some men excel others in manly qualities and Olowo-aiyé[1] had these qualities to the full.

It was a never-to-be-forgotten day in our house when my father had finished his preparations to go hunting in this forest and it was now time to bid farewell to all his relatives. The medicine-men were gathered together indoors and the elephant-killer hunters were gathered together on the veranda, while the children had taken refuge on the roof. All sorts of people were met together in the courtyard, the goats scattered hither and thither, women were weeping, men were weeping, men of worth could find no words to speak, men of honor sat with glum faces. But my father got himself ready like a European soldier, he tied medicines to his body like a diviner, he walked as one going to a wrestling bout and he stood firm as policemen stand before their commander.

When it was now time to start, he called all the household together and spoke to them saying, "The time has now come that I must go to the place where mighty men go, to the dwelling-place of strange creatures, to the place which is dark before me. I shall leave well-being behind me and go to meet trouble. But trials are the father of fortune-making and a good name is better than a new wife. If I endure today's difficulties I shall find fortune in the future. If I return with joy from the Forest of the Lord my name will long be heard of in the world. You my people, never think meanly of yourselves. Always aim at something which is important. A man who aims at achieving something important, even if he fails to achieve his aim will achieve something nearly as important. But the man who only aims to achieve something unimportant has no standing in the assembly of the mighty. He who prays for ten fine gowns, even if he fails to get ten he will get eight, and he who prays for six pairs of trousers, even if he fails to get six he will get five. But he who prays to God for one pair of trousers, if he gets two pairs he must indeed give thanks to Almighty God.

"I see you all here with glum faces, it is true, but my own heart is strong and firm like a shiny stone in the river. Progress is far from the man of two minds, and I am not in two minds as I go on my way. By the power of Almighty God who created me I shall surely return home. The man of two minds imagines in the morning that death is coming upon him and by midday he is dead, yet he might well have lived several days more in this world. A man's heart is his priest. Let me be going. Greet all the people of my house and see to my affairs in my absence. So now a man goes on his way. Tell all the people from me that a man of might has gone as a man of might to where men of might go, a man of note has gone as a man of note to where men of note resort. Let neither children nor elders, if they are gentlefolk, say that travellers in the Forest of the Lord do not return, and let all honorable people the world over be awaiting the return of a great man."

So spake Olowo-aiyé and then set off on his way to the Forest of the Lord. His eyes had changed their color, they were blood red. In his haste he almost forgot one important medicine contained in a small medicine-

---

1. **Olowo-aiyé** (ō lō′ wō ī′ yā).

calabash, and this medicine was such that if he did not take it with him finding his way to the forest would itself be difficult. The mouth of this calabash was plugged with cuckoo, *aluko* and vulture feathers and with red parrot-plumes, and its sides were stained with many sorts of blood. My own father's father had first owned it and he had obtained it from the belly of a python. For before we were born many of our family had been hunters and our grandfather whom I have just mentioned was the first man from our town to go hunting in the Forest of Spirits. It was then that he killed this python and found this wonderful medicine-calabash inside it. If a person pronounces a charm over this calabash and mentions the name of the place where he is going, the wind will blow on these feathers and they will point in the direction of the place. Indeed, my friend, if I had not forgotten the charm I would teach you it, because it is not more than five and twenty words in length, and after teaching you the charm I would search out the calabash and give it you.

The Forest of the Lord is very far, indeed it is two whole days' journey from our town. There are some big wildernesses on the way and also large rivers, which flow swiftly and sound mightily as they fall over rocks. There are many plants on the way, both those which are good and those which are harmful. Countless thousands of thorn trees bar the way as one walks along and filthy litter of every sort conspires with troublesome creepers twined about the trees to fall down on people's heads as they pass by. Furthermore, the wild animals do not let one rest. Brown monkeys and baboons and other monkeys with long tails jump from tree to tree. Their faces are like those of human beings and so too are the nails on their fingers. Truly monkeys resemble human beings closely; it seems as if the Creator made them relatives of each other.

Many different things are found in the wilderness. There are countless great trees and tall palms with the mistletoes which cling to them, and animals which live on the tops of the big palms. There are sharp-beaked birds whose attention is fixed on the base of the palm leaves so as to lose no chance of finding nuts to eat. There are squirrels which frequent the creepers, slender snakes looking round for dark recesses in which to hide, vipers lurking under the grass, pythons which inhabit the banks of rivers, and numerous poisonous snakes which hide in holes. There are snails which love damp places and tortoises which crawl under dried leaves. There is the coucal which flies at a middle height and the dove which frequents the high places. This bird plays the part of the cockerel in the wilderness, reminding the hunters of the time.

There are trees which have long since fallen to the ground and which have no more strength and which are covered with mushrooms. There are the paths of various animals, which differ from each other. The path of the mouse is narrow and smooth, but the path of the wild-boar is broad and flat. My friend, hearsay is not equal to experience and you yourself should experience the trials which beset one in the wilderness. All these difficulties my father had to endure as he made his way to the Forest of the Lord. But yet—and it is I who say it—all these things which I have described amounted to nothing compared with his experiences when he reached this forest.

On the first night after my father left home he slept on the way and by the time the sun was high in the sky on the next day he had almost reached his destination. At three o'clock in the afternoon he came to a forest which bordered on the Forest of the Lord itself. The name of this forest was the "Wilderness of Silence," because of all places under the sky that place is the most silent. A solitary sprite lives in this forest and he is fiercer than a clap of thunder. This sprite will not allow anyone to pass through to the Forest of the Lord. He gives the hunters much trouble and yet he is no more than two feet tall. He lives inside an ant-hill and he is indeed an imp of Satan who always bears with him a scourge.

When my father reached this forest everywhere was as silent as the grave. All the leaves on the trees were drooping and not one struck against another, as if there was not the slightest breeze. All the branches of the trees stood stock-still as when soldiers stand before their commander. The creepers were doubled up like sick men and the animals had rejected the place as a haunt. The birds had flown away each to his own place and every living thing was as dejected as a debtor who sits pondering on his debt. The whole forest was as still as when some great bereavement has befallen a man and his friends and acquaintances sit quiet.

Indeed, my friend, since in all this evil forest there was only my father with this little imp who lived inside an ant-heap, my father's passage through this place was fraught with difficulties. After my father had wandered about for some time in this great wilderness he and this small imp came in sight of each other. That was indeed a notable day when those two sighted each other, when injury met trouble, when hobgoblin met sprite, when two lions came face to face. The name of this imp was the "Little Devil of the Ways." He wore no coat and he wore no trousers; he had no hat on his head and tied no cloth round his loins, for it was with leaves that the wretch covered his nakedness. He had only one eye and that was wide and round like a great moon. He had no nose at all because his eye was so much bigger than the ordinary bounds of an eye. His mouth was as wide as a man's palm and his teeth were like those of a lion, and these teeth were red as when a lion has just finished eating a meal of raw meat. The sprite's body was covered with hair like a garment and resembled that of a European dog. A long tuft of hair grew on the top of his head. From his shoulder there hung a scourge and from his neck a great bag which filled one with fear. This bag was smeared all over with blood and on this blood was stuck the down of birds, while various medicines were attached to its sides—medicine-calabashes, fish-bones and parrot-plumes, cuckoo and *aluko* feathers, cowrie money used in olden days,[2] the horns of various animals large and small, including a horn of

---

2. cowrie money . . . days: The brightly colored shells of a small mollusk were formerly used as money throughout West Africa.

the antelope which devours okra on the farms, and also feathers of the bush-fowl which roams about in the wilderness. All these things were attached to the great bag carried by the little imp of the ant-hill, whose name is the Little Devil of the Ways.

As he approached his legs made a thin rattling noise because of a mass of snail shells which had been cut into small pieces shaped round like shillings and which had been strung together like beads and arranged on his legs by the imp from his ankles to his knees. His fingers were all covered with iron rings which were dark like the fingers of a woman who dyes with indigo. Ah! I tell you the truth, this was a very evil sprite.

When my father appeared on this side and the sprite appeared yonder the two of them stopped and looked at each other, because when elephant meets elephant needs must that trees crash down on each other. The sprite was advancing and my father was going on to meet him. When they had almost come up to each other they again stopped and looked at each other—things were about to happen. Little Devil was the first to speak. He opened his great mouth and said—

"Who are you? What are you? What do you amount to? What do you rank as? What are you looking for? What do you want? What are you looking at? What do you see? What are you considering? What affects you? Where are you coming from? Where are you going? Where do you live? Where do you roam? Answer me! Human being, answer me in a word! One thing is certain—you have got into trouble today, you have climbed a tree beyond its topmost leaves, you have fallen from a height into a well, you have eaten an unexpected poison, you have found a farm-plot full of weeds and planted ground-nuts in it. You man without understanding, you do not know that the lion and the antelope do not meet, that the leopard and the ox do not make friends together, and that on the day a cat spies a mouse the life of that mouse comes to an end. You saw me and I saw you, you were approaching and I was approaching, and yet you did not take to your heels. You walked in my presence as if you had no care. Are you not afraid? Does not your heart thump with alarm? Have you never heard of me? Has no one told you about me? The skulls of greater men than you are in my cooking-pot and their backbones are in the corner of my room, while my seat is made from the breast-bones of those who are thoughtless.

"I am the little imp of the ant-hill, whose name is the Little Devil of the Ways. Because a dispute arose between me and another in heaven they said I had acted dishonestly towards the Almighty and so those heavenly beings determined that I must leave my abode there. So I left heaven and went beneath the earth and I lived for a hundred years with the dead who are beneath the earth and I learned much wisdom among them. It was then that I learned that of the many deaths which the people of the world die very few are preordained from heaven. The people of the world bring death on each other by their own hands. A fool may kill one man unintentionally, another can be killed by overwork unintentionally, another can be killed by laziness unintentionally, another can be killed by gluttony unintentionally, while another can be killed by greed unintentionally. Sometimes a cunning man seeks a way to kill his neighbor but instead of that neighbor he himself goes off to the other world. Sometimes a false friend seeks a way to kill another and himself goes to the other world. Sometimes a rich man seeks a way to kill a poor man and himself goes off to the other world. Sometimes again a man of low degree seeks a way to kill a man of high degree and himself goes off to the other world. The loose talker plays with death, the prodigal plays with death, the gadder-about plays with death, the haughty man plays with death and so too does the trickster. Why is this? It is because the Creator gazes at the creature along with the work of his hands and his manner of life among other creatures, and the Creator will surely give the creature the reward of the work of his hands whatever changes there may be in circumstances, either in this world or in the next.

"I am the little imp of the ant-hill, whose name is the Little Devil of the Ways. When I left the dwelling-place of the dead I came to this Wilderness of Silence and made an ant-hill my dwelling-place. In this wilderness I found animals, here too I found birds, and here too I found spirits, but all these I have driven away, so that I no longer have anyone to live with. I alone am here and I eat the leaves of the forest. But today, now that I have unexpectedly found you, I give thanks, because my luck has brought me something. It is many a long day since I have had human flesh to eat. When I have killed you I shall enjoy your flesh for three days. With your skull I shall make okra-stew, with your breast-bone I shall make vegetable-stew, and your buttocks will make thick fat in pepper-stew. What is left of you I shall put aside in my house, in the ant-hill. Ah! I give thanks to the Lord today, I give thanks to all the deities today. I give thanks to all the spirits of the world, I give thanks to the lucky medicines inside my bag, and further I give thanks to that important sprite, Prince of the Forest, the imp who rules the ant-hill, who is my kinsman."

This was how the sprite spoke to my father, and my father answered as it is fitting that one strong man should answer another. He looked the Little Devil of the Ways up and down as when an impudent woman with a contemptuous glance looks at her husband and said, "He who tries to lift up rain in a sieve deceives himself. He who stands in the way of a railway train will find himself in Kingdom come. An elder who sees a snake and does not run is in a hurry to die. The animal which looks disdainfully at a hunter will sleep by the hearth-stones. The person who puts his trust in war involves himself in trouble.

"Any sprite who disregards me will find himself travelling from place to place in the other world. It is I who say so. Today I tell you sprites of the Forest of the Lord that when the Creator created all things which are in the world he made man to be their head. I want you to know today that pride is the beginning of destruction. Pride it is which precedes a fall. It is contrary to the laws of men and is opposed to the ordinances of God. Instead of me becoming your prey I can give your flesh to the beasts of the forest and turn you into food for the birds which fly among the trees. It is true that you have been meeting with men and turning them into inhabitants of your cooking-pot. But, Little Devil of the Ways, do not forget that some cocks are bigger than other cocks, some goats are bigger than other goats, some sheep are bigger than other sheep, some birds are bigger than other birds, some people are bigger than other people, some hunters are bigger than other hunters. It is I who tell you, I am stronger than those you have met before; I am not of their rank, I am of the rank of their fathers. You are puffed up with pride. You little sprite of the ant-hill, you Little Devil of the Ways. I am above the rank of your great-grandmother. To hell with you! What do you amount to? To hell with you seven times! You are in trouble today. Get ready, let us grapple with each other."

My friend, my father had barely finished speaking these words when the two of them began grappling with each other. This was a hard fight when a man met a spirit, and the whole forest resounded. The Little Devil of the Ways was tough and so too was Olowo-aiyé, my father, that hero who lived in this world and entered into combat with a being from the other world. When the fight first began Little Devil was trying to find an opportunity to cling to my father's hips and press his back against a thorny tree, and also to lift his leg on to his shoulder and push him on to the bushes and so injure his opponent. But this proved very difficult, because just as he had these ideas, so my father had other ideas. He was trying to find a way to lift Little Devil on to his shoulder, to get the dwarf sprite clear from the ground, to lift the wretch right above his head, to throw the rascal half a league away, so that Little Devil should travel from one place in the other world to another. But these attempts failed, because just as he was exerting himself like a lion, so Little Devil was exerting himself like an elephant and a great cloud of dust rose up in the face of the sky. The earth began to shake and the sound of their trampling feet was more than that of ten men. They glared at each other and grasped each other tightly as when a creeper clings to a tree on the farm, and both were panting like a hunter's dog. This was a hard day for the little sprite of the ant-hill, whose name is Little Devil of the Ways.

Presently, this wicked hobgoblin jumped at my father and clung to his middle, and when my father was struggling to grasp him by the leg he jumped on to his shoulder and grasping my father by the neck he began to beat him about the ears with great violence. This angered my father and he pushed the sprite along until he came to a thorny tree-trunk and then violently pushed him against the thorns. This caused the wicked sprite to give a loud yell and to jump down from my father's shoulder. So then my father gripped him by both ankles and he lifted Little Devil above his head and threw him forward in fury, hoping to smash the wretch's skull. But this plan failed. When my father looked in front of him, this creature was again standing firm and laughing and looking at my father as if the fight had only just begun.

My father now became weary of this struggle and he thrust his hand into his bag and was searching for a charm inside it when his eye suddenly lighted on an ancestral flute which we used to keep at our home. So he took this flute and began to blow it and the sound of this flute filled the whole place. He spoke of how God is the ordainer of victory and how He is the owner of all things which exist both in this world and in the next— the wealth of the sons of men and the treasures beneath the earth and everything which is on the face of the sea and in the sky. He spoke also of how there is no hindrance in the way of the Almighty. Everything which the Creator wishes to do He can do and no one can hinder the Almighty from exalting whom He wishes. My father described with his flute how the deceitful rises in the morning dark green like a plantain by the water-side, but when the sun is high he dries up like wood and by the evening he has withered completely away. The man of intrigue tells his friends that he has got himself a suit of clothes, but when the just man appears he points his finger at the other saying he is stark naked.

Such were the words of the songs which my father sang full of compassion on the day that he and the little sprite of the ant-hill met each other, and the songs were echoed throughout the forest. Now this flute was sweeter than a king's flute and as the song of the flute was a lament it could not fail to enter the recesses of the sprite's brain. The true man humbled the false, the Little Devil dropped his head like a banana-leaf, the sprite of the ant-hill began to look down on the ground pensively and the little creature opened his mouth and spoke, saying:

"The sons of men have changed and wise men have appeared among them. Much time has passed since I came here to make my dwelling-place and no one hitherto has tried to change my heart. But since the time that God created me I have noticed that the patient man never ends up with regret, but only he who foolishly lets patience be ruined. From today onwards I will not behave roughly towards people of the world, I will not be irritable with the sons of men, I will not be peevish with animals, I will not be rough with the leaves of the forest. For your words have changed my heart and I will not behave as a boor any more. But do not ever think that it is merely a spirit of laziness which leads me to utter these words. If you think so, then we must agree that you do not understand my words. You will be like one who calls a sheep an ox or a lorry[3] a bicycle or this world the next world. The patient man sees a quarrel and draws back and the fool thinks he is a coward, but when the patient man enters a quarrel, all the fools topple over like trees. I thank you for the lament which you sang, a song full of wisdom which reminded me of my Creator. If it were not for this song which you sang I would have fought for three whole days, because I have fought so before. I have fought a battle for three months, I have fought one for six months, I have fought one for a whole year, I, the little sprite of the ant-hill, whose name is the Little Devil of the Ways."

So the sprite spoke and my father put his anger aside and they greeted and shook hands with each other, and each went off in his own direction. But according to the law of nature a fight does not pass without the

---

3. **lorry:** a truck.

fighter suffering some injury, whether the fighter turn out the winner or the loser. My father had scraped his back against a tree, had torn his hunter's wallet, had lost an important charm, and had smashed his pipe. So too Little Devil had suffered hurt, two of his teeth had been dislodged, one of his rings was lost, and his leg was sprained, so that he walked like one suffering from guinea-worm.[4] That is why wise people rank quarrels with poison and avoid them every day, because quarrels are not proper for human beings, they are like fish-bones in the throat. But foolish people are in the habit of lighting a European torch and looking for quarrels all over the town.

So Olowo-aiyé went on his way and traveled on, he and God, and when he had nearly passed through the Forest of Silence he came to a little flowing stream which was bright and cool. There my father stopped and poured water on his body, and after that he ate some ripe bananas and took a cola-nut from his wallet and slipped it into his mouth. His mind was now at rest like the mind of a man who has contracted a debt of two pounds but the Lord has preserved his secret and he unexpectedly finds an opportunity of making ten pounds.

Less than ten minutes after leaving this stream my father had left the Forest of Silence behind him and had come out to a wide, open place. The verdure there was fresh and green like the front of a European's house, bushes were more numerous there than tall trees and each tree and bush in all that neighborhood was very beautiful, standing as they did with rounded shapes. Some were white and some were dark and some were like a rainbow, which has both bright and dark colors. A broad roadway went on straight ahead, that is, the path which my father was following had now become bigger. Great stones were arranged on the right and left sides of this road. Behind these stones bushes had been planted along the road and these were in flower and were very beautiful. My friend, as the proverb says: "When one's peer in age dies it is a warning to one's self." When Olowo-aiyé saw these things he knew that the Forest of the Lord was near, so my father girded himself like a man.

The wise man and the fool appear the same in a time of enjoyment but in a time of trouble the wise man stands out clearly. My father behaved like a wise man at this moment. He carefully placed his belongings on the ground and went beneath one of those trees and prostrated himself before God, saying:

"O God who created me. O Lord who created the Forest of the Lord, O marvelous One who created every marvel, O Creator who created every hunter that lives in the world, the time has now come that I want you to be my support. Some men come into the world and when they leave the world their name passes away with them. These men pass through the world like a snake over a rock and we see no trace of them. Others come

---

4. **guinea-worm:** a thread-like parasitic worm, common in tropical regions, which grows to a length of several feet. It infests domestic animals as well as man.

into the world and when they leave the world their evil name remains behind them, as when a black spot comes on to a white cloth and the washerman washes the cloth until it almost tears and the spot merely stands out more clearly. Please, my Creator, do not make me like one of these people. I humbly beg today that you make me like one of those people who come into the world and are like a moon which shines benignly for generation after generation. Their name remains after they are gone and those coming after them compete as in a race to be like them. As I go on my way today, grant that I may return like a man, so that when my time comes to die people will not be asking each other after I am gone, 'Was this man ever born?' "

This was how Olowo-aiyé spoke, and the Lord heard in the other world, because there is no man who is equal to an angel and there is no supporter equal to God. So my father went on his way singing and whistling and striding along like a soldier.

He had not long started on his way when he looked in front and saw two women coming along the road talking and laughing and slapping their hands as is the habit of countless women. These two women behaved as if they had made their home in that neighborhood and were enjoying their life in that forest. Indeed they were dressed in fine clothes as if they were in the middle of a town. One of them was light in color and was tall and stout, with the appearance of a married woman, but the second was somewhat slender and not very tall. She was dark in color and her teeth were white like fresh maize. Both of them were good-looking, their manner of speaking was that of gentlefolk, and their manner of walking was that of people who live at ease.

When they met my father he greeted them and they answered him in the restrained way which it is proper to use in answering someone with whom one is not acquainted. My father then went on his way and they went on theirs. But anyone would wonder how two gentlefolk such as these came to be in this wilderness, and this thought led my father to glance back to look at them. But at that very moment the younger of the two women also looked back and when their glances met they smiled at each other and then again set off on their way. The second time that my father looked back, his eyes again met those of this woman. Now at this time my father had as yet no wife, but was unmarried. Nevertheless he braced himself and again went on his way. But when it was now the third time that he looked back and this woman also looked back and he smiled and she smiled and the teeth of this beautiful woman were white like a wall which has been whitewashed, then Olowo-aiyé turned round, the hero turned his back on the Forest of the Lord and followed after this woman. May the Lord save the sons of men from women who cause trouble, who wear their head-ties forward on the head.

When my father began to approach her, this woman stood still but her companion walked on a little and stood away at some distance because when a man and a woman want to have a private conversation a third person is bound to be a hindrance to them. See, my friend, be careful in your behavior. If you accompany a companion to the house of his betrothed wife, think deeply before you attempt to take part in any conversation which they are having together, otherwise you will be like a dirty spot on a white cloth, and though they may have a smile on their faces in talking to you they are bound to be saying in the secret places of their hearts, "This rascal will not let us enjoy our private talk."

When my father came up to this woman he greeted her, "I hope your household is prosperous, I hope you are well, I hope no trouble affects you." The other gave him favorable replies. After answering his greetings the woman asked with a smile, "Have I not been acquainted with you before somewhere?" My father answered, "Yes, I have that feeling too. Is it your compound which is at the end of our yard?" And in fact a black-smith's compound lay at the back of us, and a girl who was a witch had been living there before Olowo-aiyé began wandering about the forests as a hunter. It was some time since my father had seen this girl. It turned out that this girl had left their compound, she and her elder sister, and had come to live in the Forest of the Lord. It was only when my father asked about this that he came to understand the circumstances. The woman answered him as follows:

"It is true that I am that girl called Ajediran[4] who used to live in the blacksmith's compound. When a quarrel broke out one day the people of our compound told lies about us and declared that it was we who had devoured their children. Yet at the time of which I am speaking I and my sister had not yet become witches. The children of men gave us a name which we did not deserve, and by the time three months had passed all the people throughout our town had come to believe that we were witches. Can the sons of men be so foolish? As soon as two or three people have said something everyone else will give up thinking for themselves and will be repeating something which to them is mere hearsay. So the sons of men gave me and my sister a name which we did not deserve. In the end we became angry and sought witchcraft and found it, and in our rage we turned ourselves into witches and have remained so until today. So you see that there are some people in the world who are like a protruding root in the middle of a path and who are a stumbling-block to the children of the Lord. When a person is not behaving in a deceitful way they will say he is behaving so, until the person concerned makes up his mind that, since the sons of men say he acts in a way in which he does not act, he might as well act so in fact. This is one of the most important causes of stumbling for those whom the Lord has created to live on the face of the earth.

"I tell you, man of might, that when my sister and I finally became witches we caused people great affliction, because we devoured young and old. We killed important people in the assembly. In the end this affair filled the Lord God with anger, because although the sons of men had behaved foolishly before, we too had now behaved stupidly like monkeys. So one morning one who was a past master in witchcraft and fiercer even than we,

---

4. **Ajediran** (ä jā´ dē rän).

cornered us in our compound and gave us battle and drove us away, so we ran here to the Forest of the Lord. I can never forget this affair as long as I live, because had it not been for this I should by now have found a man to marry me. Because of this I beg you earnestly, you handsome hunter, do not think shame of me because of the question which I shall ask. I want you to remember that the evil custom of the sons of men does not permit a woman to choose the husband whom her heart desires. It is men who have the right to speak first to ask a woman to marry them. If a woman wants to marry a man it is a difficult matter for the woman to express her wish. This custom of the children of men inflicts hardship upon one half of them, and yet, as the proverb says, if a man sees a snake and a woman kills the snake provided the snake does not escape there is no offence committed. I want you to understand clearly that if a woman is attracted to a man and reveals to the man her wish, no offence is committed. It is ignorant people who say that a woman who herself woos a man must have base desires. Before a woman would venture to do so the fire of love in the bottom of her heart must be stronger than the fire of a furnace. Without a doubt, you mighty hunter, you are not one of those ignorant people. You attract me greatly and I want you to be my husband and myself to be your wife, so that our going-out and our coming-in may be one."

See, my friend, the surprising thing in this story is that this woman's sweet words caused my father to taste love for the first time in his life. Love boiled up and covered his eyes like palm wine inside a calabash, and so for the sake of beauty Olowo-aiyé forgot his character, for the sake of bright eyes he forgot wisdom, for the sake of white teeth he caused himself to become the husband of a witch. From that day forward my father took trouble as a burden on his back and took trouble to be his wife.

DISCUSSION QUESTIONS

1. Were you satisfied with the ending of this story, or were you disappointed? Explain your answer.

2. In an epic, a hero, who is the champion of the people, goes off to do battle with a supernatural force. Often he or she is aided by magic and often he or she is tempted by a seductress or a seducer. How do these elements fit the story "The Forest of the Lord"?

3. Does Olowo-aiyé's encounter with his future wife in the Forest of the Lord remind you of another story? Explain.

4. A common element of folk tales is the inclusion of proverbs. Reread "The Forest of the Lord" and point out as many proverbs as you can.

5. An allegory is a story that symbolically represents something else. If this story were viewed as an allegory, who would Olowo-aiyé represent and what would his journey represent?

SUGGESTION FOR WRITING

In stories like "The Forest of the Lord" it is common for the hero to encounter many tests and obstacles during his journey. What further tests or obstacles might Olowo-aiyé encounter if his journey were to continue? Write a new episode in which Olowo-aiyé is put to the test again. Your episode may be as short as one paragraph or as long as you choose. Make sure your episode answers the following questions: What test or obstacle does Olowo-aiyé encounter? What danger does this obstacle or test represent? How does Olowo-aiyé triumph over this test or obstacle? What lesson, if any, does Olowo-aiyé learn?

ALFRED HUTCHINSON
(1924–1972)

A lfred Hutchinson's exciting but difficult life as a young man is vividly pictured in his autobiography, *Road to Ghana* (1960), which was published following his escape from South Africa to England via Zambia, Malawi, Tanganyika (now Tanzania), and Ghana. His autobiography is considered by some critics to be one of the finest studies ever published of the experience of living under the racist apartheid system in South Africa. Born in South Africa, Hutchinson was the grandson of a Swazi chief on his mother's side and an Englishman on his father's. He was educated in South Africa and taught for a while before he was arrested and imprisoned for his connection with the 1952 Defiance Campaign. In 1956 he was again arrested and charged with high treason. When the prosecution temporarily withdrew the indictment, he fled to Ghana without a passport. There he married an Englishwoman, Hazel Slade. Hutchinson lived in England for almost a decade, teaching in various schools in London. He moved to Nigeria in 1971 and died of a heart attack there in 1972. At a special memorial service, the South African writer Dennis Brutus, a close friend of Hutchinson's said "[Hutchinson was] one of the long list of talented black writers driven into exile by the inhumanities of apartheid, and doomed to die there." The excerpt below tells of a part of Hutchinson's escape to Ghana. ■

ABOARD AN AFRICAN TRAIN

The station[1] was full of migrant miners returning home. Escorts taking the men home stood herding them. These were the men of the Mzilikazi (Witwatersrand Native Labour Association)[2] who were returning home after their contracts in the mines. And the station belonged to them. They wore patchwork trousers and miner's hob-nailed boots and sombreros of all descriptions: yellow, orange, black, red. They tugged the hats down with knotty hands. They wore cheap wire spectacles or goggles, some on their noses, others on their foreheads. Their socks were tattered, did not match, and some had tops only. Some wore battered khaki shorts and were barefoot, and one of them was on crutches. Loaves of bread were tied to bundles standing on the ground. They swaggered a bit and looked at

---

1. **The station:** at Mafeking in the Union of South Africa, about 150 miles west of Johannesburg, where Hutchinson's journey began.

2. **Witwatersrand Native Labour Association:** Witwatersrand, the region around Johannesburg, produces much of the world's gold.

us, the surface people, with contempt, and they looked at women with a terrible longing in their eyes.

"These can kill you," said the woman beside me reading the look.

I pulled out the fish and chips and the loaf of bread from my paper bags and asked the man from Salima to eat with me. We ate slowly and washed the food down with cold drinks. Railway policemen walked up and down the platform among the miners and stopped to chat with the escorts who had the W.N.L.A. brass letters on their caps glittering in the morning sun. The woman at my side chattered with a dry ecstasy in her voice about the terrible look the miners had in their eyes.

A man came pushing a wagon with various articles on it. He was selling. The man from Salima bought soap and razor blades, and I bought soap and razor blades too. But then I made the mistake of taking the articles from the wagon.

"Don't touch!" the man shouted at me. "Don't touch!" I said I was sorry. "Don't touch! Wait till you're given!"

A railway policeman wandered up to us. I made a profusion of apologies and the man from Salima made more on my behalf. I slunk back to the bench and buried myself in a newspaper.

A howl, a whoop, tore me from the newspaper. A train, laden with migrant workers, was coming into the station headed for the mines. The windows were packed with black faces. An answering howl and whoop rose from the train as the train pulled to a stop. Then the men on the platform broke ranks and their boots crunched the ground as they swarmed to the windows of the train going to the mines. The whoop rose again and again, a terrifying jellying sound. It churned and boiled and twisted with a nameless agony—rejection, welcome, derision—bundled into one. The miners going home swaggered as they interrogated the newcomers. They cuffed them. And some of the men on the train returned blow for blow. At various points actual fights threatened and a railway policeman cuffed and clouted the returning miners where the cuffing and clouting had gone too far. The eyes were red and blank with a nameless agony. It was stupid, senseless, terrifying. What had been done to the poor people, I kept thinking in despair. And the whoop rose and fell, jellying and uncertain and crackling with the despair of fallen leaves. They swore and cursed. They cuffed and clouted and chatted a bit. And clouted and jeered.

The Bulawayo[3] train pulled in at ten o'clock. The men from Mzilikazi lifted their bundles to their shoulders and heads and formed an Indian file. There was a fourth class on the train and the miners packed into the fourth-class carriages. We trooped into the third-class. I did not want to lose sight of the man from Salima. There were six of us in the compartment: the man from Salima, an old man wearing wire spectacles, a sickly looking chap with an expensive green hat, a boy in a shoddy green jacket

---

3. **Bulawayo:** a city in southwestern Rhodesia (now Zimbabwe).

and cheap gray hat, and a big, black, old woman. It was an African train except for the driver and the conductor.

The train swung westward. I wondered when we should reach Francistown and how it would go at the nearby border of the Union and Bechuanaland.[4] I sat tense as the train swung with slow looping movements, like an African woman playing with her hips. We were swinging westward towards the desert. The land grew dry and tedious and the grass and trees were withered and coated with brown dust. There was no urgency in that train: it swung and rocked and we swung and rocked with it. We looked out of the window, glancing at each other's faces as we did so. But no one spoke for a long time.

"Hai," said the sickly chap with the green hat, "the train of Nyasaland!"[5]

That began the conversation. We all began to complain about the slowness of the train. The old man in the wire spectacles said that he had been days on the train already. He was from Cape Town and uttered a word or two in Xhosa—the African language spoken in Cape Town. He was returning to Nyasaland and asked the others where they were going. Except for the old black woman who was going to Salisbury, we were all going to Nyasaland. Even the old woman originally came from Salima, the home of my coal-black friend.

"A person only works for train fare," said the old man taking a pinch of snuff from a Royal Baking Powder tin.

We agreed that we only worked for the train fare back home. But I thought that a single ticket from Johannesburg to Salisbury for £2 13s. 11d. was very cheap, notwithstanding the class we were travelling. The sickly man pursed his singularly thin lips tightly as if fighting back pain. He had a look of world-wiseness in his eyes which the others in the compartment did not have. There was something knowing and mocking in those eyes. They did not ask me what I was going to do in Blantyre[6] and that made me feel easy. But I was thinking about the border and dreading what might happen. If the news of my escape had leaked, there I would surely be arrested and turned back. The train swung easily like an African woman slowly swinging her hips. In trepidation I waited for the border. The train swung on and on and on until surely we had crossed the border. There was no border post: no checking of passes[7] or customs. I was in Bechuanaland. One hurdle had been jumped. Anything could still happen.

----

4. **the Union . . . Bechuanaland:** The former British territory of Bechuanaland, now the Republic of Botswana, forms part of the northern border of the Union of South Africa.

5. **Nyasaland:** The former British territory of Nyasaland, now the Republic of Malawi, lies between Tanzania, Zambia, and Mozambique.

6. **Blantyre:** a city in southern Malawi.

7. **checking of passes:** Under South African law at this time, blacks had to carry an identification card, or "pass," and produce it on demand, or else be subject to arrest.

In the compartment next to ours a man was taking his Union wife and two children with him to Nyasaland. The woman and the children were a pitiful sight. The children were half blind with filth and dirty sores. Flies swarmed round their eyes and the woman, exhausted with hunger and neglect, did not even wave the flies from the children. The man sat. He too was prostrated by helplessness.

It grew hot on the train and the lavatory began to stink. Dirt began to pile in the corridors and flies buzzed. At the sidings desert women and children, insubstantial and wraithlike in their trailing, shapeless, dirty white dresses, came to sell homemade cold drinks in bottles, bottled tea, scones and hunks of dubious meat. The meat was too much for the price they asked and we asked why among ourselves and decided not to buy it. At intervals through the morning and afternoon a man in a guard's cap came to the door and pointed the spout of a kettle at us, stood silent for a long time and then went his way. He was selling tea, they said. But he did not utter a sound.

We swung throughout the day and the shadows of the thorn trees lengthened with the dipping western sun. Past Atloss, Artesia, Gaberones, Pilane. . . . At intervals the train stopped for a long time for no apparent reason, and the white driver got out and sat African-wise on a stone chatting to other whites, or made water on the bushes at the side of the railway. It was the all-African train. And then again we swung onward carrying miners and new blue Massey-Harris tractors and water tanks with us. I stood in the corridor a long time looking at the thirsty land, at the tedious thorn trees and bare hills.

A man came to lean against the window.

"Going to Nyasa?" he said. I nodded. "Going to fetch horse medicines?" I spread my hands dubiously and shrugged to say that perhaps I was fetching "medicines" of luck for horse racing. "Ah, don't deny it. Don't tell me—I know!" The man laughed. "In two months you'll have a shop and a motor car. The medicines of Nyasaland are strong," he said with pride, "but don't let them cheat you. You must get out of the towns. Not Blantyre—right out—away from the towns."

I winked an eye and he winked back. That meant he understood. It was the life. I had found an explanation for going to Nyasaland: I was going to buy horse-racing *mutis*.[8] He would never know that I had never seen the inside of a race course and didn't gamble because I hadn't the nerve for it. The woman who had spoken about the look in the miners' eyes came to the window. She was going to Nyasaland, she told me, to her husband. She had been to visit her people in Orlando. She was itching for a flirtation and I hastily gave her trail. As the evening grew she stood in the corridor with a strong young Nyasa. She had hooked her man.

A chap speaking Xhosa collared me again and again for a cigarette. He

---

8. **mutis:** good luck charms (from a Zulu word for *herb*).

was a Nyasa returning home but he wanted very much to be "Xhosa." He was full of city-talk and this frightened me off. I did not want to be identified with the city. There was a pretty young girl in the next compartment going home to Bulawayo. She was Zulu-breed, strong-thighed and solid—a descendant of Mzilikazi's, who had blazed a bloody trail north, fleeing the wrath of the Zulu monarch, Tshaka.[9] She was thickly powdered and tortured the chaps of the train with her city ways and inaccessibility. She broke into a jive, there in the corridor, to one or both of the gramophones playing simultaneously in different compartments. And the men groaned listening to the gramophone records, and said it took them "back there"—meaning Johannesburg—which they had probably never seen.

I found the man from Salima adding sums of money with a stub of a pencil and some paper. He was adding £15 10s. plus £15 10s. The first time he got it wrong. The second time it was right. There was something strange about this man in the brown jacket frayed at the sleeves and the fawn trousers which were thin at the knees. He was solid, unequivocally honest, I thought looking at him. He had a terrific self-containedness—like a man long used to living and relying on himself.

The sickly man was huddled in a corner.

"How's it?" I said to the sick man.

"That woman has finished me, S'bali (brother-in-law). She's killed me," he said, trying to smile through the pain, while carefully brushing the expensive green hat with the palm of his hand. "I've left her—left her with house, furniture, three children and all."

"Yours?" I said, meaning the children.

"Yes, S'bali, two boys and a girl."

The trouble had started, he said, when he spoke of going to Nyasaland for a time. The city woman would not hear of it, especially as she knew that he had two wives and children in Nyasaland. She didn't want to lose her "milch-cow." Nyasas were regarded as "milch-cows" by Johannesburg women, he explained. She had immediately procured *mutis* to stop him from going. And his illness had started. She had even confiscated his pass in order to stop his departure. He had told her to keep it if she wanted to: he was going. He thought he would get better in Nyasaland. I thought he was suffering from T.B.

"When did you leave Nyasaland, S'bali?" I said.

"Long ago, S'bali. In 1952."

"Six years ago!" I said. "That's a long time!"

The old man turned his wire spectacles to me.

"What do you say of me, S'bali," he said, calling me brother-in-law also. "Fourteen."

"Fourteen!"

---

9. **Mzilikazi . . . Tshaka:** The Zulu chief Tshaka conquered all of Natal province in southwestern South Africa in the 1820s. His rivals fled north and south. Mzilikazi went north and colonized Matabeleland in what is now Zimbabwe.

"I left a baby boy, S'bali. He's a man now."

I turned to Moses Banda, the man from Salima. He had left home six years ago. Mweli, the sick man, six. Moyo, the youth, three. The old man, fourteen. These were long times to be away from home, especially from a wife and children.

"That's too long," I said.

"We can't help it, S'bali," said Mweli. "It's hard to get into the Union and the longer you stay the better."

"Blantyre?" said Granny looking at me. "That's just next door. He is from Salima—where I come from," she said, pointing at my friend. "You can take a good wife there," she added. I expressed interest. "Not Blantyre—no, no. The women are all crooks. They'll eat your money and when it's finished, leave you! Get to Salima and get a good Thonga girl. She'll look well after your things." I told Granny that my grandmother had been a Thonga like her, and she promptly married me to someone—most likely a relation of hers. She invited me to spend a few days at her home in Salisbury. From the time of the "marriage" Granny referred to me respectfully as Mkwenyana (son-in-law).

Granny started scolding Moyo, the youth. The big hulking, ugly woman had a heart of gold. Granny, I thought, had been too long away from home and wanted to scold someone and had picked on Moyo because he was the youngest in the compartment.

"You'll get lost, you!" she said to the boy, who was adjusting his hat to a jaunty angle. That hat was the symbol of his manhood and throughout the day I watched him fuss over it.

"I won't. I know. I'll take a bus from Lusaka to Mzimba."

"This child is lost, Mkwenyana," said Granny, turning to me. "He doesn't know where he is going. He says he is going to Mzimba but here he is going to Lusaka."

"I'm not lost," said Moyo with dignity. "I know. I left that way."

Moses Banda, the man from Salima, was again adding sums of money. They looked like the same figures he had been adding all the time. Whenever he got tired of listening to us or looking out of the window, he pulled out his pocket book and pencil and the addition started. I turned from Banda to Moyo who had put on his wisest airs.

"Are you sure you won't get lost?" I said.

"He doesn't know anything," said Granny.

Moyo had left home in 1955 in a band of fourteen other boys. They had taken a bus from Mzima to Lusaka and from Lusaka a train to Bolawayo. In order to avoid the pass blitz at Plumtree they had walked in the bush from Bulawayo to Mafeking—a journey that took a month. Then from Mafeking in the Union of South Africa, they caught a train to Johannesburg. He had never worked in Johannesburg, the city of his dreams, but had been sent to a farm in Delmas. I asked him whether he would return to the Union.

"Never. When I want work, it will be Bulawayo," he said.

Moyo bent down and pulled his suitcase from under the seat and opened it. I peeped inside. There was an old blanket, two or three battered torches,[10] and, at the bottom of the case, a quantity of sprouting potatoes. He pulled out a Farmer's Weekly Diary of 1957 and a stub of a pencil and began making squiggles on it. He made sounds, incomprehensible sounds, as he made the meaningless squiggles. I thought I heard him say *verdomde* (damned)—Afrikaans which he had most certainly picked up on the potato fields. Granny shook her head pitying the poor boy who would get lost. He took out his ticket and looked at it, making incomprehensible sounds. Moyo couldn't even read the fare he had paid for his ticket home. Moyo had been South. Poor Moyo.

The train swung like a buxom African woman coquettishly flouncing her hips and we swung with it. Moyo adjusted his hat in case it had lost the correct angle. Mweli sat looking at nothing out of his sick eyes. And the old man sat looking at the night through the window. Moses Banda had made a new column of figures: the same figures. He had been a tailor at Iscor near Pretoria for six years. Now he was returning home with three tailor's sewing machines and other things. It was his money which he kept adding over and over again. I had thought he was a miner with hands like that.

The gramophones played in the swinging train. People who had never seen Johannesburg said that the songs reminded them of the city. The woman who had itched for a flirtation clung to her young muscled man, and the young girl of Zulu breed with her thickly powdered pretty face played hard-to-get and wrought havoc with the young men's hearts. And the train swung northward through the night. The train swung into Francistown, still in Bechuanaland, at five-thirty in the morning. We were approaching Plumtree where our passes would be checked. I grew restless and a flutter of panic drove me to ask to see my companions' passes. Granny did not have one and was defiant about it. She had travelled like that for many years. What was this newfangled thing of passes about, she said. The passes were all different from one another and different from mine. They said mine would do; that it was more official than all.

At Plumtree Rhodesian African policemen in black fezzes and big black boots jumped on the train and asked for our passes. I steadied my hand as I handed mine. The policeman glanced at me and handed it back. I almost sighed with relief. Granny glared at the young policeman. "Granny, where's your pass?"

"What pass? I've been travelling like this long before you were born! Child, ask your mates for a pass!"

"Get a pass next time, Granny," said the young policeman walking out of the compartment.

I had crossed the border into Southern Rhodesia. Someone whispered in Zulu: "*Zishile* (it's burnt)," which meant that someone was in trouble. I peeped into the corridor and right next door an African policeman had mounted guard over the door. A white official had been sent for. The man

---

10. torches: flashlights.

taking his wife and two children to Nyasaland had not taken passes for them. I was terror-stricken. Now there would probably be a recheck on the passes, and questionings. And it wouldn't take much to prove that I was no Nyasa returning home. I should be arrested and handed back to the Union. I couldn't resist peeping into the corridor, and when I next peeped a white official was there. But the man only received a warning—not even a fine.

One of the men returning to Nyasaland began a conversation with the African policeman in the corridor about conditions in the Union. "There's not a bush, not even grass to hide in," the man was saying. "Here at least you can hide behind a bush. It's like a road, and a policeman sees you miles off." The policeman looked at the bushes in silence.

"But there are Nyangas (medicine men)—where do they get the roots from then?" said the policeman.

"There are quacks galore. . . . As you say, where would they dig the roots from?" said the returning man. "There are quacks without number, that's true."

Then the man from Johannesburg told the policeman about the pass laws. A garden boy had been picked up for a pass right in the garden where he worked and his missis looked for him in vain. A servant who had been sent to the greengrocer's had been picked up for a pass with basket and vegetables and the missis found him after a search at the police station.

"I used to hear it was nice," said the policeman.

"Then go and see for yourself," said the man returning from the Union.

"No," said the Rhodesian policeman. "I'm all right here."

DISCUSSION QUESTIONS

1. In the first paragraph Hutchinson says of the migrant miners returning home: "they swaggered a bit and looked at us, the surface people, with contempt . . ." Who are "the surface people"? Why do you think the miners feel contempt for them?

2. The author tells how long each of the people in his compartment had been away from home. Why do you think this point is important to him?

3. Most of the passengers on the train are returning home to their native countries after working for a long time in South Africa. Do you get the impression that they were happy working in South Africa? Why or why not?

4. How does Hutchinson create increasing tension in this account of his journey to freedom? What is the point of greatest tension in the account?

SUGGESTION FOR WRITING

In this account, Alfred Hutchinson describes how he used deception to achieve a greater good. He flees South Africa without a valid passport in order to escape unfair prosecution. Have you ever used deception in order to achieve a greater good, or do you know someone who has? What were the circumstances and what was the outcome? Write a paragraph in which you describe such a situation—either your own or that of someone you know.

JOMO KENYATTA

(1893–1978)

Jomo Kenyatta, the son of a poor Kikuyu farmer, was born at Ichaweri, Kenya, and was educated at a Scottish mission school. He was active in politics at an early age and soon became leader of the first nationalist movement in Kenya. He lived and traveled extensively in Europe from 1931 to 1946 and studied at both Moscow University and at the London School of Economics. In 1938 Kenyatta published *Facing Mount Kenya,* a book in which he tried to demonstrate how tribal life had been disrupted by the coming of the Europeans. Returning to Kenya in 1946, he campaigned ceaselessly for African rights and independence for Kenya. In 1953 he was sentenced to seven years in prison by the British for being involved in the Mau Mau terrorist organization, a charge he vociferously denied. Kenyatta saw his dream fulfilled in 1963 when Kenya became independent. Subsequently, he became the first president of the Republic of Kenya. As president, he developed Kenya's economy and tried to unite the mixed population of Africans, Arabs, Asians, and Europeans. In his last years Kenyatta was known to his people as *Mzee,* the grand old man. He died in 1978. ■

THE GENTLEMEN OF THE JUNGLE

Once upon a time an elephant made a friendship with a man. One day a heavy thunderstorm broke out, the elephant went to his friend, who had a little hut at the edge of the forest, and said to him: "My dear good man, will you please let me put my trunk inside your hut to keep it out of this torrential rain?" The man, seeing what situation his friend was in, replied: "My dear good elephant, my hut is very small, but there is room for your trunk and myself. Please put your trunk in gently." The elephant thanked his friend, saying: "You have done me a good deed and one day I shall return your kindness." But what followed? As soon as the elephant put his trunk inside the hut, slowly he pushed his head inside, and finally flung the man out in the rain, and then lay down comfortably inside his friend's hut, saying: "My dear good friend, your skin is harder than mine, and as there is not enough room for both of us, you can afford to remain in the rain while I am protecting my delicate skin from the hailstorm."

The man, seeing what his friend had done to him, started to grumble; the animals in the nearby forest heard the noise and came to see what was the matter. All stood around listening to the heated argument between the man and his friend the elephant. In this turmoil the lion came along roaring, and said in a loud voice: "Don't you all know that I am the King of the Jungle! How dare anyone disturb the peace of my kingdom?" On hearing this the elephant, who was one of the high ministers in the jungle kingdom, replied in a soothing voice, and said: "My lord, there is no disturbance of the peace in your kingdom. I have only been having a little discussion with my friend here as to the possession of this little hut which your lordship sees me occupying." The lion, who wanted to have "peace and tranquility" in his kingdom, replied in a noble voice, saying: "I command my ministers to appoint a Commission of Enquiry to go thoroughly into this matter and report accordingly." He then turned to the man and said: "You have done well by establishing friendship with my people, especially with the elephant, who is one of my honorable ministers of state. Do not grumble any more, your hut is not lost to you. Wait until the sitting of my Imperial Commission, and there you will be given plenty of opportunity to state your case. I am sure that you will be pleased with the findings of the Commission." The man was very pleased by these sweet words from the King of the Jungle, and innocently waited for his opportunity, in the belief that naturally the hut would be returned to him.

The elephant, obeying the command of his master, got busy with other ministers to appoint the Commission of Enquiry. The following elders of the jungle were appointed to sit in the Commission: (1) Mr. Rhinoceros; (2) Mr. Buffalo; (3) Mr. Alligator; (4) The Rt. Hon. Mr. Fox to act as chairman; and (5) Mr. Leopard to act as Secretary to the Commission. On seeing the personnel, the man protested and asked if it was not necessary to include in this Commission a member from his side. But he was told that it was impossible, since no one from his side was well enough educated to understand the intricacy of jungle law. Further, that there was nothing to fear, for the members of the Commission were all men of repute for their impartiality in justice, and as they were gentlemen chosen by God to look after the interests of races less adequately endowed with teeth and claws, he might rest assured that they would investigate the matter with the greatest care and report impartially.

The Commission sat to take the evidence. The Rt. Hon. Mr. Elephant was first called. He came along with a superior air, brushing his tusks with a sapling which Mrs. Elephant had provided, and in an authoritative voice said: "Gentlemen of the Jungle, there is no need for me to waste your valuable time in relating a story which I am sure you all know. I have always regarded it as my duty to protect the interests of my friends, and this appears to have caused the misunderstanding between myself and my friend here. He invited me to save his hut from being blown away by a hurricane. As the hurricane had gained access owing to the unoccupied space in the hut, I considered it necessary, in my friend's own interests, to turn the undeveloped space to a more economic use by sitting in it myself; a duty which any of you would undoubtedly have performed with equal readiness in similar circumstances."

After hearing the Rt. Hon. Mr. Elephant's conclusive evidence, the Commission called Mr. Hyena and other elders of the jungle, who all supported what Mr. Elephant had said. They then called the man, who began to give his own account of the dispute. But the Commission cut him short, saying: "My good man, please confine yourself to relevant issues. We have already heard the circumstances from various unbiased sources; all we wish you to tell us is whether the undeveloped space in your hut was occupied by anyone else before Mr. Elephant assumed his position?" The man began to say: "No, but—" But at this point the Commission declared that they had heard sufficient evidence from both sides and retired to consider their decision. After enjoying a delicious meal at the expense of the Rt. Hon. Mr. Elephant, they reached their verdict, called the man, and declared as follows: "In our opinion this dispute has arisen through a regrettable misunderstanding due to the backwardness of your ideas. We consider that Mr. Elephant has fulfilled his sacred duty of protecting your interests. As it is clearly for your good that the space should be put to its most economic use, and as you yourself have not yet reached the stage of expansion which would enable you to fill it, we consider it necessary to arrange a compromise to suit both parties. Mr. Elephant shall continue his occupation of your hut, but we give you permission to look for a site where you can build another hut more suited to your needs, and we will see that you are well protected."

The man, having no alternative, and fearing that his refusal might expose him to the teeth and claws of members of the Commission, did as they suggested. But no sooner had he built another hut than Mr. Rhinoceros charged in with his horn lowered and ordered the man to quit.[1] A Royal Commission was again appointed to look into the matter, and the same finding was given. This procedure was repeated until Mr. Buffalo, Mr. Leopard, Mr. Hyena and the rest were all accommodated with new huts. Then the man decided that he must adopt an effective method of protection, since Commissions of Enquiry did not seem to be of any use to him. He sat down and said: "Ng'enda thi ndagaga motegi," which literally means "there is nothing that treads on the earth that cannot be trapped," or in other words, you can fool people for a time, but not for ever.

Early one morning, when the huts already occupied by the jungle lords were all beginning to decay and fall to pieces, he went out and built a bigger and better hut a little distance away. No sooner had Mr. Rhinoceros seen it than he came rushing in, only to find that Mr. Elephant was already inside, sound asleep. Mr. Leopard next came in at the window, Mr. Lion, Mr. Fox and Mr. Buffalo entered the doors, while Mr. Hyena howled for a place in the shade and Mr. Alligator basked on the roof. Presently they all began disputing about their rights of penetration, and from disputing they came to fighting, and while they were all embroiled together the man set the hut on fire and burned it to the ground, jungle lords and all. Then he went home, saying: "Peace is costly, but it's worth the expense," and lived happily ever after.

---

1. **quit:** leave; depart.

DISCUSSION QUESTIONS

1. Did you correctly predict that the man would get even with the jungle animals? If not, what did you think would happen?

2. Kenyatta said of this animal fable, "The relation between the Kikuyu and the Europeans can well be illustrated by this Kikuyu story." An allegory is a narrative in which the plot, characters, and setting represent something apart from their meaning in the story. If this fable is viewed as an allegory, who is the man? Who is the King of the Jungle? Who are Mr. Elephant, Mr. Rhinoceros, and the other jungle animals?

3. Allegorically, what does the Commission of Enquiry represent, and what is the significance of the fact that Mr. Elephant and his wife serve a dinner to the commission before it gives its verdict?

4. What is the allegorical significance of the following statement: ". . . the members of the Commission . . . were gentlemen chosen by God to look after the interests of races less adequately endowed with teeth and claws. . . ."? What is the allegorical significance of Mr. Elephant's statement that he took over the man's hut because he considered it necessary to "turn the undeveloped space to a more economic use"?

SUGGESTION FOR WRITING

After being kicked out of all of his huts by the jungle animals, the man sits down and concludes that you can fool people for a time, but not forever. How does this proverb fit the end of the story, and what allegorical significance does it have? Write one or two paragraphs in which you discuss both of these questions.

CAMARA LAYE

(1928–1980)

Novelist, short-story writer, and autobiographer Camara Laye was born into the Malinke tribe in Guinea. At the age of eighteen he left western Africa for further schooling in France. He was working in a factory in Paris when he wrote his first book, an autobiographical novel entitled *The Dark Child*. Laye was one of those rare men who had many different influences working upon him—from the tribal customs of his ancestors to the sophistication of a Paris education—and who managed to make the best of these influences a part of himself and of his writing. There is no rancor in what he wrote, only love.

One of the first black African authors to receive world-wide recognition, Laye created much controversy with his writing. Western readers found his spiritual and lyrical descriptions of rural African tribal life very appealing. Radical African critics, however, criticized Laye for not being more political. They publicly chastised him for not speaking out against French colonialism. In 1965 Laye was forced into exile because of his hostility toward the Guinean government. He eventually settled in Senegal where he lived until his death in 1980. ■

from THE DARK CHILD

Translated by James Kirkup, Ernest Jones, and Elaine Gottlieb

The following excerpt from The Dark Child *depicts Laye's own early life in a West African society whose culture is of mingled Islamic and ancient African traditions. The first-person narrator finds himself by heredity a member of the Guinea caste of coppersmiths, a craft aristocracy. In a culture where ritual and custom had governed life for generations, he grows up in a time of change.*

I

I was a little boy playing around my father's hut. How old would I have been at that time? I can not remember exactly. I must still have been very young: five, maybe six years old. My mother was in the workshop with my father, and I could just hear their familiar voices above the noise of the anvil and the conversation of the customers.

Suddenly I stopped playing, my whole attention fixed on a snake that was creeping around the hut. After a moment I went over to him. I had taken in my hand a reed that was lying in the yard—there were always some lying around; they used to get broken off the fence of plaited reeds that marked the boundary of our concession—and I thrust it into his mouth. The snake did not try to get away: he was beginning to enjoy our little game; he was slowly swallowing the reed; he was devouring it, I thought, as if it were some delicious prey, his eyes glittering with voluptuous bliss; and inch by inch his head was drawing nearer to my hand. At last the reed was almost entirely swallowed, and the snake's jaws were terribly close to my fingers.

I was laughing. I had not the slightest fear, and I feel sure that the snake would not have hesitated much longer before burying his fangs in my fingers if, at that moment, Damany, one of the apprentices, had not come out of the workshop. He called my father, and almost at once I felt myself lifted off my feet: I was safe in the arms of one of my father's friends.

Around me there was a great commotion. My mother was shouting hardest of all, and she gave me a few sharp slaps. I wept, more upset by the sudden uproar than by the blows. A little later, when I was somewhat calmer and the shouting had ceased, my mother solemnly warned me never to play that game again. I promised, although the game still didn't seem dangerous to me.

My father's hut was near the workshop, and I often played beneath the veranda that ran around the outside. It was his private hut, and like all our huts built of mud bricks that had been pounded and molded with water; it was round, and proudly helmeted with thatch. It was entered by a rectangular doorway. Inside, a tiny window let in a thin shaft of daylight. On the right was the bed, made of beaten earth like the bricks, and spread with a simple wicker-work mat on which lay a pillow stuffed with kapok. At the rear, right under the window where the light was strongest, were the tool-boxes. On the left were the boubous[1] and the prayer-rugs. At the head of the bed, hanging over the pillow and watching over my father's slumber, stood a row of pots that contained extracts from plants and the bark of trees. These pots all had metal lids and were profusely and curiously garlanded with chaplets of cowry shells; it did not take me long to discover that they were the most important things in the hut; they contained magic charms—those mysterious liquids that keep the evil spirits at bay, and, if smeared on the body, make it invulnerable to every kind of black magic. My father, before going to bed, never failed to smear his body with a little of each liquid, first one, then another, for each charm had its own particular property: but exactly *what* property I did not know: I had left my father's house too soon.

From the veranda under which I played I could keep an eye on the workshop opposite, and the adults for their part could keep an eye on me. This workshop was the main building in our concession, and my father was generally to be found there, looking after the work, forging the most important items himself, or repairing delicate mechanisms; there he received his friends and his customers, and the place resounded with noise from morning to night. Moreover, everyone who entered or left our con-

---

1. *boubous:* loose cotton garments, draping the whole figure.

cession had to cross the workshop. There was a perpetual coming and going, though no one seemed to be in any particular hurry; each had his bit of gossip; each lingered at the forge to watch. Sometimes I came near the door, but I rarely went in; everyone there frightened me, and I would run away as soon as anyone tried to touch me. It was not until very much later that I got into the habit of crouching in a corner of the workshop to watch the fire blazing in the forge.

My private domain at that time was the veranda that encircled my father's hut, my mother's hut, and the orange tree that grew in the middle of the concession.

As soon as you crossed the workshop and went through the door at the back, you would see the orange tree. Compared with the giants of our native forests, the tree was not very big, but its mass of glossy leaves cast a dense shade that kept the heat at bay. When it was in flower a heady perfume pervaded the entire concession. When the fruit first appeared we were only allowed to look: we had to wait patiently until it was ripe. Then my father, who as head of the family—and a very large family it was—governed the concession, gave the order to pick the fruit. The men who did the picking brought their baskets one by one to my father, who portioned them out among the people who lived in the concession and among his neighbors and customers. After that we were permitted to help ourselves from the baskets and we were allowed as much as we liked! My father was open-handed; in fact, a lavish giver. Any visitor, no matter who he was, shared our meals; since I could never keep up with the speed at which such guests ate I might have remained forever hungry if my mother had not taken the precaution of putting my share aside.

"Sit here," she would say, "and eat, for your father's mad."

She did not look upon such guests with a kindly eye. There were too many for her liking, all bent on filling their bellies at her expense. My father, for his part, ate very little; he was an extremely temperate man.

We lived beside a railroad. The trains skirted the reed fence of the concession so closely that sparks thrown off from the locomotive set fire to it every now and then which had to be quickly extinguished so that the whole concession would not go up in smoke. These alarms, frightening yet exciting, made me aware of the passing trains. And even where there were no trains—for in those days the railroad was dependent on a most irregular water traffic—much of my time was spent watching the iron rails. They glistened cruelly in a light which nothing in that place could relieve. Baking since dawn, the roadbed was so hot that oil which dropped from the locomotives evaporated immediately, leaving no trace. Was it the oven-like heat or the smell of oil—for the smell remained in spite of everything—which attracted the snakes? I do not know. But often I came upon them crawling in that hot roadbed. It would have been fatal if they had gotten into the concession.

Ever since the day when I had been forbidden by my mother to play with snakes I ran to her as soon as I saw one.

"There's a snake!" I would cry.

"What? Another?"

And she would come running to see what sort of snake it was. If it was just a snake like any other snake—actually they were all quite different—she would immediately beat it to death; and, like all the women of our country, she would work herself into a frenzy, beating the snake to a pulp. The men contented themselves with a single hard blow, neatly struck.

One day, however, I noticed a little black snake with a strikingly marked body. He was proceeding slowly in the direction of the workshop. I ran to warn my mother, as usual. But as soon as she saw the black snake she said to me gravely:

"My son, this one must not be killed: he is not like other snakes, and he will not harm you; you must never interfere with him."

Everyone in our concession knew that this snake must not be killed—everyone except myself, and, I suppose, my little playmates, who were still ignorant children.

"This snake," my mother added, "is your father's guiding spirit."

I gazed dumbfounded at the little snake. He was proceeding calmly toward the workshop, gracefully, very sure of himself, and almost as if conscious of his immunity; his body, black and brilliant, glittered in the harsh light of the sun. When he reached the workshop, I noticed for the first time a small hole in the wall, cut out level with the ground. The snake disappeared through this hole.

"Look," said my mother, "the snake is going to pay your father a visit."

Although I was familiar with the supernatural, this sight filled me with such astonishment that I was struck dumb. What business would a snake have with my father? And why this particular snake? No one was to kill him because he was my father's guiding spirit! At any rate, that was the explanation my mother had given me. But what exactly was a "guiding spirit"? What were these guiding spirits that I encountered almost everywhere, forbidding one thing, commanding another to be done? I could not understand it all, though their presences surrounded me as I grew to manhood. There were good spirits, and there were evil ones; and more evil than good ones, it seemed. And how was I to know that this snake was harmless? He was a snake like the others: black, to be sure, with extraordinary markings—but for all that a snake. I was completely perplexed, but I did not question my mother: I had decided that I must ask my father about it, as if this were a mystery to be discussed only between men, a mystery in which women had no part. I decided to wait until evening to speak to him.

Immediately after the evening meal, when the palavers[2] were over, my father bade his friends farewell and sat under the veranda of his hut; I seated myself near him. I began questioning him in a dilatory manner, as all children do, regarding every subject under the sun. Actually I was no more talkative than on other evenings. Only this evening I withheld what troubled me, waiting for the opportunity when—my face betraying noth-

---

2. **palavers:** conversations.

ing—I might ask the question which had worried me so deeply from the moment when I first saw the black snake going toward the workshop. Finally, unable to restrain myself any longer, I asked:

"My father, what is that little snake that comes to visit you?"

"What snake do you mean?"

"Why, the little black snake that my mother forbids us to kill."

"Ah!" he said.

He gazed at me for a long while. He seemed to be considering whether to answer or not. Perhaps he was thinking about how old I was, perhaps he was wondering if it was not a little too soon to confide such a secret to a twelve-year-old boy. Then suddenly he made up his mind.

"That snake," he said, "is the guiding spirit of our race. Can you understand that?"

"Yes," I answered, although I did not understand very well.

"That snake," he went on, "has always been with us; he has always made himself known to one of us. In our time, it is to me that he has made himself known."

"Yes," I said.

And I said it with all my heart, for it seemed obvious to me that the snake could have made himself known to no one but my father. Was not my father the head man in our concession? Was it not my father who had authority over all the blacksmiths in our district? Was he not the most skilled? Was he not, after all, my father?

"How did he make himself known?" I asked.

"First of all, he made himself known in the semblance of a dream. He appeared to me several times in sleep and told me the day on which he would appear to me in reality: he gave me the precise time and place. But when I really saw him for the first time, I was filled with fear. I took him for a snake like any other snake, and I had to keep myself under control or I would have tried to kill him. When he saw that I did not receive him kindly, he turned away and departed the way he had come. And there I stood, watching him depart, wondering all the time if I should not simply have killed him there and then; but a power greater than I stayed my hand and prevented me from pursuing him. I stood watching him disappear. And even then, at that very moment, I could easily have overtaken him; a few swift strides would have been enough; but I was struck motionless by a kind of paralysis. Such was my first encounter with the little black snake."

He was silent a moment, then went on:

"The following night, I saw the snake again in my dream. 'I came as I foretold,' he said, 'but thou didst not receive me kindly; nay, rather I did perceive that thou didst intend to receive me unkindly: I did read it thus in thine eyes. Wherefore dost thou reject me? Lo, I am the guiding spirit of thy race, and it is even as the guiding spirit of thy race that I make myself known to thee, as to the most worthy. Therefore forbear to look with fear upon me, and beware that thou dost not reject me, for behold, I bring thee good fortune.' After that, I received the snake kindly when he made himself known to me a second time; I received him without fear, I received him with loving kindness, and he brought me nothing but good."

My father again was silent for a moment, then he said:

"You can see for yourself that I am not more gifted than other men, that I have nothing which other men have not also, and even that I have less than others, since I give everything away, and would even give away the last thing I had, the shirt on my back. Nevertheless I am better known. My name is on everyone's tongue, and it is I who have authority over all the blacksmiths in the five cantons. If these things are so, it is by virtue of this snake alone, who is the guiding spirit of our race. It is to this snake that I owe everything; it is he who gives me warning of all that is to happen. Thus I am never surprised, when I awake, to see this or that person waiting for me outside my workshop: I already know that he will be there. No more am I surprised when this or that motorcycle or bicycle breaks down, or when an accident happens to a clock: because I have had foreknowledge of what would come to pass. Everything is transmitted to in the course of the night, together with an account of all the work I shall have to perform, so that from the start, without having to cast about in my mind, I know how to repair whatever is brought to me. These things have established my renown as a craftsman. But all this—let it never be forgotten—I owe to the snake, I owe it to the guiding spirit of our race."

He was silent; and then I understood why, when my father came back from a walk he would enter the workshop and say to the apprentices: "During my absence, this or that person has been here, he was dressed in such and such a way, he came from such and such a place and he brought with him such and such a piece of work to be done." And all marveled at this curious knowledge. When I raised my eyes, I saw that my father was watching me.

"I have told you all these things, little one, because you are my son, the eldest of my sons, and because I have nothing to hide from you. There is a certain form of behavior to observe, and certain ways of acting in order that the guiding spirit of our race may approach you also. I, your father, was observing that form of behavior which persuades our guiding spirit to visit us. Oh, perhaps not consciously: but nevertheless it is true that if you desire the guiding spirit of our race to visit you one day, if you desire to inherit it in your turn, you will have to conduct yourself in the selfsame manner; from now on, it will be necessary for you to be more and more in my company."

He gazed at me with burning eyes, then suddenly heaved a sigh.

"I fear, I very much fear, little one, that you are not often enough in my company. You are all day at school, and one day you will depart from that school for a greater one. You will leave me, little one. . . ."

And again he heaved a sigh. I saw that his heart was heavy within him. The hurricane-lamp hanging on the veranda cast a harsh glare on his face. He suddenly seemed to me an old man.

"Father!" I cried.

"Son . . ." he whispered.

And I was no longer sure whether I ought to continue to attend school or whether I ought to remain in the workshop: I felt unutterably confused.

"Go now," said my father.

I went to my mother's hut. The night was full of sparkling stars; an owl was hooting nearby. Ah! What was the right path for me? Did I know yet where that path lay? My perplexity was boundless as the sky, and mine was a sky, alas, without any stars. . . . I entered my mother's hut, which at that time was mine also, and went to bed at once. But sleep did not come and I tossed restlessly on my bed.

"What's the matter with you?" asked my mother.

"Nothing."

No. I couldn't find anything to say.

"Why don't you go to sleep?" my mother continued.

"I don't know."

"Go to sleep!" she said.

"Yes," I said.

"Sleep . . . Nothing can resist sleep," she said sadly.

Why did she, too, appear so sad? Had she divined my distress? Anything that concerned me she sensed very deeply. I was trying to sleep, but I shut my eyes and lay still in vain: the image of my father under the hurricane-lamp would not leave me: my father who had suddenly seemed so old and who was so young, so lively—younger and livelier than the rest of us, a man no one could outrun, who was swifter of limb than any of us. . . . "Father! . . . Father! . . . !" I kept repeating. "What must I do if I am to do the right thing?" And I wept silently and fell asleep still weeping.

After that we never mentioned the little black snake again: my father had spoken to me about him for the first and last time. But from that time on, as soon as I saw the little snake, I would run and sit in the workshop. I would watch him glide through the little hole in the wall. As if informed of his presence, my father at that very instant would turn his eyes to the hole and smile. The snake would go straight to him, opening his jaws. When he was within reach my father would stroke him and the snake would accept the caress with a quivering of his whole body. I never saw the little snake attempt to do the slightest harm to my father. That caress and the answering tremor—but I ought to say: that appealing caress and that answering tremor—threw me each time into an inexpressible confusion. I imagined I know not what mysterious conversations: the hand inquired and the tremor replied. . . .

Yes. It was like a conversation. Would I too converse that way some day? No. I would continue to attend school. Yet I should have liked so much to place my hand, my own hand, on that snake, and to understand and listen to that tremor too; but I did not know whether the snake would have accepted my hand, and I felt now that he would have nothing to tell me. I was afraid that he would never have anything to tell me.

When my father felt that he had stroked the snake enough he left him alone. Then the snake coiled himself under the edge of one of the sheepskins on which my father, facing his anvil, was seated.

II

Of all the different kinds of work my father engaged in, none fascinated me so much as his skill with gold. No other occupation was so noble, no other needed such a delicate touch. And then, every time he worked in gold it was like a festival—indeed it was a festival—that broke the monotony of ordinary working days.

So, if a woman, accompanied by a go-between, crossed the threshold of the workshop, I followed her in at once. I knew what she wanted: she had brought some gold, and had come to ask my father to transform it into a trinket. She had collected the gold in the placers[3] of Siguiri where, crouching over the river for months on end, she had patiently extracted grains of gold from the mud.

These women never came alone. They knew my father had other things to do than make trinkets. And even when he had the time, they knew they were not the first to ask a favor of him, and that, consequently, they would not be served before others.

Generally they required the trinket for a certain date, for the festival of Ramadan or the Tabaski[4] or some other family ceremony or dance.

Therefore, to enhance their chances of being served quickly and to more easily persuade my father to interrupt the work before him, they used to request the services of an official praise-singer, a go-between, arranging in advance the fee they were to pay him for his good offices.

The go-between installed himself in the workshop, tuned up his cora, which is our harp, and began to sing my father's praises. This was always a great event for me. I heard recalled the lofty deeds of my father's ancestors and their names from the earliest times. As the couplets were reeled off it was like watching the growth of a great genealogical tree that spread its branches far and wide and flourished its boughs and twigs before my mind's eye. The harp played an accompaniment to this vast utterance of names, expanding it with notes that were now soft, now shrill.

I could sense my father's vanity being inflamed, and I already knew that after having sipped this milk-and-honey he would lend a favorable ear to the woman's request. But I was not alone in my knowledge. The woman also had seen my father's eyes gleaming with contented pride. She held out her grains of gold as if the whole matter were settled. My father took up his scales and weighed the gold.

"What sort of trinket do you want?" he would ask.

"I want. . . ."

---

3. **placers:** mineral deposits.

4. **Ramadan . . . the Tabaski:** Mohammedan observances.

And then the woman would not know any longer exactly what she wanted because desire kept making her change her mind, and because she would have liked all the trinkets at once. But it would have taken a pile of gold much larger than she had brought to satisfy her whim, and from then on her chief purpose in life was to get hold of it as soon as she could.

"When do you want it?"

Always the answer was that the trinket was needed for an occasion in the near future.

"So! You are in that much of a hurry? Where do you think I shall find the time?"

"I am in a great hurry, I assure you."

"I have never seen a woman eager to deck herself out who wasn't in a great hurry! Good! I shall arrange my time to suit you. Are you satisfied?"

He would take the clay pot that was kept specially for smelting gold, and would pour the grains into it. He would then cover the gold with powdered charcoal, a charcoal he prepared by using plant juices of exceptional purity. Finally, he would place a large lump of the same kind of charcoal over the pot.

As soon as she saw that the work had been duly undertaken, the woman, now quite satisfied, would return to her household tasks, leaving her go-between to carry on with the praise-singing which had already proved so advantageous.

At a sign from my father the apprentices began working two sheepskin bellows. The skins were on the floor, on opposite sides of the forge, connected to it by earthen pipes. While the work was in progress the apprentices sat in front of the bellows with crossed legs. That is, the younger of the two sat, for the elder was sometimes allowed to assist. But the younger—this time it was Sidafa—was only permitted to work the bellows and watch while waiting his turn for promotion to less rudimentary tasks. First one and then the other worked hard at the bellows: the flame in the forge rose higher and became a living thing, a genie implacable and full of life.

Then my father lifted the clay pot with his long tongs and placed it on the flame.

Immediately all activity in the workshop almost came to a halt. During the whole time that the gold was being smelted, neither copper nor aluminum could be worked nearby, lest some particle of these base metals fall into the container which held the gold. Only steel could be worked on such occasions, but the men, whose task that was, hurried to finish what they were doing, or left it abruptly to join the apprentices gathered around the forge. There were so many, and they crowded so around my father, that I, the smallest person present, had to come near the forge in order not to lose track of what was going on.

If he felt he had inadequate working space, my father had the apprentices stand well away from him. He merely raised his hand in a simple gesture: at that particular moment he never uttered a word, and no one else would: no one was allowed to utter a word. Even the go-between's voice was no longer raised in song. The silence was broken only by the panting of the bellows and the faint hissing of the gold. But if my father never actually spoke, I know that he was forming words in his mind. I could tell from his lips, which kept moving, while, bending over the pot, he stirred the gold and charcoal with a bit of wood that kept bursting into flame and had constantly to be replaced by a fresh one.

What words did my father utter? I do not know. At least I am not certain what they were. No one ever told me. But could they have been anything but incantations? On these occasions was he not invoking the genies of fire and gold, of fire and wind, of wind blown by the blast-pipes of the forge, of fire born of wind, of gold married to fire? Was it not their assistance, their friendship, their espousal that he besought? Yes. Almost certainly he was invoking these genies, all of whom are equally indispensable for smelting gold.

The operation going on before my eyes was certainly the smelting of gold, yet something more than that: a magical operation that the guiding spirits could regard with favor or disfavor. That is why, all around my father, there was absolute silence and anxious expectancy. Though only a child, I knew there could be no craft greater than the goldsmith's. I expected a ceremony; I had come to be present at a ceremony; and it actually was one, though very protracted. I was still too young to understand why, but I had an inkling as I watched the almost religious concentration of those who followed the mixing process in the clay pot.

When finally the gold began to melt I could have shouted aloud—and perhaps we all would have if we had not been forbidden to make a sound. I trembled, and so did everyone else watching my father stir the mixture—it was still a heavy paste—in which the charcoal was gradually consumed. The next stage followed swiftly. The gold now had the fluidity of water. The genies had smiled on the operation!

"Bring me the brick!" my father would order, thus lifting the ban that until then had silenced us.

The brick, which an apprentice would place beside the fire, was hollowed out, generously greased with Galam butter. My father would take the pot off the fire and tilt it carefully, while I would watch the gold flow into the brick, flow like liquid fire. True, it was only a very sparse trickle of fire, but how vivid, how brilliant! As the gold flowed into the brick, the grease sputtered and flamed and emitted a thick smoke that caught in the throat and stung the eyes, leaving us all weeping and coughing.

But there were times when it seemed to me that my father ought to turn this task over to one of his assistants. They were experienced, had assisted him hundreds of times, and could certainly have performed the work well. But my father's lips moved and those inaudible, secret words, those incantations he addressed to one we could not see or hear, was the essential part. Calling on the genies of fire, of wind, of gold and exorcising the evil spirits—this was a knowledge he alone possessed.

By now the gold had been cooled in the hollow of the brick, and my father began to hammer and stretch it. This was the moment when his work as a goldsmith really began. I noticed that before embarking on it he never failed to stroke the little snake stealthily as it lay coiled up under the sheepskin. I can only assume that this was his way of gathering strength for what remained to be done, the most trying part of his task.

But was it not extraordinary and miraculous that on these occasions the little black snake was always coiled under the sheepskin? He was not always there. He did not visit my father every day. But he was always present whenever there was gold to be worked. His presence was no surprise to *me*. After that evening when my father had spoken of the guiding spirit of his race I was no longer astonished. The snake was there intentionally. He knew what the future held. Did he tell my father? I think that he most certainly did. Did he tell him everything? I have another reason for believing firmly that he did.

The craftsman who works in gold must first of all purify himself. That is, he must wash himself all over and, of course, abstain from all sexual commerce during the whole time. Great respecter of ceremony as he was, it would have been impossible for my father to ignore these rules. Now, I never saw him make these preparations. I saw him address himself to his work without any apparent preliminaries. From that moment it was obvious that, forewarned in a dream by his black guiding spirit of the task which awaited him in the morning, my father must have prepared for it as soon as he arose, entering his workshop in a state of purity, his body smeared with the secret potions hidden in his numerous pots of magical substances; or perhaps he always came into his workshop in a state of ritual purity. I am not trying to make him out a better man than he was—he was a man and had his share of human frailties—but he was always uncompromising in his respect for ritual observance.

The woman for whom the trinket was being made, and who had come often to see how the work was progressing, would arrive for the final time, not wanting to miss a moment of this spectacle—as marvelous to her as to us—when the gold wire, which my father had succeeded in drawing out from the mass of molten gold and charcoal, was transformed into a trinket.

There we would be. Her eyes would devour the fragile gold wire, following it in its tranquil and regular spiral around the little slab of metal which supported it. My father would catch a glimpse of her and I would see him slowly beginning to smile. Her avid attention delighted him.

"Are you trembling?" he would ask.

"Am I trembling?"

And we would all burst out laughing at her. For she would be trembling! She would be trembling with covetousness for the spiral pyramid in which my father would be inserting, among the convolutions, tiny grains of gold. When he had finally finished by crowning the pyramid with a heavier grain, she would dance in delight.

No one—no one at all—would be more enchanted than she as my father slowly turned the trinket back and forth between his fingers to display its perfection. Not even the praise-singer whose business it was to register excitement would be more excited than she. Throughout this metamorphosis he did not stop speaking faster and ever faster, increasing his tempo, accelerating his praises and flatteries as the trinket took shape, shouting to the skies my father's skill.

For the praise-singer took a curious part—I should say rather that it was direct and effective—in the work. He was drunk with the joy of creation. He shouted aloud in joy. He plucked his *cora* like a man inspired. He sweated as if he were the trinket-maker, as if he were my father, as if the trinket were his creation. He was no longer a hired censer-bearer, a man whose services anyone could rent. He was a man who created his song out of some deep inner necessity. And when my father, after having soldered the large grain of gold that crowned the summit, held out his work to be admired, the praise-singer would no longer be able to contain himself. He would begin to intone the douga, which is sung only for celebrated men and which is danced for them alone.

But the douga is a formidable chant, a provocative chant, a chant which the praise-singer dared not sing, and which the man for whom it is sung dared not dance before certain precautions had been taken. My father had taken them as soon as he woke, since he had been warned in a dream. The praise-singer had taken them when he concluded his arrangements with the woman. Like my father he had smeared his body with magic substances and had made himself invulnerable to the evil genies whom the douga inevitably set free; these potions made him invulnerable also to rival praise-singers, perhaps jealous of him, who awaited only this song and the exaltation and loss of control which attended it, in order to begin casting their spells.

At the first notes of the *douga* my father would arise and emit a cry in which happiness and triumph were equally mingled; and brandishing in his right hand the hammer that was the symbol of his profession and in his left a ram's horn filled with magic substances, he would dance the glorious dance.

No sooner had he finished, than workmen and apprentices, friends and customers in their turn, not forgetting the woman for whom the trinket had been created, would flock around him, congratulating him, showering praises on him and complimenting the praise-singer at the same time. The latter found himself laden with gifts—almost his only means of support, for the praise-singer leads a wandering life after the fashion of the troubadours of old. Aglow with dancing and the praises he had received, my father would offer everyone cola nuts, that small change of Guinean courtesy.

Now all that remained to be done was to redden the trinket in a little water to which chlorine and sea salt had been added. I was at liberty to leave. The festival was over! But often as I came out of the workshop my mother would be in the court, pounding millet or rice, and she would call to me:

"Where have you been?" although she knew perfectly well where I had been.

"In the workshop."

"Of course. Your father was smelting gold. Gold! Always gold!"

And she would beat the millet or rice furiously with her pestle.

"Your father is ruining his health!"

"He danced the *douga*."

"The *douga!* The douga won't keep him from ruining his eyes. As for you, you would be better off playing in the courtyard instead of breathing dust and smoke in the workshop."

My mother did not like my father to work in gold. She knew how dangerous it was: a trinket-maker empties his lungs blowing on the blow-pipe and his eyes suffer from the fire. Perhaps they suffer even more from the microscopic precision which the work requires. And even if there had been no such objections involved, my mother would scarcely have relished this work. She was suspicious of it, for gold can not be smelted without the use of other metals, and my mother thought it was not entirely honest to put aside for one's own use the gold which the alloy had displaced. However, this was a custom generally known, and one which she herself had accepted when she took cotton to be woven and received back only a piece of cotton cloth half the weight of the original bundle.

VI

I was very young when I began school, first attending the Koran school, and, shortly afterwards, transferring to the French. Neither my mother nor I had the slightest suspicion how long I would be a student in the latter. Had she known, I am sure she would have kept me at home. Perhaps my father knew already.

Immediately after breakfast my sister and I would start out, carrying our books and notebooks in a raffia[5] satchel. On the way we would be joined by our friends, and the closer we got to school the more of us there would be. My sister walked with the girls, I stayed with the boys. Like all young boys we loved to tease the girls, but they gave as good as they got, and when we pulled their hair they fought back, scratching and biting us, although this did not dampen our enthusiasm noticeably. There was, however, a truce between my sister and myself; her friend, Fanta, also let me alone, but I did not return the compliment.

One day when we were alone in the school yard, she asked me, "Why do you pull my hair?"

"Because you're a girl."

"I don't pull yours."

I stopped to think for a moment. Only then did I realize that she was the only one, with the exception of my sister, who didn't.

"Well, why don't you?" I asked.

"Because!"

---

5. raffia: the fiber from leaf stalks of palms.

"Because! What kind of an answer's that?"

"I wouldn't hurt you, no matter what."

"Well, I'm going to pull *your* hair."

But then it seemed foolish to do it when none of my classmates was around. She burst into laughter when I did not carry out my threat.

"You just wait until school's out," I threatened.

But again I did not make good my threat. Something restrained me, and from then on I rarely bothered her. My sister was not long in noticing this.

"I don't see you pulling Fanta's hair," she said.

"Why should I? She leaves me alone."

"Yes, I've noticed."

"Then, why should I?"

"Oh, I don't know. I thought there might be some other reason."

What was she getting at? I shrugged my shoulders. Girls were crazy; all girls were.

"Oh, Fanta makes me sick," I said. "And you make me sick too."

She only laughed at me.

"Now, you watch out," I said. "If you don't stop laughing—"

She avoided my grasp and shouted from a distance: "Fanta! Fanta!"

"Oh, shut up."

She paid no attention to me, and I rushed at her.

"Fanta! Fanta!"

Unfortunately I couldn't find a stone to throw at her, but I made a resolution to take care of that matter later.

Once at school, we went straight to our seats, boys and girls side by side, their quarrels over. So motionless and attentive did we sit, that it would have been wonderful to see what would have happened had we stirred. Our teacher moved like quicksilver, here, there, everywhere. His flow of talk would have bewildered less attentive pupils; but we were extraordinarily attentive. Young though we were, we regarded our school work as a deadly serious matter. Nothing that we learned was old or expected; all came as though from another planet, and we never tired of listening. But even if we had wearied, this omnipresent teacher would never have given us an opportunity to interrupt. Interruption was out of the question; the idea did not even occur to us. We wanted to be noticed as little as possible, for we lived in continual dread of being sent to the blackboard.

This was our nightmare. The blackboard's blank surface was an exact replica of our minds. We knew little, and the little that we knew came out haltingly. The slightest thing could inhibit us. When we were called to the blackboard we had to take the chalk and really work, if we were to avoid a beating. The smallest detail was of the utmost importance, and the blackboard magnified everything. If we made one downward stroke not precisely of the same height as the others, we were required to do extra lessons on Sunday, or were sent during recess to the first grade for a caning—a caning, I should add, one did not easily forget. Irregular downward strokes made our teacher furious. He examined our exercises under a magnifying glass, and dealt out his blows accordingly. He was indeed quicksilver, and he wielded his rod with joyous *élan*.[6]

This was how things were in the primary grades. There were fewer beatings in the upper classes; other kinds of punishment, no more pleasant, took their place. I underwent a vast variety of punishments in that school, and only one thing did not vary—my anguish. One's love of knowledge had to be very strong to survive these ordeals.

For second-year students, the customary punishment was sweeping the school yard. It was then that we comprehended how truly spacious that yard was, what an enormous number of guava trees it possessed. It seemed to us certain that the trees had been planted there for the specific purpose of littering the ground, for certainly we never received any of the fruit. In the third and fourth years our punishment was to work in the kitchen garden; and it would have been difficult to find cheaper labor. During our last two years, the school authorities had such confidence in us—a confidence, I might add, we would have gladly foregone—that we were entrusted with the herd of cattle which belonged to the school.

This last task was no sinecure.[7] The herd we tended was famous for miles around. Did a farmer have a vicious cow, it inevitably ended up in our herd. There was a good reason for this; the farmer, desperate to be rid of the beast, would accept almost any price, and the school authorities were only too anxious to take advantage of such a windfall. So the real reason was stinginess, and the result was that our school owned the most complete collection of sly, ornery creatures in existence. When we cried out, "Right!" it was just natural for them to veer left.

The way they galloped about in the bush, it seemed as if a swarm of flies were constantly irritating them. We galloped after them, incredible distances. They were always much more intent on wandering off, or battling among themselves, than foraging for food. However, their picturesque behavior was no pleasure to us. We knew that, on our return, the school authorities would carefully survey their bellies to see how well they had eaten. And woe to us should the stomachs of those raw-boned creatures not be full.

But heaven help us indeed, should a single head be missing from this, the devil's own herd. We would return home at nightfall, exhausted, since we had to whip them into a lather in order to get them to move at all in the right direction. This, of course, did not improve the dispositions of these fantastic animals. To make up for their not having eaten very much, we would gorge them with water. Footsore, we would appear with the entire herd. We would not have dared come back without every one of them. The consequences would have been too dreadful.

---

6. *élan:* enthusiasm.

7. **sinecure:** a job that requires little or no work.

That's how it was with our teachers—at any rate, when things were at their worst—and it is understandable enough that we could scarcely wait to finish school and receive that famous certificate of studies which proclaimed us "learned." And yet it seems that as yet I have scarcely said anything about the dark side of our school life, since the worst was what the older pupils made us younger ones suffer. These older students—I can not call them "comrades" since they were older and stronger than we, and less strictly supervised—persecuted us in every conceivable way. They were a haughty lot, and with reason, since no doubt they were repaying the treatment they had themselves received: excessively harsh treatment is not precisely the best method of inculcating kindness.

I remember—my hands and fingertips can not forget—what lay in store for us when we returned to school after vacation. The guava trees in the yard would be in leaf again and last year's leaves would be strewn about the ground in scattered heaps. In places there would be great piles of them.

"Sweep these up," the director would say. "This yard must be cleaned immediately."

Immediately! And there was enough work there, damnable work, for more than a week. There was more work than there should have been, since the only tools we had were our hands—our hands, and our fingers, and our fingernails.

"Now, be quick about it," the director would say to the older students, "or you'll be hearing from me."

At an order from the older boys, we would line up like peasants about to reap a field, but we did not work like peasants; we worked like galley slaves. This in a school yard! There were open spaces between the guava trees, but there was also a place where the guava trees grew so close together that their branches intertwined. Here the sun did not penetrate, and the acrid odor of decay lingered when the weather was fine.

Even when the work was not proceeding as quickly as the director had ordered, the older boys refused to help. They considered it easier to pull branches from the trees with which to beat us. Guava wood is extremely flexible, and when skillfully handled the whips whistled as they moved through the air; our backs felt as though they were on fire. Our flesh smarted, and tears fell from our eyes.

There was only one way to avoid these blows, and that was to bribe our tyrants with the lunches we had brought from home; the savory cakes of Indian corn, the wheat, the *couscous* made of meat or fish. If we had any money, that also changed hands. Anyone who refused to give up his lunch, mindful of his empty stomach, found himself the recipient of a dreadful beating. It was administered so violently, in such a diabolical rhythm, that even a deaf man would have understood that these blows were given not to speed up the work but to extort food and money.

Occasionally one of us, worn out by the deliberate cruelty, would dare to complain to the director. The director would become very angry, but the punishment he inflicted on the culprits was nothing compared to what they had administered. At any rate, our complaints did nothing to remedy the situation. Possibly it would have been wiser to have informed our parents of what we were undergoing, but somehow or other this never occurred to us. Perhaps we remained silent because of pride, or because of loyalty to the school. I know now that whatever the reason, it was stupid of us to keep silent. Such beatings were utterly alien to my people's passion for independence and equality.

One day, one of my playmates, Kouyaté Karamoko, having been the recipient of a particularly brutal beating, declared that he had had enough of this sort of thing. Kouyaté was extremely small and thin—so small that we joked that he must have the stomach of a bird, that is, a gizzard. One thing is certain, whether Kouyaté was the owner of a gizzard or some other form of stomach, he put very little into it. He cared only for fruit and at lunch was satisfied if he were able to trade his *couscous* for guavas and oranges. This minimum even he required, and it was obvious that, if he were forced to give up his fruit, he would inevitably have to turn in his gizzard for something smaller, perhaps the stomach of an insect. This did not bother the older boys; their insistent demands forced Kouyaté into a rigorous period of fasting. That day, hunger, in combination with the welts on his buttocks, made him rebel.

"I've taken all I intend to," he sniffled through his tears. "I'm going to tell my father."

"It won't do you any good to make a fuss," I said.

"You really don't think it will?"

"Don't forget that the older boys—"

But he would not let me finish.

"I don't care—I'm going to tell him," he shouted at the top of his voice.

"For heaven's sakes, keep your voice down."

He was my best friend, and I was afraid that this outburst would only earn him another beating.

"You know my father—you know he'll do something."

I knew Kouyaté's father well; he was one of the most respected praise-singers in the district. Although he no longer practiced his profession, he had a special standing in the community—a sort of scholar and praise-singer emeritus. There was no house that was not open to him.

"Kouyaté, your father's an old man."

"A very strong man," he replied proudly, drawing his thin little body up to its full height.

"You're being stupid," I warned him.

He left off whining, and I finished the conversation by telling him to do as he pleased.

The next day, no sooner had Kouyaté arrived at the school yard than he went over to Himourana, the boy who had thrashed him so brutally the day before.

"My father is most anxious to meet the upper form boy who has been kindest to me. I thought of you at once. Can you come to dinner this evening?"

"I'll be happy to," Himourana said.

Himourana's brutality was only matched by his stupidity. He was probably a glutton as well.

And that evening, sure enough, the dunce showed up at Kouyaté's concession. One of the most sturdily built in Kouroussa, it had only one gate, and the wall around it, instead of being made of reeds, was constructed of masonry with pieces of broken glass strewn along the top. One entered or left it only by permission of the master of the house. That evening Kouyaté's father came to open the gate in person, and, when Himourana had entered it, it was carefully bolted behind him.

"Do sit down," said Kouyaté's father. "Our whole family is expecting you."

Himourana glanced quickly at the cooking utensils, which seemed to promise a most satisfactory meal, and sat down in the yard. He prepared himself for the compliments that were about to be addressed to him. And then Kouyaté arose.

"Father," he said, pointing at the guest. "That's the one who always takes my food and money."

"Now, now, Kouyaté, that's not a nice thing to say," his father replied. "Are you sure you're telling the truth?" And he turned to Himourana. "Young man, you hear what my son has said? What do you have to say in your defense? Do speak quickly. I don't have too much time to give you, but I don't want to be ungenerous."

It was as if a thunderbolt had dropped at Himourana's feet. He couldn't understand a word of what was being said. He thought only of fleeing, which would have been a reasonable enough idea if there had not been that wall. One had to be as big a boob as Himourana to attempt to put the idea into execution. He was caught before he had taken ten steps.

"Now, get this into your head," Kouyaté's father said. "I am not sending my son to school for you to make a slave out of him."

And then Himourana found himself raised aloft by his arms and legs and held extended, while Kouyaté's father gave him a sound thrashing. Shamefaced, his rear end aflame, he was then permitted to go.

The next day at school the story of Himourana's punishment spread like wildfire. It created a scandal. Never before had such a thing happened, and we could scarcely believe that it had happened. All of us younger boys felt that Kouyaté's father had avenged us. The upshot was that the older boys held a meeting and decided that Kouyaté and his sister, Miriama, were to be ostracized. The edict was extended to us younger students—we also were not to talk to our playmate. However, we noted that they were very careful not to touch either Kouyaté or his sister, and even the stupidest of us was aware that they were afraid. An era had ended, we sensed, and we prepared to breathe the air of liberty.

At noon I went up to Kouyaté, having decided to defy our oppressors.

"Be careful," he said. "You know what's likely to happen."

"Oh, to hell with them."

I gave him the oranges I had brought for lunch.

"Do go away. I'm afraid they'll beat you."

I had no time to answer. Several of them were coming toward us, and I hesitated, unable to decide whether to run or not. I made my decision, and suddenly I felt their blows upon me. Then I ran, and didn't stop until I had come to the other end of the school yard. I cried as much from anger as from pain. When I had left off crying, I found Fanta sitting next to me.

"What are you doing here?"

"I've brought you a wheat-cake."

I took it and ate it almost without noticing what I was eating, although Fanta's mother was famous for making the best wheat-cakes in the district. When I had finished I went and drank some water and washed my face. Then I returned and sat down again.

"I don't like you to sit beside me when I'm crying," I said.

"Were you crying? I didn't notice."

I looked at her. She was lying. Obviously to spare my pride. I smiled at her.

"Do you want another wheat-cake?" she asked.

"No, I'm too angry. Doesn't it make you angry, too?"

"Yes," and her eyes filled with tears.

"I hate them!" I cried. "You can't imagine how I hate them. Do you know what I'm going to do? I'm going to quit school. I'm going to grow up fast, and then I'm going to come back. And for every beating I've received, I'm going to pay them back with a thousand."

She stopped crying and looked at me admiringly.

That evening I sought out my father under the veranda.

"Father, I don't want to go to school any more."

"What?"

"No," I said.

But by this time the scandal had gone the rounds of the concessions in Kouroussa.

"What's going on in that school?" my father asked.

"I'm afraid of the older boys."

"I thought you weren't afraid of anyone."

"I'm afraid of them."

"What do they do to you?"

"They take away our money and eat our lunches."

"Do they? And they whip you?"

"Yes."

"Yes, I'll have a word with those bullies tomorrow. So that's what's up?"

The next day my father and his apprentices accompanied me to school, and they stood with me at the school door. Each time one of the older boys passed, my father asked, "Is that one of them?"

"No," I answered, although there were many among them who had beaten and robbed me. But I was waiting for one boy in particular, the one who had treated me most savagely. When I saw him I cried, "There's the worst of all."

Without further ado, the apprentices threw themselves on him and stripped him bare. They handled him so roughly that my father had to come to his rescue.

"The director and I are going to have a chat about you," he said. "What I want to find out is whether you bigger fellows are here for any other reason than to beat up the smaller boys and steal their money."

That day the business of not speaking to Kouyaté or his sister ended. They played with us, and none of the older boys attempted to interfere. They did not even seem to notice us. Was a new era beginning? It seemed so. The older boys kept to themselves; it seemed almost, since we were the more numerous, that they were the ones who were being ostracized. That they were none too pleased with the way things were going was evident. And certainly they were in none too happy a situation. Up to now their parents had been unaware of their nasty practices. If the parents were informed—and there was a very good chance that everything would become public—the culprits could expect only scoldings and punishments.

When school was recessed that afternoon, my father arrived. As he had said he would, he went immediately to the director who was in the yard with the other teachers. Without bothering to say: "Good-day," my father asked, "do you have any idea what's going on in this school?"

"Why, of course I do," the director answered. "Everything's proceeding as it should."

"Then the older boys are supposed to whip the younger ones and steal their money? Are you blind, or is that really your intention?"

"Why don't you stay out of what doesn't concern you?"

"Doesn't concern me? Is it no concern of mine that my son is treated like a slave?"

"It most certainly is not."

"That you shouldn't have said!"

And my father marched closer to the director.

"Now I suppose I'm to be beaten the way your apprentices beat one of my students this morning," said the director.

He put up his fists. He was a strong man but quite fat, and my father, who was slender and quick, would have had no trouble with him at all. In fact, he did knock him down, but the assistants pulled them apart before the thing really got under way.

The director stood feeling his jaw and saying nothing; and my father, having dusted himself off, took me by the hand and led me from the yard. I walked proudly beside him to our concession. But later I felt much less proud, when, walking by myself in the city, I heard people say as I passed, "Look! There's the boy whose father beat up the director in the school yard."

This was not at all comparable to the incident in which Kouyaté's father had been involved. This was a scandal, occurring as it had in the presence of the teachers and students, and with the director as the principal victim. No, it was not at all like the other, and it seemed to me lucky if it should end with no more than my being expelled from school. I hurried back to my father.

"Why did you have to fight with him? I'll never be able to go back again!"

"But that's what you want! Didn't you say so yourself?" And my father laughed loudly.

"I don't see anything to laugh about."

"Sleep well, little dunce. If we don't hear the put-put of a certain motorcycle at our gates by tomorrow, I shall complain to the district administration."

There was no need to make this complaint. The next day, sure enough, the director's motorcycle drove up to our gate. He came in, and my father, as well as the rest, greeted him amiably: "Good evening, sir."

A chair was offered the guest, and he and my father sat down. At a motion from the latter we withdrew and watched from a distance. Their conversation appeared to be friendly, and evidently it was, for from that time on, my sister and I experienced no further horrors at school.

Yet, for all that, the scandal was not hushed up. A few months later the director was forced to resign because of a petition signed by all of the parents. The rumor had gotten about that he was using some of the students as houseboys for the convenience of his wives. These students had been boarded with him by their parents so that they might receive special attention, and their board had been paid for with cattle. I don't know if anything further came of it. All I know is that it was the straw that broke the camel's back, and that we were never again bullied by the older boys.

DISCUSSION QUESTIONS

1. What Malinke tribal rituals or customs are revealed in the first two chapters of Laye's account?

2. Why do you think Laye's father worried about the fact that Laye would not be in his company enough?

3. Based on what you learned in this selection, how would you describe the role of women in Malinke tribal society?

4. Compare Laye's description of school life with your own experiences in school. What is similar? What is different?

SUGGESTION FOR WRITING

Which chapter, or part of a chapter, from this excerpt of Camara Laye's autobiography did you enjoy most—Chapter 1, 2, or 6? Why was it your favorite? Write a paragraph in which you explain why you enjoyed a particular part of this autobiography and what you learned from it.

WILLIAM MODISANE
(born 1923)

William Modisane, poet, short-story writer, autobiographer, novelist, and journalist, was born and raised in the slum Sophiatown, a suburb of Johannesburg, South Africa. After being educated in local schools, he became a reporter for a Johannesburg newspaper and then worked for a while on *Drum* magazine. Modisane soon found life unbearable under the oppressive apartheid system of South Africa. Before his escape from South Africa through Tanganyika and then to Europe, Modisane remarked, upon looking at his newborn baby, that he felt remorseful "for bringing such innocence into the world to perpetuate the work of the devil." This feeling is mirrored in much of his writing, including his autobiography, *Blame Me on History* (1963). Modisane's many short stories deal with one man's response to the social and political horrors of South Africa before apartheid ended. While most of his writing centers upon a powerful protest theme, his first short story, "The Dignity of Begging," is satirical and free from the bitterness seen in his later work. ■

THE DIGNITY OF BEGGING

The magistrate raises his eyes above the documents and plunges them like daggers into my heart. His blue eyes are keen: my heart pounds like the bass of a boogie-woogie.

"I'm sick to death of you . . . heartily sick. There's not a native beggar on the streets whose full story I don't know," the magistrate says. "I've watched some of you grow up. There isn't one I haven't tried to rehabilitate many times. Some I was forced to send to jail, but they always come back . . . they come back to the goose that lays the golden egg."

These are fighting words. The magistrate sounds as though he's going to put us away for a few weeks. My only regret is that Richard Serurubele has to share my fate. If only the magistrate knew that he is not a parasite like the rest of us, that he's what is called an exploited beggar. He was crippled by an automobile accident, and since then his parents have made capital out of it. They use him to beg so they can balance the family budget. They never show him the comfort of love. Relentlessly they drive him, like an animal that has to work for its keep and feed. He is twenty-one. Dragging one foot along, he is an abject sight who has all the sadness of the world in his face. He looks many times older than my mother-in-law.

---

1. **Modisane:** (mō di sä′ nä).

"You beggars make it difficult for me to do my duty, and in spite of my failure to rehabilitate you, I always believe in giving you another chance. . . . A fresh start, you might call it. But I'm almost certain that you'll be back here in a few days."

The magistrate is getting soft, I can see my freedom at a distance of an arm's stretch. Here is my chance to put on my act. A look of deep compunction and a few well-chosen words can do the trick. I clear my throat and squeeze out a tear or two.

"Your honor, most of us beg because we've been ostracized by our families; they treat us as though we were lepers," I say, wiping off a tear. "They want us to look up to them for all the things we need. They never encourage us to earn our own keep. Nobody wants to employ us, people are more willing to offer us alms rather than give us jobs. All they do is show us pity. . . . We don't want to be pitied, we want to be given a chance to prove that we're as good as anybody else."

I can see from the silence in the court that everybody is deceived. . . . Everybody is filled with a sense of self-reproach. The magistrate is as mute as the undertaker's parlor. I can read pity on the faces of all the people in the court; perhaps the most pathetic is my own. I am magnificent . . . an answer to every film director's dream. I know I have said enough . . . enough to let us out, that is.

"I understand you have matriculated, your name is Nathaniel, isn't it?" He turns a page of the report prepared by a worker in the Non-European Affairs Department. "Yes, here we are. Nathaniel Mokgomare, the department recommends that you be sent to a place where you will be taught some useful trade. I want you to report to Room 14 at the department's building tomorrow morning."

This is not what I had bargained for; my brilliant idea has boomeranged. Why must I take a job when I can earn twice a normal wage begging? After all, what will horses do if I take a job? I *must* uphold the dignity of begging. Professional ethics forbid all beggars from working.

"As for you, Richard Serurubele, I'll let you go this time, but mark my words: the next time you appear before me, I'll have you sent to the Bantu Refuge.[2] Now get out of here, both of you."

If the magistrate had seen the big grin on my face as we leave the court, he would have thrown my deformed carcass in jail and deliberately lost the key. He does not see it though.

With the exception of a few loose ends everything has gone according to schedule, but my friend Serurubele is just about the most miserable man on earth. The trouble with him is he lacks imagination, but then of course, not everybody is as bright as I am. He always seems to be looking at the dull side of life, a vice coupled with an appalling brand of honesty most bishops would swear didn't exist.

---

2. **the Bantu Refuge:** one of the tracts of land allotted by the South African government to the African tribes. They are similar in many respects to America's Indian reservations.

"One of these days I'm going to kill myself," Serurubele says. "I can't go on like this, I'm tired of living off other people. Why did this have to happen to me? Tell me, Nathan. Why?"

How this man expects me to answer a question like this is beyond me. For one unguarded moment I almost tell him to send his Maker a telegram and ask Him all about it, but my gentler nature sees the harm such an answer might do.

"I don't know," I say, abruptly. "Things like this just happen; it's not in us to question why. Nature has a way of doing things, but even then she gives something in return. . . . at least I think so. . . . But how should I know, anyway?"

This is the one time I cannot find something concrete to say; I want to show him that there is compensation for his disability, but I just cannot lay my hands on it. This, I remember, is what made me leave home.

I left because my parents did not understand. They almost made a neurotic out of me; but today I wonder if it wasn't my own sensitivity which gave their actions then their seemingly absurd proportions. They seemed afraid to walk about freely; everybody sat down as if the house was full of cripples. I was treated like a babe in arms. All the things I wanted were brought to me, I was not even allowed to get myself water to drink. This excessive kindness gradually began to irritate me. . . . It became a constant reminder that I didn't belong, that I was an invalid. It then became apparent that they would soon put the food into my mouth which they had already chewed for me, and push it down my throat. These thoughts of inadequacy drove me from home.

A new life opened for me. I got myself a wife, two bouncing boys and a property at Pampoenfontein, also a room at Sophiatown[3] complete with piano. Within two years I had begged well over a few hundred pounds. The money has been used wisely. Only one problem confronts me now, I want enough money to provide for my old age. . . . The two boys are also to be considered.

"For Christ's sake, Nathaniel," Serurubele says, "what's wrong with you. Why are you always so wrapped up in your thoughts. . . . this is where I stay, remember?"

I say goodbye to him and go to my room. After having something to eat I settle down to some hard thinking. There are all sorts of insurances and societies, unions and what have you, which protect workers. Why not a beggars' union? I could rally all the beggars of the city into one union with some professional name like "The United Beggars' Union," into whose funds every beggar would contribute ten shillings a week. In the city of Johannesburg alone, there are over a hundred beggars and if they

---

3. **Sophiatown:** the Colored location in Johannesburg. Under South Africa's system of apartheid (See footnote on page 23), whites, blacks, and Coloreds (people of mixed ancestry) had to live in their own districts. The districts for non-whites were called *locations*. Sophiatown was a particularly notorious slum, which has since been destroyed in urban renewal.

could all be talked over, a capital of about two-thousand-four-hundred pounds could be realized in one year.

What a brilliant idea . . . an inspiration of genius. Sometimes I feel depressed that the world has not had the vision to realize the potentialities of my genius . . . possibly it cannot accommodate Einstein and myself in the same generation. Anyway, so much for that.

I could promise to offer each a bonus of ten pounds a year. That would be smart. . . . No beggar could resist such an offer. Maybe I should promise to buy each a property somewhere cheap, say, buy one property a year for the needy ones like Serurubele, equip him with third-rate tools and interest him in turning out junk that nobody will care to give a second look at. The scheme would be costly, but at least it would go far in enlisting their confidence. Only one would get the property; the others would wait patiently until I get religion.

The following morning I'm at Room 14 bright and early. A white man with a bored expression on his face is sitting behind a big mahogany desk. I tell him my name. He takes some paper and writes on it. He tells me to go to the address written on the paper.

The faint showers that were falling outside have become heavier, and as I go out I say something nasty about the weather. A brilliant idea strikes me as a well-dressed lady is walking towards me. She looks like a mobile gold mine ready to be tapped. . . . In fact, I can almost see the gold nuggets in her teeth. I put on a gloomy face, bend lower than usual and let my deformed carcass shiver. She stops and looks at me as if she's responsible for my deformity.

"Why, you poor boy, you're freezing to death," she says, with melodrama. "Here, go buy yourself something to eat."

I feel the half-crown piece in my hand and give her the usual line of how the good Lord will bless her, and send her tons and tons of luck: but from the way she's dressed, she appears to have had more than her share of luck.

I play this trick all the way to the address I'm given, and by the time I get there, I count well over ten half-crowns. Not bad, I say to myself; at this rate I can become the richest and most famous beggar in the city. To think the department wants to pin me behind a desk! The idea is criminal, to say the least.

One of these days when I'm on my annual leave, I hope to write a book on begging, something like a treatise on the subject. It will be written with sensitivity and charm, brimful with sketches from life, and profusely illustrated with colored photographs, with easy-to-follow rules on the noblest and oldest occupation in the world: Begging! It will be a textbook for all aspiring beggars, young and old, who will reap a wealth of knowledge from my personal experiences and genius. In fact, I think it will be the only one of its kind in world literature. Even millionaires will take up begging as a pastime to color their humdrum existence.

It will naturally begin with a history of the art from its ancient crudity of maiming children as a preparation in their education, right up to the contemporary age of beggars who are driven to the city in the latest American cars. . . . beggars with a bank balance big enough to impress the Receiver of Revenue. I can almost see it on the best-seller list for several months. This reverie almost causes me to lose my way.

I find the place and go in. My heart just misses a beat when I see the large number of people inside. Some, if not most, are deformed monstrosities like myself. What could be sweeter? I can see my plan taking shape.

The man in charge starts explaining the elementary principles of the typewriter. I pretend to be interested and ask many unnecessary questions, but intelligent enough to impress him. By five o'clock I'm running over the keyboard like a brilliant amateur.

On my way home I go via Serurubele's corner. He is still there and looking as miserable as ever. I suggest that we go home. I lure him to my room and when we get there I begin playing a certain tarantella like Rubinstein, only my rendering is in a major flat. Either my piano recital is good or my friend just loves bad sounds.

"You can have a house like this and everything that goes with it; it's yours for the taking. Why beg for other people when you can do it for yourself?"

"I've got to help with the rent and the food," he says. "How do you think I'm going to get a house like this? I can't just wish for it."

"You don't have to, you must plan and work for it like I did. I have a plan that will give it to you in less than a year. . . . Listen."

I then start explaining to him about the society with particular emphasis on the good it will do to all beggars. I see his teeth sparkling behind thick lips. I put him in charge of organizing them for our first meeting.

Last night I dreamed I was at the race course and I saw the winning double as plain as I see my twisted leg. I raid my savings in the room and make my way to Turffontein. When I get there I start scouting around for policemen. None are about and a soothing satisfaction comes with the realization that I shall not bother myself with police badges. I put a pound win on two and seven, a double in the first leg. As I'm making my bet, a man with eyes as big and lethargic as an owl's is standing next to me and beaming like a blushing groom.

I'm too nervous to watch the race, so I decide to walk about and appreciate the scenery. Suddenly I feel as though someone is staring at me. I turn round and look straight at Miss Gallovidian, a welfare worker, who has the uncanny habit of showing up at the most unexpected places. I don't need a fortuneteller to tell me I'm in trouble. She has a notorious record of having safely deposited more than twelve beggars in the Refuge. My only chance is to get out of here before she can find a beefy policeman. I'm walking to the gate when I hear people talking about two and seven. I even forget the trouble Miss Gallovidian is going to bring me. I run as fast as a man with a twisted leg can to the Bookie. Only six tickets were sold, the loud speaker was saying, only I'm not interested.

As the Bookie is handing me the money Blushing Groom seems even happier than I am. His crooked teeth, which are dulled by tobacco, click every time the Bookie counts a hundred. His greasy lips are watering while a pair of bloodshot eyes are blinking with a dull brilliance. It hurts my eyes to look at him. I have hardly put the money in my pocket, when gruesome pats me on the back and says, nice and loud: "We made it!"

I must have been a fool not to have been wise as to why Blushing Groom was acting the perfect chaperon.

"That's fine," I say. "What have we made?"

"Don't be bashful," he says, "we caught the richest double. Come, this calls for a celebration." He extends a hand, and all the time he's smiling as if his wife has given birth to quadruplets.

"Look, pal," I say. "It's a good try. I couldn't have done better myself. This is the perfect set-up, isn't it? Well, I've got news for you: I caught that double alone, I don't know you and I don't care to. Go get yourself another piece of cheese. . . . I'm not that easy."

This ape suddenly stops smiling and looks at me like I had the plague. His broad, flat nose starts puffing out steam like an angry Spanish bull (only I'm not in the mood to make fancy passes like a toreador). All in all, he looks positively fierce, like the animal in the simile.

"Six-hundred and seventy pounds is a lot of money," he shouts. "Nobody's going to cheat me out of my share. You being a cripple. . . ."

"Shut up!" I yell. "Never call me that again, you . . . You!" I swing a right cross to his face, but this ape is smart. He blocks it and lands a hard one on my chin. I rock back and land flat on my sitters, while jungle tom-toms beat out a solid conga in my head. After a while my head clears and I get up, burning with rage. If I only had the strength, I would tear this ape apart.

Blushing Groom has put on quite a show; we have a good audience. Some white folks are threatening to beat his brains out. . . . I sincerely hope they do.

Suddenly I see a police badge jostling its way through. This is no place for me! I dash and start zigzagging through the people. A junior confusion starts, with everybody trying to give way. I run a few minutes, stumble and fall on my face. The policeman bends down and grabs me firmly by the arm and whispers: "Look, John, let's not have trouble. Come along quietly and everything will be just fine."

Under the circumstances I have no choice but to submit. My mother always told me never to resist arrest, let alone striking a uniformed officer of the law. Me and my money part company after Blushing Groom had preferred charges. My submission causes me to spend a not-so-glorious weekend at the Bantu Refuge. My transfer there being arranged by the thoughtful sergeant in the charge office, who out of pure love could not have me thrown in with hardened criminals . . . what with the place filled with housebreakers, extortioners, professional pickpockets and a generous assortment of other unsavory characters. Frankly, I hoped he would mind his own business. I might even have started a crap game and made me some money.

"I am almost certain that you will be back here in a few days," the magistrate had said. Somebody ought to tell him he has a great future . . . reading palms. He looks at me and a grin spreads over his pancake-like face. This place must be short of magistrates; why has it got to be the same one all the time?

"Beggars who play the horses are a dangerous nuisance. They misuse the kindness that is shown to them."

Just my luck: now I have to listen to a lecture on morals. The magistrate looks pleased with himself, and I don't like it. Miss Gallovidian looks at me and smiles like a proud victress. She probably expects a promotion for this. I'm called on to the stand.

Some man with a thin face asks me to raise my right hand and swear to tell the truth. After saying my piece, the prosecutor starts questioning me as if he's promised thirty per cent of Blushing Groom's cut. After his session with me, he calls Blushing Groom to the stand.

"Do you know this man?" the prosecutor says.

"No, sir."

"How was it then you put up ten shillings to bet the horses with him?"

"I was losing all morning when I decided to try somebody's guesses. I met him, and we started talking."

"Did anybody see you talking to him?"

"I don't know, but somebody must have."

"Then what happened?"

"I asked him if he had a tip. He said he had one straight from the horse's mouth . . . A sure thing, he said. I then asked him if I could put up ten shillings. He agreed. I was afraid to make the bet, so I gave him the money and walked over to the Bookie's stand with him where he placed a pound win on two and seven."

"Why were you afraid to make the bet?"

"I thought he was luckier than I was . . . besides, I had been losing all morning."

"Why did you strike him?"

"He was trying to cheat me out of my share, and tried to hit me when he couldn't."

The magistrate looks at me with something like contempt in his eyes. I won't have to put on a show for him this time. I might just as well kiss half my money goodbye. Blushing Groom's story is watertight.

"I'm thoroughly disappointed with you," the magistrate says. "I didn't know you were a thief too. I don't believe you could have made that bet alone; beggars haven't got so much money. I believe his story, things like this do happen. The money will be shared equally between the two of you."

"I don't believe you could have made that bet alone." What a cheek! I'll have that hobo know I make more money in one week than he does in a month. I don't believe you. . . . Good God!

I feel like committing mass murder as the court hands Blushing Groom three hundred and thirty-five pounds of my money. This prehistoric beast has a swell racket. A few more jobs like this and he can retire and buy himself a villa on the Riviera.

Blushing Groom is magnificent, inspiring awe. He is completely uncompromising, thoroughly unscrupulous, without qualms or a conscience. He has wholly realized the separateness of good and evil and attained a purity in evil worthy of honest appraisal. He would not allow himself to be swayed from cheating me by my being a cripple. If I were allowed to choose a brother, he would be my only choice.

I take my share of the money and clear out before the magistrate and Miss Gallovidian cook up another charge against me. On my way home I find it difficult to resist the temptation of stopping at some busy corner and doing my stuff. I might make up for some of the money, but I just happen to be wearing my best and have been a beggar long enough to know that people don't give money away to beggars who are dressed better than they. People who give alms to beggars do so to establish their superiority over the receiver, and like I said: I'm not an apprentice beggar.

When I get home I find a letter from my wife.

"Our son, Tommy, is sick. Please come home. . . ."

I become afraid and anxious for my Tommy, and even the kind words of my outsize landlady fail to move me.

I had to wait for something like this to show me the folly of my ways. A man's place is next to his wife and family. I had hoped that some day I would be able to provide my boys with a decent education, to grow them like normal boys, not just sons of a helpless cripple. . . . to find a place for them in the sun. I might be a big shot beggar but as a husband and father, I stink.

"If I should not see my friend Serurubele, will you. . . ."

"Yes, I'll explain to him. I'll always have your room for you if you should ever want it again."

Deep down I know that I will want it again. I have three hundred and thirty-five reasons why I should. Blushing Groom and the gullible public of Johannesburg will live in my mind for ever. . . . I have to come back. I owe it to the profession.

DISCUSSION QUESTIONS

1. The narrator of "The Dignity of Begging," Nathaniel Mokgomare, is a rascal from the lower ranks of South African society. Find examples in the story of ways he proves himself a rascal.

2. Late in the story Nathaniel has the tables turned on him. Explain how he is tricked by another rascal.

3. The narrator, Nathaniel, makes several satirically humorous statements in this story. Point out a few examples of this kind of humor.

4. At the end of the story, Nathaniel is filled with remorse for the way he has treated his wife and children. Do you think he really will reform? Explain your answer.

SUGGESTION FOR WRITING

"The Dignity of Begging" is a satire, a literary strategy that uses humor to ridicule or put down human folly or vice. How does this definition apply to the humor in "The Dignity of Begging"? Write a short essay in which you analyze the satire in this story. What is ridiculed in the story? How is humor used to expose this vice? Include examples from the story in your essay.

ES'KIA MPHAHLELE
(born 1919)

E s'kia (Ezekiel) Mphahlele[1] was born in the slums of South Africa and had a difficult early life. In the fifth grade he was branded "backward" by the principal of his school, an assessment that was reinforced by Mphahlele's relatives. Despite his early setbacks, Mphahlele had a ferocious desire to learn. In 1940 he received a teacher's certificate and became a high-school teacher in Johannesburg. But because he organized resistance against the country's policies toward educating Africans, he was banned from teaching there. Later he taught at University College of Ibadan, Nigeria, and at University College, Nairobi, Kenya. In 1957 Mphahlele went into exile and spent time in Nigeria, France, Zambia, and the United States. During his two stays in the U.S. he received a doctorate from the University of Denver (1968) and honorary doctorates from the universities of Pittsburgh (1983) and Colorado (1994). Though he considered himself an exile, Mphahlele never lost his commitment to his native country. In 1977, after his first stay in the U.S., Mphahlele returned to South Africa. At that time he was discouraged to discover that social conditions had deteriorated further, including increased detentions, tensions, and suffering for black South Africans. Today Mphahlele is considered one of Africa's most respected educators. A writer of fiction, autobiographies, and essays, he is one of the leading literary voices from South Africa. He is the author of collections of short stories, including *Man Must Live* (1946) and *The Living and the Dead* (1961); two autobiographies, *Down Second Avenue* (1959) and *Afrika, My Music* (1984); and essays on literature and politics, *The African Image* (1962). ■

THE MASTER OF DOORNVLEI[2]

The early summer rain was pouring fiercely. In the mud-and-grass church house a bird flitted from one rafter to another, trapped. All was silent in the church except for a cough now and again that punctuated the preacher's sermon. Now and then, to relieve the gravity of the devotional moment, a few members of the congregation allowed themselves to be ensnared by the circling movements of the bird.

But only a few of them. Most of the people had their eyes fixed on the elderly preacher, as if they were following the motion of every line on each lip as he gave his sermon. In any case, he did not have a booming voice,

---

1. **Mphahlele** (mə fä lä′ lä).
2. **Doornvlei** (dürn′ vlā).

like his deacon's (a point on which the old man was often plagued by a feeling of inferiority). So his listeners always watched his lips. One or two older women at the back screwed up their faces to see him better.

A nine-year-old boy was particularly charmed by the lost bird, and his eyes roved with it. Then he felt pity for it and wished he could catch it and let it out through the window which it missed several times. But the preacher went on, and his listeners soared on the wings of his sermon to regions where there was no labor or sweat and care.

Suddenly the boy saw the bird make straight for a closed window and hit against the glass and flutter to the floor. It tried to fly but could not. He went to pick it up. He hugged it and stroked it. He looked about, but the people's faces looked ahead, like stolid clay figures. Why are they so cold and quiet when a bird is in pain? he asked himself.

It lay quiet in his hand, and he could feel the slight beat of the heart in the little feathered form.

"And so, brothers and sisters," the preacher concluded, "the Holy Word bids us love one another, and do to others as we would that they do to us. Amen." He asked his flock to kneel for prayer.

At this time Mfukeri,[3] the foreman of Doornvlei Farm on which the makeshift church was built, came in. He looked around and spotted his target—a puny wisp of a boy with scraggy legs, the boy with the bird in his hand.

When he took the boy out the people continued to kneel, unperturbed, except for the raising of a head here and there; perhaps just to make sure who the victim was this time. As the two went out the boy's rather big waistcoat that dangled loosely from his shoulders, flapped about.

It was common for Mfukeri to butt in at a prayer session to fetch a man or woman or child for a job that needed urgent attention. The congregants were labor tenants, who in return for their work earned the few square yards of earth on which they lived, and a ration of mealie-meal,[4] sugar, and an occasional piece of meat.

When they complained about such disturbances to the farmer, Sarel Britz, he said: "I'm just to my laborers. I favor nobody above the rest. Farm work is farm work; I often have to give up my church service myself."

The boy tried to protect the bird. He could not keep it on his person, so he put it under a tin in the fowlrun before he went about the work Mfukeri had directed him to do. The rain continued to pour.

The following day the boy took ill with pneumonia. He had got soaked in the rain. On such days the little mud-and-grass houses of the laborers looked wretched: as if they might cave in any time under some unseen load. The nearest hospital was fifty miles away, and if the workers wanted

---

3. **Mfukeri** (mə fū kā´ rē).

4. **mealie-meal:** corn meal.

to see the district surgeon, they would have to travel twenty-five miles there and back. The district surgeon could only be seen once a week.

The boy ran a high temperature. When he was able to speak he asked his mother to go and see how his bird fared in the fowlrun. She came back to tell him that the bird had been found under a tin, dead. That same night the boy died.

When the news went round, the workers seemed to run berserk.

"It has happened before . . ."

"My child—not even ten yet . . . !"

"Come, let's go to Sarel Britz . . . !"

"No, wait, he'll be angry with us; very angry . . ."

"We can also get angry . . ."

"Yes, but the White man is very powerful . . ."

"And truly so—where do we get work if he drives us off the farm . . . ?"

"He wants our hands and our sweat—he cannot do that . . ."

"He beats us, and now he wants to kill us . . ."

"Send him back to Rhodesia—this Mfukeri . . . !"

"Yes, we don't do such things on this farm . . ."

"By the spirits, we don't work tomorrow until we see this thing out . . . !"

"Give us our trek-passes[5] . . . ! Save our children . . . !"

"Ho friends! I am not going with you. I have children to look after . . . !"

"That is why we are going to Sarel Britz . . . !"

"Come, friends, let's talk first before we march to the master of Doornvlei."

Tau Rathebe, who could read and write, rallied the workers to an open spot not far from the main gate. Grim and rugged farm workers; shaggy; none with extra flesh on him; young and old, with tough sinewy limbs. Those who were too scared to join the march kept in the bushes nearby to watch. Women remained behind.

The men were angry and impatient. "We want Mfukeri away from Doornvlei, or we go, trek-pass or none!" was the general cry, echoed and re-echoed.

And they marched, as they had never done before, to the master's house.

Britz and Mfukeri were standing on the front verandah, waiting. It was to be expected: the foreman had already gone to warn Britz. Apart from what knowledge he had about Tau Rathebe, it was plain from the early morning that the workers were not prepared to work.

"What is it, men?"

"The people want Mfukeri sent away," said Tau. "He has been using his sjambok[6] on some workers, and now old Petrus Sechele's son is dead, because Mfukeri took him out in the rain. I've warned him about this before."

---

5. **trek-passes:** Under South African law, blacks must carry an identification card, or "pass," and produce it on demand, or else be subject to arrest. By witholding their passes, white employers can keep their black laborers in virtual slavery.

6. **sjambok** (shäm′ bok): a heavy leather whip.

"I'll think about it. You're asking me to do a difficult thing; you must give me time to think."

"How long?" asked Tau.

Sarel Britz felt annoyed at the implied ultimatum and Tau's insolent manner; but he restrained himself.

"Till noon today. Just now I want you to go to your work. I'm just, and to show it, Mfukeri is not going to the fields until I've decided."

They dispersed, each to his work, discontented and surly. When Mfukeri left Sarel Britz in conference with his mother, the usually smooth and slippery texture on the foreman's face, peculiar to Rhodesian Africans, looked flabby.

"I've told him not to use the *sjambok*, but he insists on doing it, just because I forbid it," said Britz when he had gone.

"Reason?" Marta Britz asked.

"Just to make me feel I depend on him."

"He never behaved like this when your father was alive. Once he was told he must do a thing or mustn't he obeyed."

There was a pause during which mother and son almost heard each other's thoughts.

"You know, Mamma, when I was at university—on the experimental farm—I knew many Black and Colored folk. Thinking back on the time, now, makes me feel Pa was wrong."

"Wrong about what?"

"About Kaffirs[7] being children."

"But they are, my son. Your father himself said so."

"No, one has to be on the alert with them. One can't afford to take things for granted."

"How are they grown up?"

Sarel went and stood right in front of her. "Yes, Ma, they're fully grown up; some of them are cleverer and wiser than a lot of us Whites. Their damned patience makes them all the more dangerous. Maybe Mfukeri's still somewhat a child. But certainly not the others. Take today, for instance. A coming together like this has never been heard of on a White man's farm. And they've left everything in the hands of their leader. No disorder. They're serpent's eggs, and I'm going to crush them." He paused.

"I didn't tell you that Mfukeri has been keeping an eye on this Tau Rathebe. We've found out he was deported from Johannesburg. Somehow slipped into this farm. And now he's been having secret meetings with three or four of our Kaffirs at a time, to teach them what to do like today."

"So! Hemel!"[8]

"So you see, Ma, Papa was wrong. I'm going to keep a sharp eye on the swine. But first thing, I'm ready to drive Rathebe away; out with him tomorrow."

---

7. **Kaffirs:** black South Africans, a term of abuse.

8. **Hemel:** Heavens! [Afrikaans]

At noon the master of Doornvlei made his double decision known: that Tau Rathebe was to leave the farm the following morning, and that Mfukeri had been warned and would be given another chance—the last.

This caused a stir among the laborers, but Tau Rathebe asked them to keep calm.

They wanted to leave with him.

"No. The police will take you as soon as you leave Doornvlei. You can't go from one farm to another without a trek-pass," he reminded them.

He left Doornvlei . . .

Sarel Britz felt confused. He kept repeating to himself what he had said to his mother earlier. These are no children, no children . . . they are men . . . I'm dealing with the minds of men . . . My father was wrong . . . All my boyhood he led me to believe that black people were children . . . O Hemel, they aren't . . . ! He had begun to see the weakness of his father's theory during his university years, but it was the incident with Rathebe that had stamped that weakness on his mind.

Harvest time came, and Doornvlei became a little world of intense life and work. The maize triangle of South Africa was buzzing with talk of a surplus crop and the threat of low prices.

"A big crop again, Mfukeri, what do you say?" said Britz.

"Yes, baas,"[9] he grinned consent, "little bit better than last year."

"You know you're a good worker and foreman, Mfukeri. Without you I don't know how I'd run this farm."

"Yes, baas. If baas is happy I'm happy."

"Since Rathebe left there's peace here, not so?"

"Yes, baas, he makes too much trouble. Long time I tell baas he always meet the men by the valley. They talk a long time there. Sometime one man tell me they want more money and food. I'm happy for you, baas. The old baas he say I must help you all the time because I work for him fifteen years. I want him to rest in peace in his grave."

Britz nodded several times.

The Rhodesian foreman worked as hard as ever to retain the master's praise. He did not spare himself; and the other workers had to keep up with his almost inhuman pace.

"Hey you!" Mfukeri shouted often. "You there, you're not working fast enough." He drove them on, and some worked in panic, breaking off mealie cobs and throwing them with the dexterity of a juggler into sacks hanging from the shoulder. Mfukeri did not beat the workers any more. On this Sarel Britz had put his foot down. "Beat your workers and you lose them," his father had often said. But every servant felt the foreman's presence and became jittery. And the army of black sweating laborers spread out among the mealie stalks after the systematic fashion of a battle strategy.

Sometimes they sang their songs of grief and hope while reaping in the autumn sun. Sometimes they were too tired even to sing of grief; then

---

9. baas (bäs): master. [Afrikaans]

they just went on sweating and thinking; then there was a Sunday afternoon to look forward to, when they would go to the village for a drink and song and dance and lovemaking.

Sarel Britz became sterner and more exacting. And his moods and attitude were always reflected in his trusty Mfukeri. Britz kept reminding his tenants that he was just; he favored no one above the others; he repeated it often to Mfukeri and to his mother. He leaned more and more on his foreman, who realized it and made the most of it.

Back at university the students had had endless talks about the Blacks. Britz had discussed with them his father's theory about allowing the Black man a few rungs to climb up at a time; because he was still a child. Most of his colleagues had laughed at this. Gradually he accepted their line of thinking: the White man must be vigilant.

Often when he did his accounts and books, Sarel Britz would stop in the middle of his work, thinking and wondering what he would do if he lost much of his labor, like the other farmers. What if the towns continued to attract the Black laborer by offering him jobs once preserved for the White man. Would the Black workers continue to flow into the towns, or would the law come to the farmer's rescue by stopping the influx?

Sarel Britz lived in this fear. At the same time, he thought, it would break him if he paid his workers more than forty shillings a month in order to keep them. A mighty heap of troubles rose before his eyes, and he could almost hear the shouts and yells of labor tenants from all the farms rising against their masters.

The threat became more and more real to Britz. But Mfukeri consoled him. Britz had lately been inviting him to the house quite often for a chat about doings on the farm. If only that Kaffir didn't know so much about the farm so that he, Britz, had to depend on him more than he cared to . . . "Come to the house tonight, Mfukeri, and let's talk," he said, one afternoon in late autumn.

"All right, baas."

Mfukeri went to see his master. He wondered what the master had to say. He found him reclining comfortably on his chair. Mfukeri could not dare to take a chair before he was told to sit down—in the same chair he always sat on.

"Thank you, baas."

After a moment of silence, "What do you think of me, Mfukeri?"

"Why do you ask me, baas?"—after looking about.

"Don't be afraid to say your mind."

"You're all right, baas."

"Sure?"

"Yes, baas." They smoked silently.

"You still like this farm?"

"Very much, baas."

"I'm glad. You're a good foreman—the only man I trust here."

Mfukeri understood Britz. He wanted to assure his master that he would never desert him, that he was capable of keeping the tenants together. Hadn't he spied cleverly on Tau Rathebe and avoided an upheaval?

The foreman felt triumphant. He had never in his life dreamed he would work his way into a White man's trust. He had always felt so inferior before a White man that he despised himself. The more he despised himself the sterner and more ruthless he became towards his fellow-workers. At least he could retain a certain amount of self-respect and the feeling that he was a man, now that his master looked so helpless.

As the foreman sat smoking his pipe, he thought: "How pitiable they look when they're at a Black man's mercy . . . I wonder now . . ."

"All right, Mfukeri," said the master. The Rhodesian rose and stood erect, like a bluegum tree, over the White man; and the White man thought how indifferent his servant looked; just like a tree. To assert his authority once more Britz gave a few orders.

"Attend to that compost manure first thing tomorrow morning. And also the cleaning up of the chicken hospital; see to that fanbelt in the threshing machine."

"Yes, baas, goodnight."

He was moving towards the door when Britz said, "Before I forget, be careful about Donker mixing with the cows. It wasn't your fault, of course, but you'll take care, won't you?"

"Yes." He knew his master regarded his bull Donker as inferior stock, and felt hurt.

It was a bewildered Britz the foreman left behind. The farmer thought how overwhelming his servant was when he stood before him. Something in him quaked. He was sensitive enough to catch the tone of the last "baas" when Mfukeri left: it was such an indifferent echo of what "baas" sounded like years before.

Mfukeri kept a bull with a squatter family on a farm adjoining Doornvlei. Labor tenants were not allowed to keep livestock on the farm on which they themselves worked, because they were paid and received food rations. Mfukeri's friend agreed to keep Donker, the bull, for him. It was a good bull, though scrub.

Two days later Sarel Britz was roused from his lunch-hour sleep by noise outside. He ran out and saw workers hurrying towards a common point. In a few moments he found himself standing near Mfukeri and a group of workers. In front of the barn Britz's pedigree stallion, Kasper, was kicking out at Donker, Mfukeri's bull. Donker had the horse against the barn wall, and was roaring and pawing the earth.

Kasper kicked, a quick barrage of hoofs landing square on the bull's forehead. But the stocky Donker kept coming in and slashing out with his short horns. Normally, there would be ecstatic shouting from the workers. They stood in silence weaving and ducking to follow the movements of the fighters. They couldn't express their attitude towards either side, because they hated both Britz and Mfukeri; and yet the foreman was one of them.

The stallion tried to turn round, which was almost fatal; for Donker charged and unleashed more furious lightning kicks. Master and foreman watched, each feeling that he was entangled in this strife between their animals; more so than they dared to show outwardly. Sarel Britz bit his lower lip as he watched the rage of the bull. He seemed to see scalding fury in the very slime that came from the mouth of the bull to mix with the earth.

He didn't like the slime mixing with the sand: it looked as if Donker were invoking a mystic power in the earth to keep his forehoofs from slipping. Once the hoofs were planted in the ground the bull found an opening and gored Kasper in the stomach, ripping the skin with the upward motion of the horn.

Sarel Britz gave a shout, and walked away hurriedly.

When Mfukeri saw Kasper tottering, and his beloved bull drawing back, an overwhelming feeling of victory shot through every nerve in him. What he had been suppressing all through the fight came out in a gasp and, with tears in his eyes, he shouted: "Donker! Donker!"

There was a murmur among some of the onlookers who said what a pity it was the horse's hoofs weren't shod; otherwise the ending would have been different.

Kasper was giving his last dying kicks when Britz came back with a rifle in his hand. His face was set. The workers stood aside. Two shots from the rifle finished off the stallion.

"Here, destroy the bull!" he ordered Mfukeri, handing him the gun. The foreman hesitated. "I said shoot that bull!"

"Why do you want me to shoot my bull, baas?"

"If you don't want to do it, then you must leave this farm, at once!"

Mfukeri did not answer. They both knew the moment had come. He stood still and looked at Britz. Then he walked off, and coaxed his bull out of the premises.

"I gave him a choice," Sarel said to his mother, telling her the whole story.

"You shouldn't have, Sarel. He has worked for us these fifteen years."

Sarel knew he had been right. As he looked out of the window to the empty paddock, he was stricken with grief. And then he was glad. He had got rid of yet another threat to his authority.

But the fear remained.

DISCUSSION QUESTIONS

1. The second sentence of the story reads: "In the mud-and-grass church house a bird flitted from one rafter to another, trapped." Knowing what you know about the rest of the story, what does that bird symbolically represent?

2. The first character Mphahlele introduces is a nameless minor one—a nine-year-old boy. Is he used as a symbolic representative of the rest of his community, or is he merely the cause of the later conflict in the plot, or is he both?

3. In what ways are Mfukeri and Sarel Britz alike?

4. Allegorically, the battle between Kasper the horse and Donker the bull stands for more than a barnyard struggle. What does the battle between these two animals represent? Explain your answer.

5. Why do you think the bystanders remain neutral during the battle?

6. In the last two paragraphs of the story, Sarel Britz is grief-stricken, then glad, and finally fearful. Why is he grief-stricken? Why is he glad? Why is he fearful?

SUGGESTION FOR WRITING

Note the title of this story. Who is the master of Doornvlei? Is it Sarel Britz, the owner of the farm, or Mfukeri, the foreman, or both? Write a short essay in which you defend one of these three options. Support your argument with evidence from the story.

ABIOSEH NICOL
(1920–1994)

A distinguished physician, educator, and ambassador from Sierra Leone, Dr. Davidson Nicol used the pen name Abioseh Nicol for his literary works. He completed medical school at Cambridge University in England and then returned to Sierra Leone to teach college, eventually becoming head of the University College of Sierra Leone. He later served as Sierra Leone's representative to the United Nations and as President of the United Nations Security Council.

Although highly educated and widely honored for his professional accomplishments, Nicol retained his interest in the simple life of the African villagers. His writings focus on tribal traditions and the daily struggles of village life. His most best known works of fiction are *Two African Tales* and *The Truly Married Woman and Other Stories,* from which the following story is taken. ■

LIFE IS SWEET AT KUMANSENU

The sea and the wet sand to one side of it; green tropical forest on the other; above it the slow tumbling clouds. The clean round blinding disc of sun and the blue sky, covered and surrounded the small African village, Kameni.

A few square mud houses with roofs like helmets, here thatched and there covered with corrugated zinc where the prosperity of cocoa and trading had touched the head of the family.

The widow Bola stirred her palm oil stew and thought of nothing in particular. She chewed a kola nut rhythmically with her strong toothless jaws and soon unconsciously she was chewing in rhythm with the skipping of Asi, her granddaughter. She looked idly at Asi as the seven-year-old brought the twisted palm-leaf rope smartly over her head and jumped over it, counting in English each time the rope struck the ground and churned up a little red dust. Bola herself did not understand English well, but she could count easily up to twenty in English for market purposes. Asi shouted six and then said nine, ten. Bola called out that after six came seven. And I should know, she sighed. Although now she was old and her womb and breasts were withered, there was a time when she bore children regularly every two years. Six times she had borne a boy child and six times they had died. Some had swollen up and with weak plaintive cries had faded away. Others had shuddered in sudden convulsions, with burning skins, and had rolled up their eyes and died. They had all died. Or rather he had died, Bola thought, because she knew it was one child all the time[1] whose spirit had crept up restlessly into her womb to be born and to mock her. The sixth time Musa, the village magician whom time had transformed into a respectable Muslim, had advised her and her husband to break the bones of the quiet little corpse and mangle it so that it couldn't come back to torment them alive again. But she held on to the child, and refused to let them handle it. Secretly she had marked it with a sharp pointed stick at the left buttock before it was wrapped in a mat and they had taken it away. When, the seventh time she had borne a son, and the purification ceremonies had taken place, she had turned it slyly to see whether the mark was there. It was. She showed it to the old woman who was the midwife and asked her what that was, and she had forced herself to believe the other who said it was an accidental scratch made whilst the child was being scrubbed with herbs to remove placental blood. But this child had stayed. Meji, he had been called. And he was now thirty years of age and a second-class clerk in Government offices in a town ninety miles away. Asi, his daughter, had been left with her to do the things an old woman wanted a small child for, to run and take messages to the neighbors, to fetch a cup of water from the earthenware pot in the kitchen, to sleep with her and be fondled.

She threw the washed and squeezed cassava leaves into the red boiling stew, putting in a finger's pinch of salt, and then went indoors, carefully stepping over the threshold to look for the dried red pepper. She found it, and then dropped it, leaning against the wall with a little cry. He turned round from the window and looked at her with a twisted half smile of love and sadness. In his short-sleeved, open-necked white shirt and gray gabardine trousers, a gold wrist watch and brown suede shoes, he looked like the pictures in African magazines of a handsome clerk who would get to the top because he ate the correct food, or regularly took the correct laxative, which was being advertised. His skin was grayish brown and he had a large red handkerchief tied round his neck.

"Meji, God be praised," Bola cried. "You gave me quite a turn. My heart is weak and I can no longer take surprises. When did you come? How did you come? By lorry,[2] by fishing boat? And how did you come into the house? The front door was locked. There are so many thieves nowadays. I'm so glad to see you, so glad," she mumbled and wept, leaning against his breast.

Meji's voice was hoarse, and he said: "I am glad to see you too, Mother," beating her back affectionately.

Asi ran in and cried "Papa, Papa," and was rewarded with a lift and a hug.

"Never mind how I came, Mother," Meji said, laughing, "I'm here, and that's all that matters."

---

1. **it was one child all the time . . . :** Among West African peoples, the belief exists of a spirit-child who does not live to maturity but returns to its mother's womb in a series of rebirths.

2. **lorry:** a truck.

"We must make a feast, we must have a big feast. I must tell the neighbors at once. Asi, run this very minute to Mr. Addai, the catechist, and tell him your papa is home. Then to Mami Gbera to ask her for extra provisions, and to Pa Babole for drummers and musicians. . . ."

"Stop," said Meji raising his hand. "This is all quite unnecessary. I don't want to see anyone, no one at all, I wish to rest quietly and completely. No one is to know I'm here."

Bola looked very crestfallen. She was proud of Meji, and wanted to show him off. The village would never forgive her for concealing such an important visitor. Meji must have sensed this because he held her shoulder comfortingly and said: "They will know soon enough. Let us enjoy each other, all three of us, this time. Life is too short."

Bola turned to Asi, picked up the packet of pepper and told her to go and drop a little into the boiling pot outside, taking care not to go too near the fire or play with it. After the child had gone, Bola said to her son, "Are you in trouble? Is it the police?"

He shook his head. "No," he said, "it's just that I like returning to you. There will always be this bond of love and affection between us, and I don't wish to share it. It is our private affair and that is why I've left my daughter with you," he ended up irrelevantly, "girls somehow seem to stay with relations longer."

"And don't I know it," said Bola. "But you look pale," she continued, "and you keep scraping your throat. Are you ill?" She laid her hand on his brow. "And you're cold, too."

"It's the cold wet wind," he said, a little harshly. "I'll go and rest now if you can open and dust my room for me. I'm feeling very tired. Very tired indeed. I've traveled very far today and it has not been as easy journey."

"Of course, my son, of course," Bola replied, bustling away hurriedly but happily.

Meji slept all afternoon till evening, and his mother brought his food to his room, later took the empty basins away. Then he slept again till morning.

The next day, Saturday, was a busy one, and after further promising Meji that she would tell no one he was about, Bola went off to market. Meji took Asi for a long walk through a deserted path and up into the hills. She was delighted. They climbed high until they could see the village below in front of them, and the sea in the distance, and the boats with their wide white sails. Soon the sun had passed its zenith and was half way towards the west. Asi had eaten all the food, the dried fish and the flat tapioca pancakes and the oranges. Her father said he wasn't hungry, and this had made the day perfect for Asi, who had chattered, eaten, and then played with her father's fountain pen and other things from his pocket. They soon left for home because he had promised they would be back before dark; he had carried her down some steep boulders and she had held on to his shoulders because he had said his neck hurt so and she must not touch it. She had said: "Papa, I can see behind you and you haven't got a shadow. Why?"

He had then turned her round to face the sun. Since she was getting drowsy, she had started asking questions, and her father had joked with her and humored her. "Papa, why has your watch stopped at twelve o'clock?" "Because the world ends at noon." Asi had chuckled at that. "Papa, why do you wear a scarf always round your neck?" "Because my head would fall off if I didn't." She had laughed out loud at that. But soon she had fallen asleep as he bore her homewards.

Just before nightfall, with his mother dressed in her best, they had all three, at her urgent request, gone to his father's grave, taking a secret route and avoiding the main village. It was a small cemetery, not more than twenty years or so old, started when the Rural Health Department had insisted that no more burials take place in the backyards of households. Bola took a bottle of wine and a glass and four split halves of kola, each a half sphere, two red and two white. They reached the graveside and she poured some wine into the glass. Then she spoke to the dead man softly and caressingly. She had brought his son to see him, she said. This son whom God had given success, to the confusion and discomfiture of their enemies. Here he was, a man with a pensionable clerk's job and not a farmer, fisherman or a mechanic. All the years of their married life people had said she was a witch because her children had died young. But this boy of theirs had shown that she was a good woman. Let her husband answer her now, to show that he was listening. She threw the four kola nuts up into the air and they fell on the grave. Three fell with the flat face upwards and one with its flat face downwards. She picked them up again and conversed with him once more and threw the kola nuts up again. But still there was an odd one or sometimes two.

They did not fall with all four faces up, or with all four faces down, to show that he was listening and was pleased. She spoke endearingly, she cajoled, she spoke sternly. But all to no avail. Then she asked Meji to perform. He crouched by the graveside and whispered. Then he threw the kola nuts and they rolled a little, Bola following them eagerly with her sharp old eyes. They all ended up face downwards. Meji emptied the glass of wine on the grave and then said that he felt nearer his father at that moment than he had ever done before in his life.

It was sundown, and they all three went back silently home in the short twilight. That night, going outside the house near her son's room window, she found, to her sick disappointment, that he had been throwing away all the cooked food out there. She did not mention this when she went to say goodnight, but she did sniff and say that there was a smell of decay in the room. Meji said he thought there was a dead rat up in the rafters, and he would clear it away after she had gone to bed.

That night it rained heavily, and sheet lightning turned the darkness into brief silver daylight, for one or two seconds at a time. Then the darkness again and the rain. Bola woke soon after midnight and thought she could hear knocking. She went to Meji's room to ask him to open the door, but he wasn't there. She thought he might have gone out for a while and been locked out by mistake. She opened the door quickly, holding an oil lamp upwards. He stood on the verandah, curiously unwet, and refused to come in.

"I have to go away," he said hoarsely, coughing.

"Do come in," she said.

"No," he said, "I have to go, but I wanted to thank you for giving me a chance."

"What nonsense is this?" she said. "Come in out of the rain."

"I did not think I should leave without thanking you."

The rain fell hard, the door creaked and the wind whistled.

"Life is sweet, Mother dear, good-bye, and thank you."

He turned round and started running.

There was a sudden diffuse flash of lightning and she saw that the yard was empty. She went back heavily, and fell into a restless sleep. Before she slept she said to herself that she must see Mr. Addai next morning, Sunday, or, better still, Monday, and tell him about this in case Meji was in trouble. She hoped Meji would not be annoyed. He was such a good son.

But it was Mr. Addai who came instead, on Sunday afternoon, quiet and grave, and saw Bola sitting on an old stool in the verandah, dressing Asi's hair in tight thin plaits.

Mr. Addai sat down and, looking away, he said: "The Lord giveth and the Lord taketh away." And soon half the village were sitting round the verandah and in the yard.

"But I tell you, he was here on Friday and left Sunday morning," Bola said. "He couldn't have died on Friday."

Bola had just recovered from a fainting fit after being told of her son's death in town. His wife, Asi's mother, had come with the news, bringing some of his property. She said Meji had died instantly at noon on Friday and had been buried on Saturday at sundown. They would have brought him to Kameni for the burial. He had always wished that. But they could not do so in time as bodies did not last much after a day.

"He was here, he was here," Bola said, rubbing her forehead and weeping.

Asi sat by quietly. Mr. Addai said comfortingly, "Hush, hush, he couldn't have been, because no one in the village saw him."

"He said we were to tell no one," Bola said.

The crowd smiled above Bola's head, and shook their heads. "Poor woman," someone said, "she is beside herself with grief."

"He died on Friday," Mrs. Meji repeated, crying. "He was in the office and he pulled up the window to look out and call the messenger. Then the sash broke. The window fell, broke his neck and the sharp edge almost cut his head off; they say he died at once."

"My papa had a scarf around his neck," Asi shouted suddenly.

"Hush," said the crowd.

Mrs. Meji dipped her hand into her bosom and produced a small gold locket and put it round Asi's neck, to quieten her. "Your papa had this made last week for your Christmas present. You may as well have it now."

Asi played with it and pulled it this way and that.

"Be careful, child," Mr. Addai said, "it was your father's last gift."

"I was trying to remember how he showed me yesterday to open it," Asi said.

"You have never seen it before," Mrs. Meji said, sharply, trembling with fear mingled with anger.

She took the locket and tried to open it.

"Let me have it," said the village goldsmith, and he tried whispering magic words of incantation. Then he said, defeated, "It must be poor-quality gold; it has rusted. I need tools to open it."

"I remember now," Asi said in the flat complacent voice of childhood.

The crowd gathered round quietly and the setting sun glinted on the soft red African gold of the dangling trinket. The goldsmith handed the locket over to Asi and asked in a loud whisper: "How did he open it?"

"Like so," Asi said and pressed a secret catch. It flew open and she spelled out gravely the word inside. "ASI"

The silence continued.

"His neck, poor boy," Bola said a little wildly, "that is why he could not eat the lovely meals I cooked for him."

Mr. Addai announced a service of intercession after vespers that evening. The crowd began to leave quietly.

Musa, the magician, was one of the last to leave. He was now very old and bent. In times of grave calamity, it was known that even Mr. Addai did not raise objection to Musa being consulted.

He bent over further and whispered in Bola's ear: "You should have had his bones broken and mangled thirty-one years ago when he went for the sixth time and then he would not have come back to mock you all these years by pretending to be alive. I told you so. But you women are naughty and stubborn."

Bola stood up, her black face held high, her eyes terrible with maternal rage and pride.

"I am glad I did not," she said, "and that is why he came back specially to thank me before he went for good."

She clutched Asi to her. "I am glad I gave him the opportunity to come back, for life is sweet. I do not expect you to understand why I did so. After all, you are only a man."

DISCUSSION QUESTIONS

1. When did you first suspect that Meji was dead? What details does the author use to suggest that there is something eerie about Meji's visit?

2. How is this story different from a typical "ghost story"? Consider the ghost's motivation for returning to life and the general impact the story makes on the reader.

3. Why did Bola mark her sixth baby with a pointed stick?

4. What is the significance of the last sentence in the passage below?

> Asi shouted six and then said nine, ten.
> Bola called out that after six came seven.
> And I should know, she sighed.

5. Only Musa, the village magician, shares with Bola the secret of her son Meji's death and reappearance, and yet he does not understand her. How would you characterize their different views of life?

SUGGESTION FOR WRITING

Imagine that you are an anthropologist collecting information on some of the customs and beliefs that prevail in the African village of Kameni. You have just conducted an interview with the widow Bola, who answered all of your questions patiently. Write a script of the conversation you just had.

GRACE A. OGOT

(born 1930)

Grace Ogot was born in the Central Nyanza district of Kenya. A member of the Luo tribe, Ogot attended a girls' elementary school and high school before training as a nurse both in Uganda and England. Ogot has worked as a nurse in Uganda and England, a scriptwriter and announcer for the British Broadcasting Corporation, a public relations officer for the Air India Corporation, and a delegate to the General Assembly of the United Nations. She is a founding member of the Writers' Association of Kenya and has served as its president. Ogot is known internationally primarily as a short-story writer. Her first published volume of short stories was *Land Without Thunder* (1968). A later collection, *The Island of Tears,* was published in 1980. In her writing, Ogot is faithful to the Luo tribal laws and wisdom. She believes it is her mission to pass along the folk tales of the Luo people to the younger generation. ■

THE RAIN CAME

The chief was still far from the gate when his daughter Oganda saw him. She ran to meet him. Breathlessly she asked her father, "What is the news, great Chief? Everyone in the village is anxiously waiting to hear when it will rain." Labong'o held out his hands for his daughter but he did not say a word. Puzzled by her father's cold attitude Oganda ran back to the village to warn the others that the chief was back.

The atmosphere in the village was tense and confused. Everyone moved aimlessly and fussed in the yard without actually doing any work. A young woman whispered to her co-wife, "If they have not solved this rain business today, the chief will crack." They had watched him getting thinner and thinner as the people kept on pestering him. "Our cattle lie dying in the fields," they reported. "Soon it will be our children and then ourselves. Tell us what to do to save our lives, oh great Chief." So the chief had daily pleaded with the Almighty through the ancestors to deliver them from their great distress.

Instead of calling the family together and giving them the news immediately, Labong'o went to his own hut, a sign that he was not to be disturbed. Having replaced the shutter, he sat in the dimly lit hut to contemplate.

It was no longer a question of being the chief of hunger-stricken people that weighed Labong'o's heart. It was the life of his only daughter that was at stake. At the time when Oganda came to meet him, he saw the glittering chain shining around her waist. The prophecy was complete. "It is Oganda, Oganda, my only daughter, who must die so young." Labong'o burst into tears before finishing the sentence. The chief must not weep. Society had declared him the bravest of men. But Labong'o did not care any more. He assumed the position of a simple father and wept bitterly. He loved his people, the Luo,[1] but what were the Luo for him without Oganda? Her life had brought a new life in Labong'o's world and he ruled better than he could remember. How would the spirit of the village survive his beautiful daughter? "There are so many homes and so many parents who have daughters. Why choose this one? She is all I have." Labong'o spoke as if the ancestors were there in the hut and he could see them face to face. Perhaps they were there, warning him to remember his promise on the day he was enthroned when he said aloud, before the elders, "I will lay down my life, if necessary, and the life of my household, to save this tribe from the hands of the enemy." "Deny! Deny!" he could hear the voice of his forefathers mocking him.

When Labong'o was made chief he was only a young man. Unlike his father he ruled for many years with only one wife. But people mocked him secretly because his only wife did not bear him a daughter. He married a second, a third and a fourth wife. But they all gave birth to male children. When Labong'o married a fifth wife, she bore him a daughter. They called her Oganda, meaning "beans," because her skin was very smooth. Out of Labong'o's twenty children, Oganda was the only girl. Though she was the chief's favorite, her mother's co-wives swallowed their jealous feelings and showered her with love. After all, they said, Oganda was a girl whose days in the royal family were numbered. She would soon marry at a tender age and leave the enviable position to someone else.

Never in his life had he been faced with such an impossible decision. Refusing to yield to the rain-maker's request would mean sacrificing the whole tribe, putting the interests of the individual above those of the society. More than that. It would mean disobeying the ancestors, and most probably wiping the Luo people from the surface of the earth. On the other hand, to let Oganda die as a ransom for the people would permanently cripple Labong'o spiritually. He knew he would never be the same chief again.

The words of Nditi, the medicine-man, still echoed in his ears. "Podho, the ancestor of the Luo, appeared to me in a dream last night and he asked me to speak to the chief and the people," Nditi had said to the gathering of tribesmen. "A young woman who has not known a man must die so that the country may have rain. While Podho was still talking to me, I saw a young woman standing at the lakeside, her hands raised above her head. Her skin was as a tender young deer's. Her tall slender figure stood like a lonely reed at the river bank. Her sleepy eyes wore a sad look like that of a bereaved mother. She wore a gold ring on her left ear and a glittering brass chain around her waist. As I still marvelled at the beauty of this young woman, Podho told me, 'Out of all the women in this land, we have chosen this one. Let her offer herself a sacrifice to the lake mon-

---

1. **the Luo:** an agricultural people living in the flat land around Lake Victoria in western Kenya.

ster! And on that day, the rain will come down in torrents. Let everyone stay at home on that day, lest he be carried away by the floods.' "

Outside there was a strange stillness, except for the thirsty birds that sang lazily on the dying trees. The blinding midday heat had forced the people into their huts. Not far away from the chief's hut two guards were snoring away quietly. Labong'o removed his crown and the large eagle-head that hung loosely on his shoulders. He left the hut and, instead of asking Nyabogo the messenger to beat the drum, he went straight and beat it himself. In no time the whole household had assembled under the *siala* tree where he usually addressed them. He told Oganda to wait a while in her grandmother's hut.

When Labong'o stood to address his household his voice was hoarse and tears choked him. He started to speak but words refused to leave his lips. His wives and sons knew there was danger, perhaps their enemies had declared war on them. Labong'o's eyes were red and they could see he had been weeping. At last he told them, "One whom we love and treasure will be taken away from us. Oganda is to die." Labong'o's voice was so faint that he could not hear it himself. But he continued, "The ancestors have chosen her to be offered as a sacrifice to the lake monster in order that we may have rain."

For a moment there was dead silence among the people. They were completely stunned; and as some confused murmur broke out Oganda's mother fainted and was carried off to her own hut. But the other people rejoiced. They danced around singing and chanting, "Oganda is the lucky one to die for the people; if it is to save the people, let Oganda go."

In her grandmother's hut Oganda wondered what the whole family was discussing about her that she could not hear. Her grandmother's hut was well away from the chief's court and much as she strained her ears, she could not hear what they were saying. "It must be marriage," she concluded. It was an accepted custom for the family to discuss their daughter's future marriage behind her back. A faint smile played on Oganda's lips as she thought of the several young men who swallowed saliva at the mere mention of her name.

There was Kech, the son of an elder in a neighboring clan. Kech was very handsome. He had sweet, meek eyes and roaring laughter. He could make a wonderful father, Oganda thought. But they would not be a good match. Kech was a bit too short to be her husband. It would humiliate her to have to look down at Kech each time she spoke to him. Then she thought of Dimo, the tall young man who had already distinguished himself as a brave warrior and an outstanding wrestler. Dimo loved Oganda, but Oganda thought he would make a cruel husband, always quarrelling and ready to fight. No, she did not like him. Oganda fingered the glittering chain on her waist as she thought of Osinda. A long time ago when she was quite young Osinda had given her that chain and, instead of wearing it around her neck several times, she wore it round her waist where it could permanently stay. She heard her heart pounding so loudly as she thought of him. She whispered, "Let it be you they are discussing, Osinda the lovely one. Come now and take me away. . . ."

The lean figure in the doorway startled Oganda who was rapt in thought about the man she loved. "You have frightened me, Grandma," said Oganda laughing. "Tell me, is it my marriage you were discussing? You can take it from me that I won't marry any of them." A smile played on her lips again. She was coaxing her grandma to tell her quickly, to tell her they were pleased with Osinda.

In the open space outside the excited relatives were dancing and singing. They were coming to the hut now, each carrying a gift to put at Oganda's feet. As their singing got nearer Oganda was able to hear what they were saying: "If it is to save the people, if it is to give us rain, let Oganda go. Let Oganda die for her people and for her ancestors." Was she mad to think that they were singing about her? How could she die? She found the lean figure of her grandmother barring the door. She could not get out. The look on her grandmother's face warned her that there was danger around the corner. "Mother, it is not marriage then?" Oganda asked urgently. She suddenly felt panicky, like a mouse cornered by a hungry cat. Forgetting that there was only one door in the hut, Oganda fought desperately to find another exit. She must fight for her life. But there was none.

She closed her eyes, leaped like a wild tiger through the door, knocking her grandmother flat to the ground. There outside in mourning garments Labong'o stood motionless, his hands folded at the back. He held his daughter's hand and led her away from the excited crowd to the little red-painted hut where her mother was resting. Here he broke the news officially to his daughter.

For a long time the three souls who loved one another dearly sat in darkness. It was no good speaking. And even if they tried, the words could not have come out. In the past they had been like three cooking-stones, sharing their burdens. Taking Oganda away from them would leave two useless stones which would not hold a cooking-pot.

News that the beautiful daughter of the chief was to be sacrificed to give the people rain spread across the country like wind. And at sunset the chief's village was full of relatives and friends who had come to congratulate Oganda. Many more were on their way, coming, carrying their gifts. They would dance till morning to keep her company. And in the morning they would prepare her a big farewell feast. All these relatives thought it a great honor to be selected by the spirits to die in order that the society might live. "Oganda's name will always remain a living name among us," they boasted.

Of course it was an honor, a great honor, for a woman's daughter to be chosen to die for the country. But what could the mother gain once her only daughter was blown away by the wind? There were so many other women in the land, why choose her daughter, her only child? Had human life any meaning at all?—other women had houses full of children while Oganda's mother had to lose her only child!

In the cloudless sky the moon shone brightly and the numerous stars glittered. The dancers of all age groups assembled to dance before Oganda, who sat close to her mother sobbing quietly. All these years she had been with her people she thought she understood them. But now she discovered that she was a stranger among them. If they really loved her as they had always professed, why were they not sympathetic? Why were they not making any attempt to save her? Did her people really understand what it felt like to die young? Unable to restrain her emotions any longer, she sobbed loudly as her age-group got up to dance.

They were young and beautiful and very soon they would marry and have their own children. They would have husbands to love and little huts for themselves. They would have reached maturity. Oganda touched the chain around her waist as she thought of Osinda. She wished Osinda were there too, among her friends. "Perhaps he is ill," she thought gravely. The chain comforted Oganda—she would die with it around her waist and wear it in the underground world.

In the morning a big feast of many different dishes was prepared for Oganda so that she could pick and choose. "People don't eat after death," they said. The food looked delicious but Oganda touched none of it. Let the happy people eat. She contented herself with sips of water from a little calabash.

The time for her departure was drawing near and each minute was precious. It was a day's journey to the lake. She was to walk all night, passing through the great forest. But nothing could touch her, not even the denizens of the forest. She was already anointed with sacred oil. From the time Oganda received the sad news she had expected Osinda to appear any moment. But he was not there. A relative told her that Osinda was away on a private visit. Oganda realized that she would never see her dear one again.

In the afternoon the whole village stood at the gate to say goodbye and to see her for the last time. Her mother wept on her neck for a long time. The great chief in a mourning skin came to the gate barefooted and mingled with the people—a simple father in grief. He took off his wrist bracelet and put it on his daughter's wrist, saying, "You will always live among us. The spirit of our forefathers is with you."

Tongue-tied and unbelieving Oganda stood there before the people. She had nothing to say. She looked at her home once more. She could hear her heart beating so painfully within her. All her childhood plans were coming to an end. She felt like a flower nipped in the bud never to enjoy the morning dew again. She looked at her weeping mother and whispered, "Whenever you want to see me, always look at the sunset. I will be there."

Oganda turned southwards to start her trek to the lake. Her parents, relatives, friends and admirers stood at the gate and watched her go. Her beautiful, slender figure grew smaller and smaller till she mingled with the thin dry trees in the forest.

As Oganda walked the lonely path that wound its way in the wilderness, she sang a song and her own voice kept her company.

"The ancestors have said Oganda must die;
The daughter of the chief must be sacrificed.
When the lake monster feeds on my flesh,
The people will have rain;
Yes, the rain will come down in torrents.
The wind will blow, the thunder will roar.
And the floods will wash away the sandy beaches
When the daughter of the chief dies in the lake.
My age-group has consented,
My parents have consented,
So have my friends and relatives;
Let Oganda die to give us rain.
My age-group are young and ripe,
Ripe for womanhood and motherhood;
But Oganda must die young,
Oganda must sleep with the ancestors.
Yes, rain will come down in torrents."

The red rays of the setting sun embraced Oganda and she looked like a burning candle in the wilderness.

The people who came to hear her sad song were touched by her beauty. But they all said the same thing: "If it is to save the people, if it is to give us rain, then be not afraid. Your name will forever live among us."

At midnight Oganda was tired and weary. She could walk no more. She sat under a big tree and, having sipped water from her calabash, she rested her head on the tree trunk and slept.

When she woke up in the morning the sun was high in the sky. After walking for many hours she reached the *tong,* a strip of land that separated the inhabited part of the country from the sacred place—*kar lamo.* No lay man could enter this place and come out alive—only those who had direct contact with the spirits and the Almighty were allowed to enter this holy of holies. But Oganda had to pass through this sacred land on her way to the lake, which she had to reach at sunset.

A large crowd gathered to see her for the last time. Her voice was now hoarse and painful but there was no need to worry any more. Soon she would not have to sing. The crowd looked at Oganda sympathetically, mumbling words she could not hear. But none of them pleaded for her life. As Oganda opened the gate a child, a young child, broke loose from the crowd and ran towards her. The child took a small ear-ring from her sweaty hands and gave it to Oganda, saying, "When you reach the world of the dead, give this ear-ring to my sister. She died last week. She forgot this ring." Oganda, taken aback by this strange request, took the little ring and handed her precious water and food to the child. She did not need them now. Oganda did not know whether to laugh or cry. She had heard mourners sending their love to their sweethearts, long dead, but this idea of sending gifts was new to her.

Oganda held her breath as she crossed the barrier to enter the sacred land. She looked appealingly at the crowd but there was no response. Their minds were too preoccupied with their own survival. Rain was the precious medicine they were longing for and the sooner Oganda could get to her destination the better.

A strange feeling possessed the princess as she picked her way in the sacred land. There were strange noises that often startled her and her first reaction was to take to her heels. But she remembered that she had to fulfill the wish of her people. She was exhausted, but the path was still winding. Then suddenly the path ended on sandy land. The water had retreated miles away from the shore, leaving a wide stretch of sand. Beyond this was the vast expanse of water.

Oganda felt afraid. She wanted to picture the size and shape of the monster, but fear would not let her. The people did not talk about it, nor did the crying children who were silenced at the mention of its name. The sun was still up but it was no longer hot. For a long time Oganda walked ankle-deep in the sand. She was exhausted and longed desperately for her calabash of water. As she moved on she had a strange feeling that something was following her. Was it the monster? Her hair stood erect and a cold paralyzing feeling ran along her spine. She looked behind, sideways and in front, but there was nothing except a cloud of dust.

Oganda began to hurry but the feeling did not leave her and her whole body seemed to be bathing in its perspiration.

The sun was going down fast and the lake shore seemed to move along with it.

Oganda started to run. She must be at the lake before sunset. As she ran she heard a noise coming from behind. She looked back sharply and something resembling a moving bush was frantically running after her. It was about to catch up with her.

Oganda ran with all her strength. She was now determined to throw herself into the water even before sunset. She did not look back but the creature was upon her. She made an effort to cry out, as in a nightmare, but she could not hear her own voice. The creature caught up with Oganda. A strong hand grabbed her. But she fell flat on the sand and fainted.

When the lake breeze brought her back to consciousness a man was bending over her. "O . . . !" Oganda opened her mouth to speak, but she had lost her voice. She swallowed a mouthful of water poured into her mouth by the stranger.

"Osinda, Osinda! Please let me die. Let me run, the sun is going down. Let me die. Let them have rain."

Osinda fondled the glittering chain around Oganda's waist and wiped tears from her face. "We must escape quickly to an unknown land," Osinda said urgently. "We must run away from the wrath of the ancestors and the retaliation of the monster."

"But the curse is upon me, Osinda, I am no good for you any more. And moreover the eyes of the ancestors will follow us everywhere and bad luck will befall us. Nor can we escape from the monster."

Oganda broke loose, afraid to escape, but Osinda grabbed her hands again. "Listen to me, Oganda! Listen! Here are two coats!" He then covered the whole of Oganda's body, except her eyes with a leafy attire made from the twigs of *bwombwe*. "These will protect us from the eyes of the ancestors and the wrath of the monster. Now let us run out of here." He held Oganda's hand and they ran from the sacred land, avoiding the path that Oganda had followed.

The bush was thick and the long grass entangled their feet as they ran. Halfway through the sacred land they stopped and looked back. The sun was almost touching the surface of the water. They were frightened. They continued to run, now faster to avoid the sinking sun.

"Have faith, Oganda—that thing will not reach us."

When they reached the barrier and looked behind them, trembling, only a tip of the sun could be seen above the water's surface.

"It is gone! It is gone!" Oganda wept, hiding her face in her hands.

"Weep not, the daughter of the chief. Let us run, let us escape."

There was a lightning flash in the distance. They looked up, frightened. That night it rained in torrents as it had not done for a long, long time.

DISCUSSION QUESTIONS

1. It is commonly thought that in traditional societies rulers desired sons that would succeed them. Labong'o in this story was mocked because he had no daughter. What does this imply about the position of women in this tribal community? Offer reasons why you think this might be so.

2. To *foreshadow* an event is to show or indicate that event before it happens. Foreshadowing is a common literary device used by authors to give readers a hint of what will happen later in a story. In what way is Osinda's attempted rescue of Oganda foreshadowed early in this story?

3. Find evidence in this story to indicate that it is important that the wishes of the ancestors be granted by the tribal community. For additional help in answering this question recall what you learned about tribal beliefs in Peter Abrahams's essay "The Blacks" and Birago Diop's poem "Forefathers."

4. When the villagers dance for Oganda to keep her company during her night vigil, she wonders to herself why they are not sympathetic, why they don't try to save her. What reason is given in the story for their rejoicing? What additional reason can you think of that might make them feel happy (or relieved)?

5. Do Oganda and Osinda escape at the end of the story? Does the fact that it rains indicate that they do not escape? Has the author made it clear what happens to them one way or another? Defend your opinion with evidence from the end of the story.

SUGGESTION FOR WRITING

Reconsider Discussion Question 5 and think about the comments it provoked during class discussion of this story. How would you change the ending to make it absolutely clear what happens to Oganda and Osinda? Write your own new ending to this story in which you make it clear either that they escape or that they die. If you decide that they escape, explain how they do so and predict what becomes of them. If you decide that they die, explain how they are thwarted from escaping and identify the agent of their death.

LENRIE PETERS
(born 1932)

Lenrie Peters is a poet, novelist, and doctor. He was born in Bathurst, Gambia, and as a young man lived for a while in Sierra Leone, his parents' native home. He studied medicine at Cambridge University in England, and during this time served as president of the African Students Union. After receiving his degree, Dr. Peters first worked at a hospital in Northampton, England, and then returned to Gambia where he opened a private practice. His first book, *Poems,* was published in 1964. A later volume, *Selected Poetry* (1981), includes poems from earlier editions as well as new material. In his poetry, Dr. Peters concentrates on issues concerning the entire continent of Africa rather than issues related specifically to his own country. Despite a sense of estrangement that pervades some of his poetry, he voices a strong spirit of self-respect and personal dignity. ■

HOMECOMING

The present reigned supreme
    Like the shallow floods over the gutters
Over the raw paths where we had been,
    The house with the shutters.

5   Too strange the sudden change
    Of the times we buried when we left
The times before we had properly arranged
    The memoirs that we kept.

Our sapless roots have fed
10   The wind-swept seedlings of another age.
Luxuriant weeds have grown where we led
    The Virgins to the water's edge.

There at the edge of the town
    Just by the burial ground
15   Stands the house without a shadow
    Lived in by new skeletons.

That is all that is left
    To greet us on the homecoming
After we have paced the world
20   And longed for returning.

PARACHUTE

Parachute men say
The first jump
Takes the breath away;
Feet in the air disturbs
5   Till you get used to it.

Solid ground
Is now where you left it.
As you plunge down
—Perhaps head first—
10 As you listen to
Your arteries talking,
You learn to sustain hope.

Suddenly you are only
Holding an open umbrella
15 In a windy place.
As the warm earth
Reaches out to you,
Reassures you
The vibrating interim is over,

20 You try to land
Where green grass yields,
And carry your pack
Across the fields.

The violent arrival
25 Puts out the joint.
Earth has nowhere to go:
You are at the starting point;

Jumping across worlds
In condensed time—
30 After the awkward fall,
We are always at the starting point.

DISCUSSION QUESTIONS

1. In the last stanza of the poem "Homecoming" the speaker indicates
that he—and perhaps someone else as well—has been away from
home (paced the world) for some time. Who might that person be?

2. According to the first four stanzas, what is left of the speaker's home upon his return?

3. The first five stanzas of the poem "Parachute" describe the experience of parachuting to the ground. What concluding point does the speaker make in the fifth stanza about parachuting?

4. In the last stanza, stanza six, the speaker changes his focus to something other than parachuting. What point does he make in this stanza?

SUGGESTION FOR WRITING

The first three stanzas of the poem "Homecoming" are four-line stanzas in which lines 1 and 3 rhyme and lines 2 and 4 rhyme. Try your hand at writing a poem with a similar structure. You may make your poem as many stanzas as you like but try for at least two stanzas. Each stanza should contain four lines with alternating lines rhyming. Choose any subject you wish for your poem, or write about home as Lenrie Peters does in "Homecoming."

RICHARD RIVE

(1931–1989)

Born in the slum quarter of Cape Town, South Africa, Richard Rive attended local schools until high school, at which time he won a municipal scholarship. Rive began writing short stories while still a student. He graduated from the University of Cape Town in 1949. Rive early discovered the fascination of Shakespeare and Dickens, and on it built himself a secure reputation in Africa and abroad as a teacher and writer. Though he believed in the importance of European writers, he also believed that South African students needed something more immediate to their own experiences. However, he disagreed with those African writers—particularly writers of the Negritude movement (see page xvii)—who argued that true African literature must embrace the primitive tribal tradition. "I cannot recognize palm-fronds and nights filled with the throb of the primitive," he said. "I am buses, trains, and taxis. I am prejudice, bigotry, and discrimination. I am urban South Africa." In 1962 Rive traveled throughout Africa and Europe studying current literary trends. In 1965 he attended Columbia University in New York, and in 1971 he attended Oxford University in England. Among his works are *African Songs* (1963), a collection of short stories; *Emergency* (1964), a novel; *Selected Writings* (1977), a collection of essays, stories, and plays; and *Writing Black* (1981), an autobiography. In his short stories, Rive's subject matter was slum life, protest, racial prejudice, and color snobbery. He made his home in South Africa and never considered exile, even though his own work was banned in his country. He died in 1989. ∎

AFRICAN SONG

Muti knew when he felt angry. There would be something hard in his throat, and he would clench the hands tightly so that the veins stood out. But this time he knew that he was not angry but afraid. His mouth felt dry and there was a clamminess in the palms of his hands. Somehow Muti could feel, or rather sense that they were going to meet the Police. Yet when the blue uniforms entered the dilapidated meeting-place he was as surprised as if he had not expected them. He stared as if bewitched as they marched in and covered all entrances. And Muti knew it was not an anger he felt but a deep fear which he could not understand. He was far more afraid of the blue uniforms and glistening buttons than of the fact that he had no pass.[1] There were useless regrets now that he had come to the

---

1. **no pass:** Under South Africa's apartheid system, blacks were forced to carry an identification card, or "pass," and produce it on demand or else be subject to arrest.

meeting, useless regrets that he had not first learned the ways of the Big City and got a pass. He only felt a numbness and a terror. His tongue felt enormous and his mouth felt dry. Muti eyed Mpisa and noticed how calmly he took it. But his uncle had a pass and Muti had none. Muti could almost feel Mpisa imploring him to keep calm. But how could one keep calm when there were Policemen at the door, and Policemen at the window. Some his own color and some who were white?

And then everyone was standing and Muti watched fascinatedly as the people sang; but still he sat because he had no pass. And what Muti knew must happen was happening because the blue uniforms were coming nearer, as this one shuffled in his pocket for a pass; and that one had terror in his eyes because he knew he had not one; and still another was calm like Mpisa. And still the people sang. And Muti felt a great calm come over him like a warrior feels before battle, and he clambered clumsily to his feet.

And already this one was led away because he had no pass and that one lifted the hand in protest. But one must not lift the hand in protest. And still the people sang. And Muti was filled with the wonder of it all and was not afraid of the prison walls and the blue uniforms. And then in a hoarse voice Muti also began singing the song of Africa, and not one Muti sang but a hundred Mutis, ten thousand Mutis, and they all sang the song that was Africa.

And as they sang there was a deep calm.

> *And this is what they sang.*
> *Nkosi Sikelel' Afrika* . . . . .

which means God bless Africa. God bless the sun-scorched Karoo[2] and the green of the Valley of a Thousand Hills. God bless the mountain streams that chatter impudently when they are high in the hills and are young, but roll lazily from side to side like old women in the Great Plains. And the dry pans which twist their tortured bosoms to the hot skies. And the mighty waters that hurl themselves against her shores and mockingly retreat only to come again with a new energy as if to engulf the mielies[3] and the land and the villages and the towns, even great Africa itself. God bless the cataracts that taunt the solemn rocks, and the African sky that spits blood in the evening. And the timeless hills where the shy roebuck rears its tragic eyes and the dassie[4] sips in silent pools. And the blue krantzes[5] where man has still to breathe. God bless this Africa of heat and

---

2. **Karoo:** A karoo is a dry tableland. The Great Karoo is a plateau three or four thousand feet high, in the southern part of the Cape province in South Africa.

3. **mielies** (mē´ lēs): corn. [Afrikaans]

4. **the dassie:** an African rabbit.

5. **krantzes:** cliffs.

cold, and laughter and tears, and deep joy and bitter sorrow. God bless this Africa of blue skies and brown veld,[6] and black and white and love and hatred, and friend and enemy.

For where there was rich laughter there is now sorrow and indifference. And where the eyes were shot with joy for the richness of the soil, there is now a gloom, for the mielies are no longer thick on the stalk. And before the milk lapped the sides of the calabashes, but now they are dry and the milk does not spill over the sides. And even those in the Great Cities who had laughter in their eyes and remembered their ancestors, and the land and the people, now speak in whispers and no longer remember their ancestors, and the land and the people. For now the land is without joy.

There is a heavy mist over all the land, and the mist is thick so that the eye can hardly see through, but where it does lift, one can see sorrow and weariness which only Africa can understand. For the ancient koppies[7] are weary, and the veld is no longer gay, and the people are tired, and the mielies bend their heads and weep.

God bless this Africa, this Africa which is part of us. God protect this Africa. God have mercy upon Africa.

> *And still they sang.*
> *Maluphakonyisw' Upshondo Lwayo . . . . .*

which is lift up our descendants. And Muti thought of himself and wondered if he were a better man than his father, and his father's father and the many before him. For he felt like the Great Bird that flies higher and higher till it is a brother to the sun and can see the land even before the White man came. And then Muti climbed higher like the Bird and saw the land even before the White man came.

But Muti did not understand. Where were the cities and the towns and the villages? And the buildings and the shops? And where were the ones who lived in the cities and the towns? And the White ones and the Black ones? For Muti saw nothing but the burning veld and the flat koppies and the hardy renosterbos.[8] And when he searched even further for his own people, he found them at last, and then his heart burst with pride. For he saw proud warriors with plumes of ostrich feathers, and shaking armlets which clicked as they raised the hands. And these warriors were huge ones and proud, and lifted high the legs and stamped upon the earth so that the ground shook. For they danced the dance of the young men and it was a vigorous dance and required much strength. And they were fearsome to behold.

---

6. veld: a grassland with scattered trees.

7. koppies: hills.

8. renosterbos: the rhinoceros bush, a small South African shrub, thought to be a favorite food of the rhinoceros.

And Muti also saw the small ones that hide in the sand and the bushes. But these one must not look upon for they hunt the crab and the shell-fish and eat the flesh of the dassie. And Muti felt no man should look upon them and so he turned away his head as if he did not see, and gazed upon the warriors. And he heard them roar out, "He is one who sees everything. No he is a lion for he hunts alone and kills many!" And that is what Muti heard them shout and it pleased him.

And then like the Great Bird, Muti saw the workers in the field, and the huts and the women threading the beads. And the beads were of many colors like the stones which the sun splits, red and yellow and orange. And Muti admired their hair which was stiff with the clay of the river, and he saw they were buxom and pleasant to behold. And there were cows and fat-tailed sheep. And there was much beer and much laughter and plenty to eat.

But Muti also saw the days that were lean, when the gourds were empty and the animals panted heavily. And then there was much throwing of bones and this one was sacrificed and that maiden must spill her blood for the gods were angry.

And Muti was filled with a shame lest those warriors should see him. And he wanted to hide his face lest the tillers of the soil might see him, or the crab-hunters laugh derisively. What if they saw how frightened he was because he had no pass. But they could not feel frightened because they did not know the ways of the White Ones. And then Muti did not feel so ashamed.

> *And still the people sang.*
> *Yiwa Nemithandazo yayo nyi Sikelele . . . . .*

And this means hear our prayers and bless them. And now Muti again saw the look on the face of the Old-one and felt the sadness in her heart. And like one in a dream he saw from afar and heard from afar.

"I am going away, my Mother."

And she had said nothing but only stared at him with ageless eyes.

"I have decided to go away, my Mother."

And she had stared and said nothing.

"I will find work and make much money, for there is not much money in the soil. And when I find work I will have much money in my hands so that you will laugh, my Mother. And then," and he had winked slyly, "then there will be a wife."

And then she had sighed as if from a great distance and said,

"It is well."

But he felt it was not well and he wanted her to ask why it was not well, why he left the land of the fathers, and the fields and the cow, but she only said,

"It is well."

"But I shall not go to Johannesburg, my Mother, for that place is not good. I shall go to some other place." And she said,

"I have a brother in Cape Town, he will be good to you."

And then he said,

"It is good, I will not go to Johannesburg." For he was filled with a great anger and said aloud, "And am I a mole that I must climb into the ground and dig the earth?"

But she said,

"No you are not a mole, you are a man."

And then he laughed and slapped his thighs and was pleased that she had said that, and he said,

"Ho, Mother, you are indeed a good one."

But when he went for the pass he was not a man for the White one in the office was angry and his face was red so that one could count the wrinkles. And at first Muti felt that the White man was angry because he was leaving the land of his fathers, and the fields and the cow. But when the White man asked him to go to the Great City, Muti did not want to, for there one becomes a mole.

But there are ways to get a pass if one has money, and so Muti sold the cow, and then Muti came to Cape Town.

Ho but this is a beautiful place, and the Great Water is bigger than many dams. And there are people who travel far on the Great Waters. And if one works well and has a pass one can also go on the Great Water to the land of the White ones. And there is a big mountain that is flat like a Karoo koppie but higher than many kraals.[9]

And Muti remembered the bull-necked White man and was afraid because he still had no pass. But there are ways to get a pass if one has money, and at the meeting would be his own people, and Mpisa would be there who knew the ways of the City and could speak the language of the White ones.

But Mpisa told him to be careful until he had a pass, especially of those in the blue uniforms, and that was why there was a clamminess in his throat when they entered the meeting.

And still the people sang.
Yiza Moya, Yiza Moya, Oyingcwele . . . . .

And still Muti sang these words which mean forward spirit, forward spirit which art holy. And as he sang he felt as if he could burst with pride and love. For he felt proud of this Africa, but his pride was tinged with a shame, and his love was not a true love. And as he sang he had a wonderful vision of the Africa of years hence, maybe ten years, maybe a hundred, though his vision was of two kinds, and this was the first vision.

He saw the face of a Black man and the face was grinning so that he could count the teeth. And the Black man was laughing in the face of another and this other man was a White man. But there was no malice in

---

9. kraals (kräls): native villages.

the laughter and the White one nodded and grinned back. And there was much merriment and slapping of backs. And then the vision changed to the Great Cities. And there were houses of plenty and shops laden with the produce of the earth, and there were many people passing up and down without any fear in their faces. And Muti almost laughed for the wonder of it when he saw how they did the work that men and women always do, only this time black men and women were also doing such work, and white men and women also, and brown men and women. And they ate and drank and cooked the foods and made merry, and everyone was full of laughter, and Muti himself laughed with the sheer wonder of it that the black and the white and the brown could so laugh together.

And then Muti saw the fields, and the maize was thick and the grapes hung in clusters on the vine, and there stood a black man with a hoe in his hand straightening his back, and he spoke to a white man, who lifted his work-soiled hands to scan the horizon. And there was much more than laughter, an understanding of the soul, of the land. And this was the first vision.

But there was a second vision. And now Muti saw a black face that was filled with smoldering anger, and there were tiny wrinkles around the eyes and mouth which were not good. And this time the mouth was clenched tightly and one could not count the teeth. For this time it looked into a white face that turned away. And then Muti had a vision of the Great Cities. But this cannot be, for everywhere there were black faces, and the policemen were black, and the people were black, and the one who takes your money was black, and the women who were hurrying, and the men. But where were the others? The white ones and the brown ones? And Muti was filled with a great disbelief. And a great sorrow overcame him when he saw that they were hardly there, but the few who remained were doing the things that black men used to do. And on the land there were no white ones, and in the Great Cities there were no white ones, and Muti was still filled with the disbelief.

And this was the second vision of Muti.

Nkosi Sikelele Thina Lusapho Lwakho . . . . .

And still the people sang these words which mean God bless us Thy children. God bless the children of Africa, for Africa is old but still a child; for she is old in sorrow and suffering but young in laughter and merriment. For the world does not understand Africa, even as a mother that flings the child from her breast. And the land suffers, and the people suffer and the children. God bless the children of Africa whose eyes are not so bright and in whose voices there is not much laughter, for the children are part of Africa, the children are Africa.

Go and see the child in the fields where the maize bends its head. Can you not see that the eye is dimmer and the mouth that of an old man? Can you not see that the soul is wizened and that the laughter is full of sad meaning? For Africa is old in its youth, and grey in its childhood. For even the baby is old in suffering and knows when the breast is dry and the calabash is empty, and the dust is thick on the bed of the river. And the father grunts and turns away the head. And the children have seen the tears in the eyes of the mother and they have also wept silently although they still do not understand. And these are the children of Africa, who are old men and women, but laugh with the voice of youth.

God bless the children in the Great Cities, for they have no beards but are as men. And there is sadness in Africa for the children who no longer play in the streams but follow the ways of the Great Cities. And the laughter of the veld is lost in the sorrow of the towns, and the little ones swagger and laugh insolently. And there is a knife in the hand and hatred in the eye, and mistrust, for the ways of the Great Cities are not good.

God bless us Thy children, make us also ageless but make us part of Africa. God bless our descendants who will be the people of Africa. God bless the cities, and the towns, and the villages. God make us to see a great light so that the ways of man may become better ways. God bless the people and the children, and the veld, and the koppies and the krantzes. God bless Africa.

And still the people sang and the blue uniforms came nearer and Muti knew that he had no pass. But still as they sang Muti's face was lit up with a great light.

God Bless Africa . . . . .
And another man who had no pass was led silently away.
Maluphakonyisw' Upshondo Lwayo . . . . .
And Muti felt as if he could burst with all the pride and love.
Hear our prayers and bless them . . . . .
And still the uniforms came nearer and the brass buttons glowed as the lamps caught them.
Yiza Moya, Yiza Moya, Oyingcwele . . . . .
Forward spirit, Forward spirit, which art holy.
Nkosi Sikelele . . . . .
And Muti could hardly contain himself for the love he felt for his people.
Thina Lusapho Lwakho . . . . .
God bless us Thy children, with a hoarse voice and a body that trembled all over. And then, as the blue uniforms stood before him, the last triumphant note.
Nkosi Sikelel' Afrika!

DISCUSSION QUESTIONS

1. The story line of "African Song" is slight. However, note the title. Might it explain a purpose other than simply relating a story? Explain.

2. Muti recounts two visions of the future he has while he is singing. Explain each vision he has.

3. Although this story may be slight, it does contain the one essential ingredient of all plot—conflict. What is the immediate conflict in this story? How does Rive build the tension and drama of this conflict as the story approaches its end?

SUGGESTION FOR WRITING

Do you have a favorite song, one that makes you feel good, that inspires you? What is it about that song that inspires you? Is it the words? the melody? Choose a favorite song, one that is special to you, and write a short essay about it. In your essay describe the ideas that are expressed in the song and explain what it is about the song that makes you feel good.

NO ROOM AT SOLITAIRE

Now Fanie van der Merwe[1] had every right to be annoyed. Here he stood, owner of the only hotel in Solitaire, wiping glasses in an empty bar on Christmas Eve. The owner of the only canteen till Donkergat, and facing empty tables and chairs. Well, not quite empty, because old Dawie Volkwyn[2] sat sullen and morose at the counter. But then Dawie Volkwyn always sat sullen and morose at the counter. Fanie couldn't remember when Dawie had not sat on the very same stool opposite the kitchen door. To have the only canteen for miles around empty on Christmas Eve.

It was obviously done for spite. Oom Sarel[3] always did things for spite. Take the case of Marietjie Louw[4] when she went out with Dawie. His argument with Fanie had started with politics. Oom Sarel had sat at the counter, the way he always sat, holding forth on every subject. God's gift to South African politics, Fanie had mumbled under his breath. Fanie had kept calm until Oom Sarel had said that Kaffirs[5] could not be educated beyond Std. II.[6] Fanie had been annoyed, very annoyed, and had quoted the case of Witbooi's[7] cousin. Now Witbooi's cousin had reached Std. VI

---

1. Fanie van der Merwe (fä′ nē vän dir mir′ və).

2. Dawie Volkwyn (dä′ ve vülk′ van).

3. Oom Sarel (üm sä′ rel). The word *Oom* means "uncle" and is loosely applied to any older man.

4. Marietjie Louw (mä′ rē kē lōv).

5. Kaffirs: black South Africans, a term of abuse.

6. Std. II: Standard II is roughly equivalent to the fourth grade in American schools, Standard VI to the eighth grade.

7. Witbooi (vit′ bü ē).

at a school in Cape Town. Oom Sarel had insisted that it was unheard of, and if it were so it was deliberately done by the missionaries or the English or something like that. Fanie had added that Witbooi's cousin could read and write in Afrikaans[8] even better than some of the white bywoners.[9] Oom Sarel had become very red about the neck and had said he would not drink in a bar owned by a Communist. Then he had walked out. Now many had walked out before, but Oom Sarel was different. He owned Bo-Plaas, the richest maize farm in the District, and had already been to Johannesburg twice and sometimes visited Hermanus in the Cape for his holidays.

So it was obviously done for spite. Otherwise why should Oom Sarel have a Christmas Eve braaivleis[10] and invite everyone in Solitaire except Fanie van der Merwe and, well, and Dawie Volkwyn? The free boere-wors[11] and brandy were given to lure away all his customers. Louw Viljoen and Daantjie Pretorius and Jan Mostert and them. Fanie would have loved to be there. He would have closed the bar and given Witbooi the evening off. But then, he had been pointedly ignored.

So now he halfheartedly wiped glasses on Christmas Eve and surveyed the deserted canteen. Only Dawie. But then no one ever invited Dawie anywhere. Though in spite of his drinking and bad reputation with women, Dawie Volkwyn knew life. And when he had had sufficient brandy, he would belch, lean back comfortably, narrow his eyes, and hold forth on religion, politics, the English, why the world was going to the dogs, and Marietjie Louw. He was certain that Marietjie was a little more than interested in him, but her father thought Dawie too old at fifty. Marietjie herself must be well over forty, and there was no prospect of a husband in sight.

"Ja,[12] Dawie," said Fanie sitting opposite him, "so goes the world." Dawie made no reply, so Fanie opened a bottle of brandy and filled two glasses. They drank in silence, each occupied with his own thoughts.

Fanie filled again. "It is hard when there is no business."

Another long silence, while they sipped their brandy. After the third glass Dawie replied.

"I hear Oom Sarel slaughtered two oxen."

"Ja."

"And three lambs, and fowls and geese."

"*Ja.*"

"And Oom Sarel bought all the wine and brandy from Cohen in Donkergat."

---

8. **Afrikaans:** the Dutch dialect spoken in South Africa.

9. **bywoners** (bā vô′ nirs): sharecroppers. [Africaans]

10. **braaivleis** (brīv′ lās): a barbecue. [Africaans]

11. **boerewors** (bür′ vürs): a type of sausage. [Africaans]

12. **Ja** (yä): yes.

"*Ja*," repeated Fanie fatalistically. He began to have serious doubts about the ability of Witbooi's cousin to read and write in Afrikaans. He would have to ask his kitchen boy. Witbooi's cousin was beginning to mess up his business.

"I never could have thought my bar would be empty on Christmas Eve."

"So goes the world."

Fanie poured Dawie another drink.

"Well here's to Christmas. *Veels geluk.*"[13]

"*Veels geluk.*"

"A long time ago in Bethlehem."

"Ja," said Dawie, looking far back in time, far beyond his fifty years. "It was a long time ago."

"But He will return."

"It says so in the Book."

"*Ja.*"

"In Revelations."

"He will come in all His glory."

"And the trumpets shall sound."

"But I've been thinking, Fanie."

"*Ja?*"

"When He first came they didn't know Him."

"So?"

"It stands so in the Book."

"I know."

"How will we know Him when He comes again?"

"You are speaking dangerous things."

"What if He is not a White man?"

"He is a White man!"

"I know," Dawie said weakly.

They slipped back into silence and Fanie automatically refilled the glasses.

"How will we recognize Him?"

"There will be signs, Dawie."

"Like what?"

"It stands in the Book."

Fanie hoped that Louw Viljoen, Jan Mostert, and Daantjie Pretorius would still come in for a quick one, even if Oom Sarel's wine was free. So he bought it from Cohen in Donkergat. Sheer spite.

"Fanie, I'm not a religious man."

"I know, Dawie."

"I'm not a church-going man."

"I know."

"But I like to ask questions."

"*Ja.*"

---

13. **Veels geluk** (vels ge' lük): congratulations.

"How will we know Him when He comes again?"

"It stands in the Book."

"What does it say?"

"You must read it in the Book."

"I'm not a reading man."

"Ja." Fanie felt that the conversation was leading nowhere, and decided to revert to the subject of Witbooi's cousin. "Do you believe Kaffirs can read?"

"I don't know, Fanie."

"If they went to school in Cape Town?"

"Maybe."

"That's what I told Oom Sarel."

"And so?"

"Called me a kaffir-boetie."[14]

"Wragtig."[15]

"And a Communist."

"That is bad."

"So I told him about Witbooi's cousin."

"Ja?"

"You know him?"

"No."

"He passed Std. VI."

"That can be."

"Then Oom Sarel walked out on me."

Both men moodily sipped at their glasses. Dawie wondered whether Marietjie Louw was also at Bo-Plaas and if she was thinking of him. Fanie hoped Louw Viljoen and Daantjie Pretorius would drop in after the braaivleis. After all he liked Louw.

"Baas."[16]

Louw was argumentative, but one could get on with him.

"Baas!"

"Ja, Witbooi?"

"There is a man with a woman outside who want to see the baas."

"Tell them to come in."

"Baas, they are from my people."

"Tell them to go to hell." He turned back to Dawie. "Kaffirs are becoming more and more cheeky."

"That is true."

"A lazy bunch of good-for-nothings."

"I agree with you."

"But that doesn't mean some can't read and write."

"True."

---

14. **kaffir-boetie** (käf´ ər bü´tē): a white person who is sympathetic to blacks.

15. **Wragtig** (räg´ tē): truly.

16. **Baas** (bäs): master.

"In Afrikaans."

"That is so."

"Take Witbooi's cousin."

"Ja. Witbooi's cousin."

The kitchen boy reappeared, greatly agitated.

"Baas, the man say it is serious."

"Chase them away."

"I tried to, baas."

"Tell them I'll come with my shotgun."

"It's no use, baas."

"Get rid of them."

"I try again, baas."

Fanie removed a fresh bottle of brandy from the shelf and removed the tinsel expertly with his teeth. He twisted the corkscrew in and pulled. He refilled the two glasses, feeling much better, even jovial.

"Now take Witbooi's cousin."

"Ja."

"Now there's a clever Kaffir."

"Must be."

"He works in an office in Cape Town."

"Ja?"

"Writes letters for his boss."

"Wragtig!"

"And at the end of the month he sends out accounts."

"Some of these people can do it."

"But Oom Sarel can't understand."

"Oom Sarel is difficult."

Witbooi tapped Fanie lightly on the sleeve.

"Please, baas, come and see."

"What?"

"The man and woman at the back door."

"Didn't you chase them away?"

"I can't, baas."

"Verdomp!¹⁷ Bring my shotgun!"

"Ja, baas."

"Kom, Dawie, let's get rid of them."

Dawie was reluctant to shift from the half-full bottle of brandy, but had to be careful not to annoy Fanie. He climbed unsteadily to his feet and swayed behind the hotelkeeper through the canteen and kitchen.

In the doorway stood a bearded man of an indefinite age, holding a donkey by a loose rein. A black woman sat groaning on the stoep.¹⁸

"Ja?" said Fanie.

"My wife, she is sick."

"So what is wrong?"

---

17. **Verdomp** (vir dômp´): damn! [Africaans]

18. **Stoep** (stüp): a veranda. [Africaans]

"She is sick, baas."

"But what is the matter?"

"She is going to have a child."

"I am not a verdomde[19] midwife."

"I look for a doctor, baas."

"Yes?"

"There is no one in the dorp."[20]

"So what can I do?"

"They all at Bô-Plaas, baas."

"So?"

"I need help, baas, my wife is sick."

"Go to Bo-Plaas."

"She is sick, baas."

"Come on, get away."

"Please, baas."

"Voertsek!"[21] Fanie turned on his heels, followed by Dawie. They set-tled down to their disturbed drink.

"As if I'm a verdomde midwife."

"Kaffirs are getting more cheeky."

"They come to me of all people."

"Wragtig."

"I run a hotel, I don't deliver babies."

"That's the worst of these people."

Suddenly Fanie's eyes gleamed with a sadistic delight. "I hope they go to Bo-Plaas."

"Ja."

"That would put Oom Sarel in his place."

"That would."

"And the woman must give birth right there."

"Ja, that would be very funny."

"Please, my baas."

Fanie turned around, annoyed at Witbooi.

"They're still here, baas."

"Huh?"

"They won't go away."

"Chase them."

"They want a place to rest."

"There's no room."

"In one of the shelters, baas."

"There's no place."

"The woman is very sick."

Fanie downed his brandy at one gulp and then drank two more in

---

19. **verdomde** (vir dôm′ də): damned. [Africaans]

20. **dorp** (dôrp): town. [Africaans]

21. **Voertsek!** (vùrt′ sek): get away, a term of abuse. [Africaans]

quick succession. "There's no room!" he repeated, then stared, amazed, at Dawie, who had begun to laugh hysterically in a high-pitched giggle.

"And what do you find so funny?"

"There's no room," Dawie repeated, "no room in the inn."

"And so?"

"Can't you see, man?"

"No."

"It's Christmas Eve."

"Allewereld!"[22]

"The Kaffir had a donkey."

"Ja, ja!" Fanie burst out in a guffaw, but there was a false ring. He choked, spluttered, and then burst into a fit of coughing. He recovered and laughed till the tears streamed down his cheeks. Dawie laughed dutifully. "No room at the inn."

"Ja, that is very funny."

Fanie was suddenly silent. Dawie stilled a half-hearted attempt to laugh.

"Come, let's go and see," Fanie said suddenly.

"The Kaffir?"

"Ja."

"All right."

"Bring the brandy along."

"And the glasses."

They got up unsteadily and walked to the back door. Fanie looked ash gray under his leathery skin. There was no one at the door.

"Witbooi!"

No reply.

"Witbooi!!"

The servant appeared suddenly, as if from nowhere.

"Baas?"

"Where's the man?"

"I don't know, baas."

"You're lying."

"It's true, baas."

"Where are they?"

"The woman is very sick."

"So where did they go?"

"I put them in the stable, baas."

"Hemelsnaam!"[23]

"Allewereld!"

Fanie and Dawie slowly looked at each other and then, at the same time, timidly looked toward the sky to see whether there was a bright star.

---

22. **Allewereld!** (äl′ ə wə relt): literally, the whole world; an exclamation.

23. **Hemelsnaam!** (he′ məls näm): an exclamation; literally, Name of heaven!

DISCUSSION QUESTIONS

1. What reasons does Fanie give for refusing to help the black African couple? Do you think these are his only reasons? Explain your answer.

2. Parts of this story bear a striking resemblance to the Christmas story of the Nativity, a point that both Fanie and Dawie recognize. Do they appear comfortable with the comparison? Explain your answer.

3. Are Fanie and Dawie confirmed racial bigots or are they more complex than that? Use evidence in the story to support your opinion.

4. In what way do Fanie and Dawie undergo a change in their attitudes at the end of the story?

SUGGESTION FOR WRITING

Think of a simple classic story that you have enjoyed in the past. It could be a fairy tale like "Cinderella," or a folk tale like "Paul Bunyan and Babe, the Blue Ox," or any other famous story that you have enjoyed. Rewrite the story in your own words, set it in the present, and substitute new characters for the old ones. However, leave most of the plot essentially the same. As you prepare your story, ask yourself these questions: What elements of the classic story will I use? What elements will I ignore? How will I end the story?

JAMES D. RUBADIRI
(born 1930)

Malawi, where James David Rubadiri taught and wrote, was once Nyasaland. After Nyasaland was united with North and South Rhodesia in 1953, Rubadiri stood with the African population who agitated against federation. In the rioting of the Nyasaland crisis of 1959, Rubadiri was arrested but not jailed. After his release he went to England, where he had studied earlier, to work for a time as a broadcaster. Upon his return to Malawi, he became an English teacher. In 1963 he was named ambassador to the United States and to the United Nations. He held these posts until 1965. Rubadiri is a poet, novelist, and anthologist. His publications include *No Bride Price* (1967), a novel; and *Poems from East Africa* (1971), a collection of poems by fifty black African poets. His poetry has appeared in a variety of collections, including *Modern Poetry from Africa* and *New African Literature and the Arts.* In his writing Rubadiri aims to interpret the thoughts and experiences of his people. Rubadiri returned to the United Nations in 1995 and currently serves as ambassador from Malawi. ∎

Henry Morton Stanley, the American journalist who in 1871 found the Scottish missionary David Livingstone on the shores of Lake Tanganyika in central Africa, continued his explorations in later years. On his next expedition in 1875 he visited King Mutesa of Buganda, a region northwest of Lake Victoria and now a part of Uganda, and won admission for Christian missionaries to that area. This eventually led to the establishment of a British protectorate there.

STANLEY MEETS MUTESA

Such a time of it they had;
The heat of the day
The chill of the night
And the mosquitoes that followed.
5 Such was the time and
They bound for a kingdom.

The thin weary line of carriers
With tattered dirty rags to cover their backs;
The battered bulky chests
10 That kept on falling off their shaven heads.

Their tempers high and hot
The sun fierce and scorching
With it rose their spirits
With its fall their hopes
15 As each day sweated their bodies dry and
Flies clung in clumps on their sweat-scented backs.
Such was the march
And the hot season just breaking.

Each day a weary pony dropped,
20 Left for the vultures on the plains;
Each afternoon a human skeleton collapsed,
Left for the Masai[1] on the plains;
But the march trudged on
Its Khaki leader in front
25 He the spirit that inspired.
He the light of hope.

Then came the afternoon of a hungry march,
A hot and hungry march it was;
The Nile and the Nyanza
30 Lay like two twins
Azure across the green countryside.
The march leapt on chaunting[2]
Like young gazelles to a water hole.
Hearts beat faster
35 Loads felt lighter
As the cool water lapt their sore soft feet.
No more the dread of hungry hyenas
But only tales of valor when
At Mutesa's court fires are lit.
40 No more the burning heat of the day
But song, laughter and dance.

The village looks on behind banana groves,
Children peer behind reed fences.
Such was the welcome
45 No singing women to chaunt a welcome
Or drums to greet the white ambassador;
Only a few silent nods from aged faces
And one rumbling drum roll

---

1. **Masai** (mä sī'): a nomadic people of East Africa.

2. **chaunt:** variation of the word *chant*.

James D. Rubadiri   **209**

To summon Mutesa's court to parley
50   For the country was not sure.

The gate of reeds is flung open,
There is silence
But only a moment's silence—
A silence of assessment.
55   The tall black king steps forward,
He towers over the thin bearded white man
Then grabbing his lean white hand
Manages to whisper
"*Mtu mweupe karibu*"
60   White man you are welcome.
The gate of polished reed closes behind them
And the West is let in.

DISCUSSION QUESTIONS

1. Study the title of the poem and the headnote that precedes it. Who is the focus in stanza three, lines 23–26? Who is the focus in the last stanza, lines 55–60?

2. The obvious or surface meaning of line 6—"They bound for a kingdom"—is that the expedition was headed in the direction of King Mutesa's kingdom. Based on what you learned in the headnote of the poem, what further meaning might the poet imply by using the construction "bound for"?

3. In the fifth stanza, the speaker reports that Stanley's party received a subdued welcome because "the country was not sure." What do you think the country was not sure of?

4. What is the literal meaning of the last line, "And the West is let in"? What is the symbolic significance of this line?

SUGGESTION FOR WRITING

Have you ever had the desire to explore an unknown part of the world or at least a part of the world with which you are unfamiliar? If you were given an opportunity to go on an expedition, where would you go and what would you hope to accomplish? Write a short essay in which you explain what kind of expedition you would undertake, why you would choose such an expedition, and what you would hope to learn.

MABEL SEGUN

(born c. 1938)

A native Nigerian, Mabel Segun was educated in grammar school in Lagos and then attended University College in Ibadan. She has worked as a teacher, as editor of *Hansard* (the daily report) of the Western Nigerian parliament, and has been in charge of overseas publicity in the Information Services of Western Nigeria. She has written poems, articles, and one novelette for children, *My Father's Daughter* (1965). Segun's poetry is characterized by lively imagery and serves as a vigorous protest medium, in which she sees Africans as "infants overblown / poised between two civilizations." Her poetry has been published in the African journal *Black Orpheus* and in anthologies in Africa, Europe, and the United States. ■

THE PIGEON-HOLE

How I wish I could pigeon-hole myself
and neatly fix a label on!
But self-knowledge comes too late
and by the time I've known myself
5   I am no longer what I was.

I knew a woman once
who had a delinquent child.
She never had a moment's peace of mind
waiting in constant fear,
10   listening for the dreaded knock
and the cold tones of policeman:
"Madam, you're wanted at the station."
I don't know if the knock ever came
but she feared on right till
15   we moved away from the street.
She used to say,
"It's the uncertainty that worries me—
if only I knew for certain . . ."

If only I knew for certain
20   what my delinquent self would do . . .
But I never know
until the deed is done
and I live on fearing,
wondering which part of me will be supreme—

25   the old and tested one, the present
      or the future unknown.
      Sometimes all three have equal power
      and then
      how I long for a pigeon-hole.

CONFLICT

      Here we stand
      infants overblown,
      poised between two civilizations,
      finding the balance irksome,
5   itching for something to happen,
      to tip us one way or the other,
      groping in the dark for a helping hand
      and finding none.
      I'm tired, O my God, I'm tired,
10   I'm tired of hanging in the middle way—
      but where can I go?

DISCUSSION QUESTIONS

1. What is the meaning of *pigeon-hole* in line 1 of "The Pigeon-Hole"? What does the speaker say about herself in this stanza?

2. What does the speaker say about herself in the third stanza? What do you think "delinquent self" means in line 20?

3. Stanza 2 represents an interruption in the poem. Here the speaker talks about a woman she knows. Do you think this stanza adds anything to the poem, or does it detract from the poem as a whole? Explain your opinion.

4. Explain line 2 of "Conflict." What is an "infant overblown"?

5. This poem can be thought of as being a complaint from an emerging black nation or a complaint from an emerging social class. With this in mind, explain the first 8 lines.

6. In line 10, what is "the middle way"?

7. In what ways are the ideas in this poem similar to those in "The Pigeon-Hole"?

SUGGESTION FOR WRITING

It is likely that in these two poems Mabel Segun's point of reference is her daily life in Nigeria and her political knowledge of the emerging nations of Africa, but the ideas in these poems also have universal applications. Do you ever find yourself being influenced by your past—your behavior and beliefs when you were younger? On the other hand, do you also find yourself thinking about the future and what it will bring? Write a short essay in which you assess your growth as an individual at this point in your life. Discuss to what extent you are still influenced by your past and what your worries about and hopes for the future are.

LÉOPOLD SÉDAR SENGHOR

(born 1906)

Léopold Senghor has won success as a poet, linguist, teacher, and diplomat. He is very much a black poet, singing the beauty of his blackness, of his cultural heritage, of his people's closeness to nature. He makes much use in his poetry of imagery of the night and the moon, the protective ancestral presences in his imagery. He was born a Catholic in the small village of Joal, Senegal, a land in which the majority is Muslim. He attended a Catholic missionary school in a nearby village for his elementary education, a seminary in Dakar for a few years, and a secondary school in Dakar. He then was awarded a scholarship to study in France, where he became the first West African to complete his degree at the Sorbonne in Paris.

During this time Senghor became a central figure among the African and West Indian students living in Paris. His friendship with Aimé Césaire and Léon Dumas led to the founding of the Negritude movement (see page xvii). During World War II Senghor, who had joined the French army, was caught by the Germans and held as a prisoner of war for two years. In 1960, when Senegal became an independent nation, Senghor was installed as the first president of that country. In 1980 he retired from politics and in 1983 he was elected to the prestigious Académie Française. From 1945 to 1978 Senghor published numerous volumes of poems. They are collected in one volume titled *Poemes,* which was published in 1982. ■

PRAYER TO THE MASKS

Masks! O Masks!
Black mask red mask, you black and white masks
Masks with the four points from which the Spirit blows
I greet you in the silence!
5   And not you the last, lion-headed Ancestor
You guard this place forbidden to all laughter of woman, to every
    smile that fades
You give forth this air of eternity wherein I breathe the breath of
    my Fathers.
Masks with maskless faces, bereft of every dimple as of every wrinkle
Who have fashioned this image, this face of mine leaning over the
    altar of white paper
10   In your image, hear me!

Behold, Africa of the empires is dying—it is the agony of a
    pitiable princess
And also Europe to whom we are bound by the navel.
Fix your immutable eyes upon your children who are commanded
Who give their lives like the poor man his last garment.
15 May we answer Present at the rebirth of the World
As the leaven[1] which is necessary to the white flour.
For who would teach rhythm to the dead world of machines and
    of cannons?
Who would raise the cry of joy to awaken the dead and the
    orphans at dawn?
Speak, who would restore the memory of life to the man with gut-
    ted hopes?
20 They call us the men of cotton, of coffee, of oil
They call us the men of death.
We are the men of dance, whose feet regain vigor in striking the
    hard earth.

NIGHT OF SINE[2]

Woman, rest on my brow your soothing hands, your hands softer
    than fur.
Up above the swaying palm trees scarcely rustle in the high night
    breeze.
Not even a lullaby.
Let the rhythmic silence cradle us.
5 Let us listen to its song, let us listen to the beat of our dark blood,
    let us listen
To the deep pulse of Africa beating in the midst of forgotten
    villages.
Now the weary moon sinks toward her bed in the quiet sea
Now the bursts of laughter grow sleepy, the story-tellers themselves
Are nodding their heads like babies on the backs of their mothers
10 Now the feet of the dancers grow heavy, and heavy the voices of
    the alternating choruses.

This is the hour of stars and of the night who dreams
And reclines on the hill of clouds, wrapped in her long milky
    cloth.

---

1. leaven: a substance that causes expansion of dough; an element that produces an altering or
transforming influence.

2. Sine: The region of Sine-Saloum, so called because it lies between the Sine and the Saloum
rivers in Senegal, was the home of Senghor's tribe.

The roofs of the huts gleam tenderly. What do they say, so confidentially, to the stars?
Inside, the fire dies out among intimate smells bitter and sweet.
15 Woman, light the lamp of clear oil, that the Ancestors may gather
about and talk like parents when children are sleeping.
Let us listen to the voices of the Ancients of Elissa.[3] Like us,
exiled,
They did not want to die and let the torrent of their seed be lost
in the desert sands.
Let me listen in the smoky hut where welcome spirits visit,
My head on your breast which is warm like a *dang*[4] just taken
steaming from the fire,
20 Let me breathe the smell of our Dead, let me recall and repeat
their living voice, let me learn to
Live before descending, deeper than a diver, into the lofty depths
of sleep.

BE NOT AMAZED

Be not amazed beloved, if sometimes my song grows dark,
If I exchange the lyrical reed for the Khalam or the tama[5]
And the green scent of the ricefields, for the swiftly galloping war
drums.
I hear the threats of ancient deities, the furious cannonade of the
god.
5 Oh, tomorrow perhaps, the purple voice of your bard will be silent
for ever.
That is why my rhythm becomes so fast, that the fingers bleed on
the Khalam.
Perhaps, beloved, I shall fall tomorrow, on a restless earth
Lamenting your sinking eyes, and the dark tom-tom of the mortars below.
And you will weep in the twilight for the glowing voice that sang
your black beauty.

---

3 the Ancients of Elissa: Senghor's family came from the village of Elissa in Portuguese Guinea.

4. dang: a variety of couscous, a dish made from coarsely ground flour, sometimes with the
addition of meat or vegetables.

5. Khalam . . . tama: The Khalam is a type of lute. The tama is a small drum, held in the armpit,
and played with a stick. The pressure of the arm on a system of tighteners allows subtle
variations of tone.

DISCUSSION QUESTIONS

1. Note the title in "Prayer to the Masks." Who are the masks to whom this poem is addressed?

2. What message does the speaker bring to the masks?

3. Explain the simile in lines 15-16.

4. In line 22, what do you think "we are the men of dance" means?

5. Describing the peace of his tribal home in "Night of Sine," Senghor remembers earlier members of the tribe who, like himself, had wandered far. What situation is described in the first two stanzas of this poem?

6. Note line 16. What do you think "Like us, exiled" might be a reference to? (See footnote 3 and Senghor's biography for help.)

7. In lines 5–6 and in the last stanza, what does the speaker recommend that he and his beloved do before falling asleep?

8. In "Be Not Amazed," why may the speaker's song grow dark?

9. What does the speaker predict might happen to him?

10. Senghor's poetry often voices a nostalgia for an Africa that because of colonialism and changing cultures is rapidly disappearing. With this idea in mind, what other meaning can you find in the poem?

SUGGESTION FOR WRITING

As one of the Negritude poets (see page xvii), Léopold Senghor believed strongly in rediscovering the cultural values of Africa. Reread "Prayer to the Masks," "Night of Sine," and "Be Not Amazed." After studying these poems, write a short essay explaining how each of these poems deals with the theme of rediscovering the cultural values of Africa. Support your ideas with evidence from each poem.

WOLE SOYINKA
(born 1934)

Wole Soyinka—playwright, poet, novelist, critic, lecturer, actor, musician, producer, teacher, translator, politician, and publisher—is the first black African to become famous around the world as a dramatist. He is also the first black African to win the Nobel Prize in literature (1986). Soyinka was born in Ijebu-Isara, Western Nigeria, to Yoruba parents, both of whom were teachers. He grew up in the nearby city of Abeokuta and received his early education there. After studying at the University of Ibadan, Soyinka attended the University of Leeds in England, where he received a degree in English literature in 1957. He then worked as a play reader for two years at the Royal Court Theatre in London. In 1960, when Nigeria became independent, Soyinka returned to his native country. During the next seven years, Soyinka established two theatre companies; worked with other traveling companies; wrote seven plays, a novel, and a volume of poetry; and conducted literary research. In 1967, when Nigeria became embroiled in civil war, Soyinka, who opposed the conflict, was imprisoned until the war ended in 1970. Soyinka spent the next five years in self-imposed exile in Ghana, England, and the United States. Soyinka returned to Nigeria in 1976 and took a position as professor of comparative literature and dramatic arts at the University of Ife, where he remained until his retirement in 1985. Throughout his career Soyinka has combined a remarkable literary output—more than twenty plays, four volumes of poetry, three autobiographies, two novels, and many critical essays—with an intense interest in politics. In all of this work, he is committed above all to human freedom and justice. ∎

FADO[1] SINGER

My skin is pumiced to a fault
I am down to hair-roots, down to fiber filters
Of the raw tobacco nerve
Your net is spun of sitar[2] strings
5   To hold the griefs of gods: I wander long
In tear vaults of the sublime
Queen of night torments, you strain
Sutures of song to bear imposition of the rites
Of living and of death. You
10   Pluck strange dirges from the storm

---

1. fado (fä´ du): a mournful Portuguese folk song.

2. sitar: an Indian guitar with a long neck and varying number of strings.

Sift rare stones from ashes of the moon, and ride
Night errands to the throne of anguish
Oh there is too much crush of petals
For perfume, too heavy tread of air on mothwing
15   For a cup of rainbow dust
Too much pain, oh midwife at the cry
Of severance, fingers at the cosmic cord, too vast
The pains of easters for a hint of the eternal.
I would be free of your tyranny, free
20   From sudden plunges of the flesh in earthquake
Beyond all subsidence of sense
I would be free from headlong rides
In rock reams and volcanic veins, drawn by dark steeds
On gray melodic reins.

SEASON

Rust is ripeness, rust
And the wilted corn-plume;
Pollen is mating-time when swallows
Weave a dance
5   Of feathered arrows
Thread corn-stalks in winged
Streaks of light. And, we loved to hear
Spliced phrases of the wind, to hear
Rasps in the field, where corn leaves
10   Pierce like bamboo slivers.
Now, garnerers we,
Awaiting rust on tassels, draw
Long shadows from the dusk, wreathe
Dry thatch in woodsmoke. Laden stalks
15   Ride the germ's decay—we await
The promise of the rust.

I THINK IT RAINS

I think it rains
That tongues may loosen from the parch
Uncleave roof-tops of the mouth, hang
Heavy with knowledge.
5   I saw it raise
The sudden cloud, from ashes. Settling

They joined in a ring of gray; within
The circling spirit.
O it must rain
10 These closures on the mind, binding us
In strange despairs, teaching
Purity of sadness.
And how it beats
Skeined transparencies on wings
15 Of our desires, searing dark longings
In cruel baptisms.
Rain-reeds, practiced in
The grace of yielding, yet unbending
From afar, this, your conjugation with my earth
20 Bares crouching rocks.

DISCUSSION QUESTIONS

1. If the "I" in "Fado Singer" is the speaker, who is the "you"? (Note especially lines 4 and 9–10.)

2. What is the effect of the singer's music on the speaker? Cite words and phrases from the poem to support your opinion.

3. What time of year is celebrated in "Season"? What words suggest this time of year?

4. In line 16, what is "the promise of the rust"?

5. In line 1, why does the speaker think "It Rains"?

6. In line 9, why does the speaker say it must rain?

7. What are *reeds*? What might *rain-reeds* be?

8. Do you think rain is being used symbolically in this poem? Explain.

SUGGESTION FOR WRITING

For poet Wole Soyinka, rain is a good thing, or it can lead to good things. What is your general reaction to rain? Do you view it as a nuisance? Does it make you feel sad? Do you consider it a necessary evil? Are there any times when rain makes you feel happy? Write one or two paragraphs in which you describe your own reactions to rain. How many different reactions do you have. Be sure to explain the circumstances for each one.

EFUA T. SUTHERLAND

(1924–1996)

Born in Ghana (then called the Gold Coast) and educated for a time in England, Efua Theodora Sutherland made a major contribution during her lifetime to the world of theater and art in her native country. Sutherland grew up in a Christian family and was exposed at an early age to European influences in her home town of Cape Coast. She was also exposed to the world of classical Greek drama through productions at a local boys' school. Sutherland spent much of her life on a self-described journey of discovery to learn more about the people of Ghana, particularly the people of rural Ghana, with whom she was unfamiliar. Early in her career she taught school. Increasingly, however, she devoted more of her energies to drama and the theater. At about the same time that Ghana achieved independence (1957), Sutherland founded the Ghana Experimental Theatre and the Ghana Drama Studio. She also was the founder of the Ghana Society of Writers, and she helped to establish the magazine *Okyeame* to encourage new writers in Ghana. In 1963 she was granted a research appointment in African literature and drama at the University of Ghana's Institute of African Studies. In later years she was involved with the Children's Drama Development Project and the National Commission on Children. In 1991 she was awarded an honorary doctorate from the University of Ghana. She died in 1996 after a long illness. During her lifetime, Sutherland wrote numerous short stories, poems, plays, and children's books. Her work is infused with passion, impatience, and the agony of her people. ■

EDUFA

CHARACTERS

ABENA, *Edufa's sister*
EDUFA
SEGUWA, *a matronly member of the household*
AMPOMA, *Edufa's wife*
KANKAM, *Edufa's father*
CHORUS *of women from the town*
SENCHI, *Edufa's friend*
SAM, *an idiot servant*

> SCENE: *The courtyard and inner court of* EDUFA's *expensive house. The two areas are linked by wide steps. The inner court is the ground floor of the house. Here, towards the back, and slightly off center, a slim pillar stands from floor to ceiling. Back of this pillar is a back wall. There are also two*

flanking walls, left and right. Short flights of steps between back and side walls lead into EDUFA's *rooms on the left, and guest rooms on the right. A door in the right wall, close to the courtyard steps, leads into the kitchen. There are three, long, boxlike seats, which match the color of the pillar. Two of these are close to the courtyard steps, against the side walls; one is right of the pillar.*

An atmosphere of elegant spaciousness is dominant.

For Act Three, the seats are shifted to more convenient positions, and light garden chairs, a trestle table, and a drinks trolley are moved in.

People in the audience are seated in EDUFA's *courtyard. The gate by which they have entered is the same one the chorus and other characters use as directed in the play.*

PROLOGUE

ABENA *is sitting on a side seat, her head in her lap, her cloth wrapped round her for warmth. She is gazing into a small black water-pot which stands on the step below her. Another pot, red, stands on the floor beside her. She tilts the black pot, measuring its contents with her eyes. Then she looks up, sighs wearily, and rubs her eyes as if she can no longer keep sleep away.*

ABENA (*beginning slowly and sleepily*).
Night is long when our eyes are unsleeping.
Three nights long my eyes have been unsleeping,
Keeping wakeful watch on the dew falling,
Falling from the eaves . . .

> *She glances anxiously round the inner court, rises, goes towards the steps leading to* EDUFA's *rooms, hesitates, and turns back.*

And dreaming.
Dreamlike views of mist rising
Above too much water everywhere.
I heard tonight
A voice stretched thin through the mist, calling.
Heard in that calling the quiver of Ampoma's voice.
Thought I saw suddenly in the restless white waters
The laterite red of an anthill—jutting
And rocking.
A misty figure on its topmost tip,
Flicking her fingers like one despairing.
I panicked, and came to this door, listening,
But all was silence—
Night is so deceiving when our eyes
Are robbed too long of sleep.

O child of Ama,
Child of Ama in the night
Is wandering,
Crying, "Mm-m-m-m,
How my mother is pondering."
O child of Ama,
Why is she wandering,
Why wandering,
Why wandering in the night
Like the dying?
Meewuo!

She keeps up the last bars of the song for a while, patting the black pot
with one hand and her own arm with the other, in a manner suggestive
of self-consolation. Presently, she looks into the sky again.

But my last night of wakefulness is over. (*She rises, tipping the black pot.*) The last drop of dew has fallen. There's enough dew water in the pot. (*She picks up the pot and tilts the red one.*) And here is stream water from the very eye of the spring where the red rock weeps without ceasing. (*Gesturing towards* EDUFA's *rooms*) My brother Edufa, your orders are done though I obey without understanding. . . . (*Walking about*) Here in this house, where there was always someone laughing, suddenly no one feels like smiling. I've never known such silence in my brother's house. Mm? It is unnatural. From rising until sleep claimed us again at night, people came through our gate, for who doesn't know my brother Edufa in this town? Benevolent one, who doesn't love him? Old and young, they came. They brought laughter. Those who brought sadness returned with smiles, comforted.

Why then does brother shut our gate to stop such flow of friends? Mm? True that Ampoma, his wife, is unwell; but if she is unwell, should we not open our gate? She is not mortally ill; but even so, just let it be known, and sympathy and comforting gifts would flow in from every home. So much does the whole town hold her dear. (*Yawning*) Oh well . . . I don't even know what it is that ails her. Their door is barred, and my brother says nothing to me. (*Yawning again*) Ha! Tired. (*She picks up the red pot also, carrying the two pressed against her body.*) Well . . . I place these at his door . . . (*She places them at the top of the steps.*) . . . and make my way . . . to . . . (*Yawning*) sleep. I don't know why I should be so sad.

She crosses, humming her song, and goes out through the kitchen door.

ACT ONE

EDUFA's hands reach out and pick up the pots. He is heard issuing instructions urgently to someone inside.

EDUFA. Pour first the dew water, and then the stream water, over the herbs in the bathroom. Quickly. Then bring out fire for the incense.

Outside the courtyard walls a chorus of women is heard performing.

CHORUS (*chanting to the rhythm of wooden clappers*).
Our mother's dead,
Ei! Ei—Ei!
We the orphans cry,
Our mother's dead,
O! O—O!
We the orphans cry.

The chanting repeats. As the voices, the clack-clack accompaniment, and the thudding of running feet recede, SEGUWA *comes hurriedly out of* EDUFA's *rooms. She listens as she crosses to the kitchen, and is clearly disturbed by the performance. Her brief absence from the court is filled in by the chanting, which becomes dominant once again as the chorus returns past the house. She comes back, carrying a brazier in which charcoal fire is burning in a small earthen pot. She hesitates by the kitchen door, still preoccupied with the performance outside. At the same time* EDUFA *rushes out in pyjamas and dressing gown. He carries a box of incense and has the air of a man under considerable mental strain.*

EDUFA. Why are they doing a funeral chant? They are not coming towards this house? (*To* SEGUWA) You've spoken to no one?

SEGUWA (*with some resentment*). To no one. My tongue is silenced. (*Pause*) It must be for someone else's soul they clamor.

The chanting fades.

EDUFA (*composing himself*). No, they are not coming here. (*Pause*) Put the fire down. (SEGUWA *places the fire close to the central seat.* EDUFA *rips the box open and flings incense nervously on the fire.*) Keep the incense burning while Ampoma and I bathe in the herbs.

SEGUWA. It seems to me that the time has come now to seek some other help. All this bathing in herbs and incense burning—I don't see it bringing much relief to your wife, Ampoma, in there.

EDUFA. Doubting?

SEGUWA. I'm not saying I doubt anything. You have chosen me to share this present burden with you, and I'm letting my mouth speak so that my mind can have some ease. It is I myself who say I'm hardy, but how can I help having a woman's bowels?

EDUFA. Calm yourself. I cannot give in to any thoughts of hopelessness. Where is your faith? I thought I could trust it.

SEGUWA. You can trust my secrecy; that I have sworn; though what I have sworn to keep secret, now frets against the closed walls of my skull. I haven't sworn to have faith against all reason. No, not in the face of your wife's condition in that bedroom there. Let's call for help.

EDUFA (*with indications of despair*). From whom? We are doing everything we can. Also, it is Ampoma's wish that no one should be allowed to see her.

SEGUWA. And is she dead that we should be bound to honor her wishes? She is not herself. In her present state we can expect her to say childish things. The sick are like children. Let me call for help.

It is almost unnatural that even the mother who bore her should be kept ignorant of her sickness, serious as it now is. Ah, poor mother; if we could but see her now. She is probably pampering the children you've sent to her, keeping them happy, thinking she is relieving her daughter for rest and fun with you, her husband. (*Bitterly*) How you are deceived, Mother.

EDUFA. Don't fret so much. Calm yourself, will you?

SEGUWA. It is your wife who needs calming, if I may say so.

EDUFA. You've promised to stand with me in this trouble. You will, won't you? Your service and your courage these last few days have given me strength and consolation. Don't despair now. Ampoma is getting better.

SEGUWA. Better? Ho, ho. After fainting twice last night? (*Shrugs*) Ah, well, just as you say. I promised to stand with you and will. But may God help us all, for the bridge we are now crossing is between the banks of life and the banks of death. And I do not know which way we're facing. (*Pause*) Where is the incense? I'll keep it burning.

EDUFA (*relieved*). Your kindness will not be forgotten, believe me, when we can smile again in this house. (*He gives her the box. She sprinkles more incense on the fire.*) See that the gate is barred.

SCENE 2

AMPOMA *has appeared unnoticed at the top of the steps and is standing there unsteadily. There is a look of near insanity about her.* SEGUWA *sees her first and lets out a stifled scream.*

EDUFA (*hurrying to her*). Oh, Ampoma. You shouldn't leave your bed. You shouldn't come out here.

AMPOMA (*weakly*). The sun is shining on the world, and I am . . . falling. (*She totters.*)

SEGUWA. Hold her! She'll fall.

EDUFA (*only just saving* AMPOMA *from falling*). Is the gate barred?

SEGUWA (*with uncontrolled irritation*). O God! I cannot understand it. (*She picks up a wrap* AMPOMA *has dropped on the steps and starts towards the gate, but gives up in confusion, and returns to the incense-burning.*)

AMPOMA (*moving and compelling* EDUFA, *who is supporting her, to move with her*). I have come out into the bright sun. There is no warmth in my bed. And no comfort. Only darkness.

EDUFA. Sit, then. Let us sit together here. (*He urges her tenderly to the seat near the kitchen door, takes the wrap from* SEGUWA, *and arranges it round* AMPOMA's *shoulders.*) You want to be in the sun? That means you are getting well. You are. Tell yourself you are. Make your soul will your strength back again. (*Pause*) In a little while we will bathe in the herbs, and later today, at the junction between day and night, we will bathe again, the final time. Tomorrow . . . tomorrow, you will feel much better. I promise you.

AMPOMA (*dreamily*). Tomorrow? When . . . is tomorrow? (*She droops and quickly buries her face in the nape of* EDUFA's *neck.*)

EDUFA (*confused*). Tomorrow . . .

AMPOMA (*breaking free*). Oh, no! I cannot have them straying.

> SEGUWA *picks up the wrap she flings away and hovers anxiously in the background.*

EDUFA (*helplessly*). What? Who?

AMPOMA. Like two little goats. I'm leaving them. I? Two little goats struggling on the faraway hillside. I see their eyes glowing in the dark, lonely. Oh, my little boy! And you, my girl with breasts just budding! What hands will prepare you for your wedding? (*She sobs quietly.*)

SEGUWA. She is talking of her children. Thank God they are not here to see this sight.

EDUFA (*to* AMPOMA). Don't talk as if all were ending. All is not ending. It cannot end. (*To* SEGUWA) Put on more incense. (*He guides* AMPOMA *back to the seat.*)

AMPOMA (*on the way*). My bed is so full of a river of my own tears, I was drowning there. (*Helplessly*) Why do we weep so much? (*They sit.*)

EDUFA. Dreams. You only dreamed these things. Sickness plagues the mind with monstrous fantasies. Pay no heed to them. Think only of reality. . . . Think of me. Is not your bed that sunny place in which we plant our children? There has never been anything but warmth and happiness there, and never will be, as long as I live and love you so.

AMPOMA. Don't speak of it. I have strayed into the cold. Yet, how good that I should not be the one to live beyond your days. I could not live where you are not. I could not live without you, my husband.

EDUFA. Ah, loving wife.

AMPOMA. Yes. That is the truth. I have loved you.

EDUFA. You have. And I have you still to fill my days with joy. (*He puts his arm round her protectively.*)

AMPOMA (*looking at him sadly*). I am dying too young, don't you think? Look at me. (*She rises abruptly.*) What am I saying? We knew this day could come. Am I listening to the lure of his voice at this final stage? Weakening at the closeness of his flesh? (*To* EDUFA) Help me. Take your arm away from me. Why do you restrain me at your peril?

EDUFA. Come inside. You've been out here too long already.

AMPOMA (*more calmly, moving again, halting now and then*). Let me talk with you a little longer in the sun before I step into the dark, where you cannot see me. Soon my pledge will be honored. I am leaving our children motherless in your hands. Let me hear you say you love them, though I know you do.

EDUFA. I love them, Ampoma.

AMPOMA. And will you keep them from harm? Protect them?

EDUFA. How else would I be worthy of the sacred name of father? How worthy of your trust, brave woman? No harm shall come to the children that I can prevent.

AMPOMA. I fear the harm that might come to them from another woman's dissatisfied heart.

EDUFA. Ampoma, what are you saying? Another woman? I swear that in this, as in nothing else, true triumph is mine. You inspire devotion, incomparable one. There is no other woman beside you.

AMPOMA. The dead are removed. Time must, and will, soften pain for the living. If you should marry another woman, will she not envy my children because you have them with your own love and mine combined?

EDUFA. Poor Ampoma. In what unfamiliar world is your mind wandering that you speak so strangely?

AMPOMA. Promise me that you will never place them in another woman's power. Never risk their lives in the hands of another. Promise me that, and I will die without that unbearable fear here in my heart.

EDUFA. You will not die. But if it will calm you to hear it, I do promise.

AMPOMA. That you will not marry again?

EDUFA. That no other woman will cross my inner door, nor share my bed. This house will never even harbor a woman not of my own blood, at whom my eye could look without restraint.

AMPOMA. Swear it.

EDUFA. I swear it.

AMPOMA (*calmly walking away from him*). Over me the sun is getting dark. (*With great agitation*) My husband! Watch the death that you should have died. (*She frets from place to place as if escaping from him.*) Stay over there in the sun. Children! My children! If I could cross this water, I would pluck you back from the mountainside. Children! Hold my hand! (*She stretches out her hand to the vision that she alone can see.*)

EDUFA (*catching hold of her*). Oh, wife of my soul. You should never have made that fatal promise.

AMPOMA. That I loved you? My love has killed me. (*Faintness comes over her. She falls into* EDUFA's *arms.*) Children! And . . . Mother . . . Mother.

> EDUFA *takes her in, almost carrying her.*
> SEGUWA, *not quite knowing how to help, follows them.*

CHORUS (*heard again in the distance*).
Our mother's dead,
Ei! Ei—Ei!
We the orphans cry,
Our mother's dead,
O! O—O!
We the orphans cry.

> *The voices travel farther into the distance.*

SCENE 3

SEGUWA (*returning*). This is what we are living with. This weakness that comes over her and all this meandering talk. Talk of water and of drowning? What calamitous talk is that? When will it end? How will it end? We are mystified. How wouldn't we be? Oh, we should ask Edufa some questions; that is what I say. You should all ask Edufa some questions. (*She goes to the fire, throws in more incense, and withdraws from it as if she hates it.*)

I wish I could break this lock on my lips.
Let those who would gamble with lives
Stake their own.
None I know of flesh and blood
Has right to stake another's life
For his own.
Edufa! You have done Ampoma wrong,
And wronged her mother's womb.
Ah, Mother! Mother!
The scenes I have witnessed in here,
In this respected house,
Would make torment in your womb.
Your daughter, all heart for the man
She married, keeps her agonies from you.
Ah, Mother! Mother!
Edufa has done Ampoma wrong.
Tafrakye!
Some matters weight down the tongue,
But, Mother, I swear
Edufa does Ampoma wrong,
He does her wrong.

She returns angrily to the incense burning.

SCENE 4

KANKAM *enters through the gate. Hearing his footsteps,* SEGUWA *turns round in alarm. She is torn between surprise and fear when she notices who has arrived.* KANKAM *stops on the courtyard steps.*

SEGUWA (*approaching him hesitantly*). Grandfather!

KANKAM (*quietly*). Yes. It is me. Three years, is it? Three years since I walked out of that same gate, a disappointed father. Three years. Well . . . tell him I am here.

SEGUWA. Tell Edufa?

KANKAM. Yes, the man whom nature makes my son.

SEGUWA. Oh, Grandfather, do I dare? So troubled is his mood, he has ordered his gate shut against all callers.

KANKAM (*with power*). Call him.

SEGUWA (*nervously*). As for me, I'm willing enough to call him, but—

KANKAM (*an angry tap of his umbrella emphasizing his temper*). Call him! It was I who bore him.

SEGUWA (*on her knees, straining to confide*). Oh, Grandfather, help him; help him. God sent you here, I'm sure. I could tell you things—no . . .

I couldn't tell you. Oh, please forget your quarrel with him and help us all. What shall I say? Hmm. His wife, Ampoma, is sick, sick, very sick.

KANKAM. So he bars his door, just in case anyone looks in to offer help. (*Calling with authority*) Edufa! Edufa!

SEGUWA (*hurrying*). I will call him. He was bathing. (*She meets* EDUFA *coming out of his rooms.*)

EDUFA (*seeing his father and recoiling*). You? What do you want? (*His eyes shift uneasily as* KANKAM *stares hard at him. He comes down the steps.*) What do you want? Three years ago you declared me not fit to be your son and left my house. Had my position not been well evaluated in this town, you might have turned tongues against me as the man who drove his own father out of his home. What do you want now?

KANKAM (*walking deliberately to the seat near the kitchen*). Yes. It has burned down to loveless greetings between father and son, I know. What do I want? I will tell you presently. (*He sits.*) Don't let us fail, however, on the sacredness of courtesy. Had I entered the house of a total stranger, he would have given me water to drink, seeing I'm a traveller. (EDUFA *is embarrassed, but at that moment* SEGUWA *is already bringing water from the kitchen.*) I happen to be your father, and you a man in whose house water is the least of the things that overflow.

> SEGUWA *gives the water to* KANKAM, *who pours a little on the floor stylistically for libation, drinks, and thanks her. She returns to the kitchen.*

EDUFA (*awkwardly*). Well?

KANKAM. Sit down, son. Sit. (EDUFA *sits uneasily on the opposite seat.*) What do I want, you say? (*Very deliberately*) I want the courage that makes responsible men. I want truthfulness. Decency. Feeling for your fellowmen. These are the things I've always wanted. Have you got them to give? (EDUFA *rises, angry.*) I fear not, since you have sold such treasures to buy yourself the importance that fools admire.

EDUFA. If you have come only to tempt me to anger, then leave my house.

KANKAM. Oh, stop blabbering. I left before, and will do so again, but it isn't any absurd rage that will drive me out.

EDUFA. What do you want, I say?

KANKAM (*with terrible self-control*). The life of your wife, Ampoma, from you.

EDUFA (*very nervous*). And you mean by that? (KANKAM *only stares at him.*) What makes me keeper of her life?

KANKAM. Marriage . . . and her innocent love. (*A chilly pause*) Oh, I know it all, Edufa. You cannot hide behind impudence and lies, not with me. Diviners are there for all of us to consult. (EDUFA *winces.*) And deeds done in secret can, by the same process, be brought to light.

EDUFA. You know nothing. Diviners! Ho! Diviners? What have diviners got to do with me?

KANKAM. That, you must tell me. I believe in their ancient art. I know, at least, that Ampoma is sick and could die. It has been revealed to me that she could die. And why? That you might live.

EDUFA. Absurd. It is not true. . . . Ampoma is a little ill, that's all. She has fever . . . that's all. . . . Yes . . . that's all. You are deceived.

KANKAM. Deceived. That I am. Am I not? Look at me and tell me it is not true. (EDUFA's *eyes shift nervously.*) He cannot. How could he? (*Pause*) I went to my own diviner to consult him about my health. He spread his holy patch of sand, lit candles, and over his sacred bowl of water made incantation, and scrawled his mystic symbols in the sand.

I'll tell you what he saw in his divination, for it was all about you, my son. (*Advancing on* EDUFA) Four years ago you went to consult one such diviner.

EDUFA. Do you want me to take you seriously? You cannot believe all this, you who educated me to lift me to another plane of living.

KANKAM. That's all right, my man. Most of us consult diviners for our protection. All men need to feel secure in their inmost hearts.

EDUFA. I am not all men. I am emancipated.

KANKAM. As emancipated as I'll show. Your diviner saw death hanging over your life—a normal mortal condition, I would think. But what happened, coward, what happened when he said you could avert the danger by the sacrifice of another life?

EDUFA. He lies.

KANKAM. Who? Has that not been heard before? Has that not been said to many of us mortal men? Why were you not content, like all of us, to purge your soul by offering gifts of cola and white calico to the needy, and sacrificing a chicken or a sheep or, since you can afford it, a cow?

EDUFA. Are you all right, Father?

KANKAM. Beasts are normal sacrifices, but surely you know they are without speech. Beasts swear no oaths to die for others, Edufa. (*Pause*) Were you not afraid, being husband and father, that someone dear to your blood might be the one to make the fatal oath over that powerful charm you demanded and become its victim?

EDUFA. This is intolerable. I will hear no more. (*He makes for his rooms.*)

KANKAM (*with quiet menace, barring his way*). You will hear it all, unless you'd rather have me broadcast my story in the marketplace and turn you over to the judgment of the town. (EDUFA *stops, sensitive to the threat.*) My diviner does not lie. The very day itself when all this happened was clearly engraved in sand.

EDUFA (*huffily*). All right, all-seeing, prove it. (*He sits.*)

KANKAM (*standing over him*). It had been raining without relief since the night before. Dampness had entered our very bones, and no one's spirits were bright. But you were, of all of us, most moody and morose; in fact, so fractious that you snapped at your wife for merely teasing that you couldn't bear, for once, to be shut away from your precious business and society. It was as if you couldn't tolerate yourself, or us. Suddenly you jumped up and rushed out into the raging storm. That was the day you did your evil and killed your wife.

EDUFA. Great God! If you were not my father, I would call you—

KANKAM. Towards evening you returned. The rain had stopped, and we of the household were sitting here, in this very place, to catch what warmth there was in the sickly sunset. You seemed brighter then, for which change we all expressed our thankfulness. In fact, contrarily, you were cheerful, though still a little restless. How could we have known you were carrying on you the hateful charm? How could we have suspected it, when your children were playing round you with joyful cries? How could we have known it was not a joke when you suddenly leaned back and asked which of us loved you well enough to die for you, throwing the question into the air with studied carelessness? Emancipated one, how could we have known of your treachery?

EDUFA (*rising*) Incredible drivel! Incredible. Is this the man I have loved as father?

KANKAM. You had willed that some old wheezer like me should be the victim. And I was the first to speak. "Not me, my son," said I, joking. "Die your own death. I have mine to die." And we all laughed. Do you remember? My age was protecting me. (*Pause*) Then Ampoma spoke. (*Pause*) Yes, I see you wince in the same manner as you did when she spoke the fatal words that day and condemned her life. "I will die for you, Edufa," she said, and meant it too, poor doting woman.

EDUFA. Father, are you mad?

KANKAM (*shocked*). *Nyame* above! To say father and call me mad! My *ntoro* within you shivers with the shock of it!

EDUFA (*aware that he has violated taboo*). You provoked me.

KANKAM (*moving away*). All right, stranger, I am mad! And madness is uncanny. Have you not noticed how many a time the mad seem to know things hidden from men in their right minds? (*Rounding up on* EDUFA) You know you killed your wife that day. I saw fear in your eyes when she spoke. I saw it, but I didn't understand.

I have learned that in your chamber that night you tried to make her forswear the oath she had innocently sworn. But the more you pleaded, the more emotionally she swore away her life for love of you; until, driven by your secret fear, you had to make plain to her the danger in which she stood. You showed her the charm. You confessed to her its power to kill whoever swore to die for you. Don't you remember how she wept? She had spoken and made herself the victim. Ampoma has lived with that danger ever since, in spite of all your extravagant efforts to counter the potency of the charm by washings and rites of purification. (*With great concern*) Edufa, I am here because I fear that time has come to claim that vow.

EDUFA. Leave me alone, will you? (*He sits miserably.*)

KANKAM. Confess it or deny it.

EDUFA. I owe you no such duty. Why don't you leave me alone?

KANKAM. To kill? Say to myself, Father, your son wants to murder, and go? All the world's real fathers would not wish a murderer for a son, my son. Yes, in spite of my rage there is still truth of father and son between us.

EDUFA. Rest. My wife, Ampoma, is not dying.

KANKAM. If she does not die, it will be by the intervention of some great power alone. An oath once sworn will always ride its swearer. But there might still be a chance to save her.

EDUFA. Indeed, in this age there are doctors with skill enough to sell for what's ailing her, and I can pay their fees.

KANKAM (*pleading*). Confess and denounce your wrong. Bring out that evil charm. And before Ampoma and all of us whose souls are corporate in this household, denounce it. Burn it. The charm may not be irrevocably done if we raise the prayer of our souls together.

EDUFA. Will it help you if I swear that there is no ground for all your worry? And now will you let me go?

KANKAM (*with anguish*). Hush! You swear? Oh, my son, I have finished. I can do no more. Have you sunk so low in cowardice? If you must lie, don't swear about it in a house in which death is skirmishing and the ancestral spirits stand expectantly by. A man may curse himself from his own lips. Do not curse the house in which your children have to grow.

Spirits around us, why don't you help him save himself? When he went to consult the diviner, he was already doing well. You could tell.

If you looked at his new clothes, you could tell; if you looked at his well-appointed house in whose precincts hunger wouldn't dwell. Already, the town's pavements knew when it was he who was coming. Nudging announced him. Eyes pivoted to catch his smile. (*With disgust*) You could see all the ivory teeth and all the slimy way down the glowing gullets of those who were learning to call him sir. For he was doing well in the art of buying friends by street benevolence.

EDUFA (*seizing on a diversion*). Now you betray yourself. It has taken me all these years to probe the core of your antagonism. From what you say, it is clear at last that you envied me. Oh! What lengths a man will go to hide his envy.

KANKAM. Pitiful.

EDUFA. Fathers are supposed to share with pride in their sons' good fortune. I was not so blessed. My father envied me and turned enemy—even while he ate the meat and salt of my good fortune.

KANKAM. Pitiful.

EDUFA. And there was I, thinking that enemies could only be encountered outside my gates.

KANKAM. Pitiful. At my age a man has learned to aim his envy at the stars. (*Suffering*) Pity him, you spirits. He grew greedy and insensitive, insane for gain, frantic for the fluff of flattery. And I cautioned him. Did I not warn him? I tried to make him stop at the point when we men must be content or let ourselves be lured on to our doom. But he wouldn't listen. He doesn't listen. It makes me ill. Violently ill. I vomit the meat and salt I ate out of ignorance from his hand.

I have finished. (*Pause*) It wouldn't be too much to ask to see the lady before I leave?

EDUFA. She mustn't be disturbed.

KANKAM (*picking up his umbrella from the seat*). Well . . . as you wish, noble husband. There are enough women, I suppose, ready to fall for your glamor and line up to die for you. I am leaving. Forever now. (*He steps into the courtyard.*)

EDUFA. One moment. (KANKAM *turns to him hopefully.*) I hope you haven't talked like this to anyone. You could do so much harm. Unjustly.

KANKAM (*with a rage of disappointment*). Worm. Coward. You are afraid for your overblown reputation, aren't you? You are afraid that if the town got to know, they would topple you. No. I am tied by my fatherhood, even though I am not proud that my life water animated you. It is not my place to disillusion your friends. I'll let them bow to a worm. In time they are bound to know they're bowing too low for their comfort. Were this matter a simple case of crime, I would perhaps seek solution by bringing you to secular justice. As it is, to try still to save the woman's life, our remedy is more probable in the paths of prayer, which I now go to pursue away from your unhelpful presence. (*He leaves.*)

EDUFA.

Alone.

Tears within me that I haven't had the privilege to shed.

Father!

Call him back that I may weep on his shoulder.

Why am I afraid of him? He would stand with me even though he rages so.

Call him back to bear me on the strength of his faith.

He knows it all. I can swear he is too true a man to play me foul. But I could not risk confirming it. I dread the power by which he knows, and it shall not gain admission here to energize that which all is set this day to exorcise.

No, a man needs to feel secure! But, oh, how I am stormed.

Don't ask me why I did it; I do not know the answer. If I must be condemned, let me not be charged for any will to kill, but for my failure to create a faith.

Who thought the charm made any sense? Not I. A mystic symbol by which to calm my fears—that was all I could concede it.

It still doesn't make any sense. And yet, how it frets me, until I'm a leaf blown frantic in a whirlwind.

If only I hadn't been so cynical. I bent my knee where I have no creed, and I'm constrained for my mockery.

Hush, O voice of innocence! Still your whining in the wind. Unsay it. Do not swear, for I am compromised.

She who lies there must recover if ever I'm to come to rest. I love my wife, I love her. My confidence is her hope and her faith in me, mine.

So are we locked.

ACT TWO

SCENE 1

The CHORUS *is heard approaching* EDUFA's *house.*

CHORUS.

Ei! Ei—Ei!

We the orphans cry,

Our mother's dead,

O! O—O!

We the orphans cry.

They enter through the gate at a run. Their exuberance and gaiety would belie the solemn nature of their ritual observance. They stop below the courtyard steps.

CHORUS ONE (*calling*). May we enter? Are there no people in this beautiful house?

CHORUS TWO. In the house of the open gate?

CHORUS THREE. In the house of He-Whose-Hands-Are-Ever-Open?

CHORUS.
　Open Face
　Open Heart
　Open Palm,
　Edufa.

CHORUS FOUR. Come, scratch our palms with a golden coin.

CHORUS FIVE. With a golden nugget.

CHORUS. For luck and good fortune.

CHORUS ONE (*stepping up*). And Ampoma the beautiful; where is she? Woman of this house of fortune. Singing your husband's praise is singing your praises too. Tender heart who nurses him to his fortune. Stand side by side while we beat envious evil out of your house.

CHORUS. Are there no people in this beautiful house?

SEGUWA (*entering from the kitchen*). Who let you in?

CHORUS (*cheerfully*). The gate of this house is always open.

SEGUWA (*uneasily*). Well . . . greeting . . .

CHORUS. We answer you.

SEGUWA (*still hesitating at the kitchen door*). And you have come . . . ?

CHORUS ONE. We have come to drive evil away. Is the man of the house in? And the lady? We are driving evil out of town.
CHORUS.
　From every home
　From street and lane
　From every corner of our town,
　Ei! Ei—Ei!
　We the orphans cry.

CHORUS TWO (*steps up, sniffing and trying to locate the scent*). Incense.

SEGUWA (*moving quickly forward*). Whose funeral sends you out in ceremony?

CHORUS. Another's, and our own. It's all the same. While we mourn another's death, it's our own death we also mourn.

SEGUWA (*touched*). True. (*She wipes away a tear.*)

CHORUS (*crowding near her*). Oh, don't let us sadden you.

SEGUWA. There is so much truth in what you say. I would say, Do your rite and go in peace, for it is most necessary here. I would say, Do your rite and do it most religiously, for it is necessary here. I would say it, but I am not owner of this house.

CHORUS ONE. Why do you hesitate? Is Edufa not in?

SEGUWA. I am trying to make up my mind whether he should be in or out.

CHORUS TWO. Well, if a man is in, he's in; and if he is out, he's out. Which is it?

CHORUS ONE. Make up your mind, for soon, noon will be handing over its power to the indulgent afternoon, and our ritual is timed with the rigors of high noon. Which is it? Is he in or out?

SEGUWA. For driving evil out, he is in, I suppose.

CHORUS. Aha! Then call him.

SEGUWA. I will do my best to bring him out.

CHORUS TWO. Do your best?

SEGUWA. Well . . . I mean . . . Ampoma, his wife, is lying down . . . and . . .

CHORUS ONE. And it is hard for him to tear himself away. . . . Aha!

SEGUWA. Yes . . . No . . . Well . . . let me go and find out. I can make up my mind better away from your questioning eyes. (*With a gesture of invitation as she makes for* EDUFA's *rooms.*) Wait.

CHORUS. We are waiting. (*They surge into the court.*)

CHORUS ONE. What's her trouble? There was a riot in her eyes.

CHORUS TWO. We haven't come to beat her. (*Showing her clappers*) These aren't cudgels to chastise our fellow men. These are for smacking the spirits of calamity.

CHORUS ONE (*snidely*). Ampoma is lying down, she said.

CHORUS TWO (*laughing*). Sick, or lying down in the natural way?

CHORUS THREE. I would say, Simply rich. Would you not do the same in her place? Let her enjoy her ease.

CHORUS FOUR. Imagine the fun of it. (*She goes to the seat, right, and mimes lying down luxuriously, much to the enjoyment of her friends.*) O lady, lady lying in a bed of silk! What kind of thighs, what kind of thighs must a woman have to earn a bed of silk? A bed of silk, O! If I had her life to live, I wouldn't be out of bed at eleven o'clock in the morning either. Never, O!

In the middle of this fun-making, EDUFA *rushes out. He stops short at the sight. But the mood of hilarity there compels him to a show of humor.*

CHORUS (*running up to crowd round him*). Husband!

CHORUS ONE. Aha! The giver himself.

CHORUS. Greeting.

EDUFA. I answer. Well? . . . Well?

CHORUS ONE. We would not dream of passing up your house while we do our rite.

EDUFA. Whose death is it? Is the rite for a new funeral?

CHORUS ONE. No. It's for an old sorrow out of which time has dried the tears. You can say that we are doing what gives calamity and woe the final push in the back—which is a manner of speaking only, as you know—

EDUFA. And you have come here . . .

CHORUS ONE. To purge your house also in the same old manner, for calamity is for all mankind and none is free from woe.

EDUFA. Thank you. You may proceed.

CHORUS TWO (*in fun*). Then cross our palms with the gleam of luck. And give us a welcome drink. (EDUFA *motions to* SEGUWA, *who goes to the kitchen to get drinks, taking the brazier away with her.*) And let the beautiful one, your wife, know that we are here.

EDUFA. She is not very well today.

CHORUS (*genuinely*). Oh! Sorry.

EDUFA. Nothing serious. In fact she is getting better.

CHORUS (*relaxing*). Good. We greet her and wish her well.

EDUFA. She thanks you. Welcome in her name, and from myself as well. (*He takes a big gold ring off his finger and touches the palm of each of the women with it, saying:*) Good luck and good fortune to you, friends. (SEGUWA *brings drinks on a tray, which she places on the seat near the kitchen.*) And here are your drinks.

CHORUS ONE (*solemnly*). Come, friends. Let's do the ceremony for the benevolent one.

CHORUS (*becoming formal*). Evil has no place here. Nor anywhere. Away, away. (*Moving rhythmically at a slow-running pace through the court and courtyard, they perform their ritual with solemnity. Chanting.*)

Our mother's dead,
Ei! Ei—Ei!
We the orphans cry,
O! O—O!
We the orphans cry.

Speaking, at a halt.

Crying the death day of another
Is crying your own death day.
While we mourn for another,
We mourn for ourselves.
One's death is the death of all mankind.
Comfort! Comfort to us all,
Comfort!
Away evil, away.
Away all calamity,
Away!

Chanting, on the move.

Our mother's dead,
Ei! Ei—Ei!
We the orphans cry,
Our mother's dead,
O! O—O!
We the orphans cry.

During this ritual SEGUWA *stands attentively in the background.* EDUFA *remains just above the courtyard steps, intensely quiet, eyes shut in private prayer. the* CHORUS *finish up on the steps below, facing him.*

CHORUS ONE. There now. We have done. Health to you. (EDUFA *is too removed to hear her.*) Health to you, Edufa, and to your wife and all your household. (*To her companions*) See how he is moved. We have done right to come to the house of one as pious as he.

CHORUS TWO. Such faith must surely bring him blessing.

EDUFA (*stirring*). Your drinks await you.

The mood of the CHORUS *changes to lightheartedness again.*

CHORUS ONE (*as her companions collect their drinks, her own glass in hand*). That's right. Tears and laughter. That's how it is. It isn't all tears and sorrow, my friends. Tears and laughter. It isn't all want and pain. With one hand we wipe away the unsweet water. And with the other we raise a cup of sweetness to our lips. It isn't all tears, my friends, this world of humankind.

CHORUS (*drinks in hand*). May you be blessed, Edufa.

EDUFA (*hurrying them up nicely*). Drink up. Day is piling up its hours, and you must be eager to attend the business of your own homes. It was good of you to come. (*He contrives to draw* SEGUWA *aside.*) Go in there. Ampoma was sleeping. It would not do for her to walk out into this. (SEGUWA *hurries into* EDUFA's *rooms.*) You did well to come. A man needs friendship. But it's late in the morning, and you are women . . . with homes to feed.

CHORUS ONE. We will come again to greet your wife.

EDUFA (*skillfully herding them out*). Yes, yes—

CHORUS TWO. Would you sit us at your generous table? Eat with us?

CHORUS THREE. Charm us?

EDUFA. Yes. All in good time . . . some day soon.

SEGUWA (*running out happily*). Edufa! Edufa! She has asked for food.

EDUFA (*excitedly*). For food. She has?

SEGUWA (*making fast for the kitchen*). For soup. She says, I would like some fresh fish soup. Thank God.

EDUFA. Thank God. Get it.

SEGUWA. After three days without interest—

EDUFA. Get it quickly.

SEGUWA. Thank God. (*She enters the kitchen.*)

EDUFA (*calling after her*). Is there fish in the house? If not, send out instantly. Thank God. (*Stretching out his hands to the chorus*) Victory, my friends.

CHORUS one (*puzzled*). So relieved. Ampoma must be more ill than he cared to let us know. Thank God.

CHORUS TWO. He is wise not to spill the troubles of his house in public.

EDUFA (*on his way in*). Thank you, friends. I must leave you now.

SCENE 2

As EDUFA *and the* CHORUS *are leaving,* SENCHI, *carrying a small battered leather case, swings in flamboyantly, whistling to announce himself.*

SENCHI. . . . and the wanderer . . . the wanderer . . . the wanderer comes home. (*Seeing the* CHORUS) Comes in the nick of time, when everything he loves is together in one place. Friends, women, bottles . . . (*His laughter is all-pervasive.*)

EDUFA (*thrilled*). Senchi!

SENCHI (*airily to the* CHORUS). Good afternoon. My name is Senchi, and I'm always lucky. I love women and always find myself right in the middle of them. Welcome me.

CHORUS FOUR (*quite pleased*). He's quite a fellow.

SENCHI. She's right.

EDUFA. Senchi. What brings you here?

SENCHI (*stepping up to him*). Life . . . brings me here. Welcome me.

EDUFA. Indeed. You've come in excellent time.

SENCHI. And what are you doing here? Practicing polygamy? Or big-mammy? Or what? Anyone you choose to declare will be against the law. I'm in transit, as usual. May I spend the night with you?

EDUFA. But certainly. Do me the favor. It's very good to see you, and my privilege to house one as lucky as you obviously are.

SENCHI (*to* CHORUS). Now he flatters.

EDUFA. I only wish we were better prepared to receive you.

SENCHI. Impossible (*His eyes on the* CHORUS) You couldn't improve on this welcome here. All good stock, by their looks. Local breed? They're not dressed for fun and games, though, are they? Pity.

CHORUS three (*approvingly*). He's quite a fellow.

SENCHI (*sniffing*). And I smell—what is that I smell? Incense? (*To* EDUFA) Say, have you changed your religion again? What are you practicing now? Catholicism, spiritualism, neotheosophy, or what? Last time I passed through here, you were an intellectual atheist or something in that category. I wouldn't be surprised to see you turned Buddhist monk next time. (*The* CHORUS *are leaving.*) Don't go when I've only just come. (*To* EDUFA) What are they going away for?

CHORUS. Our work is finished here.

EDUFA. They've been doing a ceremony here. Don't delay them any longer.

SENCHI. Why, I smelled something all right. What are they? Your acolytes? Wait a minute. They're in mourning. Is someone dead? (*To* EDUFA) None of your own, I hope.

EDUFA. No.

CHORUS. This was an old sorrow, friend.

SENCHI. Ah! I understand. One of those "condolences" rites. Why do you people prolong your sorrows so? (*To* CHORUS) Though, I must observe, you have a funny way of going about it—drinking and sniggering. (*Very playfully*) Come on, give me those confounded sticks. I'll show you what they are good for. (*He snatches the clappers from the* CHORUS, *and a mock chase follows, during which he tries to smack them. He flings the clappers in a heap below the steps near the kitchen.*) Now, embrace me, and be done with sorrow.

CHORUS (*delighted*). Oh! Oh! We were on our way.

SENCHI. To me. (SEGUWA, *entering, sees the romping, and her single exclamation is both disapproving and full of anxiety.* SENCHI *turns to her.*) What's the matter with the mother pussy cat? Come over, lady, and join the fun.

EDUFA (*sensitive to* SEGUWA'S *disapproval*). Let the women go now, Senchi.

SENCHI. Why? That's no way to treat me.

SEGUWA (*ominously*). Edufa.

EDUFA. They can come back some other time.

SENCHI. Tonight? All of them?

SEGUWA. Edufa.

EDUFA. Let them go now. Tonight? Very well, tonight.

CHORUS THREE (*eagerly*). To eat?

SEGUWA. Edufa.

EDUFA. Yes. Why not?

SENCHI. You mean that?

EDUFA. A bit of a party, since my wife recovers . . . and—

SENCHI. Oh, how thoughtless of me. Has Ampoma been ill? And I haven't asked of her. . . . Though I've brought her a song. It's all your fault for distracting me. Sorry.

EDUFA. . . . and you too have come, my friend, and brought us luck. It seems to me that we are permitted to celebrate my good fortune—

CHORUS ONE. Expect us.

CHORUS TWO. We will be glad to help you celebrate.

EDUFA (*to* CHORUS). And to you also I owe my gratitude—

CHORUS. Expect us. (*They leave cheerfully through the gate.*)

SENCHI. Wonderful. (*He joins* EDUFA *in the court.*)

EDUFA (*with a great sigh*). Oh, Senchi! This has been quite a day.

SENCHI (*suddenly serious*). Tired? Between you and me, my friend, I'm downright weary in my b-o-n-e-s, myself. I've become quite a wanderer, you know, tramping out my life. It isn't as if I didn't know what I'm looking for. I do. But, oh, the bother and the dither. And the pushing and the jostling. Brother, if you meet one kind, loving person in this world who will permit a fellow to succeed at something good and clean, introduce me, for I would wish to be his devotedly and positively forever. Amen. But of that, more later. I'm worn out with travel. Lead me to a bed in a quiet corner for some sweet, friendly, uncomplicated sleep.

EDUFA. Won't you eat?

SENCHI. No food. Only peace, for a while.

EDUFA. As you wish. (*To* SEGUWA) Take my friend to the guest rooms overlooking the river. It's quiet there. We'll talk when you awake. No luggage?

SENCHI (*showing his battered leather case*). This is all I care about.

EDUFA (*to* SEGUWA). See that he has all he needs. And after, arrange a meal for tonight. Spare nothing. (*He hurries into his rooms.*)

SEGUWA (*grimly*). This way. (*She strides ahead to the steps leading into the guest rooms.*)

SENCHI (*catching up with her*). For the sake of a man's nerves, can't you smile? I can't stand gloom.

SEGUWA. You should have your fun another day.

SENCHI. What particular brand of fun is this you're recommending?

SEGUWA. The party tonight.

SENCHI. That? Don't call that a party, woman. Call it something like Senchi's Temporary Plan for the Prevention of Senchi from Thinking Too Hard. You don't grudge me a small relief like that, surely. (SEGUWA *wipes away a tear.*) Come on. Now what have I said? Are you one of those women who enjoy crying? I'll make a bargain with you, then. Allow me to have my rest. When I awake, I promise to make you cry to your heart's content—by singing, merely. I make songs, you know. (*Patting his leather case*) Songs for everything; songs for goodness, songs for badness; for strength, for weakness; for dimples and wrinkles; and, for making you cry. But I'll tell you a secret. I never make songs about ugliness, because I simply think it should not exist.

SEGUWA (*exasperated*). This way, please. (*She leads* SENCHI *up the steps.*)

ABENA *enters from the kitchen with a smart tray on which is a hot dish of soup. She is on her way to* EDUFA's *rooms, looking decidedly happy.*

ABENA (*stopping halfway up the steps, proudly smelling the soup*). She will like it. I used only aromatic peppers—the yellow—and the mint smells good. (EDUFA *comes out.*) Dear brother. (*She raises the tray for him to smell the soup.*)

EDUFA (*smelling*). Lovely. Little one, are you well? We haven't talked much of late.

ABENA. I'm glad she's better.

EDUFA. Oh . . . yes. You did your work well, it seems.

ABENA. My work?

EDUFA (*quickly changing the subject*). How is your young man? (*He takes the tray.*)

ABENA (*shyly*). I will see him today.

EDUFA. Good. You haven't had much of a chance lately, have you?

ABENA. No . . . er . . . Can't I take the soup in to her? I've had such thoughts. I miss her. We were so happy before all this began, stringing beads and looking through her clothes. She's going to let me wear her long golden chain of miniature barrels at my wedding—right down to my feet.

EDUFA. Let's get her up strong, then. You can see her tonight. We have guests.

ABENA (*appreciatively*). Yes. I've heard him singing.

EDUFA. It's very good to have him here.

ABENA. He sings well.

EDUFA. Some women from town are coming to eat with us tonight.

ABENA (*with childlike joy*). People here again. Laughter again.

EDUFA (*smiling, but compelling her down the steps*). Sister, come. (*Intimately*) Did you mind staying up nights? Was it very hard?

ABENA (*unburdening*). Not . . . too . . . hard. I didn't mind it inside the house, though it got so ghostly quiet at times, I almost saw my lonely thoughts taking shape before my eyes . . . becoming form in the empty air. And then, collecting the stream water . . . that . . . that in the night, and the forest such a crowd of unfamiliar presences.

EDUFA. Hush! It's over. All over. Thank you. Go out now. Enjoy yourself. Can you give us a nice meal tonight?

ABENA. Delighted.

As she goes through the kitchen door, SAM *enters through the gate, running, dodging, like one pursued. He carries a bird cage and a small tin box.*

SAM (*to an imaginary crowd towards the gate*). Thank you. Thank you. (*Gloatingly*) They didn't get me. (*Speaking to no one in particular*) An idiot's life isn't so bad. There are always people to stop children throwing stones at us. They only do that for idiots, I find. (*To the cage*) Let us tell my master that. (*Paying tender attention to what is inside the cage, he walks up a step, crosses to left, and puts the cage and the box down.*)

SEGUWA (*entering from the kitchen*). You're back.

SAM. Are you pleased to see me? (*Lifting up the cage*) Look, he is my bird.

SEGUWA (*horrified*). Don't bring it near me. It's an owl.

SAM (*blithely*). Of course. An owl is a bird.

SEGUWA. What's it doing here?

SAM. It came with me. It was an owl before; but now it's with me, it's no longer itself. It's the owl of an idiot. What we get, we possess. I caught it in a tree.

SEGUWA. Take it outside. (SAM *sulks, turning his back on her.*) Did everything go well? Did you find the place? Did you see the man? (SAM, *moving his bird cage aside, merely nods his affirmatives.*) And what's the news? (SAM's *back stiffens stubbornly.*) It's no good; he won't talk to me. I'll let your master know you're back. (*She goes into* EDUFA's *rooms, while* SAM *pays fussy attention to his owl. She returns with* EDUFA, *who is in a state of high expectancy.*) There he is . . . back.

EDUFA (*coaxingly*). Sam, are you back?

SEGUWA. I don't know what he's doing with that thing. Let him take it away.

EDUFA. What is it, Sam?

SEGUWA. An owl.

EDUFA (*terrified*). Take it out. (SAM *sulks.*) We would do well not to disturb him before we've heard what he has to say. He can get very stubborn. (*Sweetly*) Sam, come here. (SAM *doesn't budge.*) You may keep your bird. (SAM *turns to him, grinning broadly.*)

SAM (*pointing to the owl*). My owl and I had a nice thought for you on the way. When you are born again, Master, why don't you come back as an idiot? There are always people to stop children throwing stones at us. They only do that for idiots, I find.

EDUFA (*smiling in spite of himself*). All right. Now tell me quickly what I want to know. (*Anxiously*) Did you find the place?

SAM. It's an awful place. What do you send me to places like that for? Not the village itself. That is beautiful, floating in blue air on the mountain top, with a climbway in the mountain's belly going zig-zag-zig, like a game. (*He thoroughly enjoys his description.*)

SEGUWA (*impatiently*) He's so tiresome with his rambling.

EDUFA (*trying to be patient*). Good, you found the village. And the man?

SAM. He is a nice man, tall as a god. And he fed me well. You don't give me chicken to eat, but he did. (*Thinks a bit*) What does such a nice man live in an awful house like that for? That's the awful part.

EDUFA (*very anxiously*). Never mind. What did he say?

SAM. Ah! (*Secretively*) Let me fetch my box of goods. (*He fetches the tin box and sets it down before* EDUFA.) First, three pebbles from the river. (*He takes out these pebbles.*) Catch them. (*He throws them one by one to* EDUFA.) One. Two. Three. (EDUFA *catches them all.*) Good! They didn't fall.

EDUFA (*intensely*). I understand that. We mustn't let Ampoma fall to the ground.

SAM (*taking out a ball of red stuff*). With this, make the sign of the sun on your doorstep where your spirit walks in and out with you. Come, I know you are not much of an artist. I'll do it for you the way the man showed me. (*He walks importantly to the steps leading to* EDUFA's *rooms, and as he draws a raying sun boldly on the riser of the first step:*) Rays! Everywhere . . . you . . . turn.

SEGUWA (*with awe*). Ampoma talks so much of the sun.

EDUFA. Yearningly.

SAM (*returning to the box*). And then came the part I didn't understand.

EDUFA (*hoarsely*). Yes . . . quickly, where is it?

SAM. Here it is in this bag. (*He produces an old leather pouch which is spectacularly designed and hung with small talismans.*)

EDUFA (*trembling*). Give it to me.

SAM. Now listen. He says burn it.

> EDUFA *snatches the pouch from him.*

EDUFA (*to* SEGUWA). Get fire—in the back courtyard. Quickly.

> SEGUWA *leaves in haste.*

SAM (*with emphasis*). The man says, Burn it with your own hands, before you bathe in the herbs for the last time.

EDUFA (*with eyes shut*). We're saved. (*Then he becomes aware again of the waiting* SAM.) Well done, Sam. You may go.

SAM. I won't go to that awful house again.

EDUFA. No. Get something to eat. And rest. You are tired. (SAM *picks up the box and walks eagerly to the bird cage.*) But . . . Sam. You must let that bird go.

SAM (*aggrieved*). My owl? Oh, Master, he is my friend. He's the bird of an idiot. He likes us. He and I had a nice thought for you on our way—

EDUFA (*threateningly*). Take it out of here! Out.

SAM. Oh . . . (*He picks up the bird cage and goes out of the gate muttering sulkily.*) We'll stay outside. . . . If they won't have us in, we won't eat. . . . We will starve ourselves. . . . We . . .

EDUFA (*gripping the pouch in his fists with violence*). This is the final act. I will turn chance to certainty. I will burn this horror charm and bury its ashes in the ground: the one act that was still hazard if left undone.

ACT THREE

SCENE 1

A trestle table covered with a fresh white cloth is moved into the court, close to the central seat. So is a loaded drinks trolley. The seats left and right are shifted in. Wicker garden chairs provide additional seating.

   ABENA *and* SEGUWA *are preparing for the party, obviously enjoying doing it with some taste. They move in plates, cutlery, serviettes, wine glasses, etc., pursuing their work without paying more than momentary attention to any distractions.*

   SENCHI *and* EDUFA *appear from the guest rooms.* EDUFA *is in evening dress but has yet to put on his jacket.* SENCHI *looks noticeably absurd in a suit that is not his size. He brings his leather case, which he soon places carefully against the trestle table.*

SENCHI. I'm grateful to you for listening to all my talk.

EDUFA. If it helps, I'm happy to listen. What can I do more?

SENCHI. Every now and then I feel this urge to talk to somebody. It helps me to dispose of the dust of my experiences. And that's when I come here. There are not many people with enough concern to care about what accumulates inside a man. (*He indicates his heart.*) You and Ampoma both listen well, though I must say that you, being so solid and so unemotional, lack the rain of her sympathy.

EDUFA. That's your secret, then. I've never told you I admire you although you can't show a balance in the bank, have I?

SENCHI. No.

EDUFA. I do. You're so relaxed and normally so convincing with your laughter. Yet, you do puzzle me somewhat. Don't you think it is important to have solidity? Be something? Somebody? Is being merely alive not senseless?

SENCHI. What is this something, this somebody that you are? Give it name and value. I'm not being disparaging; I'm seeking.

EDUFA. I don't know. I thought I did until it got so confusing. I . . . Ask the town. They know who Edufa is and what he's worth. They can count you out my value in the homes that eat because I live. Yes, my enterprises feed them. They rise in deference from their chairs when they say my name. If that isn't something, what is? And can a man allow himself to lose grip on that? Let it go? A position like that? You want to maintain it with substance, protect it from ever-present envy with vigilance. And there's the strain that rips you apart! The pain of holding on to what you have. It gives birth to fears which pinch at the heart and dement the mind, until you needs must clutch at some other faith. . . . Oh, it has driven me close to horror . . . and I tell you, I don't know what to think now.

SENCHI (*who has been listening with concern*). We make an odd pair of friends, to be sure. You, with your machines growling at granite in your quarries to crumble and deliver to you their wealth; and I, trying to pay my way in the currency of my songs. But perhaps that, like many statements we are capable of expressing, is merely grasping at extremes of light and dark, and missing the subtle tones for which we haven't yet found words.

EDUFA. Yes, I do have my moments when I'm not quite as solid as you think, when solidity becomes illusory.

SENCHI. But you do give an impression of being settled and satisfied, which is what I'm not.

EDUFA. I wish I could, like you, dare to bare myself for scrutiny. (*Pause*) I'm being compelled to learn however, and the day will come, I suppose.

SENCHI. Ah, yes. We commit these thoughts to the wind and leave it to time to sift them. (*Snapping out of his serious mood*) I'm ready for immediacy which is this evening's light relief. Where are the ladies?

EDUFA. Don't worry; they will not miss this chance to dine at Edufa's house.

SENCHI (*preening*). Do I look noticeable? (*Making much of his ill-fitting suit*) I've never gone hunting in fancy dress before.

EDUFA (*really laughing*). Oh, Senchi, you're so refreshing, you ass.

SENCHI. Yes, call me ass. Always, it's "You're an ass!" Seldom does a man say, "I am an ass." That takes courage. But you're right. I am an ass, or I would be wearing my own suit.

EDUFA. Come on. You don't mind wearing my suit?

SENCHI. I do. It's the same as a borrowed song, to me. Singing other people's songs or wearing other people's suits, neither suits me.

EDUFA (*teasing*). Well, you're in it now.

SENCHI. Being an ass, I am. However, it will serve for an evening of foolery. (*A flash of seriousness again*) Tell me, do you understand, though?

EDUFA. What, Senchi?

SENCHI (*earnestly*). You see, it's like this. My own suit may be shabby, but its shabbiness is of my making. I understand it. It is a guide of self-evaluation. When I stand in it, I know where I stand and why. And that, strangely, means to me dignity and security.

EDUFA. There, you're getting very serious. Have a drink.

SENCHI. A drink. Ah, yes. (*Stopping short at the trolley*) Oh, no, not before I have greeted Ampoma with breath that I have freshened in my sleep.

> *He sits.* EDUFA *serves himself a drink.*

SCENE 2

EDUFA. Our guests will soon arrive. Before they do, I have an act of love that I must make tonight.

SENCHI. You surprise me. Can't you wait? You?

EDUFA. It is a gesture of pure pleasure such as my heart has never before requested.

SENCHI. I don't need telling about the pleasure of it. What I'm saying is, Can't you wait? You?

EDUFA. Just now you judged me unemotional.

SENCHI. Don't worry; after this confessional, I absolve you of the charge.

EDUFA. You see, I've never stinted in giving my wife gifts. Gold she has and much that money can buy. But tonight I'm a man lifted up by her love, and I know that nothing less than flowers will do for one such as she is.

SENCHI. Applause. Talk on.

EDUFA (*to* ABENA). Fetch the flowers, sister. (*She goes into the kitchen.*)

SENCHI (*watching her go*). You make me feel so unmarried, confusing Senchi's Plan for the Ruination of Women. You're driving me to sell my freedom to the next girl that comes too near me.

EDUFA. Don't do that. Learn to love, my friend.

ABENA *returns with a beautiful bouquet of fresh flowers and
hands it to* EDUFA.

SENCHI. Lovely.

EDUFA (*to* ABENA). Little one, you who are soon to marry, I'm giving
you a chance to look at love. Take these flowers in to Ampoma. (*He
speaks emotionally into the flowers.*) Tell her that I, her husband, send
them, that it is she who has so matured my love. I would have
presented them myself, but I have learned the magic of shyness and
haven't the boldness to look into her eyes yet.

ABENA *embraces him happily and takes the flowers from him.*

SENCHI. Applause! Standing ovation! This is the first graceful act I've
ever seen you do. (*As* ABENA *walks away*) Keep the door open as you
go, and let my song keep tune to this moment of nobility. (*He sings.*)
Nne
Nne Nne
Nne
Nne Nne
O Mother
Nne
Nne Nne

ABENA, *turning in appreciation of the song, drops the flowers, which fall on
the step with the sign of the sun on it.*

ABENA. Oh! (*She quickly retrieves the flowers.*)

EDUFA (*becoming tense*). For God's sake, be careful.

SENCHI (*continuing after the incident*).
If I find you
Nne
Nne Nne
I'll have to worship you
Nne
Nne Nne
I must adore you
Nne
Nne Nne
O Mother
Nne
Nne Nne

EDUFA, *enchanted by the song, attempts to join quietly in the refrain.*

She's wonderful
She's wonderful
O Mother
She's wonderful

Yes, if I find you
Nne
Nne Nne
I'll have to worship you
Nne
Nne Nne
I must adore you
Nne
Nne Nne
O Mother
Nne
Nne Nne

EDUFA. Very good, Senchi.

> SEGUWA *is so affected by the song that she is sobbing quietly*
> *behind the table.*

SENCHI (*noticing her*). That is the wettest-eyed woman I've ever seen.
(*He goes to her.*) Oh, sorry; I promised to make you cry, didn't I?
There now, are you happy?

SEGUWA. That's a song after my own heart.

SENCHI. After mine also.

> *There is a sudden ripple of laughter from* EDUFA'*s rooms.*

EDUFA (*elatedly*). That is her laughter. That is Ampoma. I love her.
(ABENA *returns.*) Is she happy?

ABENA. Radiant. She was standing before the mirror when I entered,
looking at her image, her clothes laid out on the bed beside her.
Seeing the flowers mirrored there with her, she turned to greet their
brightness with her laughter. Then she listened to your song with her
eyes shut and sighed a happy sigh. She listened to your message
attentively and said, "Tell my husband that I understand."

EDUFA (*glowing*). She does. I know. She loves. I know.

ABENA. "Tell Senchi," she said, "that all will be left to those who dare to
catch in song the comfort of this world."

SENCHI. That, I have understood.

ABENA. And she will join you later, she says.

EDUFA. Yes, she is able to, tonight. Great heart-beat of mine, it is good
to be alive. (*Briskly*) Senchi, a drink now?

> *They go to the drinks.*

ABENA. Everything is ready to serve, brother. And I am awaited.

EDUFA (*affectionately*). Go; you have earned your moment.

SENCHI (*watching her approvingly*). Little sister, buxom sister. I ought to think of marrying that girl.

EDUFA (*smiling*). Too late. You have lost her to another.

SENCHI. Too bad. I'm always ending up blank. But, never mind now. (*Declaiming*) I will make do with ephemerals. Turn up the next page in Senchi's chronicle of uncertainties. (*He gets a drink.*)

SCENE 3

SENCHI (*at the trolley, his back to the courtyard*). They are coming.

EDUFA (*turning round and seeing nobody*). How do you know?

SENCHI (*also turning round*). I'm highly sensitized, that's all. I can feel women twenty miles away, minimum range.

> The CHORUS *enter through the gate, talking. They are dressed, even overdressed, for the evening.*

CHORUS ONE. That was exciting, dodging those prying eyes in town.

EDUFA (*to* SENCHI). You win. They are here.

CHORUS TWO. Won't they be surprised tomorrow when they learn that we too have been invited here.

CHORUS THREE. There they are, waiting for us.

SENCHI (*to* EDUFA, *meaning his suit*). Do I look noticeable?

EDUFA (*sharing the fun*). I don't stand a chance beside you.

CHORUS ONE. How do I look?

CHORUS FOUR. Fine. (*With relish*) Look at that table. It is good simply to see.

CHORUS TWO (*also impressed*). Ei!

SENCHI. Is there a roadblock there? Come on; I never allow women to keep me waiting.

CHORUS (*in fun below the courtyard steps*). Is there anybody in this beautiful house?

SENCHI (*pleased*). A lively flock, eh? They have a sense of humor. That's a good beginning.

EDUFA (*coming forward*). Good evening.

CHORUS. We answer you.

SENCHI (*meeting them*). Embrace me.

CHORUS ONE (*flirtatiously*). Do you always do things in such a hurry?

SENCHI. That's a good one. That is a rollicking good one. Lady, for that much perkiness, I'm yours . . . momentarily.

EDUFA (*enjoying it*). Senchi. Ladies, it's very good of you to come, and thank you for this morning's kindness.

CHORUS ONE. We trust your wife keeps well. Shall we be seeing her this evening?

EDUFA. Certainly. She will join you presently.

CHORUS ONE. Accept this little gift for her from all of us here. (*She hands the gift to him.*)

CHORUS TWO. We were making so much noise here this morning we hope we didn't disturb her in any serious way.

EDUFA. Oh, no. On her behalf, I thank you. Sit wherever you like. (*The chorus choose seats.* CHORUS FOUR *sits close to the set table, eyeing everything.*) This is indeed most pleasant. I'll get you drinks. (*He places the gift on the table and gets busy with drinks.*)

SENCHI (*startling* CHORUS FOUR *at the table*). We are not quite eating yet, you know.

CHORUS FOUR (*naïvely*). It looks so pretty.

SENCHI. You look prettier than forks and knives and stiffbacked serviettes; that is sure.

CHORUS FOUR (*uncomprehending*). Servietttes?

SENCHI. Yes, these things. (*Taking her by the hand to the seat near the kitchen*) Sit over here with me. I have other things I rather think it will be interesting to try to negotiate with you. May I hold your hand? Or is that considered adultery in these parts? (*They sit.*) I always try to get the local customs straight before I begin negotiations.

EDUFA (*handing out drinks*) Senchi, give the lady a drink at least.

SENCHI assists him.

CHORUS FOUR. Lady! Ei, that's nice.

SENCHI (*pleased with her*). She is positively c-u-t-e.

CHORUS TWO (*confidentially to chorus three*). This is all as we imagined it. Better even.

CHORUS THREE (*full of curiosity*). Who is his friend?

SENCHI (*at the trolley*). Aha! I have ears like a hare, you know. Before a woman can say "Senchi," I come to the summons of her thought. I'm acutely sensitive. Edufa, she wants to know who I am. Tell her I'm a

Efua T. Sutherland   253

neo-millionaire in search of underdeveloped territories. (*The* CHORUS *respond with laughter.*) They applaud. They do have a sense of humor. Fine. (*Fussily*) Drinks all round, and who cares which is what. (*He hands a drink to* CHORUS FOUR.)

EDUFA. I do. Everyone gets exactly what she wants.

The drinks are settled. SENCHI *sits in a central position.*

SENCHI (*raising his glass ceremoniously*). We have it in hand. (*A moment of awkward silence as people drink.*) Now, what's the silence for? This is a party. Shall we play games?

CHORUS ONE. What games?

SENCHI. Party games.

EDUFA. Excuse me. I'll see if Ampoma is ready. (*He goes to his rooms.*)

SENCHI (*rising promptly*). That's kind of you, Edufa. (*To* CHORUS) He is a most considerate, kindhearted man when I'm around.

Let's make the best of our opportunities. Now, let me see. We will not play Musical Chairs; that, being a little colonial, is somewhat inappropriate here. But I'm open to suggestion . . . and . . . if you like, inspection too. (*The* CHORUS *laugh heartily as he strikes poses.*) They merely laugh, which is no way to encourage me. Hm . . . (*He plays at thinking seriously.*) Do you like songs?

CHORUS (*enthusiastically*). Yes.

SENCHI (*liking this*). That means I can entertain you in songs, eh?

CHORUS. Yes.

SENCHI. Do you like stories?

CHORUS. Yes.

SENCHI. That means I must tell them, eh?

CHORUS. Yes.

SENCHI. What do I get for all of this, from you?

CHORUS ONE. We laugh for you.

SENCHI. And with me?

CHORUS. Oh, yes.

SENCHI. Yes. Yes. Do you never say No?

CHORUS. No.

SENCHI. Brilliant conversation. Senchi, you must make better headway. (*Pauses reflectively*) Oh, yes, you are. They say they don't ever say No.

CHORUS ONE. Isn't he funny!

> *She and the others have been enjoying a private joke centered on*
> SENCHI's *ill-fitting suit.*

SENCHI. Oh, madam, that's unkind.

CHORUS ONE. It's your suit . . . pardon me . . . but your suit . . .

SENCHI. That kind of joke should thoroughly frustrate a man. But I must admit it is most intelligent of you. I don't know whether you realize how positively brilliant your observation is. Well now, what next? I have an idea. I sing a bit, you know.

CHORUS (*eagerly*). Ah!

SENCHI. Does that mean, Sing?

CHORUS. Yes.

SENCHI. Yes! We will all sing my song. Listen; it's easy.

> *He sings snatches of the song for* AMPOMA, *encouraging the*
> CHORUS *to participate. They try.*

CHORUS ONE. It's sad.

SENCHI. So it is. But, quickly before you start crying all over me, here is a rumpus song all right. We will have the foolery for which I'm fitly suited tonight. Here is the story of it. A traveller's tale. I'm a bit of a traveller, you know. (*He poses for effect.*)
   And I came to this city called Bam, and there was this man; whether he is mad or simply stark raving poor, I couldn't ascertain. But he impressed me; I can tell you that. Wait a minute; I've written his story down. (*He takes some sheets of paper out of his leather case.*) I'm a bit of a writer, you know. (*The* CHORUS *nudge each other.*)
   A man claimed insane walks through the city streets. No prophet nor priest costumed in fancy gown is he; but he too, afire with zeal, feels that men must heed his creed—or at the least applaud the wit with which he calls them sons of a bitch. (*He looks round for approval. The faces round him are getting blank with incomprehension. He becomes more declamatory.*)
   He raves through the city streets at sane passers-by. And what does he say? He feels that heed ought to be given to his preaching, or at the least, applause must greet his singular screeching:
   "Gentlemen, show me a thought you've thought through, and I'll bow to you right low and grant you a master's due.
   "Feather-fine ladies with hips that rhyme, who the blazes minds your children's manners at this time?
   "Left, right, left, does not feed a nation. I'd rather have you roaring drunk at a harvest celebration."
   Oh, he is a character, an absolute word-exhibitor. But, Ladies, where is your laughter? Aren't you amused?

CHORUS (*quite blank*). We are listening.

SENCHI. Good. I thought myself that his words should sound good on a trumpet. (*He takes a small trumpet out of his leather case.*) Come on, procession! (*He begins to blow a tune to the words in quotation above. The CHORUS are swept into the fun. They are dancing round after him, procession style, when edufa enters, now in his jacket.*) Join up, Edufa. Procession.

EDUFA *complies.* SENCHI *alternates between the trumpet and singing the words. Presently, the whole group is singing to his accompaniment. AMPOMA appears unnoticed at the top of the steps. She is tastefully dressed in a delicate color, looking very much like a bride. She watches the romping scene briefly, with a mixture of sadness and amusement, before she descends at a point when the group is taking a turn in the courtyard.*

EDUFA (*seeing her*). Ah, friends, my wife!

The singing and dancing come to an abrupt halt.

SENCHI (*with profound admiration*). Ampoma. Mother.

CHORUS. Beautiful.

AMPOMA (*graciously*). I'm sorry I was not up to welcome you, Senchi.

SENCHI. You are here now, Ampoma, and well. I couldn't wish for more.

AMPOMA. That was your singing. It is a lovely song.

SENCHI. Yes, for such as you a man must sing. The song is yours, made in the strain of your name, my gift to you. (*He takes a sheet of music out of his pocket.*) Take it. (*She does.*) And accept me as yours, devotedly and positively forever. . . . Amen!

The CHORUS practically applaud.

CHORUS ONE. Isn't he a character!

AMPOMA (*to the CHORUS*). I didn't know about the women being here. Thank you for your company. I hope my husband is honoring your presence here.

CHORUS. We are most happy to be here.

EDUFA. There is a gift they brought for you.

AMPOMA. How kind. (*Pensively*) So many rays of kindness falling on me, each with its own intensity . . . (*Brightening*) I respond with warm heart . . . and hand. (*She shakes hands hurriedly and nervously with the CHORUS.*)

EDUFA (*whispering to her*). Your hand is trembling. You're sure you're not cold? I'll fetch you a wrap.

AMPOMA (*with cheerfulness*). No, I'm well wrapped in your affection, and that is warm enough. My friends, you see I have a most affectionate husband.

SENCHI. We will have to name this the night of fond declarations.

EDUFA (*a little nervously*). Had we better eat now?

AMPOMA. Yes, our friends must be hungry . . . and it is getting late.

SENCHI. Escort her to her chair there. (*He starts the* CHORUS *singing again and moving in mock procession into the court.* AMPOMA *joins in the game. Suddenly she loses her balance and barely avoids a fall. Only her hand touches the ground as she steadies herself.* SENCHI *springs to her support.*) Oh, sorry.

EDUFA (*worried*). Be careful with her. (*He escorts her to a chair by the pillar.*) Sit down, Ampoma, please. (SEGUWA, *who sees the fall as she is bringing in a dish of food, is frozen in her tracks. This so unnerves* EDUFA *that he speaks harshly to her.*) Where's the food? Why are you standing there? Bring it. (*He gives attention to* AMPOMA.)

AMPOMA. I'm all right. Please don't shout at her. She has nursed me well.

SENCHI. No, Edufa, don't. That woman's tears are too ready to fall.

From this stage, a strange mood develops in AMPOMA. *She frequently talks like one whose mind is straying.*

AMPOMA (*fast*). Friends, eat. My husband provides well. I hope you're happy here. Why am I sitting down? (*She rises.*) I must feed you. (*As she quickly passes plates of food served by* SEGUWA) Eat. We must eat to keep the body solidly on its feet. I wasn't able to cook for you myself. (*Pause*) That's sad. A woman must serve her husband well. But I'm sure the food is good. We never serve anything but the best to our friends. Eat. You don't know how good it was to hear you fill this house with merriment. Eat.

Everyone is served. AMPOMA *sits down and receives a plate from* EDUFA, *who has been watching her anxiously.*

SENCHI (*to* CHORUS FOUR). You may eat now. (EDUFA *sits down beside* AMPOMA, *but his mind is not on his food.*) Ampoma, I need your rare counsel. Which of these five women shall I take to wife, lawfully?

AMPOMA (*laughing gaily*). Oh, Senchi, bless you. Which one catches your eye everywhere you turn, like I catch Edufa's eye? That's the one you should have.

The women avert their eyes, eating busily.

SENCHI (*looking round*). No hope.

EDUFA (*at the table*). Here is wine. (*Like one about to propose a toast*) This evening is a celebration unpremeditated.

SENCHI (*sitting up*). Speak, husband, speak.

EDUFA. There is nowhere I would rather be, nothing more than this I would rather be doing. Join with me in drinking to the health of my lovely wife, whom I publicly proclaim a woman among women and friend among friends.

SENCHI. Applause. Vote of thanks!

EDUFA. Drink. To her health.

CHORUS and SENCHI (*rising, each with glass in hand*). To your health, Ampoma.

CHORUS ONE (*instinctively formal*). In all directions we let our libation pour. Your husband is true and rare. Live together blessedly to the end of your days. Health to you.

CHORUS. Health to your children. Health to your house.

AMPOMA (*deeply shaken*). I will have some wine now. Thank you, my friends.

EDUFA (*serving her*). Here.

SENCHI. And enough of solemnity. You're making her pensive.

They all sit.

EDUFA (*with unconcealed concern*). Ampoma.

AMPOMA. I'm all right. (*She rises. She is not all right.*) It is a moving thing to feel a prayer poured into your soul. But now it's over. (*Pause*) Give me some wine. (*Now straining for a diversion, she moves forward to gaze into the sky above the courtyard.*) The night is usually full of stars. Where are they all tonight? Senchi, can't you sing them out in a riot?

SENCHI (*beside her, parodying*). Little stars; little, colossal, little stars. How I wonder where you are. How I wonder why you are. How I wonder which one of you is my star, and why you fizzle.

AMPOMA (*very pleased*). That's good. Oh, Senchi.

CHORUS ONE. He is never at a loss for things to say.

CHORUS TWO. It's extraordinary.

EDUFA. If he could settle down, he could become a poet.

AMPOMA (*seriously*). He is one already, no matter how he roams.

SENCHI (*touched*). Thank you, Ampoma.

AMPOMA (*returning to her chair*). Eat, friends, it's late.

CHORUS TWO. But you are not eating.

AMPOMA. I have fed all I need. And there is no time. Very soon I must embrace my husband before you all, answering the affection into which he draws me. (*She rises hastily and loses her balance again, just avoiding a fall, steadying herself with her hand.*)

EDUFA (*supporting her and very disturbed*). Don't trouble, I implore you.

SENCHI (*to* AMPOMA). Sorry. (*Trying to relax the tensing atmosphere*) But, come on, Edufa. Let her embrace you. I haven't ever seen Ampoma breaking through her shyness. Besides, if she embraces you, then I can embrace all the others; and so the night makes progress swingingly.

AMPOMA (*embracing* EDUFA). Women, I hope you don't think me without modesty. (*Taking up a position*) We spend most of our days preventing the heart from beating out its greatness. The things we would rather encourage lie choking among the weeds of our restrictions. And before we know it, time has eluded us. There is not much time allotted us, and half of that we sleep. While we are awake, we should allow our hearts to beat without shame of being seen living. (*She looks magnificent and quite aloof. Then she speaks more quietly.*) My husband, you have honored me by your words and by your precious gift of flowers. I wish to honor you in return, in language equally unashamed. (*She beckons to* SEGUWA, *who since* AMPOMA*'s near fall has been expressing her alarm in the background.*) Go to my room. On my bed there is a casket. Bring it to me. (SEGUWA *complies.*)

CHORUS TWO. Many women would like to be in a position to say what you have said here, Ampoma.

SENCHI. Therefore, I should not neglect to pay attention to my preliminary surveys which will prepare the way for such contracts to be signed. (*He eyes the* CHORUS *playfully.*) Shall we change seats? (*As he changes seats to sit by another woman*) I have been camping too long in one place and getting nowhere.

SEGUWA returns with the casket.

EDUFA (*confused and uncomfortable*). What's this?

AMPOMA (*opening the casket and taking out some smart waist beads*). Waist beads, bearing the breath of my tenderness.

CHORUS (*nonplussed, eyes popping, but laughing*). Oh! Oh!

EDUFA (*astounded, embarrassed, but not displeased*). Ampoma!

SENCHI (*beside himself*). Great! Whew!

AMPOMA (*inscrutable*). Women, you understand, don't you, that with this I mean to claim him mine? And you are witnesses. My husband, wear this with honor. (*She surprises* EDUFA *by slipping the beads round his neck. His first reaction is shock.*) With it I declare to earth and sky and water, and all things with which we shall soon be one, that I am slave to your flesh and happy so to be. Wear it proudly, this symbol of the union of our flesh.

> The CHORUS *and* SENCHI *are making the best of a most astonishing situation by laughing at* EDUFA's *discomfiture.*

EDUFA (*attempting to hide his embarrassment behind a smile*) Why, Ampoma . . . Well . . . what can I say . . . (*He removes the beads as soon as she lets go.*)

SENCHI. That's rich. Oh, Ampoma, you are the most terrific woman I have ever seen. Don't stand there so foolishly, Edufa. Do something. Say something. I would sweep her up in my arms, take wings, and be gone.

AMPOMA (*very abruptly*). Excuse me, friends, I must leave you. I hope you will tell the town what I have done without considering it gossip. If I had wished it not to be known, I would not have done it here before you. Take my hand in yours quickly. (*She shakes hands with the women in great haste.*) I am happy that you came. . . . I do not know you well, but you are women and you give me boldness to commit my deepest feelings to your understanding. (*She is hurrying away.*) Sleep well when you return to your own homes.

CHORUS (*chilled*). Good night, Ampoma. Good night.

EDUFA (*miserably*). I must see her in. (*He catches up with her before she reaches the steps.*) Are you all right?

AMPOMA (*brightly*). Oh, yes. It's such a relief to feel so well at last.

> *She takes his hand, looks round, and seems to be wanting to linger.* EDUFA *attempts to lead her away.*

SENCHI (*to* CHORUS). You have seen truth.

CHORUS ONE. I couldn't have believed it if my own eyes hadn't witnessed it. Ampoma?

SENCHI. Just do what she recommends, that's all.

> EDUFA *and* AMPOMA *are going up the steps.*

AMPOMA. Thank you, but don't leave our friends. I want to go in alone.

EDUFA. As you wish, my dear, but—

AMPOMA. I want to; please don't leave them now.

EDUFA (*reluctantly*). I'll make it very brief and join you presently. (*He comes down.*) Ah, Senchi, she's all but taken my breath away.

(AMPOMA *falls on the step with the sign of the sun on it, causing* SEGUWA *to scream.* EDUFA *runs to his wife, yelling with horror.*) No! Ampoma! No!

SENCHI (*helping to lift up* AMPOMA). Why didn't you take her up the steps?

CHORUS TWO. She's been unsteady all the time. She's not recovered yet, is she?

EDUFA (*unaware of anyone else's presence*). There, Ampoma, there. You didn't fall all the way to the ground. I will not let you fall. No! No! No! Not to the ground. To the ground? No! Lean on me. You shouldn't have come out. I shouldn't have permitted it. Oh! No! (*He is taking her up.*)

SENCHI (*with great concern*). Take her in. It wasn't a big fall, fortunately. (*Helplessly*) Sleep well, Ampoma. (AMPOMA *turns to look at him with a wistful smile. He is left standing alone on the steps, deeply puzzled.*) That's strange. . . . (*He comes down.*) Well, sit down, ladies. (*Obviously trying to pretend the atmosphere of panic doesn't exist*) I don't blame Edufa for overdoing his concern. He's a man caught in the spell of high romance. Why, if I were in his shoes, I would be even more wildly solicitous. (*He thinks this over, forgetting the presence of the* CHORUS *meanwhile.*) In his shoes? No, not that. I'm wearing his suit, I openly confess, but his shoes I wouldn't wear. I, Senchi, must at all times maintain a genuine contact with the basic earth in my own shoes. (*Shaking himself out of his reflection*) Have a drink. (*But he cannot move.*) She didn't fall too badly, did she? Perhaps she shouldn't be up yet.

CHORUS ONE. I'm thinking the same, remembering her action here.

CHORUS TWO. You saw it? The tension beneath the smile?

CHORUS THREE. She was unhappy.

CHORUS ONE. But she was happy also, strangely.

> *It is now that* SEGUWA *is noticed wandering in the courtyard with gestures of desperation.*

SENCHI (*unnerved*). Woman, you are too excitable. What are you fussing around for like a hen wanting somewhere to lay an egg? (SEGUWA *looks at him as if she's afraid he'll hit her.*) Control yourself.

SEGUWA. I cannot any more. She fell. Did you count? Oh! The thought! She fell three times, and each time she touched the ground. Oh! Oh!

> *The* CHORUS *converge on her.*

CHORUS ONE. What do you mean?

SENCHI. Oh, come off it. My goodness, she didn't break any bones. Ampoma wouldn't forgive you for making her seem so fragile.

SEGUWA. She fell off the sign of the sun; and the sun itself is blanked, and it is dark.

CHORUS (*with urgency*). What sign?

SEGUWA (*out of control*). Bad signs. They would pose no menace if no oath had been sworn and we were free to read in her present condition normal disabilities for which remedy is possible. As it is, the reality of that oath makes Edufa for all time guilty, no matter how or when she meets her end.

SENCHI. Don't talk to us in fragments, woman.

SEGUWA. I thought we could cancel out the memory. (*Rushing towards the steps*) But I see the sign of the three pebbles, and on the third fall she fell on the sign of the sun, to the ground. (*She points out the sign of the sun.*)

CHORUS (*crowding round*) What is it?

SENCHI. What is this, woman?

SEGUWA (*hiding her face in her hands and turning away*). It shouldn't be there to plague our memory, deluding us from the path of reason.

SENCHI. This woman is unstable. I wouldn't have her running about my house if I had one. But. . . what is this sign?

SEGUWA (*terrified*). I don't know. I have told you nothing. Get out. I know nothing about it. Why did you come feasting here tonight? Get out! Get out, all of you. (*She rears up against the wall, pointing at the* CHORUS.) Or are you eager to take Ampoma's place? Can you pay the price of sharing Edufa's bed? Nothing less than your lives? Oh, he is most dangerous.

She dashes off into EDUFA'*s rooms. The* CHORUS *and* SENCHI *hover round the steps, staring at the sign of the sun.*

CHORUS (*several voices*). She's terrified.

SENCHI. So is Edufa. Does a fall call for these flights of terror? Such hysteria? (*He scrutinizes the sign, and his distress increases.*) I should break in there and demand explanation.

CHORUS ONE. Do you remember this morning, at our ceremony, that woman's haunted look, her strangeness?

CHORUS TWO. Her fighting to say whether Edufa was in or out?

CHORUS ONE. And Edufa himself. If there wasn't something terribly wrong, would he have been so conspicuously relieved when Ampoma asked for food?

SENCHI. Do you mean that all this happened here?

CHORUS THREE. Yes, this morning, in our presence.

SENCHI (*grimly to himself*). To me, also, he has shown some strange disturbances of spirit this day. . . . And then, Ampoma's wandering mind tonight, her . . . But let's not run on so. We know nothing until I go in there. (*He is about to force his way into* EDUFA's *rooms when* SEGUWA *rushes out. She cringes when she sees him and flees into the courtyard, her fist in her mouth as if to stifle an outcry.*) Where's Edufa? Woman, speak. What's happening here?

CHORUS. Talk to us. Tell us.

They and SENCHI *press in on* SEGUWA *as she roams with her hand pressed against her mouth. She suddenly notices the clappers that the* CHORUS *used in the mourning rite, seizes them, and thrusts them impulsively at the* CHORUS.

SEGUWA (*bursting out*). Don't ask me to talk. Help me. You have come to do the rite, have you not? Do it quickly, I implore you.

SENCHI (*at the top of the step*). Edufa!

SEGUWA. What is there left of sacredness?

CHORUS. By the souls of our fathers, speak.

SEGUWA. It is that evil charm on which the oath was sworn. We cannot ever forget it. We cannot reason without it now.

SENCHI. What? Charms in Edufa's house?

CHORUS. What charm?

SENCHI. Edufa! It's Senchi.

SEGUWA. And yet he burned it. But the deed was done. He buried it, but it was her he buried.

CHORUS. Buried?

SEGUWA. Oh, speak, tongue! Women, you did your ceremony here, but you left the evil one himself behind you. Edufa. He is in there with his victim. This is the day when Edufa should have died. Another has died for him: his wife, Ampoma. She loved him, and she has died to spare his life.

CHORUS ONE. Died? For him? People don't die that kind of death.

CHORUS. Died? No. We have eaten here with her, laughed with her.

SENCHI (*helplessly*). Groans in there . . . like one who stifles agony lest he shed unmanly tears. I fear it is the worst, my friends.

SEGUWA. Coward! Coward! Coward! He is a cursed man. Go. Tell the town about the man who let his wife die for him. (*She breaks down.*) Then go and tell her mother. Oh, Mother! Will someone go and tell her mother, for I cannot look her in the face. I cannot look those motherless children in the face.

CHORUS. You lie. We will not believe you.

SEGUWA. Come, I'll show you where he buried it.

> *She strides ahead to take them to the back courtyard. Just at this point* EDUFA *comes out, a man clearly going out of his mind. The* CHORUS *run up to crowd below the steps.*

CHORUS ONE. Oh, Edufa. Has this woman fed from your hand, who now maligns you so?

> SEGUWA *has fled at sight of* EDUFA.

CHORUS. We implore you, tell us she lies. We do not believe her, pious one. Tell us she lies.

SENCHI. Friend, what is this?

EDUFA (*dejectedly on the steps*). If you see my father, call him back that I may weep on his shoulder.

CHORUS. Great God, is it true that she is dead?

SENCHI (*shaking him*). Edufa. Friend. What's all this about charms?

EDUFA (*violent, his voice unnatural*). I burned it. (*He slouches helplessly on the steps.*)

SENCHI. Stand up, man. What in the name of mystery is it all about?

CHORUS ONE. Do you hear him? He buried it, he says. There was something then? Edufa, is it true what this woman says? That Ampoma is dead, and in your place?

EDUFA. . . . and buried . . . (*Wildly*) I told her not to swear. I did not know that harm could be done. I did not know it. (*Looking belligerently at* SENCHI, *and not recognizing him*) Who are you? Why are you looking at me?

SENCHI (*sadly*). Senchi.

CHORUS ONE. He is raving.

EDUFA. I told her not to swear. I didn't know that harm could be done.

CHORUS. Not to swear, or harm could be done. Alas!

SENCHI (*seizing hold of him*). Tell me all, Edufa.

> *The owl hoots outside.*

EDUFA (*wildly*). Didn't he take that bird away? (*He looks at* SENCHI *dangerously.*) Who are you? Don't restrain me. (*Straining with more than natural strength*) Where is my leopard skin? I'll teach Death to steal my wives. (*So strong that* SENCHI *can no longer restrain him*) Death, I will lie closely at the grave again, and when you come gloating with your spoil, I'll grab you, unlock her from your grip, and bring her safely home to my bed. And until then, no woman's hand shall touch me.

CHORUS. She is dead. (*They rush into* EDUFA's *rooms.*)

SENCHI (*with infinite sadness*). There, Edufa, there . . . don't rave so. No . . . not this. (*He attempts to hold him again.*)

EDUFA (*wrenching himself free*). The last laugh will be mine when I bring her home again. I will bring Ampoma back. Forward, to the grave. (*He moves in strength towards the back courtyard, roaring.*) I will do it. I am conqueror! (*His last word, however, comes as a great questioning lament.*) Conqueror . . . ?

He runs out by way of the back courtyard. The CHORUS *return mournfully.* SENCHI *makes his way past them into* EDUFA's *rooms.*

CHORUS (*several voices together, and a single voice every now and then, as they make their way out through the gate; rendered at a slow dirge tempo*).
Calamity.
That we should be the witnesses.
Do not restrain your tears,
Let them stream,
Make a river of sorrow, for Ampoma is dead.
We do not know how,
We do not understand,
But she is dead.

Will someone go and tell her mother!
Edufa! Edufa!
How is it possible
That she is dead?

They can be heard beating their clappers after the chanting. SENCHI *returns. He stands alone on the steps.*

SENCHI. Blank. I have ended up blank once again. All that is left, the laughter of the flowers in her lifeless arms and the lingering smell of incense. (*He descends.*) And over me, the taut extension of the sky—to which I raise my song. Will someone go and tell her mother? (*He sings.*)
And if I find you
I'll have to worship you
I must adore you
Nne
Nne Nne
O Mother
Nne
Nne Nne

The End.

DISCUSSION QUESTIONS

1. According to the classical definition of a tragic hero, the protagonist is a person better than ourselves who through some error in judgment, weakness of character, or twist of fate suffers crushing defeat or death. Explain how the character Edufa fits this description.

2. Might Ampoma also fit the classical definition of a tragic hero? Explain your answer.

3. From the very beginning of the play to the end, the fear of Ampoma's death hangs like a dark cloud over the proceedings. Does this fact make her eventual death more, or less, tragic—more, or less, painful to accept? Explain your opinion.

4. Contrast Seguwa and Senchi. What purpose does each serve in the play?

5. *Edufa* is based on the Greek legend of Admetus and Alcestis which is immortalized in Euripedes' play *Alcestis*. Find in your school library a plot summary of *Alcestis* (either in a book of famous literary plots or in an encyclopedia like *Encyclopaedia Britannica*). Read the plot summary and then explain the major difference between it and *Edufa*.

SUGGESTION FOR WRITING

In the original Greek legend upon which *Edufa* is based, Alcestis, the equivalent of Ampoma, is rescued in the end and saved from death. Can you do the same for Ampoma? Can you figure out a way to come to her aid and bring a happy ending to *Edufa*? Create a new ending for *Edufa* in which some force for good—either an existing character in the play or a new one you add to the cast—rescues Ampoma from death. For the sake of simplicity, deal only with the events that happen near the end of the play—perhaps the last half of the last scene—and create your new ending in prose. If you would prefer the challenge of writing dramatic dialogue, you may do so, but it is not mandatory.

TSEGAYE GABRE-MEDHIN

(born 1935)

Tsegaye Gabre-Medhin was born in Ambo, Ethiopia. He attended the Blackstone School of Law in Chicago and also studied drama in England, France, and Italy. In 1966 Tsegaye became the acting director of Ethiopia's Haile Selassie Theatre in Addis Ababa. Tsegaye is a playwright, novelist, poet, and essayist, and is generally considered to be one of the finest Ethiopian writers in the English language. His novel, *Oda-Oak Oracle,* is thought by many critics to be the best fiction in English to come from Ethiopia. At the 15th Congress of World Poets held in England in 1997, Tsegaye's poetry was honored and his essay "Poetry Conquered the Darkness and the World Was Saved" was presented. ■

HOME-COMING SON

Look where you walk, unholy stranger—
this is the land of the eighth harmony
in the rainbow: Black.
It is the dark side of the moon
5   brought to light;
this is the canvas of God's master stroke.

Out, out of your foreign outfit, unholy stranger—
feel part of the great work of art.
Walk in peace, walk alone, walk tall,
10   walk free, walk naked.
Let the feelers of your motherland
caress your bare feet,
let Her breath kiss your naked body.
But watch, watch where you walk, forgotten stranger—
15   this is the very depth of your roots: Black.

Where the tom-toms of your fathers vibrated
in the fearful silence of the valleys,
shook in the colossus bodies of the mountains,
hummed in the deep chests of the jungles.
20   Walk proud.

Watch, listen to the calls of the ancestral spirits, prodigal son—
to the call of the long-awaiting soil.
They welcome you home, home. In the song of birds
you hear your suspended family name,
25 the winds whisper the golden names of your tribal warriors,
the fresh breeze blown into your nostrils
floats their bones turned to dust.
Walk tall. The spirits welcome
their lost-son-returned.
30 Watch, and out of your foreign outfit, brother,
feel part of the work of art.
Walk in laughter, walk in rhythm, walk tall,
walk free, walk naked.
Let the roots of your motherland caress your body,
35 let the naked skin absorb the home-sun and shine ebony.

DISCUSSION QUESTIONS

1. What color is emphasized in this poem? Find four places in the poem where the color is mentioned or alluded to? Why do you think the speaker emphasizes this color?

2. Note the title "Home-Coming Son" and the three references in the poem to a "stranger." Who is coming home? Where is home? Where do you think the stranger has been?

3. In the poem the speaker is addressing the stranger. What is the speaker trying to tell the stranger?

SUGGESTION FOR WRITING

Have you ever spent a relatively long period of time away from your home and friends? Perhaps you moved to another part of the country for a while. Perhaps you spent a year studying abroad or part of a summer at a camp. How did it feel to get back home? Were you happy? disoriented? Did you feel out-of-it for a time? Did you have to readjust? Write a few paragraphs in which you describe how it felt to be back home. If you haven't experienced such a situation, imagine what it would be like to leave home for a period of time and write about that. What do you take for granted at home? What would you miss most? What would you most enjoy about being away?

MATALA MUKADI TSHAKATUMBA

(born c. 1940)

Born a member of the Mulubu tribe in the Lower Congo (now Zaire), Tshakatumba began to write during his school years in Boma, a practice that continued throughout his years at the University of Liege in Belgium, where he studied political science beginning in 1965. That year a selection of his poetry appeared in the publication *Afrique*: "Baobob," Deception," "A Kanika" ["To Kanika"], and "Prière sans echo" ["Prayer Without an Echo"]. Two of his poems were later anthologized in *The African Assertion* by Austin J. Shelton (1968). In 1969 he published a volume of his work entitled *Réveil dans un nid de flammes* ["Waking Up in a Burning Nest"]. In the selection that appears here, Tshakatumba addresses a black woman, a symbolic figure who invokes mother Africa. ■

MESSAGE TO MPUTU ANTOINETTE, GIRL OF THE BUSH, FRIEND OF MY CHILDHOOD

African sister black sister
you who do not know Damas or Mackay
you who must learn Césaire and Senghor[1]
you who are ignorant of the boundaries of your continent
and in the half-light go to draw water
like an ancient goddess
wearing an Edenic smile
at the only spring in the neighborhood
it is for you above all that I labor
it is for you that the cold benumbs me
sister of the sapodilla tree[2] loving sister
Africa will be the fruit of our accord.

---

1. **Damas . . . Mackay . . . Césaire . . . Senghor:** Léon Damas (1912–1978), Claude Mackay (1890–1948), Aimé Césaire (born 1913), and Léopold Sédar Senghor (born 1906). All were black poets who have celebrated the beauty of black women. They were among the young students who founded the Negritude movement in Paris in 1934. See the article on page xvii.

2. **sapodilla tree:** a tropical evergreen.

Tireless gazelle
who wanders at the close of day
through the hushed thickets of dead wood you gather
O black woman! guileless sister
your beauty touches me your beauty enchants me
like the blue wave simmering
in your unfathomable depths
To see moored beneath the intertwined lianas
a continent moored in a trance
where the tom-toms beat out the rhythm of life
O loving friend in the giant encrusted lokumé:[3]
Africa will be what together we make it.

———
3. **lokumé:** a Central African tree.

DISCUSSION QUESTIONS

1. Make a list of all of the nature imagery that you find in this poem. What do you think is the author's purpose in using it?

2. This poem is a typical example of the verse of the Negritude school (see page xvii). One common theme is of this movement is that of Africans in exile. What details in the poem suggest that Tshakatumba is in exile?

3. For many of the Negritude poets, the black woman symbolizes Africa. How would you characterize the poet's attitude toward his childhood friend and the Africa she represents?

SUGGESTION FOR WRITING

Tshakatumba makes good use of two poetic devices in this poem: parallelism and epithet. Parallelism is the repeated use of the same grammatical structure:

> you who do not know . . .
> you who must learn . . .
> you who are ignorant . . .

An *epithet* is an adjective or adjective phrase used to describe or characterize a person or thing:

> sister of the sapodilla tree . . .
> tireless gazelle . . .

Write a short poem to a friend of your childhood (or to anyone else who is important to you) focusing on that person's good qualities and the pleasant memories you have of your time together. Pattern your poem after Tshakatumba's by using parallelism and epithet.

AMOS TUTUOLA

(1920–1997)

From modest beginnings in Abeokuta, Nigeria, Amos Tutuola eventually became a successful author and the first African writer to earn international acclaim. Although he was a bright student with a quick mind, his formal schooling ended with the unexpected death of his father, a cocoa farmer, who had been financing his education.

Hoping to earn money to pay his own school fees, Tutuola turned his hand to farming corn. That year the rains failed, and the crop yield was disappointing. He then trained as a blacksmith and served in the Royal Air Force as a coppersmith. After World War II he attempted to earn a living as a metalworker and then as a photographer, but was unsuccessful in both of these ventures. It wasn't until Tutuola took a job as a messenger that his literary career began.

Tutuola filled the long hours of boredom between errands by writing stories. His skill as a storyteller, going back to his school days, enabled him to complete his first book, *The Palm-Wine Drinkard* (1952) in only a few days. The eventual success of his first work motivated him to improve his skills as a writer, and so he began taking evening courses and studying literature and mythology.

Tutuola fascinates readers with his unusual use of English. His unique style is due in part to the fact that he writes in a language that is not his first. Somehow this language serves to create a remarkable expression of the Yoruba myths and legends he revisits in his writing. *The Palm-Wine Drinkard,* which remained his most popular work, was adapted into a successful stage production. Other works include *The Brave African Huntress* (1958), *The Wild Hunter in the Bush of Ghosts* (1982), *Yoruba Folktales* (1986), and *Pauper, Brawler, and Slanderer* (1987). The first story below is from *The Brave African Huntress.* ■

ANIMAL THAT DIED BUT HIS EYES STILL ALIVE

The big gun that stops the voices of the soldiers
Animals are surplus in the town in which the people have no teeth

As I (Adebisi, the African huntress) was traveling along in this jungle it was so I was killing all the wild animals that I was seeing on the way. When I saw that the night was approaching I shot one small animal to death. I made a big fire and I roasted this animal which was an antelope, in the fire. Before I ate it to my satisfaction it was about ten o'clock in the night. But anyhow I ate out of it as I could and I kept the rest of it near the fire which I would eat in the morning. After that I lay down near this fire and then I slept but there was nothing which was happened to me throughout this night.

When I woke up in the morning by the crying of birds and when the dove gave the sign of eight o'clock, then I ate the rest of that roasted animal. After that I hung my gun and hunting bag on my shoulder having checked the gun and saw that it was in good order. Then I started to look for the wild animals to be killed. And within three days I nearly killed the whole of the wild animals of this jungle. It was very scarcely to see one or two and I was very happy about this, but it still remained three big troubles—how to drive away all the pygmies from this jungle as they used to detain hunters in their custody. How to kill the dangerous animals who had light on eyes and how to kill a very curious and dangerous boa constrictor which was very dangerous to the hunters as well.

After I nearly killed the whole of the wild animals, I did not travel more than seven days when I came across a big wild animal. It was as big as an elephant. I had never seen the kind of this animal before. Because he had a very big head. Several horns were on his forehead. Each of the horns was as long and thick and sharp as cows' horns. Very long black and brown hairs were full this head and they were fallen downward, they were also very dirty. All the horns were stood upright on his forehead as if a person carried a bunch of sticks vertically. His beard was so plenty and long that it covered his chest and belly as well. The teeth of his mouth were so plenty and long that whenever he was eating a person who was in two miles away would be hearing the noises which they were making. Even as the teeth and the horns of his mouth and head were so fearful many of the wild animals who saw him when he was coming to kill them with all these things were dying for themselves before he would reach them instead to kill them with his teeth and horns, because they were too fearful to them.

He had two curious eyes which were as accurate as full moon of the dry season. Both were on the right part of his head as the other animals did, but each was bigger and could see everywhere without moving head. The powerful light that these eyes were bringing out could not go far or straight but they were bringing out the clear and round light. The ray of this light was always round him and it could be seen clearly from a long distance.

He had a kind of a terrible shout with which he was frightening the animals and his humming was also terrible to hear. All the rest animals were so hated and feared him that they never went near the place that he traveled for one week.

There was none part of his body which was not terrible and which was not frightened neither human being nor other creature of this world.

Immediately I saw this "super-animal" as I could call him, in that morning through the round clear light of his eyes, was that I stopped in one place and I first breathed out heavily with great fear. Because I could not escape again, I had already approached him too closely before I saw him. And at the same moment that he too saw me, although I was still quite aloof when he first saw me. He first sighted all his horns towards me and then he was running to me as fast as he could. But when I thought within myself that if I stood on the ground and shot him, he would kill me instantaneously, because my "shakabullah" gun would not be able to kill him in one shot, therefore I hastily climbed a tree to the top.

But when he ran to the place that I had stood before and he did not meet me there again. He was going round and round until when he saw me on top of this tree. As I was on top of this tree I thought that I was saved but not at all. Because at the same moment that he saw me on top of this tree, he started to bite the tree at the bottom. And to my fear within two minutes he had nearly bitten the whole bottom of this tree. When I saw that the tree was just toppling to the ground, just to save my life, I hastily jumped from there to the top of another mighty tree which was nearby. And when he saw me on top of this mighty tree again, he started to bite the bottom of it as well and he was in great anger this time because he wanted to eat me without much trouble as this.

And when I saw that this mighty tree was toppling down as well, then I hastily sold my "death," I said within myself that before this "super-animal" would kill me I must first defend myself perhaps I would be saved. Then without hesitation I shot him. But when the gun-shots hit him on the chest and hurt him as well on the hind legs. It was this time this "super-animal" became more powerful and more dangerous than ever. And it was this day that I believed that—the half-killed snake is the most dangerous. Because this animal was then shrieking and shouting and humming more terribly with angry voice than ever. His fearful humming was hearing all over the jungle.

He was jumping and dashing to the trees, rocks, etc. and within a few minutes he had broken down all the trees of that area and scattered everything in disorder with great anger. When he came back to the tree on top of which I was he started to bite the bottom of this tree until it fell down. This tree hardly fell down when he jumped on me, but I was so lucky that immediately this tree fell on hard ground, it sprang up again before it lay down quietly, I fell off from it to a little distance, so by that he missed me to grip with his paws. Of course I hit my back on another tree which was near that spot and that gave me much pain. And as I was hastily standing up he had jumped high up and as he was coming down just to cover the whole of me, hastily lay flatly on the ground and then he simply rolled along on the ground instead. Before he stood up again I had taken my cutlass[1] and I was waiting for him at once.

Within one second he had stood up, but he did not attempt to bite me this time, he wanted to hit me to death with his horns. But at the same moment that I saw what he wanted to do this time, I hastily leapt to my left when he was about to butt me with his horns and I cut him several times with my cutlass within this moment, so he simply butted a heavy rock instead when he missed me.

He hardly missed me when he turned to his back and as he was coming again with great anger, I hastily leaned my back on the stump of the big tree which he had cut down, and I exposed my chest and belly in such

---

1. **cutlass:** a sword with a short, curved blade; a machete.

a deceived way that he believed that he would not miss me as before. So as he was running furiously towards me with all his power and when he was about to reach me, I hastily leapt again to my right unexpectedly and unfortunately he simply butted the stump of that tree. So all his horns pierced this stump of tree, he could not pull them out but he was held up there helplessly, except his hind legs with which he was scattering the ground very roughly.

After I rested for a few minutes then I started to beat him with my poisonous cudgel until when he was completely powerless and then he died after some minutes. It was like that I killed this "super-animal" as I could call him. But to my surprise was that as he had already died the light of his eyes was still shining clearly and thus it was when I left there.

After I had killed this animal I started to look about for the fearful boa constrictor which my father had told me about his news that he (boa) was also very dangerous. As I was looking for this boa constrictor it was so I was killing all the wild animals which I was seeing on the way. And in a few days' time I killed the whole of them. So this time there was no more the fear of the wild animals again in this jungle except the fears of this terrible boa constrictor and the pygmies. I roamed about for several days but I did not come across this boa until one day when I traveled back to the place where I had killed "super-animal" unnoticed. But it was still a great surprise to see that the light of the eyes of this animal was still shining clearly. The flesh of his body was already decayed and the bones were already scattered on the ground but the eyes which brought out this light was still alive, the light was as clear as when the animal was still alive. So the eyes and the long hairs which were covered the skull were still on this skull as well and all the horns were still on the skull but they were still pierced the stump of that tree since the day that the animal had butted it (stump) himself.

In the first instance that I came there unexpectedly and when I saw this head with the clear light I thought that the animal had become alive after I had left there the other day. I stood before this head and I started to think of what to do with it, because the clear light which came out from the eyes was very attractively. When I thought what to do with it for a few minutes and I did not know yet so I pulled the head out of the stump. I first trimmed the hairs of the head very short then I cut those long horns very short too after that I trimmed the inside of the skull very neatly. But to my surprise when I put this skull or head on my head it was to my exact size and it seemed on my head as a cock helmet. I was seeing clearly through the eyes and the light of the eyes traveled far away in the jungle but I was then so fearful that there was not any living creature which would see me would not run away for fear because I was exactly as when that animal was alive. So when I believed that it would help me in future I wrapped it with the skin of animal and I kept it in my hunting bag. As from that day I was using it in the night as my light and I was wearing it on the head whenever I was hunting. So this wonderful head became a very useful thing at last.

DISCUSSION QUESTIONS

1. Early in the story, Adebisi explains that she must kill the dangerous animals who had "light on eyes." What do you think this phrase means?

2. What is the purpose of Adebisi's quest in this story? In other words, what does she hope to achieve? Is she successful?

3. Both Tutuola's story and D. O. Fagunwa's "The Forest of the Lord" (p. 109) are fantastic tales about hunters and quests. How would you compare the tones of these two narratives?

SUGGESTION FOR WRITING

At one time Tutuola's fellow Nigerians criticized him for using what they considered imperfect English. Try rewriting some of Tutuola's shorter paragraphs, this time using Standard English. What has been gained or lost by doing this? Which version do you prefer?

DON'T PAY BAD FOR BAD

There once lived two tight friends, named Dola and Babi. Both were ladies. Babi and Dola liked each other since when they were children. They wore the same kind of clothes and were always going everywhere together in their village and to several other villages as well. Because of this many people thought that they were twins.

Both were going everywhere together until they grew old enough to marry. But as they liked each other so much they decided to marry two men of the same family and who lived in the same house, so that they might be with each other always.

Luckily, a few days after they had thought to do so, they heard of two men who were born by the same father and mother and lived in the same house as well. So Babi married the one who was junior and Dola married to the second who was the senior. Now, Babi and Dola were very happy because they were living together in their husbands' house as when they had not married.

A few days after their marriage, Dola cleared a part of the front of the house very neatly. She sowed one kola-nut on that spot. After a few weeks the kola-nut shot out. Having seen this, she filled up one big jar with water and put it before her new kola-nut tree. Very early in the morning, Dola would go and kneel down before her tree and jar and then she would pray to the tree to help her to get a baby in time. Then after the prayer, she would drink some of the water which was inside the jar. Dola believed that there was a certain spirit who was coming and blessing the kola-nut tree and the water in the night. Having done all this then she would go back to her room before the rest of the people in the house would wake.

After some months, the kola-nut tree grew up to the height of about two feet. But unfortunately the animals of the village began to eat the leaves of the tree and this hindered its growth. One morning, Babi saw Dola, her friend, as she knelt down before the tree and jar praying. After the prayer, Babi asked: "Dola, what are you doing before that kola-nut tree and the jar?"

"Oh, this kola-nut tree is my god and I ask it always to help me to get a baby in time," Dola, pointing a finger to the tree and jar explained quietly.

But when Babi noticed that the animals had eaten the leaves of the tree, she went back to her room. She brought the head of her large pitcher from which the body had been broken away. She gave it to Dola and advised her to cover her tree with it so that the animals might not be able to eat the leaves of the tree again. Dola took it from her and thanked her greatly. Then she covered her tree with it and as from that morning the animals were unable to eat the leaves again and the tree then grew as quickly as possible in the center of the head of the pitcher.

A few years after, the tree yielded the first kola-nuts. The nuts were of the best quality in the village. For this reason the kola-nut buyers bought them with a considerable amount of money. And when the tree yielded the second and third nuts, the buyers bought them with a large sum of money as before. So in selling these nuts, Dola became a wealthy woman.

Having seen this, Babi was so jealous that one day, she asked—"Please, Dola, will you return the head of my pitcher this morning?" "What? The head of your pitcher?" Dola shouted with great shock.

"Yes, the head of my pitcher. I want it back this morning," Babi replied in a jealous voice.

"Well, the head of your pitcher cannot be returned this time unless I break it into pieces before it will be able to come out from my tree," Dola replied with a dead voice.

"The head of my pitcher must not break nor split in any part before you return it to me." Babi shouted without mercy.

"I say it cannot be taken away from the tree unless the tree is cut down!" Dola explained loudly.

"Yes, you may cut the tree down if you wish to do so, but at all costs, I want the head of my pitcher back!" Babi boomed on Dola.

"But, Babi, remember that both of us had become friends since when we were children. Therefore, do not attempt to destroy my kola-nut tree," Dola begged Babi.

"Yes, of course, I don't forget at any time that we are friends but at any rate, I want the head of my pitcher now!" Babi insisted with a great noise.

At last, when it was revealed to Dola that Babi simply wanted her tree to be destroyed so that she might not get kola-nuts to sell any more, she went to the court of law. She sued Babi for trying to destroy her tree. But when the judge failed to persuade Babi not to take the head of her pitcher back, he judged the case in favor of her, that Dola must return the head of the pitcher to her.

With great sorrow, the kola-nut tree was cut down and the head of the pitcher was taken away from the tree and returned to Babi. Babi was now very happy not because of her pitcher but of Dola's tree which was cut down. After that she and Dola entered the house and they continued their friendship as before. And Dola did not show her sorrow for her tree in her behavior towards Babi.

A few months after the tree was cut down, Babi delivered a female baby. In the morning that Babi's baby would be named, Dola gave her a fine brass ring as a present, to put on her baby's neck, because brass was one of the most precious metals in those days. Babi took the brass ring from Dola with great admiration and she put it on her baby's neck at the same time. This brass ring had been carefully molded without any joint.

Ten years passed away, when one fine morning, as Babi's baby was celebrating her tenth birthday, Dola went to Babi, and asked gently—

"Babi, my good friend, I shall be very glad if you will return my brass ring this fine morning."

"Which brass ring!" Babi sprang up and shouted.

"My old brass ring which is now on your daughter's neck," Dola pointed a finger at the girl's neck as if she was simply joking with her.

"This very brass ring, on my daughter's neck?" Babi was trembling with fear.

"Yes, please," Dola replied quietly.

"Please, Dola, my good friend, don't try to take your brass ring back, as you know, before the ring can be taken away from my daughter's neck, her head must be cut off first because it is already bigger than the ring!" Babi begged with tears.

"I don't force you to cut off the head of your daughter but I want my brass ring back without cutting it!" Dola insisted.

At last when Babi failed to persuade Dola not to take her brass ring back from her, she went to the same court of law. She sued Dola for trying to kill her daughter. Unfortunately, the case was judged in favor of Dola when she had related the story of her kola-nut tree which was cut down when Babi insisted on taking the head of her pitcher back. The judge added that the head of Babi's daughter would be cut off in the palace of the king and in the presence of the whole people of the village so that everybody might learn that jealousy was bad. Then a special day was fixed to behead Babi's daughter so that the brass ring could be taken away from her neck.

When that day came the whole people of the village gathered in the front of the palace and the king sat in the middle of the prominent people. Then the king told Babi loudly to put her ten-year-old daughter in the center of the crowd and she did so. She and her daughter stood and both were trembling with fear while the swordsman who was ready to behead her daughter stood at the back of the girl with the sword in hand and was just waiting to hear the order from the king and then to behead her. Then the king announced loudly to Babi—

"As Dola's kola-nut tree was cut down the other day when you insisted on taking the head of your pitcher back, so the head of your daughter will be cut off now, before Dola's brass ring will be taken away from your daughter's neck and given back to her."

The people were so quiet with mercy that it was a few minutes after the king had announced to Babi before they could talk to each other. And the people mumbled again with grief when the king gave the order to the swordsman to behead the daughter. But as the swordsman raised the sword up to cut the head off, Dola hastily stopped him and announced loudly—

"It will be a great pity if this ten-year-old daughter is killed, because she has not offended me but her jealous mother. And I believe, if we continue to pay bad for bad, bad will never finish on earth, therefore, I forgive what Babi has done to my kola-nut tree!"

The king and the rest of the people clapped loudly for Dola immediately after she pardoned Babi. Then everyone went back to his or her house with gladness. But Dola and Babi were still good friends throughout their lives' time.

DISCUSSION QUESTIONS

1. Compare your ideas about the concepts of giving and friendship with those expressed in the story.

2. As "Don't Pay Bad for Bad" approached its climax, were you fearful about the outcome? Did the resolution of the story satisfy you?

3. In a famous Old Testament story about the wisdom of King Solomon (see 1 Kings 3), two women both claim the same newborn child. Solomon offers to cut the child in half; horrified, the real mother surrenders her claim, whereupon Solomon awards her the infant. How is "Don't Pay Bad for Bad" like and unlike the biblical narrative?

SUGGESTION FOR WRITING

Imagine that you are a new judge in Dola and Babi's village, sent to replace the previous judge. The two friends have come to you with their dispute over the return of the brass ring that is now around the neck of Babi's young daughter. Knowing what you know about the details of this case, what would your decision be? Write an "opinion" explaining your thinking.

Acknowledgments

xi "Poem of the Conscripted Warrior" by Rui Nogar, trans. Philippa Rumsey. From *African Writing Today*, ed. Ezekiel Mphahlele.

xvii Quotation in "Negritude" from *The Encyclopedia of World Literature in the 20th Century*, ed. Wolfgang Bernard Fleischmann. New York: Frederick Ungar Publishing Co.: 1969. Reprinted by permission of The Continuum Publishing Group.

3 "How the World Changed" (Anonymous) from *Liberian Folklore*, copyright © 1966 by Doris Banks Henries. Reprinted by permission of Macmillan Co., Ltd.

4 "The Eye of the Giant" from *Tales Told in Togoland* by A. W. Cardinall. First published by the International African Institute, London. Reprinted by permission.

6 "Anansi's Fishing Expedition" from *The Cow-tail Switch and Other West African Stories* by Harold Courlander and George Herzog. Copyright 1947, © 1974 by Harold Courlander. Reprinted by permission of Henry Holt and Company, Inc.

10 "The Singing Cloak" from *Tales Told in Togoland* by A. W. Cardinall. First published by the International African Institute, London. Reprinted by permission.

12 "The Gourd Full of Wisdom" from *Tales Told in Togoland* by A. W. Cardinall. First published by the International African Institute, London. Reprinted by permission.

13 "How Hawk Learned of the Shallow Hearts of Men" (Anonymous) from *Liberian Folklore*, copyright © 1966 by Doris Banks Henries. Reprinted by permission of Macmillan Co., Ltd.

14 "The Hunter Who Hunts No More" from *Tales Told in Togoland* by A. W. Cardinall. First published by the International African Institute, London. Reprinted by permission.

14 "The Talking Skull" (Anonymous) from *African Genesis* by Leo Frobenius and Douglas G. Fox, published by Stackpole Books. Reprinted by permission.

15 "Justice" from *The Fire On The Mountain* by Harold Courlander and George Herzog, Copyright 1950 by Henry Holt & Company, © 1978 by Harold Courlander and Wolf Leslau, © 1995 by Harold Courlander. Reprinted by permission of Henry Holt and Company, Inc.

16 "Talk" from *The Cow-tail Switch and Other West African Stories* by Harold Courlander and George Herzog. Copyright 1947, © 1974 by Harold

Courlander. Reprinted by permission of Henry Holt and Company, Inc.

21 "The Blacks" by Peter Abrahams. Copyright © 1959 by Peter Abrahams. Reprinted by permission of Curtis Brown, Ltd.

22 Reprinted by permission of GRM Associates, Inc., Agents for the Estate of Ida M. Cullen. From the book *Color* by Countee Cullen. Copyright © 1925 by Harper & Brothers, copyright renewed 1953 by Ida M. Cullen.

33 From *Tell Freedom* by Peter Abrahams. Copyright © 1954 by Peter Abrahams, Renewed. Reprinted by permission of Curtis Brown, Ltd.

46 "The Lonely Soul" from *Deep Down the Blackman's Mind* by R. E. G. Armattoe, printed in *African Voices, An Anthology of Native African Writing*. Ed. Peggy Rutherford. Grosset & Dunlap: 1970.

48 "Funeral of a Whale" by J. Benibengor Blay from *An African Treasury* by Langston Hughes. Copyright © 1960 by Langston Hughes. Reprinted by permission of Crown Publishers, Inc.

52 "Night Rain" by J. P. Clark from *The African Assertion*. Copyright © 1968 by The Odyssey Press.

53 "Girl Bathing" by J. P. Clark from *The African Assertion*. Copyright © 1968 by The Odyssey Press.

55 "Men of All Continents" by Bernard Dadié, from *Poesie Vivante*, 1985. Reprinted by permission of Présence Africaine.

57 "Truth and Falsehood," from *Tales of Amadou-Koumba* by Birago Diop. Trans. Dorothy S. Blair. Reprinted by permission of Addison Wesley Longman Ltd.

61 "The Wages of Good" by Birago Diop, from *African Writing Today*. Trans. Robert Baldick.

65 "Forefathers" by Birago Diop, from *An African Treasury* by Langston Hughes. New York: Crown, 1960. Copyright © 1960 by Langston Hughes.

67 "Africa" by David Diop, trans. Anne Atik, 1987. First appeared in the anthology *Coups de Pilon*. (Présence Africaine, Paris, 1956). Reprinted by permission of Présence Africaine.

68 "Listen Comrades" by David Diop, from *Coups de Pilon*, 1987. Originally published 1956. Reprinted by permission of Présence Africaine.

68 "He Who Has Lost All" by David Diop, trans. Dorothy Blair. From *African Voices, An Anthology of Native African Writing*, ed. Peggy Rutherford. Grosset & Dunlap: 1970.

69 "Your Presence" by David Diop, from *Coups de Pilon*, 1987. Reprinted by permission of Présence Africaine.

69 "Defiance Against Force" by David Diop from *Anthologie de la nouvelle poesie negre et malgache de langue francaise*, de Léopold Sédar Senghor. © P. U. F., coll. "Quadrige," 3eme ed. 1997. Reprinted by permission.

71 *The Feud* by R. Sarif Easmon. Reprinted by permission of Addison Wesley Longman Ltd. and Mrs. Esther Easmon.

96 "Ritual Murder" by C. O. D. Ekwensi, from *African Voices, An Anthology of Native African Writing*, ed. Peggy Rutherfoord. Grosset & Dunlap: 1970.

103 "Law of the Grazing Fields" by C. O. D. Ekwensi, from *An African Treasury* by Langston Hughes. New York: Crown, 1960. Copyright © 1960 by Langston Hughes.

109 "The Forest of the Lord" chapter from *Igbo Olodumare* by D. O. Fagunwa, trans. E. C. Rowlands. From *A Selection of African Prose,* compiled by W. H. Whitely. Copyright 1945 by Thomas Nelson & Sons, Ltd. Reprinted by permission.

122 Excerpt titled "Aboard An African Train" from *The Road to Ghana* by Alfred Hutchinson. Copyright © 1960 by Alfred Hutchinson. Reprinted by permission of HarperCollins Publishers, Inc.

131 "The Gentlemen of the Jungle" from *Facing Mount Kenya* by Jomo Kenyatta. Reprinted by permission of Secker and Warburg.

135 Excerpts from *The Dark Child: The Autobiography Of An African Boy* by Camara Laye, translated by James Kirkup, Ernest Jones, and Elaine Gottlieb. Copyright © 1954 and renewed © 1982 by Camara Laye. Reprinted by permission of Farrar, Straus & Giroux, Inc.

156 "The Dignity of Begging" by William Modisane, from *African Voices, An Anthology of Native African Writing*, ed. Peggy Rutherfoord. Grosset & Dunlap: 1970.

165 "The Master of Doornvlei" from *In Corner B.* by Es'kia Mphahlele. Published first by East African Publishing, 1967. Ravan Press, Johannesburg, 1985. Reprinted by permission of Professor Es'kia Mphahlele.

174 "Life Is Sweet at Kumansenu" from *The Truly Married Woman* by Abioseh Nicol. Reprinted by permission of David Higham Associates, Ltd.

181 "The Rain Came" by Grace A. Ogot, from *Modern African Stories*, ed. Koemy and Mphahlele. Reprinted by permission of East African Educational Publishers Ltd.

190 "Homecoming" from *Satellites* by Lenrie Peters. Reprinted by permission of the author.

191 "Parachute" from *Satellites* by Lenrie Peters. Reprinted by permission of the author.

193 "African Song" by Richard Rive from *African Songs*. Copyright 1963 by Seven Seas Publishers.

200 "No Room at Solitaire" by Richard Rive from *Quartet, New Voices from South Africa*. Copyright 1963 by Richard Rive. Reprinted by permission of David Philip Publishers.

208 "Stanley Meets Mutesa" by James D. Rubadiri from *African Voices, An Anthology of Native African Writing*, ed. Peggy Rutherfoord. Reprinted by permission of Professor David Rubadiri, Ambassador and Permanent Mission of Malawi to The United Nations.

211 "The Pigeon-Hole" by Mabel Segun, from *Reflections: Nigerian Prose and Verse*, ed. Frances Ademola. Copyright 1962 by Mabel Segun. Reprinted by permission of African Universities Press.

212 "Conflict" by Mabel Segun, from *Reflections: Nigerian Prose and Verse*, ed. Frances Ademola. Copyright 1962 by Mabel Segun. Reprinted by permission of African Universities Press.

214 "Prayer to the Masks" by Léopold Sédar Senghor from *Anthologie de la nouvelle poesie negre et malgache de langue francaise*, de Léopold Sédar Senghor. © P. U. F., coll. "Quadrige," 3eme ed. 1997. Reprinted by permission.

215 "Night of Sine" by Léopold Sédar Senghor, from *Anthologie de la nouvelle poesie negre et malgache de langue francaise*, de Léopold Sédar Senghor. © P. U. F., coll. "Quadrige,"3eme ed. 1997. Reprinted by permission.

216 "Be Not Amazed" by Léopold Sédar Senghor, from *Modern Poetry from Africa*, ed. Moore and Beier.

218 "Fado Singer" from *Idanre and Other Poems* by Wole Soyinka. Copyright © 1967 by Wole Soyinka. Reprinted by permission of Hill and Wang, a division of Farrar, Straus & Giroux, Inc. and Methuen Publishing Limited.

219 "Season" from *Idanre and Other Poems* by Wole Soyinka. Copyright © 1967 by Wole Soyinka. Reprinted by permission of Hill and Wang, a division of Farrar, Straus & Giroux, Inc. and Methuen Publishing Limited.

219 "I Think It Rains" from *Idanre and Other Poems* by Wole Soyinka. Copyright © 1967 by Wole Soyinka. Reprinted by permission of Hill and Wang, a division of Farrar, Straus & Giroux, Inc. and Methuen Publishing Limited.

221 *Edufa* by Efua T. Sutherland. Reprinted by permission of Addison Wesley Longman Ltd.

267 "Home-Coming Son" by Tsegaye Gabre-Medhin. Reprinted by permission of the author.

269 "Message to Mputu Antoinette, Girl of the Bush, Friend of My Childhood" by Tshakatumba, from *The African Assertion*.

271 "Animal that Died But His Eyes Still Alive" from *The Brave African Huntress* by Amos Tutuola. Reprinted by permission of Faber and Faber, Ltd.

275 "Don't Pay Bad for Bad" by Amos Tutuola, from *Reflections: Nigerian Prose and Verse,* ed. Frances Ademola. Copyright 1962 by Amos Tutuola. Reprinted by permission of Faber and Faber Ltd.

Pronunciation Key

a	bat	ėr	her	oi	soil	ch	change		a	in along
ā	cage	i	hit	ou	scout	ng	song		e	in shaken
ä	star	ī	hit	u	up	sh	shell	ə	i	in stencil
â	dare	o	cot	u̇	put	th	think		o	in lemon
au	law	ō	old	ü	tube	TH	there		u	in circus
e	bet	ô	for			zh	pleasure			
ē	me									

Index of Authors, Titles, and Translators

Teacher's Edition / Teacher's Manual Included

LITERATURE OF

Africa

TRADITIONS IN WORLD LITERATURE

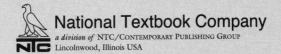

National Textbook Company

a division of NTC/CONTEMPORARY PUBLISHING GROUP
Lincolnwood, Illinois USA

Contents

LITERATURE OF AFRICA

FOLK TALES

SUMMARY

How the World Changed: This creation myth tells how Meleka (God) changed the world because of the wickedness of man. At first people and beasts lived together in the forest. People were only one color—black. They had no homes because they needed none for protection. There was no night, only day. Children wandered away periodically, frightening their parents. Because of this, Meleka added night to force children back home. People and beasts then lived together under the protection of a giant cotton tree. One day a child, playing with fire, burned down the cotton tree. The animals decided man was their enemy and fled to the forest. On another day, naughty children played in Meleka's pond, which he used as a painting bowl. As a result their black skin changed colors to white, brown, and yellow. They have remained that way ever since.

The Eye of the Giant: During a famine, a young man goes into the bush looking for food and discovers a giant with very long hair named Owuo or Death. The giant gives the young man wonderful food on the condition that he stay and work for him. The boy agrees but eventually becomes homesick. The giant allows him to go home when the boy agrees to supply the giant with his brother as a replacement. Later the boy returns, hungry for more food. His brother is missing, but once again he enjoys his time with the giant before deciding once again to return home. This time he supplies the giant with his sister and her slave as replacements. Later the boy returns yet again, hungry for more delicious food. This time he discovers that the bones of the food he has been eating are his sister's. Horrified, he escapes and warns the villagers. They approach the giant and light his hair on fire. Eventually the fire kills the giant. The boy discovers medicine at the roots of the giant's hair and sprinkles the medicine on the bones in the giant's hut. Immediately the boy's brother, sister, and slave are brought back to life. The boy also sprinkles the medicine into the eye of the dead giant, and immediately the eye opens. It is from that eye that death comes. Every time Owuo shuts that eye or blinks, a person dies.

Anansi's Fishing Expedition: Anansi the Spider, trickster hero of West African folk tales, decides to trick Anene into doing all the work on a fishing expedition. Anene, however, turns the tables on Anansi. Anene suggests that for each task needed, he will execute the task if Anansi will get tired for him. Foolish Anansi, thinking Anene is trying to get away with something, demands the reverse. So Anansi ends up cutting branches, carrying the wood, making the traps, carrying the traps to the water, and setting them. Anene does nothing but moan and groan. Anene even tricks Anansi into letting him have each day's supply of caught fish. In the end he convinces Anansi to try to sell rotting fish traps to the villagers. The villagers are so offended at Anansi's audacity that they beat him. In the end Anene explains that the episode should teach Anansi a lesson. Anansi agrees but jokingly criticizes his partner Anene for not taking the pain for Anansi's beating.

The Singing Cloak: Anansi and Chameleon were farmers who lived in the same town. One year Chameleon enjoyed a bountiful harvest while Anansi suffered a drought. Anansi asked Chameleon to sell him his farm, but Chameleon refused, so Anansi vowed revenge. Chameleon's farm had no path leading to it because Chameleon traveled instead through the grass and bushes. Anansi promptly built a path from his house to Chameleon's farm and claimed it as his own. Chameleon complained to the chief, but the chief sided with Anansi. It was now Chameleon's turn for revenge. He dug a very large, deep well and covered it with a mud roof except for one small hole. Then he made himself a wonderful cloak out of dried yam vines with flies attached to them. Whenever he walked, the cloak shook and the flies made a wonderful buzzing noise. The chief so admired the cloak that he asked to buy it, but Chameleon refused. When Anansi heard of this, he promised the chief that he would get it for him. He asked Chameleon if he could buy it and Chameleon agreed, provided Anansi would fill a hole with food in exchange. Anansi promised twice as much food, but when he started putting food in the hole he soon discovered that all the food he possessed would not fill it. He sold his livestock and all he possessed to get more food for the well but still could not fill it. When Chameleon realized that Anansi was now poor, he released him from his promise and gave him the cloak. The cloak, however, had begun to rot. A strong gust of wind released all the flies, and Anansi was left wearing only some dried vine stalks. Anansi was so ashamed that he went into hiding.

The Gourd Full of Wisdom: Anansi the Spider decided one day to hoard all wisdom for himself. So he collected all of it in a large gourd and hung it on the wall of his house. Still not satisfied, he took it into the bush to find a better hiding place. His son accompanied him. Anansi decided to place it at the top of a tall palm tree where it would be safe. However when he tried to climb the tree the large gourd kept getting in his way. His son suggested that he sling the gourd over his back to make it easier to maneuver. Anansi realized that his son was right, but he also realized that his son used wisdom to make that judgment. Anansi therefore decided that it would be better if many people rather than one had wisdom, and so he opened the gourd and scattered the wisdom on the ground for all to use.

How Hawk Learned of the Shallow Hearts of Men: One day Hawk captures Chameleon and carries him into the air. People praise the hawk for his deed and thank him for ridding them of their enemy Chameleon. Chameleon pleads with Hawk to let him go, claiming that the flattery of the people is not genuine. Hawk, however, is proud of the flattery and intends to eat Chameleon. Suddenly Chameleon grabs Hawk by the throat and overpowers him. The people then praise Chameleon for his cleverness in ridding them of the evil hawk. Chameleon whispers in Hawk's ear, "Now do you realize how shallow are the hearts of men?" From that day on Chameleon and Hawk have remained allied against the treachery of humans.

The Hunter Who Hunts No More: The narrator in this tale, a hunter, explains why he no longer hunts. One day he shot a large roan (horse) and tried to follow it as it ran off. The trail ended at a large baobab tree. The hunter explains to an old man what happened, and the old man takes the hunter through a large hole in the tree to a wonderful village of dwarfs. The village is in mourning because the eldest son of the chief is dying. He had been shot through the chest by a hunter from the narrator's village, a man that had a reputation for killing the young men of this fairy village. The villagers could not understand the motive of the hunter because they had never done him any harm. The chief's son dies and the old man and the hunter leave the fairy village and pass through the baobab tree again. There on the ground at the base of the tree lies the large roan that the hunter had shot. The narrator concludes by saying that many other hunters have witnessed the same thing.

The Talking Skull: A hunter confronts a human skull in the bush and asks what brought it there. The skull answers: "Talking brought me here." The hunter goes to the king and reports that he found a human skull who wants to know how the king's parents are. The king does not believe the skull could speak. The king asks his wise men what they think. They agree with the king and decide to send guards to the bush to learn the truth. If the hunter has lied, he is to be killed. When they get to the bush, the skull is silent. The guards kill the hunter. When the guards leave, the skull asks the hunter's head what brought him there. The dead hunter's head replies: "Talking brought me here!"

Justice: A woman asks a deaf man about her missing goats. Thinking she is looking for a water hole, he points to the river. She finds her goats there. One young goat has broken a leg. She returns to the deaf man to thank him. He thinks she is accusing him of harming her young goat, and he yells at her and slaps her. She takes him to the judge, who is deaf and also nearsighted. After everyone has told their stories, the judge announces his decision. He tells the deaf man to stop mistreating his wife. He tells the woman to not be late with her husband's meals. He tells the young goat, mistaking it for an infant, to have a long life. The crowd breaks up, pleased that justice has been served.

Talk: A man was digging yams in his garden when one of the yams said to him: "Leave me alone." The man's dog repeated it: "The yam says leave him alone." When the man tries to discipline his dog with a branch cut from a palm tree, the palm tree says: "Put that branch down!" When the man tries to throw the branch away, the branch says: "Man, put me down softly." When the man puts the branch on a stone, the stone says: "Hey, take that thing off me." When the frightened man starts to run for his village, he encounters a fisherman, a weaver, and a man bathing in the river. He tells each of them his problems. The fisherman's fish trap, the weaver's cloth, and the river that the third man is bathing in all support the yam. The four astonished men take the problem to the chief. He scolds them for disturbing the peace and sends them back to work. At the end, the chief's stool says: "Imagine, a talking yam!"

GUIDELINES FOR DISCUSSION QUESTIONS

Origin Stories

1. What details in "How the World Changed" did you find most interesting? What fascinated you about these particular details?

Students will probably have widely differing opinions on the most interesting details of this creation myth. Many might be fascinated by the idea of humans and animals living together peacefully. They might suggest that there is a romantic appeal to the idea of all of God's creatures living in peace in a forest environment with no apparent dangers to fear. Others may talk about the use of fire to separate humans from animals, the practice of children freely wandering away from their parents, or the manner in which white-, brown-, and yellow-skinned people came into the world.

2. Note the relationship of humans and animals in this tale. What point seems to be implied about how humans ought to relate to animals?

According to this myth, humans and animals lived peacefully together in the beginning. It is suggested that humans betrayed animals and that the current separateness is a fault. It is implied that humans and animals should (in a perfect world) coexist peacefully.

3. The young man in "The Eye of the Giant" is much too trustful of the giant. At what point in the proceedings should he have suspected that something was wrong?

When he first returned to the giant's hut and learned that his brother was no longer there, he should have become very suspicious.

4. This folk tale is an explanatory one because it explains why something happens or why something exists or where something came from. What is being explained in this tale?

The tale provides an account of why people die. They die because Owuo shuts or blinks his eye, and according to the tale he does this all the time.

Trickster Stories

1. In "Anansi's Fishing Expedition," what does Anansi plan to do, and how does Anene turn the tables on him?

Anansi decides to go on a fishing expedition with someone who will do all the work. Anene pretends to cooperate but actually tricks Anansi into doing the work while Anene reaps the benefits.

2. Does Anansi's last comment to Anene in the tale indicate that he has learned the humor of how he has been tricked, or does it indicate that he is still in the dark?

Students might read the ending either way. There is no way to prove one interpretation over the other. But many students will probably suggest that the comment itself is in keeping with the humor throughout the tale and that it might be reasonable to assume at this point that Anansi is poking fun at himself.

3. If there is a lesson to be learned in this folk tale, what might it be?

The lesson might be that if you set out to take advantage of someone, be careful that you yourself aren't taken advantage of.

4. In "The Singing Cloak," Anansi is clearly the villain. Is Chameleon the hero of the tale? Explain your answer.

At first glance, it seems obvious that he is the hero. He is after all victimized by Anansi and is forced to protect himself from Anansi's treachery. But some of the things that Chameleon does seem very much unhero-like. In order to fight back, he resorts to the same kind of devious trickery that Anansi employs.

5. You have no doubt heard the expressions "An eye for an eye, and a tooth for a tooth" and "Fight fire with fire." Explain how each of these expressions applies to "The Singing Cloak."

These expressions have similar but not identical meanings, and the subject of "The Singing Cloak" illustrates both of them. The first expression focuses on the rightness of revenge. It argues that if you have been abused by someone you have the right to abuse them equally in return. In the tale, Anansi strips Chameleon of his farm and so, in return, Chameleon strips Anansi of his farm. The second expression focuses on the method of revenge. It argues that you should imitate the tactics of your enemy. In the tale Anansi uses deceit and trickery (creating the path and lying about it) to get the better of Chameleon. In return Chameleon uses deceit and trickery (the deceptively large well and the singing cloak) to get even with Anansi.

6. **In "The Gourd Full of Wisdom," what does Anansi do that is consistent with his reputation as a trickster?**

Anansi becomes jealous of the fact that other people have the use of wisdom and so he devises and attempts to carry out a devious plan to hoard all the wisdom for himself.

7. **What other qualities does Anansi display in this tale that are consistent with the qualities of a hero?**

When Anansi thinks about what his son suggests to him, he reveals honesty in recognizing that what he is attempting is wrong; he uses reason to conclude that wisdom should be shared; and he demonstrates fair-mindedness in deciding to make wisdom available to all.

Moral Stories

1. **What simple point about human nature is made in "How Hawk Learned of the Shallow Hearts of Men"?**

The point made in this tale is that people are two-faced. They will say one thing one day and the opposite the next. They cannot be relied upon to be truthful or trustworthy.

2. **Do you think the portrayal of human nature in this tale is accurate? Explain your answer.**

Students will have a spirited time debating this issue in class. It would probably not be surprising if they assess the portrayal as being both accurate and not accurate. Students will be able to come up with countless examples of people they know or have heard about who have not been consistently truthful or at least who have changed their minds a lot. However, they will also argue that there are people (perhaps including themselves) who are truthful and who do not change their minds as capriciously as those in the tale do. Many students will argue that the ability to be two-faced is probably a part of human nature that most people must fight giving in to.

3. Supernatural fairy tales often use substitutions of identity—a frog turns into a prince, a hideous old hag turns into the most beautiful woman in the kingdom. Usually the substitution of identity is a reward for virtue. Is this true in "The Hunter Who Hunts No More"? Explain.

No it is not true. The dual identity of the roan / young man seems simply a fact of nature in this tale. The roan/young man is not rewarded in any way. It/he is brutally slain by an uncaring, insensitive hunter.

4. What message might be contained in this tale? Think back to the attitudes about humans and animals presented in the creation myth "How the World Changed." Do they shed any light on the message contained in this tale?

In the creation myth, humans and beasts lived peacefully together until humans betrayed the animals. The attitude in that tale seems also to be illustrated here: All of God's creatures are equally important and deserve respect. Humans and beasts should coexist peacefully in nature.

5. An exemplum is a brief tale or anecdote told to teach a lesson or moral. Exempla were especially common in Medieval sermons and are still popular with preachers around the world today. Explain how "The Talking Skull" serves as an exemplum.

This very brief tale describes an interesting situation—a man discovers a talking skull—leading to a very simple point: Be careful what you say. Idle talk can get you in trouble. It is a perfect example of a brief anecdote that teaches a lesson—the essential ingredients of an exemplum.

6. Why do you think the skull refuses to speak until after the hunter has been killed?

The obvious answer is that there would be no lesson illustrated otherwise. But it can also be argued that there is a logical reason why the skull waits. He is punishing the hunter for having lied to the king. The hunter himself illustrates the point being made: Be careful what you say.

Humorous Stories

1. The comedy of misunderstanding in "Justice" eventually reaches absurd proportions. How could the misunderstanding have been corrected at various points in the story?

First, when the woman returned to the deaf man she should have been able to realize that something was wrong with his hearing. She could have written him a note or simply ignored him and walked away. Certainly one of the bystanders should have intervened and straightened out the situation before it went to the judge. The judge, of course, was in no position to sort out the mess, but even at that point at least the judge's incompetence should have been exposed for what it was.

2. This folk tale is a satire—pointed ridicule of human folly. What is being satirized? Do you think the satire is gentle or sharp?

On the surface it appears that justice—or the lack of it—is being satirized. Everyone in the tale is the object of laughter. Everyone displays a critical lack of understanding. Everyone appears to perceive only what they want to perceive. Students may be divided on whether the satire is gentle or sharp. Again, on the surface it appears to be gentle. We are invited to laugh at everyone, including ourselves. But the implications of the satire are devastating: the tale would lead us to believe not only that genuine justice is impossible to achieve but also that the community at large is willing to accept that situation without complaint.

3. Does it matter that the human characters in "Talk" are not fully developed individuals, but rather are types—the country man, the fisherman, and so on? Why or why not?

In this short tale it would be impossible to make the characters more fully developed, and it makes no difference anyway. The focus of the tale is not on the characters, but on the absurdity of the situation.

4. What elements contribute to the humor of this tale?

The absurdity of talking yams and, by extension, all inanimate objects that talk, the repetition of what happened at regular intervals in the tale, the growing alarm of the men who encounter the talking objects, and the final twist at the end of the story all contribute to the humor.

GUIDELINES FOR ASSESSING STUDENT WRITING

1. The folk tale "Talk" is about a yam who feels mistreated and speaks out. It is also about a man who is astonished by the fact that a yam can talk. If you wanted to interpret this simple tale

very generally as an allegory, what would the situation presented in this tale symbolically represent? Write a short essay in which you discuss possible symbolic interpretations of "Talk."

It can be argued that the yam who talked in this tale can be viewed as representing any person or group of people who are ignored, mistreated, or simply taken for granted. The repetition of the abuse or disrespect at regular intervals throughout the tale reinforces the idea of the pervasiveness of the abuse or disrespect that some people receive. The fact that the chief gets in the action in this tale might suggest that even leaders and governments can be guilty of not understanding people and perhaps taking advantage of or abusing people. The talking stool at the end of the tale illustrates that leaders have their own blind spots to deal with. Some students may enjoy developing the symbolism even more. Assess students' essays on how well they relate their ideas to material in the tale.

2. **Three of the tales grouped here feature Anansi the Spider, the famous trickster character of West African folklore. Find these three tales and compare them. In a short essay, discuss the character of Anansi in each. How does Anansi differ from one story to the next? What lesson or moral (if any) is illustrated in each tale? Study the tone of each tale. What do you think is the attitude of the "authors" and listeners or readers of these tales toward Anansi? Use evidence from each tale to support your ideas.**

Students should find Anansi a fascinating literary character to discuss. In their essays they should note that although Anansi displays characteristics that are consistent from one tale to another (his reputation as a trickster, for example), his personality also varies in each of the three stories included here. In "Anansi's Fishing Expedition" he is hopelessly gullible and easily bested. In "The Singing Cloak" his actions seem more wicked and his cleverness must be matched by equal cleverness. In "The Gourd Full of Wisdom" Anansi displays uncharacteristic hero-like qualities. In analyzing possible lessons or morals in these tales, students should be able to recognize that simple greed is the focus of each and that the foolishness or danger of greed is somehow confronted in each. Reflecting on attitudes toward Anansi should provide students with fertile material for exploration. Many might conclude that the sheer variety of situations Anansi faces might qualify him as a kind of everyman of West African folklore. Assess students' essays on how well they tie their opinions to examples from each of the Anansi tales.

3. Using what you've learned about the qualities of folk tales, write a short tale that focuses on one important trait. For length, match "The Talking Skull" or "The Gourd Full of Wisdom." Keep your tale simple. Write a story about a trickster *or* a story explaining how something came about *or* a story with a moral *or* a story with supernatural elements. Don't try to do all of these things. If time permits, share your final product with the class.

It might be helpful to review the introduction to these folk tales with students and the questions throughout that deal with folk tale characteristics and techniques. Reinforce the suggestion that students keep their efforts short and simple. Encourage them to let their imaginations run loose. Remind them that no detail is too outrageous, illogical, or unbelievable for a folk tale. In determining what they will use for a subject, have students reflect on what they would enjoy focusing on—a colorful, mischievous character, an action-packed adventure, a valuable lesson, or what? Assess students' stories on the creativity of their contents and the clarity of their expression.

PETER ABRAHAMS

The Blacks

SUMMARY

In this essay, published originally by *Holiday Magazine* in 1959, Peter Abrahams, a black South African, discusses his friendship with Kwame Nkrumah, who became the first president of the new Republic of Ghana in 1960, and Johnstone Kenyatta, who became the first president of the new Republic of Kenya in 1964. Abrahams describes both men as he knew them in London in the early 1950s when they were students and then describes how each man changed after returning to Africa several years later. Abrahams also discusses the importance of the tribal African in shaping the destinies of both Nkrumah and Kenyatta. He concludes his essay with an examination of the significant characteristics of tribal Africans and observes that, though they are resistant to change, change will be imposed on them, and how they react to that change will have a powerful bearing on the future of Africa.

GUIDELINES FOR DISCUSSION QUESTIONS

1. **In the first few pages of his essay, Abrahams paints a vivid picture of the street life of Accra. List examples of sense imagery in his description that you found most memorable.**

   Abrahams provides of wealth of descriptive detail, including the following: "potent stench of the sea," "rotting fish," "houses were drab, run-down wooden structures or made of corrugated iron," "an open drainage system," street traders with "round loaves of bread and hunks of cooked meat," mammy trucks "hurtling across the countryside," a long procession of women in "white flowing robes and white kerchiefs," their faces "painted into grotesque masks made with thick streaks of black, red, white and yellow paints," the whole procession "a shivering, shaking mass," and bottles of opaque white coconut milk or palm juice with "little foreign bodies that floated" in them.
       Students may also cite other examples.

2. **Abrahams describes Nkrumah and Kenyatta as he knew them in London and then again when he meets each of them in Africa. How did Nkrumah and Kenyatta change after returning to Africa?**

Both men were strongly affected by their exposure to the ways of tribal Africans. Abrahams describes Nkrumah in London as a nervous and angry young student, filled with conflict and tension, prone to evolving fantastic schemes, and dedicated to the emancipation of Africa. When Abrahams meets him in Accra, Nkrumah appears poised and relaxed; his eyes reflect a new inner tranquillity. As the first African prime minister of the Gold Coast, he has gained much power in the tribal community and has crafted an uneasy alliance with the tribal chiefs. Abrahams notices that Nkrumah now possesses a new reserve, a new caution. He has abandoned some of his liberal principles and, consistent with tribal ways, has become intolerant of any opposition.

In London, Abrahams remembers Kenyatta as the most relaxed, sophisticated, and "westernized" of his African friends. He was cultured and enjoyed the friendship of some of the most distinguished people in English political and intellectual society. In Kenya, Abrahams notices that Kenyatta speaks with an undercurrent of bitterness and looks momentarily like a "trapped, caged animal." Kenyatta admits his bitterness and confesses that in order to be a leader he must renounce his western beliefs and assert himself in tribal terms. Abrahams describes him as "the victim both of tribalism and westernism gone sick." He is trapped between the two ways of life.

3. **What does Abrahams mean by saying that "being black is a small matter in tribal Africa"? How does this statement contrast with Abrahams's own experience as a black South African?**

To tribal Africans, color does not matter. "Color is an act of God that neither confers privilege nor imposes handicaps." Because Abrahams grew up in South Africa, he is acutely conscious of his skin color. As a Colored man, Abrahams suffered under apartheid imposed by the white government of the Union of South Africa.

4. **What is of greatest importance to the tribal African?**

What matters most to the tribal African is the complex pattern of his or her position within the tribe and his or her relationship to other members of the tribe. The most important single characteristic of tribal Africans is that they are not individuals in the western sense. They believe that their lives are completely controlled by good and evil spirits and especially the spirits of their ancestors. Also their society is an exclusive one. Anyone not in the tribe is an enemy and can never become a member. Anyone in the tribe is a permanent member. There is no way out of it except death.

5. **In the last paragraph of the essay Abrahams voices a hope that in the Africa of the future "the finer qualities of the old ways" may be fused with the new. What might be considered among the best qualities of the old ways? What is good about the new ways?**

Among the best qualities of the old ways are the tribal Africans' belief that race and color are not important, their strong loyalty to fellow members, their reliance on the family as the foundation of the group, their protection of each member, and their insistence that there are no orphans or misfits within the group. The good things that the new ways can bring are the advantages of modern technology: better roads and homes, improved sanitation, better communications, increased educational and economic opportunities, and the amenities of contemporary life. The best of the new ways could also include a tolerance toward change and an openness toward the principles of democracy.

GUIDELINES FOR ASSESSING STUDENT WRITING

Imagine that you are given the opportunity to abandon your western way of life and become a member of a tribal African group. Write two paragraphs. In the first, explain what adjustments to tribal life would be the easiest for you to make. In the second, explain what adjustments would be the hardest. Base your opinions on the description of tribal Africans that Abrahams provides.

Students' opinions will vary, but in the first paragraph most will probably mention the importance of family as something that would be an easy adjustment. Some may also mention the loyalty among tribal members and the strong sense of acceptance and protection within the the group. In the second paragraph students might offer any of the following: the practice of making human sacrifices for the betterment of the group, the sense of isolation within the group and lack of communication outside it, the loss of individual freedom and the intolerance toward dissent, the belief that your life is controlled by powers outside yourself, and the strong resistence to change of any kind. Students may also mention the lack of western amenities, though Abrahams does not discuss this specifically.

from *Tell Freedom*

SUMMARY

In this selection, taken from Peter Abrahams's autobiography, *Tell Freedom,* Abrahams recalls two events from his early childhood in rural South Africa. In part one, 5-year-old Abrahams, accompanied by his friend Andries, is sent on an errand to buy crackling (fried pork rind), which was his family's main source of meat. On their way, the two boys fight off the bitter cold by staging running contests and pitching stones. When they reach their destination Abrahams is reprimanded by the white man selling the crackling for not demonstrating proper respect when addressing a white man. On the return trip home, the two boys are overtaken by three white boys. The white boys provoke Abrahams into a fight, and he is beaten unconscious. When he recovers and goes home, he explains to his aunt and uncle (with whom he lives) what happened. He is surprised at first when they don't punish him for his actions but soon realizes that they are more worried about worse things to come. At suppertime, a white man shows up with the three white boys. He demands that Uncle Sam punish Abrahams. Although it hurts him to do it, Uncle Sam warns Abrahams never to lift his hand to a white person and then severely beats him with a belt until the white man allows him to stop.

In part two, winter ends and summer arrives. Abrahams makes friends with a young African boy named Joseph, who is a member of the Zulu tribe. Joseph's skin is much darker than Abrahams', almost black. Aunt Liza explains that there are three kinds of people. The whites come first, then the Coloreds (people of mixed race), like Abrahams, then the blacks, like Joseph. Joseph and Abrahams spend their summer together exploring the river, going swimming, fighting with sticks, racing grasshoppers, and engaging in many other activities. Joseph introduces Abrahams to his mother and Abrahams is astonished to hear that she considers Joseph the man of the house because his father is away working in the mines. Abrahams learns much from Joseph and his mother. Near the end of the summer, Joseph and his mother leave the area when Joseph's father dies in a mine accident. Abrahams is devastated by the loss of his close friend.

GUIDELINES FOR DISCUSSION QUESTIONS

1. **Which part of this selection did you enjoy more, part one about Abrahams' confrontation with the three white boys or part two about Abrahams' friendship with Joseph? Why?**

   Most students probably will choose part two over part one. Many will express anger at the events that occur in part one, although some might add that they appreciated learning about the inhumane treatment Abrahams received as a result of racial prejudice. Most students will identify with the positive experiences that Abrahams and Joseph enjoy in part two. The good times the two boys share may remind some students of wonderful summers they have spent with special friends.

2. **A novel that describes the growth of a child to maturity is called a _bildungsroman_. Why might this term be a good one to apply to this selection from Abrahams' autogiography? In what ways does Abrahams grow in this selection?**

In part one, Abrahams confronts racial prejudice at a very early age. When he tries to fight back, he is punished brutally for his efforts. He grows as a person because he learns from this experience that life is not always fair, that justice does not always prevail, and that standing up for the truth is not always rewarded. In part two, Abrahams learns much from Joseph, who is more mature for his age. Abrahams learns to appreciate the value of Joseph's friendship in spite of hearing from Aunt Liza that Joseph is supposedly inferior to Abrahams because he is darker. Joseph teaches Abrahams physical skills such as swimming and defending himself with a stick. More importantly, Joseph, by his example, teaches Abrahams to accept responsibility for dealing with serious situations—for example, acknowledging the death of Joseph's father, comforting Joseph's mother, and coming to terms with Joseph's departure.

3. **Reread the quotation from Isaiah that appears at the beginning of the selection. In what ways is the content of the quotation relevant to the selection?**

If students have difficulty interpreting the quotation accurately, offer them the following rewording: "The wrong judgment is made, and justice is denied because truth is defeated and fairness is not allowed." Students should be able to point out the unfairness of the crackling seller's treatment of Abrahams. Even more dramatically, they should recognize that the wrong judgment is made and justice is defeated when Abrahams is beaten because of his confrontation with the three white boys, a confrontation that he did not initiate. In part two, the attitude that white people come first, then Coloreds, and then blacks is unfair, unjust, and false. Some students may also point out that to Abrahams the loss of Joseph's friendship is unfair and unjust.

4. **Discuss Abrahams' meeting with Joseph. In what ways might this be considered one of the most important events in Abrahams' life?**

As discussed in question 2, Abrahams matures as a person because of his friendship with Joseph, which is reason enough to make his meeting with Joseph an important event in his life. Even more important, however, is the lesson Abrahams learns at this early age that the color of a person's skin should not be a barrier to friendship.

5. **In this selection, Abrahams describes two events from his childhood that made a lasting impression on him. Think back to your own childhood. What event made a lasting impression on you? How did it affect you?**

Students will recall many different kinds of incidents. Some might remember their first encounter with hostility from a playmate or neighbor, or the serious illness of a family member or relative, or the conquering of a childhood fear, or the shattering of a childish belief. Others might remember the special qualities of a first true friendship, the loving guidance of a parent or favorite aunt or uncle, or a decisive moment when their courage or integrity was put to the test. Encourage students to reflect on the ways in which an important event in their childhood influenced their understanding of themselves and the world they live in.

GUIDELINES FOR ASSESSING STUDENT WRITING

Compare and contrast the first part of this selection (Abrahams' confrontation with the three white boys and the consequences) with the second part (Abrahams' friendship with Joseph). You may do this by discussing both parts in one paragraph or by writing one paragraph in which you discuss part one and another paragraph in which you discuss part two. Whichever format you choose, note the weather, Abrahams' activities, and the attitudes of the people with whom Abrahams comes in contact. Also describe the difference in mood between the two parts.

Students should note that part one takes place in the bitter cold of winter; part two takes place during the warmth of summer.

In part one, Abrahams is mistreated by a white man selling crackling and by three white boys who taunt him because of his race. When he tries to fight back, he is beaten unconscious and then later punished again with a brutal beating. In part two Abrahams meets and becomes friends with a young Zulu boy. They enjoy a wonderful summer of games and adventures.

In part one Abrahams encounters people with racially bigoted attitudes. Even his aunt and uncle, out of fear for their lives, break down under the bigotry forced upon them. In part two Abrahams enjoys the warm friendship of both Joseph and his mother. They treat him with respect and love.

The mood of part one might best be described as bleak and harrowing. The weather is miserably uncomfortable, what happens to Abrahams is horrific, and the outlook for his future appears bleak indeed. In stark contrast, the mood of part two is primarily positive and uplifting. The weather is enjoyable, and Abrahams comes to treasure the wonderful times he spends with Joseph and his mother. Only at the end, when Joseph leaves, does the mood return to a somber one.

R. E. G. ARMATTOE

The Lonely Soul

SUMMARY

The speaker in this poem meets an old woman who is walking down a lonely road, talking and laughing to herself. The speaker goes on to say that if the road is long, and there are no travelers, and showers of sorrows fall down on a person walking down the road, then that person may talk by himself. The speaker concludes by recognizing that the old woman is sad, and the speaker shares her sadness.

GUIDELINES FOR DISCUSSION QUESTIONS

1. **Have you ever caught yourself talking out loud to yourself in private or in public? What were the reasons?**

   Many students will probably admit that they have talked to themselves and will offer a variety of reasons for doing so. Often people scold themselves if they feel they've done something wrong or made a mistake. They might also express anger or sadness if something goes wrong or if they've been mistreated. Also people talk to themselves when they have a lot on their minds and they're trying to sort out their thoughts.

2. **What event does the speaker in this poem describe? According to the speaker, why does the woman laugh and talk to herself?**

   The speaker describes meeting an old woman who is walking down a lonely road and talking and laughing to herself. According to the speaker, she does this "[to] keep the tears away."

3. **What does the speaker realize in the last two lines of the poem?**

   The speaker realizes that the old woman is sad and that he shares her sadness.

4. **If you look below the surface meaning of the lines, what might the long road (line 10) represent? Who might the travelers (line 11) be? What might the showers (line 13) be? Who do you think the child (line 8) is that the speaker addresses?**

The long road might represent life; the travelers might be family members and friends or acquaintances; the showers might be sad events in a traveler's life; and the child might be anyone younger than the speaker, anyone who doesn't have the years of experience that the speaker and the old woman have.

GUIDELINES FOR ASSESSING STUDENT WRITING

Is the title "The Lonely Soul" an appropriate one for this poem? Write a paragraph in which you discuss this question. Consider the identity of the lonely soul. Also consider the words and phrases and the stylistic devices the speaker uses to get across his point.

Some students may believe that a more appropriate title would be "The Lonely Old Woman," but many will recognize that, though the old woman is the obvious reference in the title, the speaker might also be considered a lonely soul since he shares the old woman's sadness. By extension, some may also recognize that any "lone wayfarer" may be referred to in the title.

The speaker uses repetition of certain words, phrases, and ideas to reinforce the title—for example, "*lonely* road," "talk *alone*," "road be *long*," "travelers *none*," "*lone* wayfarer," and "*lone* country roads." Also "talking by (or to) herself (or himself)" is repeated five times. Some students might note that the word *soul* in the title could be a pun on the word *sole* meaning "only" or "lone."

J. BENIBENGOR BLAY

Funeral of a Whale

SUMMARY

In this essay, J. Benibengor Blay describes the funeral ceremony for a whale in the town of Missibi in Ghana. As the king of the sea, the whale is sacred to the people of Missibi, who worship the sea. The morning after a violent storm, Missibi fishermen find the whale washed up on the shore. The fishermen inform the chief, and then the public is informed. Arrangements for the funeral begin immediately. People from near and far begin arriving. The whole community is involved. Bamboo huts are built for the ceremony. Cases of liquor are brought out. Musicians polish their instruments. The chief and his advisers and the women of the community dress in mourning. A long funeral procession leaves for the beach where the whale lies. At the ceremony, the chief praises the whale and begs for the whale's help in bringing health and plenty to the community. Music is played; guns and firecrackers are fired off; games are provided for the children; and the women engage in wailing contests. The men become partly or completely drunk. At the climax of the ceremony, the whale is covered with a white sheet, and the people throw pebbles or shells at it. That signals the end of the ceremony, and the people return to the town.

GUIDELINES FOR DISCUSSION QUESTIONS

1. **The immense and expensive effort put forth to honor the death of a whale must tax the Missibi community heavily. In what ways do you think it is worth it to the people of Missibi to go to this trouble?**

   First and foremost, the people of Missibi worship the sea and consider the whale to be the king of the sea. By honoring the death of the whale, they are reaffirming their faith in their beliefs. They praise the dead whale and beg it to bring them health and plenty. Also this ceremony offers a great social opportunity for members of the community to come together and unite—each in his or her own way—in a cause that is important to them.

2. What is the color of mourning in the Missibi community? How do you know?

The color of mourning is red. The narrator explains that in the funeral procession the chief and his counselors are dressed in red. Also the women are smeared with red clay and they wear pieces of red calico tied around their hair.

3. At the funeral everyone seems to have some responsibility. What are the responsibilities of the old men? the young men? the women? What do the hunters, fishermen, farmers, and priests do?

The old men make sure that traditional funeral procedures are followed. The young men keep order and play musical instruments. The women tell the story of the whale and take part in a weeping and wailing contest. The hunters fire off guns and firecrackers. The fishermen fish and cast their nets on the shore. The farmers sow seeds, and the priests play tom-toms and perform daring feats of self-mutilation.

4. Although the funeral for the whale is a time for mourning, in what ways is it also a time for celebration for the people of Missibi?

The narrator reports that in spite of the sadness of the occasion, it is a great day for the hawkers from distant parts (and others) because they will be witnessing a tradition that happens rarely if ever in a lifetime. It is an occasion for the entire community of Missibi—near and far— to come together and unite in paying homage to the whale. Drinks and food are provided for everyone. The chief and the women praise the whale. The celebration includes music and firecrackers, games for the children, and wailing contests with prizes for the women. All of the men become partly or completely drunk.

GUIDELINES FOR ASSESSING STUDENT WRITING

In one or two paragraphs, compare the funeral ceremony for the whale with funeral ceremonies you are familiar with. What obvious differences can you identify? What similarities can you identify? In your paragraph(s), discuss both the differences and the similarities.

Most students should readily recognize the differences between the ceremony for the whale and funeral ceremonies they have attended. However, after studying the details in the essay, they may be surprised to discover the number of similarities they can identify. Students should include some of the following differences and similarities in their paragraphs.

Differences: In our culture, public funerals are not given for animals. Also, most funerals are attended by family members and friends; rarely is an entire community involved. Black is the color of mourning in our culture, not red. We do not ask the deceased to intercede on our behalf and bring us health and plenty. We don't include games for the children or wailing contests with prizes for the women. Finally, our spiritual leaders don't perform feats of self-mutilation.

Similarities: It is common to have a funeral procession, sometimes to bring the body of the deceased into a house of worship for the ceremony and also to accompany the body to the gravesite for burial. It is also common to lament the loss of the person and to praise him or her in a eulogy. Often, after the ceremony, refreshments are provided for the mourners and time is provided for the family and friends to visit and celebrate the life of the deceased. Music is often included in funeral ceremonies, and at military funerals guns are fired off. At the gravesite sometimes mourners will throw a little earth or a flower or two on the coffin in the same way that people of Missibi throw pebbles and shells on the body of the whale.

J. P. CLARK

Poems

SUMMARY

In "Night Rain" the speaker wakes up in the middle of the night to discover that it is raining. He describes his mother moving food supplies to safety and putting wooden bowls and earthenware around the floor to catch the leaking drops of rain. The speaker finds the rain comforting and utilizes its soothing sounds to go back to sleep. In "Girl Bathing" the speaker describes a woman who wades into water briefly to bathe and then returns to the beach. The speaker praises the woman's beauty and, by implication, also praises her strength and dedication to her role in the community.

GUIDELINES FOR DISCUSSION QUESTIONS

1. To what does the speaker compare himself in lines 3–6 of "Night Rain"?

The speaker has awakened in the middle of the night with his belly exposed, much like a fish that has been drugged by fisherman and is floating belly up on the water.

2. What is happening in lines 15–27, and what is the speaker's mother doing?

The rain is leaking into the speaker's house and his mother is placing wooden bowls and earthenware around the floor to catch the drops. She is also moving food supplies away from the water that is leaking into the house.

3. What does the speaker mean when he refers to the "ample soothing hand" of the drumming of the rain as being "joined to that of the sea"?

The speaker means that the sea has the same soothing effect on him that the drumming of the rain has. The speaker is probably referring to the soothing sound of sea waves as they roll onto the shore.

4. Often in poetry a storm is presented as threatening or violent, inspiring fear or awe. Is that an accurate description of the speaker's reaction to the storm in "Night Rain"? Use evidence from the poem to support your answer.

No, that is not an accurate description of the speaker's reaction. In line 30 the speaker tells his brothers not to tremble, and in lines 42–47 he suggests that they roll over and let the rain and sea lull them back to innocent sleep.

5. In the poem "Girl Bathing," describe the woman's physical actions. What does she do?

She sets down a basket of cassava and wades into water up to her hips. She then dunks herself under the water, loosening her hair and washing the dirt off her back. She splashes briefly in the water and then returns to the beach.

6. As part of their program of rediscovery of authentic African culture, the French-speaking *Negritude* poets (see Introduction, page xvii) often take as their theme the beauty of black women. In "Girl Bathing" the speaker celebrates the beauty of a black woman. Do you think the speaker celebrates something more than the woman's beauty? Explain your answer with evidence from the poem.

The speaker, in addition to celebrating the woman's beauty, also celebrates her strength and dedication to her role in the community. The speaker describes "sweat and dirt long dried in every pore," suggesting that this woman engages in hard physical labor. The speaker goes on to refer to the soothing ("unguent" and "tonic") effect of the water on the woman's body, suggesting that the water restores her vitality. This African woman seems to be a symbol for the speaker of the strength and beauty of all African women and of the important role they assume in their communities.

GUIDELINES FOR ASSESSING STUDENT WRITING

Which of these two poems by J. P. Clark did you enjoy reading more? Choose one of the poems and write a paragraph in which you discuss your reasons for enjoying it. Consider the content of the poem, its imagery, and its theme.

Students who choose "Night Rain" will likely remember similar experiences of waking up in the middle of the night because of the sound of rain and then letting that sound lull them back to sleep. They may also remember a time in their own lives when they had to deal with a leaky roof, either at home, at school, at work, or on vacation. Students might mention liking the sense of peace and comfort that the poem evokes. Many will probably point out the fish image, the water drops "like orange or mango fruits" and like a broken string of beads, the immobilized owl or bat, and the "soothing hand" of the rain and the sea.

Students who choose "Girl Bathing" will probably admire the beauty of the words Clark uses to describe the woman's actions, including "lapping her thigh," "unguent flow of limbs," "ripe with joy," "teeth flashing pearls," and "iridescent . . . porcelain skin." Many will probably identify with the cooling, soothing effects of a dip in the water after hard work. They will also probably find the theme—praise of the black woman's beauty and strength—a satisfying one.

Whichever poem students choose, remind them to discuss the content, imagery, and theme.

BERNARD DADIÉ

Men of All Continents

SUMMARY

The speaker in this poem—either an individual representing the people of Africa or the "spirit" of Africa itself—addresses men and women around the world ("men of all continents"). Lines 25–30 further suggest that the speaker is specifically addressing people of good will. The speaker says that Africa has been around since biblical times ("I was there when the angel drove out the ancestor") and has suffered many tragedies ("cold in the bones," "hunger in the belly," and "the clatter of carbines"). The speaker warns people of good will that in spite of the efforts of "we who seek ourselves" and the hope in a star that "has always given a wink," evil or tragic events ("bullets") still thwart the dreams of Africans for a better future.

GUIDELINES FOR DISCUSSION QUESTIONS

1. **Who is the speaker—the "I"—of the poem? Who is being addressed—the "you"—in the poem? Who might the "we" be in lines 18–19?**

   The speaker is someone representing the people of Africa, or it is the "spirit" of Africa itself. A key line in helping to identify the speaker is line 4 ("I was an arable land"). The person(s) being addressed is (are) identified in the title of the poem "men of all continents"—specifically women and men of good will around the world. The "we" of the poem is probably the people of Africa collectively.

2. **What is the speaker saying in lines 8–12?**

   The speaker is saying that Africa is as old as biblical history—as old as the Garden of Eden, Noah and the flood, the birth of Jesus, and the death and resurrection of Jesus.

3. **What does the speaker mean by saying that "Bullets still behead the roses / in the mornings of dreams"?**

   The speaker is saying that evil or bad things still thwart good intentions or that hope is still being nipped in the bud. Specifically, the speaker might be saying that progress for a better Africa is still being blocked or set back.

GUIDELINES FOR ASSESSING STUDENT WRITING

Do you think this is a poem of hope or despair? Write a paragraph in which you argue one side or the other or perhaps both. Support your opinion with evidence from the poem.

Students who argue that this is a poem of hope will use line 23 as their primary defense. In saying "But a star has always given a wink" the speaker seems to be suggesting that there is hope for Africa's future. Students who argue that this is a poem of despair will point to the two places where the speaker says that "Bullets still behead the roses." Not only does the speaker repeat this sentiment, he also chooses to end the poem on this despairing note, and the word *still* seems to intensify the despair. Some students, however, may want to argue both sides. They might contend that the speaker intends to emphasize despair for the present but hope for the future, using the same lines for their defense. They might further argue that the speaker is cautioning people of good will who have already achieved progress ("You who hold heaven within reach") to be patient with Africa ("We who seek ourselves"). Encourage students to share their paragraphs with the class. The ideas in this poem should provoke a lively discussion.

BIRAGO DIOP

Truth and Falsehood

SUMMARY

Fene-Falsehood and Deug-Truth embark on a journey. Fene-Falsehood suggests that Deug-Truth do all the talking because people prefer the truth. They first meet a housewife who treats them badly. When Deug-Truth complains, the housewife flies into a rage. They next meet a village chief who is controlled by the children of the village. When Deug-Truth points this fact out, the offended chief banishes them. When the two travelers learn of a king who is mourning the loss of his favorite wife, Fene-Falsehood decides to take over. Leaving Deug-Truth behind, he goes to the king and promises to return the king's wife to life in exchange for one-half of the king's possessions. Through trickery, Fene-Falsehood manages to get what he wants without resurrecting the king's wife.

GUIDELINES FOR DISCUSSION QUESTIONS

1. Were you able to predict the outcome of this tale? If so, at what point in the tale did you know what would happen?

Most students will figure out what is going to happen before they reach the end of the tale. Some may realize as early as the first time that Deug-Truth is defeated that Fene-Falsehood will eventually triumph. Many will have predicted the outcome by the time Deug-Truth is defeated a second time. The method of Fene-Falsehood's victory, however, should come as a surprise to most if not all students.

2. Very often in fairy tales, events happen in threes—someone gets three wishes, there are three bears, or a knight goes on three missions. What are the three events that lead to the outcome of this tale?

First event: Fene-Falsehood and Deug-Truth meet a housewife who refuses to offer them and her husband food. When Deug-Truth complains, the wife flies into a rage. Second event: The two travellers meet children in a village who seem to be in control of passing out meat from a slaughtered bull. When Deug-Truth observes that this seems to be the case, the chief of the village is offended and banishes them. Third event: Fene-Falsehood and Deug-Truth learn of a king who is mourning the death of his favorite wife. This time Fene-Falsehood leaves Deug-Truth behind. He promises the king that he will bring back his wife and manages to trick the king into giving him one-half of his land without bringing back his wife.

3. **The dictionary defines** *paradox* **as "a seemingly contradictory statement that expresses a possible truth." What is the paradox in this tale? Why is it a paradox?**

Fene-Falsehood suggests that his traveling companion, Deug-Truth, do all the talking on their journey because people prefer the truth. The paradox is that Deug-Truth is not well received and it is Fene-Falsehood who triumphs in their dealings with people. It is paradoxical because people believe that they prefer the truth but often accept falsehood over truth anyway.

GUIDELINES FOR ASSESSING STUDENT WRITING

Can you think of a different ending for this tale? For example, what would happen if Fene-Falsehood were defeated? Think of ways to change the ending and then write a new ending for this tale. Begin your new ending with the third event in this tale, and consider these questions: How will the king learn the truth about Fene-Falsehood's deception? What will happen to Fene-Falsehood in the end? What role, if any, will Deug-Truth play? Share your ending with your classmates. Which of the new endings did you like most? Explain.

If students have difficulty coming up with ideas for a new ending for this tale, you might suggest the following questions to help get them started: What could Fene-Falsehood do to help bring about his own downfall? Could he become too confident? too greedy? In what way could the king's advisers intervene? What could Deug-Truth do to help expose Fene-Falsehood? Could other characters from earlier in the story help out—for example, the angry housewife or the offended chief who banished the two travelers? What new character could be introduced to help expose Fene-Falsehood?

The Wages of Good

SUMMARY

Diassigue-the-Alligator discovers that the channel where he lives is to be drained. He hides deep in the brush to avoid being killed by the villagers. Goné-the-Child discovers Diassigue, and Diassigue convinces Goné to roll him up in a mat and carry him to the river. When they get there, Diassigue tricks Goné into going out too deep in the river and then grabs Goné, intending to eat him. Goné protests that his good deed should not be punished, and the two agree that they will test Goné's opinion on three individuals. If they agree with Goné, Diassigue will release him. If they agree with Diassigue, Diassigue will eat Goné. The first two individuals, Nagy-the-Cow and Fass-the-Horse, tell sad tales of how their good deeds were punished. But the third individual, Leuk-the-Hare, asks for a full explanation of the circumstances before offering his opinion. When he discovers Diassigue's duplicity, he pretends not to understand what happened and asks that the two reenact the events. Once Diassigue has been rolled up in the mat, Leuk instructs Goné to take the alligator home to his family and eat him.

GUIDELINES FOR DISCUSSION QUESTIONS

1. **Do you agree with Diassigue-the-Alligator or with Goné-the-Child? In general, is a good deed repaid with a bad turn or with another good deed? Explain your answer.**

    Students may have mixed opinions on this subject. Many will argue that good deeds should be repaid with kindness or another good deed, but that often in real-life situations good deeds go unrewarded. Students might suggest that good deeds go unrewarded because some people are selfish and think only of themselves and their own welfare and comfort. Others might argue that good deeds are rewarded as often as not. You might ask students to think of examples from daily news stories of good deeds rewarded.

2. **In what way is the conflict between Goné and Diassigue a struggle between an idealist and a realist? Who is the idealist, the boy or the alligator? Who is the realist? Explain.**

    This tale is a struggle between someone who goes out of his way to be helpful without thinking of himself and someone else who selfishly and in a practical way thinks only of himself and his comfort. The child Goné is the idealist because he helps the alligator get to the river. Diassigue-the-Alligator is the realist because he selfishly accepts the boy's help and then decides to eat the boy because he is hungry.

3. **This tale illustrates the common plot device of the trickster tricked. Who is the trickster? How is the trickster tricked?**

    Diassigue is the trickster. He tricks Goné into carrying him into the deep water of the river and then captures him with the intent to eat him. In the end, Diassigue is tricked by Leuk-the-Hare. Leuk, after listening to what happened, pretends not to understand and tricks Diassigue into becoming Goné's captive.

GUIDELINES FOR ASSESSING STUDENT WRITING

Do you feel sorry for Diassigue's plight at the conclusion of the story, or do you think justice was served? Write a paragraph in which you argue either that Diassigue got what he deserved or that he should have been treated more humanely. Whichever position you take, support your opinion with reasons.

Students may be divided in their opinions about Diassigue. Many if not all of them will concede that what he attempted to do was clearly wrong, and some may argue that because it was wrong he deserved what he got. They will stress that if he had been allowed to, he would have eaten Goné and therefore deserves no mercy. They may also argue that an eye for an eye and a tooth for a tooth is appropriate in this situation. Others, while recognizing the severity of what Diassigue wanted to do, will argue that two wrongs don't make a right. Diassigue may have had evil intentions, but he hadn't yet actually acted on them. They will suggest that eating him is just as wrong as his intention to eat Goné.

Forefathers

SUMMARY

The speaker in this poem encourages his audience, fellow Africans, to listen to things—the fire's voice, the voice of water, the sobbing of trees, the murmuring wood, the flowing water, a child's crying, the weeping plant, and so on. All of these sights and sounds are evidence that their forefathers are not dead, but rather that they are everywhere around them in daily life.

GUIDELINES FOR DISCUSSION QUESTIONS

1. **Do you think that things in nature are important to the speaker of this poem? Why or why not?**

   Yes, things in nature are extremely important to the speaker. Fire, trees, water, and so on provide reminders that the speaker's ancestors are still alive in spirit.

2. **The speaker says that the dead are not gone forever, that the dead are not dead. What does he mean?**

He means that even though his ancestors have died, their spirits live on and are constantly present in daily life.

3. **One critic has suggested that this poem gives us a sense of the timelessness and unhurried pace of Africa, of a person who pauses silently listening and feeling the continuity of life. How are these ideas illustrated in the poem?**

The unhurried pace of Africa is illustrated by the speaker's instructions to listen to things in nature. To do so, an individual must stop and take time. A person can't appreciate what nature is "saying" if he or she is hurrying through the day. The timelessness and the continuity of life are illustrated by the speaker's revelation that his ancestors are present in nature. He is suggesting that the past is part of the present and will also be part of the future. Long after an individual dies, his or her spirit will still be present in the world.

GUIDELINES FOR ASSESSING STUDENT WRITING

It is obvious in this poem that the speaker's ancestors are very important to him. Who do you think this is so? Reread pages 30–31 of Peter Abrahams's essay "The Blacks." What light does he shed on this subject, and how does it relate to the ideas in this poem? After reading Abrahams' essay, write a paragraph in which you explain why ancestors are so important in the lives of tribal Africans, and also explain how this information relates to the ideas in Diop's poem.

Students should find the following information in Abrahams's essay: Tribal Africans believe that they are the living embodiment of their ancestors. Their ancestors have a powerful hold on them. The ancestors control and regulate the lives and activities of the living. If something goes wrong, it is a sign that the ancestors are angry and need to be appeased. Nothing is ever accidental in tribal life. Everything is the result of the influence of good and evil spirits that dwell everywhere around the tribal group. Tribal Africans believe that they are totally controlled by their ancestors and also protected by them. Students should also be able to recognize that these ideas are totally consistent with the ideas of the speaker in this poem, who urges his audience to pay attention to their forefathers through the reminders of them that exist all around.

DAVID DIOP

Poems

SUMMARY

These five poems by David Diop are related to one another in theme. Each poem contains in it the idea of enslavement and the fight for freedom. In "Africa" the speaker asks if Africa is defined by the bruises on its back, by the humility of the slavery of its children. The answer comes back: no, Africa is defined more appropriately as a young robust tree that yearns for freedom. In "Listen Comrades" the speaker urges his listeners to pay attention to the fight for freedom because there is hope for the future. In "He Who Has Lost All" the speaker contrasts freedom in Africa in the first stanza with colonial enslavement in the second stanza. In "Your Presence" the speaker declares his love for Africa. The references to "eyes no longer veiled with fever" and "suffering that burdens today with the taste of tomorrow" are references to slavery. Finally in "Defiance Against Force" the speaker strongly urges his listeners to resist their captors and break the bonds of slavery.

GUIDELINES FOR DISCUSSION QUESTIONS

1. In "Africa" what question does the speaker ask in lines 12–16? What answer is the speaker given in lines 17–24?

The speaker asks if Africa is defined by the humility of its enslaved position. A voice answers no. Africa is a young robust tree ("midst white faded flowers") yearning for freedom.

2. Why do you think the voice that answers describes freedom as having a "bitter flavor"?

It probably is a reference to the concern that freedom will come at a great cost in terms of pain and suffering.

3. In line 2 of "Listen Comrades" what is the "keen clamor of the Negro"?

It is the struggle for freedom and equality.

4. In line 12 the speaker says that Mamba "poured forth for us milk and light." What do you think this means?

The quotation probably means that Mamba, through his words and actions, inspired Africans to hope for a better future.

5. In the last line of the poem what are "the dreams of men"?

They are dreams of freedom and equality.

6. The two stanzas of "He Who Has Lost All" stand in stark contrast to each other. What word in the first stanza describes the condition of life depicted in that stanza? What word in the second stanza describes the direct opposite condition? What has happened to the people in the poem between stanza one and stanza two?

Liberty is the word in the first stanza. Its opposite in the second stanza is *slavery*. Between the two stanzas, the people have become enslaved by conquerors.

7. In "Your Presence" the speaker seems to be declaring his love for another person. One possible interpretation is that metaphorically the object of the speaker's love is Africa. Defend this idea using evidence from the poem (Reread David Diop's biography on page 67 for help in answering this question.)

Diop was born in France and lived most of his life in France but still considered himself African. This poem may have been written during or just after one of his visits to Africa. The phrase "in your presence," in line 1 and repeated in line 11, suggests a traveller who has been away. So also does the phrase "pain of separation" in line 2. In line 1 the speaker says he has rediscovered his name and in line 11 he has rediscovered the memory of his blood, suggesting that being in Africa has caused him to appreciate anew his heritage.

8. In "Defiance Against Force" whom is the speaker addressing? What message does the speaker give to his audience?

He is addressing Africans who are enslaved. He tells them to rise up and resist their captors.

GUIDELINES FOR ASSESSING STUDENT WRITING

All five of these poems by David Diop have a common idea running through them, although that idea is only lightly touched on in the poem "Your Presence." What is that idea and how is it treated in each poem? Write a paragraph or two in which you answer these two questions. Support your opinion with evidence from each poem.

All of these poems deal in one way or another with the idea of enslavement and the struggle for freedom. Students should be able to find ample illustrations of this idea in the poems. In "Africa" the speaker talks about the labor of slavery and the slavery of children. He also talks about the weight of humility, the red-striped back, and the whip. But in the last stanza he also talks about an Africa that has hope for freedom in its future. In "Listen Comrades" the speaker talks about leaders who have been killed in the fight for freedom but urges his comrades to continue the fight. In "He Who Has Lost All" the speaker contrasts a life of liberty in stanza one with a life of enslavement in stanza two. The central idea in "Your Presence" is the speaker's love for Africa, but even in this poem the references to "eyes no longer veiled with fever," "the snows of yesterday," the "shattered ideas," and the "suffering that burdens today" may be references to slavery. Finally, in "Defiance Against Force" the speaker urges "you who bow you who mourn" (enslaved Africans) to rise up and resist their captors.

R. SARIF EASMON

The Feud

SUMMARY

One the eve of her marriage to the warrior Luseni, the princess Nenneh Touray and her slave Poreh are kidnapped, Nenneh's father is killed, their village is burned, and most of the villagers are sold into slavery. The rival king Daimba Seisay wants Nenneh to be one of his wives. One of his other wives, Yalie Woanday, tries to convince Nenneh to cooperate, but Nenneh resists. Daimba then shows her how he treats his slaves. While viewing the slaves at work, Nenneh spots Luseni among the group and manages to whisper a secret message to him. Later that night they meet under a tree and consummate their love for each other. They also plan to escape. A month later they make an attempt along with Poreh, but, on a tip from Woanday, Daimba's sodiers stop them. In the confusion, Poreh escapes but Luseni is brutally killed.

Twenty years pass. Nenneh is now the wife of Daimba. Secretly, she meets with Poreh, Lansannah (Luseni's twin brother) and her son Luseni who was conceived the night that Nenneh and Luseni consummated their love. Seeking revenge, Nenneh takes her son Luseni with her back to Daimba's village. The two capture Daimba and Woanday and execute Daimba at the tree where Luseni had been murdered. Nenneh is so obsessed with her desire for revenge that she refuses to believe Daimba is dead. She returns to the tree to check on Daimba and is killed when lightning strikes the tree and it crushes her.

GUIDELINES FOR DISCUSSION QUESTIONS

1. **Note the title of this novella. What feud is presented in this story?**

   On one side of the feud is Nenneh Touray, the "widow" of the warrior Luseni. With her is her slave Poreh, her brother-in-law Lansannah, and her son Luseni. On the other side of the feud is King Daimba Seisay. At issue for Nenneh is revenge against Daimba for taking her prisoner, killing her father, and killing her husband-to-be Luseni.

2. **What changes do you notice in Nenneh during the twenty years the story covers? What sort of man is Daimba Seisay? What is your final impression of each of these characters?**

At the beginning of the story, Nenneh is a young and beautiful princess filled with girlish dreams of romance and her impending marriage to Luseni. After twenty years she has become embittered. Her eyes are described as sunken in their sockets and hard. Her hair is gray. She is obsessed with getting revenge on Daimba Seisay. Daimba is a powerful, ruthless king. He maliciously invades Nenneh's village, kills her father and takes some of the villagers, including Nenneh, captive. He sells the others into slavery. Later, when he discovers the truth of Luseni's identity, he brutally kills him. Within the world of tribal society, however, he justifies all of this as normal. At the end of the story, Daimba displays a curious sense of honor as he awaits his own death. He may be ruthless, but he accepts his behavior and when it is turned on him he is resigned to his fate. Nenneh is so obsessed with revenge at the end that she refuses to believe that Daimba is dead, and she brings about her own death by insisting on checking on him.

3. **After Daimba Seisay's death the narrator comments that Nenneh was "feeling lost . . . now that the prop of her life was knocked away by her enemy's death." What does this statement mean? Do you think this is a tale of justice or revenge? Explain your answer.**

The prop of Nenneh's life was her lust for revenge against Daimba Seisay. Once she attained that revenge she felt she had no more reason to go on. Students may suggest that this is a tale of both justice and revenge. Justice is served when Daimba is murdered because he was responsible for the murders of Nenneh's father and husband-to-be. But for the same reason, revenge is also attained. Nenneh dedicates herself to getting even with Daimba and with the help of her son she does.

4. **Throughout the story the narrator comments on people and society in general. Note the following quotations. What picture of African tribal life do you get from these quotations?**
   - **"Laconic and brutal as the information [of the raid] was, it was no worse than Nenneh had expected. It was the logic of the times. Her father had done the same thing to other tribes. Only she had never, never realized it had been so bad for others as it was turning out for her."**
   - **"Young though [Daimba] was, both as man and as king, absolute power had corrupted him beyond redemption."**
   - **"Poreh was made of sterner stuff than the princesses and parasites of Susu society."**

A picture emerges of a stark and brutal life. In the first quotation the narrator reveals that Nenneh was not surprised by the severity of the raid, suggesting that burning villages and kidnapping villagers was commonplace and expected of rival tribes. Being in a privileged position, Nenneh was only unaware of the severity of the treatment given to the victims of a raid. The second quotation reveals the awesome power that a leader of a tribal group wielded, and the third quotation comments on the tribal practice of keeping slaves and the rough treatment that slaves received.

GUIDELINES FOR ASSESSING STUDENT WRITING

Do you think that Nenneh was fated to die at the end of this story, or was it just a tragic coincidence that she was crushed by the tree? Write a paragraph in which you defend one of these opinions. Use evidence from the story and your understanding of tribal beliefs as best you can to support your position.

Students may be divided in their opinions regarding Nenneh's death and, of course, there is no definite right or wrong answer to this issue, but there is strong evidence in the story to justify believing that Nenneh's death was not an accident, but fated. Students will probably notice references to Allah in the story. These establish the notion that the lives of the characters are subject to the will of Allah.

As heinous as Daimba Seisay's crimes were, there is evidence in the story that his actions were understood by his enemies—that bloodshed among tribes was commonplace and expected. Nenneh's desire for revenge is considered a personal one by her brother-in-law and son. They agree to help her to avenge *her*, not her dead husband-to-be. They even ask her first if she won't consider forgiving Daimba. She is presented as so obsessed with revenge that she is not satisfied even after Daimba is dead. When she dies, from the point of view of the other characters, Allah has brought an end to the feud, as Lansannah says in the last line of the story. Students who insist that Nenneh's death was accidental will suggest that she was simply in the wrong place at the wrong time—if she had not gone back to the tree, she would not have died. They will insist that her death was the result of a freak accident of nature.

C. O. D. EKWENSI

Ritual Murder

SUMMARY

Kofi is summoned to the palace of the paramount chief, the *Omanhene*, who has died. The new *Omanhene* has not taken over yet. In a back room, a room formerly used for ritual human sacrifice, the three half-brothers of the dead *Omanhene* meet Kofi. They tell him they want him to dispose of evidence that would incriminate them in past illegal dealings. In actuality, however, they plan to kill him, and before he can escape, they do. They bury his body and go into hiding. They have arranged things so that the new *Omanhene* will be falsely blamed for killing Kofi in a ritual murder. However, the three brothers are consumed by guilt and imagine that they see Kofi's ghost haunting them. They consult a fetishman (priest) and ask for help. The police, along with the new *Omanhene*, follow the brothers and learn from the fetishman what they've done. With the reluctant help of the fetishman, the police capture the brothers in the act of digging up Kofi's grave. For his part in the capture, the fetishman takes his own life.

GUIDELINES FOR THE DISCUSSION QUESTIONS

1. **At the beginning of this story did you suspect something bad would happen to Kofi? Why or why not? If so, at what point did you become convinced?**

   Most students will probably admit that they suspected something bad would happen to Kofi. The foreshadowing of trouble is strong from the very beginning. Kofi's friends warn him and refuse to leave the palace without him. Then, when Kofi enters the palace, the scene becomes dark and foreboding, especially with the mention of the golden stool and what it stands for. Finally, those students who don't suspect anything up to this point certainly will be convinced that Kofi is in trouble when panic seizes him and he springs toward the door.

2. **The first scene takes place in the bright sunlight on the steps of a palace in a modern city; the second scene is in a dark corridor and the back room (called the black room) of the palace. What is the symbolic significance of this contrast?**

The symbolic significance centers on the bright sunshine outside the palace in this city of western law and order as contrasted with the darkness of the corridor and the black room where atrocities have occurred. After students have finished the story, they may also see the contrast as being one between the new Africa on the outside versus the old Africa represented by the black room.

3. **Between the old Africa and the new one stand certain men ready to use old traditions unscrupulously to advance their position in the new world. In this story, who are these men and what old traditions do they use unscrupulously?**

   These men are the three half-brothers of the dead *Omanhene*—Apiedu, Lampey, and Kwame. They plan to frame the new *Omanhene* for the ritual murder of Kofi, to cover themselves for past misdeeds. They kill Kofi and spread his blood over the golden stool to make it look like the new *Omanhene* sacrificed Kofi in a now forbidden ritual.

4. **Why do you think the fetishman poisons himself at the end of the story?**

   Students may be puzzled at the fetishman's actions. On the surface he wouldn't appear to have any reason for taking his own life. But there are two clues which might shed some light on this apparent mystery at the end of the story. First, the police inform him that the "ghost" the three brothers saw was actually the new *Omanhene*, no ghost at all. This news in a way undercuts the validity and importance of the help the fetishman was to have provided the three brothers, and he may have understood that. Second, he confesses to himself that he has never betrayed anyone in 80 years. He may be despondent over having violated his religious principles and think that death (including death of the old ways) is the honorable course of action.

5. **Think about the title: "Ritual Murder." Are the killings in the story ritual murders? In what way might this story be considered to be about the "murder" of the old Africa?**

   The killing of Kofi is not a ritual murder, even though his killers hoped it would look like one. The suicide of the fetishman might be considered a ritual in the loosest sense—one might argue that he was ritually giving up the old ways. The important symbolic ritual murder in this story is the victory of the new Africa over the old Africa when the police and the new *Omanhene* capture the unscrupulous brothers of the dead *Omanhene*.

GUIDELINES FOR ASSESSING STUDENT WRITING

Compare the ending of "Ritual Murder" with the ending of "The Feud." Consider these questions in your composition: What happens to Nenneh Touray at the end of "The Feud"? What happens to the three half-brothers at the end of "Ritual Murder"? What part does guilt play in either story? In what way are Nenneh and the three brothers responsible for their own demise? What part do the old traditions play in each story?

Students should be able to make the following comparisons: Both Nenneh and the three brothers die after returning to the body of the person they have killed. Guilt plays a very strong part in the actions of the three brothers. We are not told if Nenneh feels any guilt over her own actions, but her behavior would suggest that she must have felt some guilt, even though tribal custom may not include a sense of guilt for revenge murders. In both cases, the guilty parties are responsible for their own demise. One can argue that if Nenneh had not gone back, she would still be alive. If the brothers had not returned to Kofi's grave, the police would not have caught them. The old traditions in "The Feud"—an eye for an eye and a tooth for a tooth—are clung to tenaciously. It is because of the tradition of villages fighting other villages that the feud in that story is compelling and ongoing. The old traditions in "Ritual Murder"—the golden stool and what it symbolizes—are maliciously taken advantage of in an attempt to frame an innocent leader. In a larger sense, the old ways—graft and corruption—are rooted out and replaced by new ways.

The Law of the Grazing Fields

SUMMARY

According to the law of the grazing fields, a man may elope with the woman of his choice, regardless of her marital status, as long as he can get her to his home without being caught. Amina is in love with Yalla, a fine specimen of a man, but her father has promised her to Jama, a weak-kneed coward, who has offered 500 head of cattle for her. Amina and Yalla had planned to elope to his home, but have been stopped by Modio, Amina's brother. As the story opens, Amina is locked in Modio's hut. In her despair, Amina suddenly discovers that the hut is on fire. Yalla, who set the fire on purpose to distract her brothers, rescues Amina and rides away with her. The brothers pursue the fleeing couple the full five miles to Yalla's hut. As the couple approach the hut, Yalla is hit in the back with a poison arrow. Amina drags him safely the last few yards into the hut. They have made it and are now man and wife. As the story ends Yalla begs Amina to give him the antidote to the poison so he won't die. The brothers accept defeat and ride away, praising Yalla for his victory.

GUIDELINES FOR DISCUSSION QUESTIONS

1. What is the law of the grazing fields?

The law of the grazing fields states that a man may elope with any woman of his choosing, regardless of her marital status, as long as he can get her safely to his home without being caught.

2. In what sense is Amina a victim of the society in which she lives? In spite of this, in what ways does Amina show that she is a strong woman?

Amina is a victim of a society that allows men to decide whom she will marry. She is not allowed any power in making this decision and must accept whomever her father chooses for her or whoever carries her safely to his home. In spite of her circumstances, Amina shows strength in a number of ways. She strongly resists her brother when he captures her. She has the courage to try to escape with her lover and the strength and presence of mind to drag him into his hut after he has been wounded. In this way, she actively participates in her own liberation.

3. Do you think Yalla lives or dies at the end of the story?

There really is no right or wrong answer to this question, but most students will probably assume that Yalla lives. There is no reason given to believe that he will not receive the antidote in time. Besides, he and Amina have just successfully outwitted her brothers and in the last sentence of the story Yalla is praised for his manliness and courage. If the author had intended for us to believe that Yalla dies, he surely would not have ended his story on such a positive note. Those few students who argue that he dies will probably point to the place where Yalla encourages Amina to get into the hut even if he dies. The important thing, they might argue, is that Amina has escaped Jama, not whether Yalla lives or dies.

GUIDELINES FOR ASSESSING STUDENT WRITING

In what ways does this story seem similar to a story set in the Wild West of the United States? Write a paragraph in which you compare

the elements of this story—setting, plot, and characters—with a story about the Wild West.

Were it not for a few references in this story that help place it in Africa, it would be very easy to mistake it for a western short story. Students should be able to write about the following similarities: The setting, the grazing fields of the savannah, is very similar to the plains of the Wild West. The population of the savannah consists of cattlemen, who also inhabited the Wild West. The law of the grazing fields, which is the law of might, is very similar to the code of the Wild West, which emphasized possession of land and the law of might. Amina's fate is not unlike the fate of many women who became mail-order brides for men of the Wild West, although mail-order brides were willing participants in that practice. The escape from the brothers and the horse chase across the savannah are elements straight out of a Wild West thriller. Even the poison arrow seems familiar. Finally, Amina's character matches the strong women that abound in western fiction, and Yalla is the African equivalent of the male hero of western fiction. Students may offer other details that illustrate similarities between this story and a story about the Wild West.

D. O. FAGUNWA

The Forest of the Lord

SUMMARY

Olowo-aiyé decides to test his manhood by setting out on a journey to the dreaded Forest of the Lord. He ties medicines to his body and is given a rousing send-off by the people and medicine men of his village. First he comes to the Wilderness of Silence, and there he meets an evil sprite or imp named the Little Devil of the Ways. The two engage in a fierce wrestling match and it appears to be a draw, but then Olowo-aiyé retrieves a magic flute from his bag. He begins to play the flute, and the words and music charm the evil sprite, who surrenders. The two shake hands and Olowo-aiyé goes on his way. Next he meets a young woman in the Forest of the Lord. He recognizes her from his village and she tells him a story of how she became a witch. He is so charmed by her that he turns away from the Forest of the Lord and agrees to marry her. Thus, from that day forward, he "took trouble as a burden on his back and took trouble to be his wife."

GUIDELINES FOR DISCUSSION QUESTIONS

1. Were you satisfied with the ending of this story, or were you disappointed? Explain your answer.

Students may be divided on this question. Many will probably be disappointed that Olowo-aiyé does not continue his journey to the Forest of the Lord to test his manhood and suggest that the ending is unsatisfying as a result. Some, however, might be pleased that Olowo-aiyé was charmed by the witch. Some girls in particular might suggest that Olowo-aiyé got what he deserved for having such lofty ambitions.

2. In an epic, a hero, who is the champion of the people, goes off to do battle with a supernatural force. Often he or she is aided by magic and often he or she is tempted by a seductress or seducer. How do these elements fit the story "The Forest of the Lord"?

In "The Forest of the Lord" the hero is given a rousing send-off by the people of his village, he uses a magic flute to conquer the Little Devil of the Ways, and he is so charmed by a witch that he agrees to marry her.

3. **Does Olowo-aiyé's encounter with his future wife in the Forest of the Lord remind you of another story? Explain.**

Alert students will notice a resemblance to the story of Adam and Eve in the Garden of Eden. Like Adam, Olowo-aiyé turns away from the Forest of the Lord (from God) and allows himself to be tempted by the young woman (Eve). In both cases, trouble becomes a burden.

4. **A common element of folk tales is the inclusion of proverbs. Reread "The Forest of the Lord" and point out as many proverbs as you can.**

Students should be able to find many proverbs in the story, including the following: Trials are the father of fortune-making and a good name is better than a new wife. A man who aims at achieving something important, even if he fails to achieve his aim will achieve something nearly as important. He who prays to God for one pair of trousers, if he gets two pairs he must indeed give thanks to Almighty God. Progress is far from the man of two minds. A man's heart is his priest. He who tries to lift up rain in a sieve will find himself in Kingdom come. An elder who sees a snake and does not run is in a hurry to die. Pride is the beginning of destruction. The patient man never ends up with regret, but only he who foolishly lets patience be ruined. The patient man sees a quarrel and draws back. Wise people rank quarrels with poison. The wise man and the fool appear the same in a time of enjoyment but in a time of trouble the wise man stands out clearly.

5. **An allegory is a story that symbolically represents something else. If this story were viewed as an allegory, who would Olowo-aiyé represent and what would his journey represent?**

Olowo-aiyé would represent the common man or "everyman." In an allegory his journey would symbolically represent one's journey through life.

GUIDELINES FOR ASSESSING STUDENT WRITING

In stories like "The Forest of the Lord" it is common for the hero to encounter many tests and obstacles during his journey. What further tests or obstacles might Olowo-aiyé encounter if his journey were to continue? Write a new episode in which Olowo-aiyé is put to the test again. Your episode may be as short as one paragraph or as long as you choose. Make sure your episode answers the following questions: What test or obstacle does Olowo-aiyé encounter? What danger does this obstacle or test represent? How does Olowo-aiyé triumph over this test or obstacle? What lesson, if any, does Olowo-aiyé learn?

If students have trouble getting started on their episodes, ask them to think about fairy tales or other classic stories they have read in which a hero embarks on a dangerous journey. What kind of tests does that hero encounter—a fire-breathing dragon, a highwayman or bandit, a chasm filled with venomous snakes, a raging storm, an angry giant holding a village under siege, a fair maiden locked in a prison-tower, a field of poppies that induce sleep, a detour through the underworld, an evil wizard? Remind students to make sure that their stories include answers to the questions in the writing assignment.

ALFRED HUTCHINSON

Aboard an African Train

SUMMARY

In this excerpt from his book *Road to Ghana*, Alfred Hutchinson describes the beginning of his journey out of South Africa to escape unfair prosecution for his work for the African National Congress. Hutchinson first comments on the crowd of migrant miners at the train station at Mafeking. They are returning home to their native lands after doing backbreaking and dangerous work in the South African gold mines. Their faces register contempt for the "surface people"—people like Hutchinson who do not work in the mines. Hutchinson boards the train and shares a compartment with five other Africans. He is traveling without a valid passport and worries about what will happen when they cross the first border. However, no checks are made at the border and Hutchinson almost breathes a sigh of relief. Tension continues to build, nevertheless, and Hutchinson notices that the train stops at various intervals for long periods of time. One by one, Hutchinson learns a little about each of his traveling companions. All of them are returning home after spending many unhappy years in South Africa. At the Rhodesian border a policeman does check Hutchinson's pass, but only briefly. In the next car a family is stopped and interrogated but ultimately released. Hutchinson has passed his first major hurdle on his flight to freedom.

GUIDELINES FOR DISCUSSION QUESTIONS

1. **In the first paragraph Hutchinson says of the migrant miners returning home: "They swaggered a bit and looked at us, the surface people, with contempt. . . ." Who are the "surface people"? Why do you think the miners feel contempt for them?**

   The surface people are people who do not work in the mines. The miners work under miserable conditions and probably resent those people who have escaped such work.

2. **The author tells how long each of the people in his compartment had been away from home. Why do you think this point is important to him?**

He is probably acutely aware of the fact that he is leaving home by leaving South Africa, and he has no idea if he'll ever be able to return.

3. **Most of the passengers on the train are returning home to their native countries after working for a long time in South Africa. Do you get the impression that they were happy working in South Africa? Why or why not?**

No, they were not happy in South Africa. The old man says: "A person works for train fare." Moyo, the young man, confesses that he'll never return to the Union. Each of the passengers Hutchinson talks to has been disappointed in one way or another and longs to return home.

4. **How does Hutchinson create increasing tension in this account of his journey to freedom? What is the point of greatest tension in the account?**

The tension begins with the arrival of the miners and the commotion they cause. It gradually builds to the point when the train passes the first border. Periodically the train stops for long stretches of time, and Hutchinson wonders why it is going so slowly. The point of greatest tension occurs when the train reaches Plumtree at the Rhodesian border. There Hutchinson's pass is checked and a family is detained momentarily, but no action is taken by the authorities.

GUIDELINES FOR ASSESSING STUDENT WRITING

In this account, Alfred Hutchinson describes how he used deception to achieve a greater good. He flees South Africa without a valid passport in order to escape unfair prosecution. Have you ever used deception in order to achieve a greater good, or do you know someone who has? What were the circumstances and what was the outcome? Write a paragraph in which you describe such a situation—either your own or that of someone you know.

Many students will recall simple situations like lying to a friend in order not to offend that person—for example, complimenting a friend on his or her clothes when they really think that the clothes are unattractive. Some students, however, may recall more serious situations such as driving without a valid driver's license or breaking a safety law by speeding in order to get an injured person to the hospital. It may be helpful to have a brainstorming session to jog students' memories before they begin writing. Be sure to remind them that the deception, whatever it is, must be used in the service of a greater good, and not simply to avoid punishment for wrongdoing.

JOMO KENYATTA

The Gentlemen of the Jungle

SUMMARY

One day, during a hailstorm, Mr. Elephant comes to a man's hut and asks if he can put his trunk inside the hut out of the storm. The man consents, but Mr. Elephant also puts his head in and then the rest of his body and forces the man out of the hut. The two begin to argue, and other animals of the jungle gather. The King of the Jungle, Mr. Lion, demands an explanation. When he hears what has happened, he tells Mr. Elephant to appoint a commission to sort out the problem. Mr. Elephant appoints several animals to the commission but no men. The animals decide that Mr. Elephant has a right to stay in the hut, but the man is free to build himself another hut. When the man does, Mr. Rhinoceros takes it away from him. This process is repeated until all the other animals have new huts and the man still has none. One morning, when the other huts are beginning to decay, the man builds a new, bigger hut. All the animals fight to occupy it. While they are all fighting, the man sets the hut on fire, burning it down with all the animals. The man then goes home and lives happily ever after.

GUIDELINES FOR DISCUSSION QUESTIONS

1. **Did you correctly predict that the man would get even with the jungle animals? If not, what did you think would happen?**

   Most students will say that they predicted man would get even, even though they probably didn't know how he would get even. They will agree with the moral of the tale, that you can fool people for a time, but not forever. Man is clearly the hero in this tale, and it seems logical to assume that he couldn't be fooled indefinitely. A few students, if confused by the allegorical implications of the tale, might have sided with the animals and thought that the man would be tricked again at the end.

2. **Kenyatta said of this animal fable, "The relation between the Kikuyu and the Europeans can well be illustrated by this Kikuyu story." An allegory is a narrative in which the plot, characters, and setting represent something apart from their meaning in the story. If this fable is viewed as an allegory, who is the man? Who is the King of the Jungle? Who are Mr. Elephant, Mr. Rhinoceros, and the other animals?**

Allegorically, the man represents a Kikuyu native, and, by extension, all native Africans. The King of the Jungle represents the British government, perhaps the colonial governor of Kenya. Mr. Elephant, Mr. Rhinoceros, and the other animals are influential members of the colonial government (white Europeans).

3. Allegorically, what does the Commission of Enquiry represent, and what is the significance of the fact that Mr. Elephant and his wife serve a dinner to the commission before it gives its verdict?

The commission probably represents some form of the British judicial system. Clearly, Mr. Elephant's dinner for the commission is intended to influence their decision, which is Kenyatta's way of expressing his belief that the colonial judicial system in Kenya was corrupt.

4. What is the allegorical significance of the following statement: ". . . the members of the commission . . . were gentlemen chosen by God to look after the interests of races less adequately endowed with teeth and claws. . . ."? What is the allegorical significance of Mr. Elephant's statement that he took over the man's hut because he considered it necessary to "turn the undeveloped space to a more economic use"?

The first statement is Kenyatta's way of exposing the racism at the foundation of British attitudes toward native Africans. The British believed, or claimed to believe, that they were more enlightened than the native Africans and that British policies were in the best interests of the natives. The second statement, Mr. Elephant's rationale for taking over the man's hut, exposes the primary reason for Britain's interest in Kenya, and, by extension, all colonial interests in Africa. Mr. Elephant claimed he was helping the man with a problem, but in fact he lied. His real reason for occupying the hut was simply to take it over. Allegorically, Kenyatta is saying that colonial powers claim that they take over land to develop it, but actually they take it over to profit from its resources.

GUIDELINES FOR ASSESSING STUDENT WRITING

After being kicked out of all of his huts by the jungle animals, the man sits down and concludes that you can fool people for a time, but not forever. How does this proverb fit the end of the story, and what allegorical significance does it have? Write one or two paragraphs in which you discuss both of these questions.

Students might find it valuable to do some research on Jomo Kenyatta before writing their paragraphs. Kenyatta's efforts toward bringing independence to Kenya and his legal troubles with the British government should help stimulate students' thinking on this subject. Assess students' paragraphs on their ability to discuss both the literal and the allegorical elements in this fable. On a literal level, students should be able to point out that it was only a matter of time before the man would figure out that he was being taken advantage of and that he would need to do something about it if he were to survive. By fighting fire with fire, literally, he effectively disposed of his adversaries. The allegorical significance of the proverb, as it plays out in the fable, is unavoidably controversial. On a general level, Kenyatta is saying that native Africans can't be fooled indefinitely. Eventually they will discover the truth and rise up to take action. On a specific level, Kenyatta appears to be advocating violence, something he denied in real life. Students who research additional information on Kenyatta can inform the class of his legal battle with the British government, his imprisonment for involvement in the Mau Mau rebellion, and his persistent denial that he was ever involved in terrorist activities.

CAMARA LAYE

from *The Dark Child*

SUMMARY

This excerpt from Camara Laye's autobiography, *The Dark Child*, includes Chapters 1, 2, and 6, which cover episodes from Laye's early youth in Kouroussa, Guinea. In Chapter 1 Laye recounts a close call he had with a venomous snake, he discusses his relationship to his father, and he describes his father's special relationship with a small, black snake, which was believed to be the guiding spirit of the Malinke tribe. In Chapter 2 Laye relates an episode that illustrates his father's expertise as a goldsmith. A woman in the village brings some grains of gold to be crafted into a trinket. She also brings a praise-singer to flatter Laye's father with praises while he works. Laye explains the entire process of transforming the gold into an ornament, including a description of the praise-singer's *douga*, a spirited dance celebrating the completion of the work. In Chapter 6 Laye recalls his experiences as a student in the lower grades of a French school. He discusses the students' love for learning and the school's method of disciplining students. He ends the chapter with an account of how he and his friends, with the help of their parents, avenged the abuse that older bullies in the school inflicted on them.

GUIDELINES FOR THE DISCUSSION QUESTIONS

1. **What Malinke tribal rituals or customs are revealed in the first two chapters of Laye's account?**

   Laye describes the magic potions that his father smears on his body to protect and purify him while working on gold. He describes the custom of his father passing out oranges to everyone in the community. He explains the spiritual relationship of the black snake, as guiding spirit, to the Malinke tribe. He discusses the purpose of the praise-singer in the gold-making process, including the performance of the *douga*, the special dance in honor of the goldsmith, and he mentions the magical incantations that the goldsmith utters while he is working on the gold.

2. **Why do you think Laye's father worried about the fact that Laye would not be in his company enough?**

   Laye's father knew that times were changing and that Laye would eventually be leaving the community in order to further his education.

Laye's father probably realized that this action would have the effect of cutting Laye off from his culture and the traditions of that culture.

3. **Based on what you learned in this selection, how would you describe the role of women in Malinke tribal society?**

Much is implied about the role of women by the fact that little or nothing is said of them in this excerpt. Their role appears to be clearly subservient to the men of the community. From the selection we learn that they are responsible for raising the children and preparing the meals, but little else. The men have separate huts from the women, and Laye confides that his questions about the black snake will have to be answered by his father because spiritual matters such as this are too mysterious for the women.

4. **Compare Laye's description of school life with your own experiences in school. What is similar? What is different?**

Students will recognize that the teasing between the boys and girls is very familiar to them. Laye's revelation that they took their work very seriously, that they were always attentive, and that they wouldn't think of disobeying, will probably come as a surprise to some students, who may have a more relaxed attitude toward school. They may also be surprised at the stern discipline at the French school that Laye attended. They will be familiar with the bullying of older children toward the younger children, but again they'll probably be surprised that the schoolmaster attempted to defend such behavior.

GUIDELINES FOR ASSESSING STUDENT WRITING

Which chapter, or part of a chapter, from this excerpt of Camara Laye's autobiography did you enjoy most—Chapter 1, 2, or 6? Why was it your favorite? Write a paragraph in which you explain why you enjoyed a particular part of this autobiography and what you learned from it.

Students, no doubt, will be divided in their choices. Those who choose Chapter 1 will probably express astonishment, if not disbelief, at the docile behavior of the black snake in the presence of Laye's father. Those who choose Chapter 2 will probably emphasize what they learned about the process of transforming gold into ornamental objects. They may also express an interest in the role of the praise-singer. Those who choose Chapter 6 will probably register surprise at the harshness of Laye's school experiences, but they will also note the aspects of school life that apparently remain the same worldwide. Be sure to remind students to provide sound reasons for their choices and to offer their own observations on what they've learned. Encourage students who wish to write about more than one section of this excerpt to do so.

WILLIAM MODISANE

The Dignity of Begging

SUMMARY

The narrator of this story is Nathaniel Mokgomare, a professional beggar. He has been brought to court for begging and is upset that the judge might put him in jail. Luckily, he gets off with a light sentence: finding a job through the government. Even this upsets him. That night he makes plans to start a beggars' union. The next day he reports to work and manages to con the supervisor. Before arriving at work, however, he resorts to his old ways of begging for money. On the next day, he takes the money he has conned and bets it at the race track. He wins, and when he goes to collect his money, a fellow con man tricks him into sharing his winnings, even getting a judge to side with him. That night when Nathaniel gets home he finds a note from his wife pleading for financial help for her and the children. Nathaniel vows to reform, but at the end of the story he concludes that he probably will return to begging, saying that he owes it to the profession.

GUIDELINES FOR DISCUSSION QUESTIONS

1. The narrator of "The Dignity of Begging," Nathaniel Mokgomare, is a rascal from the lower ranks of South African society. Find examples in the story of ways he proves himself a rascal.

Nathaniel begs for a living because it is easier and more lucrative than holding down a regular job. He tries to worm his way out of a jail sentence by putting on a fake sob story for the judge. He is pleased with himself when he gets off with a light sentence. He spends an evening planning a bogus scheme to start a beggars' union, which would make him rich but do little to help beggars. On his way to government-forced work, he can't resist doing some more begging. He neglects his family, and when he "reforms" at the end, he even admits that it probably won't last.

2. Late in the story Nathaniel has the tables turned on him. Explain how he is tricked by another rascal.

Nathaniel goes to the race track and is conned by another man into sharing his winnings. Even though the man is lying, a judge upholds the man's right to one-half of what Nathaniel won at the track.

3. **The narrator, Nathaniel, makes several satirically humorous statements in this story. Point out a few examples of this kind of humor.**

Students should be able to find many examples. Here are a few you can suggest if students have trouble at first:
   • Why must I take a job when I can earn twice a normal wage begging?
   • I must uphold the dignity of begging. Professional ethics forbid all beggars from working.
   • Why not a beggar's union? I could rally all the beggars of the city into one union with some professional name like "The United Beggars' Union". . . .
   • I feel depressed that the world has not had the vision to realize the potentialities of my genius . . .
   • To think the department wants to pin me behind a desk! The idea is criminal, to say the least.
   • One of these days . . . I hope to write a book on begging . . . with easy to follow rules on the noblest and oldest profession in the world . . .
   • He has wholly realized the separateness of good and evil and attained a purity in evil worthy of honest appraisal. . . . If I were allowed to choose a brother, he would be my only choice.
   • Deep down I know that I will want [begging] again. . . . I have to come back. I owe it to the profession.

4. **At the end of the story, Nathaniel is filled with remorse for the way he has treated his wife and children. Do you think he really will reform? Explain your answer.**

It seems fairly certain that he will not really reform. He admits that he will probably want to return to begging, and he rationalizes that he owes it to the profession to do so.

GUIDELINES FOR ASSESSING STUDENT WRITING

"The Dignity of Begging" is a satire, a literary strategy that uses humor to ridicule or put down human folly or vice. How does this definition apply to the humor in "The Dignity of Begging"? Write a short essay in which you analyze the satire in this story. What is

ridiculed in the story? How is humor used to expose this vice? Include examples from the story in your essay.

Students should be able to recognize that both the art of begging and the sincerity of professional beggars are being satirized in this story. Nathaniel is a sneaky character who professes to be proud of his "noble" profession but who also takes delight in conning the judge into giving him a light sentence when he is brought before the court. He claims pompously that "professional ethics forbid all beggars from working," but in reality he begs instead of doing honest work because he knows he can make more money by begging. Nathaniel is a con artist in everything he says and does. He claims he left home because of "excessive kindness" bestowed on him. He hatches a plan to help beggars by starting a beggars' union, but really intends only to make himself rich. He gambles his money at the race track and then is outraged when another con artist tricks him. He can't even resist begging when he is on his way to a job the court ordered him to take. On his way home from his second appearance in court he is disappointed because he is wearing good clothes, which makes it difficult for him to be a convincing beggar. At the end of the story he makes quite a fuss over what a stinky father he has been and vows self-righteously to reform. Almost immediately he hedges on this promise. To the end, he remains a rascal who claims he owes it to the profession to be who he is.

ES'KIA MPHAHLELE

The Master of Doornvlei

SUMMARY

On a Sunday morning at Doornvlei Farm in South Africa, black African tenants who work on the farm are in church. A small boy watches a bird fly into a closed window and fall to the floor. He rescues the bird. At that point Mfukeri, the black foreman of the farm, comes into the church to retrieve the boy to do some work for him, even though it is pouring rain outside. The boy puts the bird in a safe place and goes about his work in the pouring rain. The next day he comes down with pneumonia. He asks his mother to check on the bird. His mother reports that the bird is dead. That night the boy dies too. When word gets out that the boy has died, Tau Rathebe, a leader of the tenants, rallies them to confront Sarel Britz, the white owner of the farm. They complain of Mfukeri's mistreatment of the boy and demand that Mfukeri be dismissed or they will quit the farm. Britz discusses the situation with his wife and decides to give Mfukeri a second chance but to dismiss the rabble rouser Tau Rathebe. Britz fears the potential power of the tenants, even though he has withheld their trek-passes, passes which would allow them to move freely around the country. He concludes that he'd better crush any revolt before it develops. All goes peacefully for a while. At harvest time Britz calls his trusted foreman in for a conversation. He thanks Mfukeri for his faithfulness. Silently Mfukeri is pleased. He enjoys his power over his white boss while at the same time despising himself for having to do Britz's dirty work disciplining the tenants. The more he despises himself the harder he treats his fellow tenants, in order to build himself up all the more. Britz vaguely senses the tension between him and Mfukeri and regrets that he is so dependent on the black foreman. One day Mfukeri's bull, Donker, traps Britz's prize stallion, Kasper, in the barnyard. The two animals fight furiously before Donker fatally gores Kasper in the stomach. Britz immediately shoots the dying horse. He then hands the gun to Mfukeri and orders him to kill the bull or leave the farm forever. Mfukeri refuses to kill the bull and walks away. At the end, Sarel Britz is filled with conflicting emotions—grief-stricken at the loss of his stallion; glad that Mfukeri, who was a threat to his authority, has finally gone; and still very much afraid of his tenants and their growing power.

GUIDELINES FOR DISCUSSION QUESTIONS

1. **The second sentence of the story reads: "In the mud-and-grass church house a bird flitted from one rafter to another, trapped." Knowing what you know about the rest of the story, what does that bird symbolically represent?**

   Students learn later in the story that, just like that little bird, the small boy and the rest of the tenants at Doornvlei Farm are trapped. They are stuck working for low wages because the white owner holds their trek-passes, identification cards that would allow them to leave for other jobs.

2. **The first character Mphahlele introduces is a nameless minor one—a nine-year-old boy. Is he used as a symbolic representative of the rest of his community, or is he merely the cause of the later conflict in the plot, or is he both?**

   Students should be able to recognize that the small boy is both. In terms of the plot, his death obviously is the cause of the later conflict. But on a symbolic level, his helplessness in the face of Mfukeri's inhumane treatment represents the same helpless, trapped feeling that the rest of his community experiences. The boy's death serves as a rallying point for the tenants, and they confront Sarel Britz with their grievances.

3. **In what ways are Mfukeri and Sarel Britz alike?**

   Both men have power, Britz over Mfukeri and Mfukeri over the tenants. Both men work together to keep the tenants under control. Both men are suspicious of each other, and both resent their dependence on each other. Both men battle inner demons, and both are hated by the tenants.

4. **Allegorically, the battle between Kasper the horse and Donker the bull stands for more than a barnyard struggle. Symbolically, what does the battle between these two animals represent? Explain your answer.**

   The battle of these two animals symbolically represents the battle for power and dominance between Sarel Britz and Mfukeri. Donker represents a threat to Kasper just as Mfukeri represents a threat to Britz. The fact that Donker wins the battle is related in an intriguing way to the end of the story. At the end, has Mfukeri won his battle with Britz? Students should enjoy debating this issue.

5. Why do you think the bystanders remain neutral during the battle?

The bystanders hate both men. They don't know who to support in the battle between the two animals. Since they are caught between the two men, practically speaking they lose either way.

6. In the last two paragraphs of the story Sarel Britz is grief-stricken, then glad, and finally fearful. Why is he grief-stricken? Why is he glad? Why is he fearful?

He is grief-stricken because he has lost Kasper, his prize horse. He is glad because he has gotten rid of Mfukeri, who he had come to realize was a threat to his power. He is fearful because he still has to deal with his tenants, and he is very mistrustful of their growing power.

GUIDELINES FOR ASSESSING STUDENT WRITING

Note the title of this story. Who is the master of Doornvlei? Is it Sarel Britz, the owner of the farm, or Mfukeri, the foreman, or both? Write a short essay in which you defend one of these three options. Support your argument with evidence from the story.

There is no real right or wrong answer to this question. Any of the above three options is defensible. Students who argue that Sarel Britz is the master of Doornvlei have the most obvious evidence on their side. After all, he is identified by one of the tenants in the story as the master of the farm. He is also the master in the sense that he gives orders to Mfukeri.

More importantly, he remains the master after Mfukeri leaves. Students who choose Mfukeri may have a more difficult time defending their choice. But they can raise interesting questions. We are told in the story that Mfukeri enjoys the power he exercises over his boss. And we are also told that Sarel Britz resents his dependence on Mfukeri. Who, then, is the real master? From the tenants point of view, it is Mfukeri that administers the discipline; he is their master. Also, at the end it can be argued that Mfukeri gets the better of Britz not only because Donker kills Kasper but also because Mfukeri ultimately refuses to take orders from Britz when Britz demands that Mfukeri kill Donker. Students who choose both will probably argue that there are two protagonists in the story. Britz is the obvious master, but he is reduced to fear at the end. Mfukeri, ironically, is the real master at the end when he stops taking orders and becomes his own man. Regardless of which option students choose, assess their writing on the basis of the clarity of their ideas and their ability to use evidence from the story to defend their point of view.

ABIOSEH NICOL

Life is Sweet at Kumansenu

SUMMARY

Nicol's story focuses on an old widow named Bola, who in the past had given birth to six sons, all of whom died shortly after birth. The villagers believed that all of these sons were the same person who kept reappearing. After the death of the sixth son, Bola was advised to mangle the baby's bones so that the child could not reappear and cause her any more pain. Bola refused, and she eventually had a seventh son who survived.

As the story opens, the surviving son, Meji, now 30 years old, pays an unexpected visit to his mother's house. His pallor, weariness, and avoidance of the other villagers cause his mother some concern, but she is overjoyed to see him. Shortly after he leaves, she receives the news that he has been dead for several days. It then becomes apparent that he visited her after death, making a long and difficult journey to thank her for giving him a chance to live. The story ends on a positive note, with Bola declaring that "life is sweet," even when it brings sorrow.

GUIDELINES FOR DISCUSSION QUESTIONS

1. **When did you first suspect that Meji was dead? What details does the author use to suggest that there is something eerie about Meji's visit?**

    Students will become suspicious at various points in the story, of course. The following details (in order of appearance) all indicate that there is something uncanny about Meji:
    * He enters the house even though the door is locked.
    * His skin looks "grayish" and pale.
    * His mother remarks that his brow feels cold.
    * He eats nothing.
    * His daughter notices that he has no shadow.
    * His daughter asks why his watch stopped running at twelve o'clock, and he replies that "the world ends at noon."
    * His daughter asks about the scarf around his neck, and he jokes that his head would fall off without it.
    * When they visit his father's grave, he feels nearer to his father than he ever had before.
    * His mother notices a smell of decay in his bedroom.
    * He stands in the rain but does not get wet.

2. **How is this story different from a typical "ghost story"? Consider the ghost's motivation for returning to life and the general impact the story makes on the reader.**

In a typical ghost story, the ghost returns to earth to get revenge on selected individuals or at least to scare them. The writer or teller of a ghost story usually attempts to build as much suspense as possible, making the reader anxious and fearful. In Nicol's story, the ghost comes back out of love and gratitude, and the story progresses in a simple leisurely way. There is no attempt to build suspense or fear.

3. **Why did Bola mark her sixth baby with a pointed stick?**

Bola made a mark on the baby's left buttock in order to find out if the next baby born was actually the same baby. When she saw the mark on the seventh baby, she had her answer.

4. **What is the significance of the last sentence in the passage below?**
   Asi shouted six and then said nine, ten.
   Bola called out that after six came seven.
   And I should know, she sighed.

The last sentence is a graceful transition from the present to the past. When Bola says, "I should know" that after six comes seven, she is thinking of her seventh son, the only one that lived. The rest of the paragraph recounts her personal history with the seven babies.

5. **Only Musa, the village magician, shares with Bola the secret of her son Meji's death and reappearance, and yet he does not understand her. How would you characterize their different views of life?**

Musa believes that pain is something to be avoided and therefore suggests that it would have been better if Meji had never been born. Bola believes that pain is part of life and that her brief but loving relationship with Meji was worth all the sorrow it brought.

GUIDELINES FOR ASSESSING STUDENT WRITING

Imagine that you are an anthropologist collecting information on some of the customs and beliefs that prevail in the African village of Kameni. You have just conducted an interview with the widow Bola, who answered all of your questions patiently. Write a script of the conversation you just had.

Abioseh Nicol   TM-63

Students could present any number of details about such everyday customs as the style of the houses and the kind of food eaten in Kameni, but a thorough interview would also need to mention the following beliefs, which receive considerable emphasis in the story:

- The belief about the spirit-child, who does not live to grow up but returns to his mother's womb to be born again.
- The belief that an individual can throw four split kola nuts on a grave and, if they fall with all four faces up or with all four faces down, that person can then communicate with the dead.

The questions asked by the anthropologist should be specific ("I understand that the villagers have a belief about using kola nuts to communicate with the dead. Could you explain that belief to me?"). It would also be good if the students used some follow-up questions after hearing the answer. ("Can anyone perform this ritual, or does the individual have to be related to the dead person?")

GRACE A. OGOT

The Rain Came

SUMMARY

Labong'o, the chief of the Luo tribe, is heartbroken. His village is plagued by a devastating drought that is killing the cattle and may soon kill the children. The ancestors must be appeased before it will rain again. Nditi, the medicine man, tells Labong'o that a young girl must be sacrificed in order for the Almighty to send rain. In a dream Nditi saw Labong'o's daughter, Oganda, and was told by a representative of the ancestors that she must be the one to be sacrificed. Labong'o sadly tells Oganda of her fate. Oganda resigns herself to her situation. The rest of the village rejoices because now something will be done to bring them the badly needed rain. After a night of dancing and feasting by the villagers, Oganda sets out on her journey to the sacred land and the lake where she will be sacrificed to the monster. She thinks of her lover, Osinda, and notes that he has disappeared from the village. As she gets close to the lake where the monster dwells, she notices that she is being followed. Just before plunging into the lake she is grabbed from behind by Osinda. He convinces her to escape with him. They wear coats made of leaves to hide themselves from the ancestors and the monster. When they reach the barrier of the sacred land—a place no human returns from alive—they look back and see the sun almost set. Oganda is afraid, but Osinda begs her to run with him. Lightning flashes in the distance. They look up, afraid again. That night it rains in torrents.

GUIDELINES FOR DISCUSSION QUESTIONS

1. **It is commonly thought that in primitive societies rulers desired sons that would succeed them. Labong'o in this story was mocked because he had no daughter. What does this imply about the position of women in this tribal community? Offer reasons why you think this might be so.**

   Little is said in this story about the position of women, but it would seem that if Labong'o were so desperate for a daughter women must be valued. Certainly they would be valued as potential wives and mothers, particularly for their importance in assuring future generations of the tribe. On a more alarming note, it is clear from the story that girls were valued as potential sacrifices, something that was considered to be an honor.

2. To *foreshadow* an event is to show or indicate that event before it happens. Foreshadowing is a common literary device used by authors to give readers a hint of what will happen later in a story. In what way is Osinda's attempted rescue of Oganda foreshadowed early in the story?

Early in the story, Oganda whispers a prayer to Osinda in which she says "Come now and take me away. . . ." That is exactly what he tries to do later. His rescue attempt is also vaguely hinted at the three times the reader learns that Osinda has disappeared from the community. Alert readers will suspect that there is a connection between his disappearance and Oganda's troubles.

3. Find evidence in this story to indicate that it is important that the wishes of the ancestors be granted by the tribal community. For additional help in answering this question recall what you learned about tribal beliefs in Peter Abrahams's essay "The Blacks" and Birago Diop's poem "Forefathers."

The importance of pleasing the ancestors is dealt with early in this story when Labong'o realizes that if he disobeys the ancestors the Luo people will probably be wiped off the face of the earth. The importance of pleasing the ancestors is echoed by the villagers who remind Oganda that it is an honor to be chosen as a sacrifice for appeasing the ancestors.

Students will probably remember Abrahams's discussion of the centrality of ancestors in tribal life. Tribal groups believe that their ancestors control their entire lives, that nothing happens by chance. In Diop's poem the speaker reminds his listeners that their ancestors are not dead; they are constantly around in nature influencing the daily lives of tribal people.

4. When the villagers dance for Oganda to keep her company during her night vigil, Oganda wonders to herself why they are not sympathetic, why they don't try to save her. What reason is given in the story for their rejoicing? What additional reason can you think of that might make them feel happy (or relieved)?

The villagers consider it a great honor to be chosen to die for the community. They also believe that this act will bring them the badly needed rain. Additionally, although this is not mentioned in the story, it seems logical to believe that they are secretly happy or relieved that one of them has not been chosen. Like Oganda, they probably secretly fear the prospect of dying.

5. **Do Oganda and Osinda escape at the end of this story? Does the fact that it rains indicate that they do not escape? Has the author made it clear what happens to them one way or another? Defend your opinion with evidence from the end of the story.**

Many students will believe that they have escaped, citing Osinda's last words of encouragement to Oganda, the fact that they have reached the border of the sacred land, and the fact that the narrator of the story does not say they did not escape. Students who believe that they have not escaped will point to the last sentence and ask "If they escaped, why does it rain?" Regardless of their individual positions on this issue, most if not all students should be able to recognize that the fate of the pair is not made absolutely clear.

GUIDELINES FOR ASSESSING STUDENT WRITING

Reconsider Discussion Question 5 and think about the comments it provoked during class discussion of this story. How would you change the ending to make it absolutely clear what happens to Oganda and Osinda? Write your own new ending to this story in which you make it clear either that they escape or that they die. If you decide that they escape, explain how they do so and predict what becomes of them. If you decide that they die, explain how they are thwarted from escaping and identify the agent of their death.

If students have trouble thinking of plausible new endings, suggest that they use the following questions to stimulate ideas to develop: If Oganda and Osinda escape, how do they safely cross the barrier? Where do they go? Do they continue to wear their coats of leaves? Can they hide from the ancestors forever? How will they survive? Can they ever return to the Luo community? If Oganda and Osinda die, will it be immediately? Will the sea monster rise out of the lake to trap them? Will the ancestors find another way to punish the pair? Because it rains, does that automatically mean that the pair must die? Might there be other circumstances under which the ancestors could be appeased? What would happen if it didn't rain? What would happen to the Luo community in such an event?

Assess students' stories on the clarity of expression and the creativity employed in composing plot details for their new endings.

LENRIE PETERS

Homecoming and *Parachute*

SUMMARY

In "Homecoming" the speaker explains that, after returning home from traveling to other parts of the world, little or nothing remains of what he thought he remembered. In "Parachute" the speaker describes the experience of parachuting to the ground and compares it to returning home after traveling to other parts of the world.

GUIDELINES FOR DISCUSSION QUESTIONS

1. In the last stanza of the poem "Homecoming" the speaker indicates that he—and perhaps someone else as well—has been away from home (paced the world) for some time. Who might that person be?

The speaker might be talking about any native African who has spent time in other parts of the world. It is possible that Lenrie Peters, the author of the poem, is referring to himself and/or personal friends of his. While attending school in Cambridge, England, Peters served as president of the African Students Union and knew many Africans who lived outside the continent of Africa.

2. According to the first four stanzas, what is left of the speaker's home upon his return?

Very little or nothing of what the speaker remembers about his home remains. The present reigns supreme. What the speaker remembers has been buried and changes have occurred. The house stands without a shadow (perhaps meaning without any visible reminders of its history), and it is occupied by new skeletons (people).

3. The first five stanzas of the poem "Parachute" describe the experience of parachuting to the ground. What concluding point does the speaker make about parachuting in the fifth stanza?

After the jump is concluded, you are on solid ground, back where you started from.

4. In the last stanza, stanza six, the speaker changes his focus to something other than parachuting. What point does he make in this stanza?

In this stanza the speaker is talking about living or traveling in other parts of the world (jumping across worlds). When you are through traveling, you always return to the starting point—home.

GUIDELINES FOR ASSESSING STUDENT WRITING

The first three stanzas of the poem "Homecoming" are four-line stanzas in which lines 1 and 3 rhyme and lines 2 and 4 rhyme. Try your hand at writing a poem with a similar structure. You may make your poem as many stanzas as you like but try for at least two stanzas. Each stanza should contain four lines with alternating lines rhyming. Choose any subject you wish for your poem, or as Lenrie Peters does in "Homecoming," write about home.

To help students get started, brainstorm possible subjects of importance to them. To make sure students understand the requirements of the assignment, review the structure of the first three stanzas of "Homecoming" with them or create your own one-stanza model on the chalkboard and discuss it. Assess students' poems on their creativity of ideas and expression and on how well students followed the structural requirements of the asssignment.

RICHARD RIVE

African Song

SUMMARY

Muti is afraid. He is attending a public meeting without an identification pass that would allow him and other black Africans to move about freely in the city. Policemen have entered the meeting and are systematically checking everyone for a pass. During the meeting the audience sings an inspirational African song. The first two lines of the song are "God bless Africa. Lift up our descendants." As he sings Muti thinks about his life, past and present, in Africa and his hopes for the future. At the same time, a policeman is getter closer and closer to him. As the song ends, Muti trembles because the policeman is standing right before him. Although we are not told, we assume that Muti will be arrested.

GUIDELINES FOR DISCUSSION QUESTIONS

1. **The story line of "African Song" is slight. However, note the title. Might it explain a purpose other than simply relating a story? Explain.**

   The title suggests that this story might be intended as an extended song—one of praise, inspiration, and hope for Africa. Have students track the lines of the song that the people at the meeting sing during the telling of the story. The words of the song echo some of the ideas Rive presents in the story.

2. **Muti recounts two visions of the future he has while he is singing. Explain each vision he has.**

   Muti sees two very different futures for Africa. In his first vision, black people and white people are laughing together. The stores of the great cities have plenty of food and products to sell and black people and white people are working together. Finally, the fields have an abundance of fruits and vegetables and again black people and white people are working the fields side by side. In the second vision, Muti sees black faces smoldering with anger. In the great cities there are many black people but only a few white people, and the few white people that remain are doing things that black people used to do. In this vision the white people have obviously left Africa, and the black people are angry.

3. Although this story may be slight, it does contain the one essential ingredient of all plots—conflict. What is the immediate conflict in this story? How does Rive build the tension and drama of this conflict as the story approaches its end?

Muti is attending a public meeting without possessing a required identification pass that would allow him to move freely about the city. The conflict exists in the form of a policeman in a blue uniform who has come to the meeting to check everyone's pass. The tension and drama increase as the policeman moves closer and closer to Muti. Rive further heightens the drama by alternating the policeman's movements and reports of people being led away with lines of the inspirational song that the audience at the meeting is singing.

GUIDELINES FOR ASSESSING STUDENT WRITING

Do you have a favorite song, one that makes you feel good, that inspires you? What is it about that song that inspires you? Is it the words? the melody? Choose a favorite song, one that is special to you, and write a short essay about it. In your essay describe the ideas that are expressed in the song and explain what it is about the song that makes you feel good.

You may need to coax students into recognizing the variety of possibilities they have available to choose among. Suggest, for example, that students think about the possibilities that exist in popular songs, patriotic songs, religious songs, love songs, campfire songs, folk songs, and political-protest songs. Assess students' essays on the clarity of their ideas and on students' abilities to support their choices with reasons.

No Room at Solitaire

SUMMARY

It is Christmas Eve and Fanie van der Merwe is sitting at the empty bar of his hotel. His only customer is his friend Dawie Volkwyn. Everyone else has been invited to a party. The two white men commiserate with each other. They talk about the significance of Christmas. They wonder how they will know Jesus when he comes again. Dawie asks "What if He is not a White man?" Fanie reassures him. The conversation changes. The two men discuss the intelligence of black South Africans. Despite what others may believe, they agree it is possible for black South Africans to learn to read and write. They are interrupted by Fanie's black servant, Witbooi. A black couple is at the door with a donkey. The woman is pregnant. They need help and a room. Fanie turns them down, disgusted that they would have the nerve to come to his hotel. He tells them there is no room. He and Dawie discuss the situation and laugh uncomfortably over the significance of Fanie's words "There is no room"—no room at the inn. Gradually they become more uncomfortable. Witbooi reports that the couple refuse to go away. Fanie and Dawie go to check on the couple, bringing a bottle of brandy with them. They discover that Witbooi has put the couple in the stable. Both men let out an exclamation and then check the sky to see if there is a bright star nearby.

GUIDELINES FOR DISCUSSION QUESTIONS

1. **What reasons does Fanie give for refusing to help the black African couple? Do you think these are his only reasons? Explain your answer.**

He tells them he is not a midwife and anyway there is no room. These are certainly not his only reasons. He also is offended that a black couple would request a room at his hotel.

2. **Parts of this story bear a striking resemblance to the Christmas story of the Nativity, a point that both Fanie and Dawie recognize. Do they appear comfortable with the comparison? Explain your answer.**

No they are not comfortable. They laugh over the coincidence but both are uneasy. Dawie laughs "dutifully" and Fanie's laugh has a "false ring." After thinking it over, they decide to check on the couple and even bring a bottle of brandy with them.

3. **Are Fanie and Dawie confirmed racial bigots or are they more complex than that? Use evidence in the story to support your opinion.**

Both Fanie and Dawie seem more complex. Both express racially bigoted ideas but they reject more blatantly bigoted ideas that a friend of theirs believes. The fact that they become uneasy over the way they have treated the black couple indicates that their bigotry has limits.

4. **In what way do Fanie and Dawie undergo a change in their attitudes at the end of the story?**

Clearly they have a change of heart regarding their treatment of the couple requesting a room. The fact that they go to check on the couple and bring a bottle of brandy suggests that perhaps they have decided to help the couple. At the end of the story, when the two men look at the sky to see if they can see a bright star, the reader might wonder if the two men are beginning to question some of their biases.

GUIDELINES FOR ASSESSING STUDENT WRITING

Think of a simple classic story that you have enjoyed in the past. It could be a fairy tale like "Cinderella," or a folk tale like "Paul Bunyan and Babe, the Blue Ox," or any other famous story that you have enjoyed. Rewrite the story in your own words, set it in the present, and substitute new characters for the old ones. However, leave most of the plot essentially the same. As you prepare your story, ask yourself these questions: What elements of the classic story will I use? What elements will I ignore? How will I end the story?

Other fairy tales or children's stories that might be good sources include "The Three Little Pigs," "Hansel and Gretel," "The Little Engine That Could," and "Little Red Riding Hood." You might also suggest the Old Testament of the Bible as a good source of possibilities—Adam and Eve in the Garden of Eden, Noah and the Flood, and Daniel in the Lion's Den, for example. Emphasize that students should select simple stories to rework and assess their efforts on their clarity of expression and their ability to follow the requirements of the assignment.

JAMES D. RUBADIRI

Stanley Meets Mutesa

SUMMARY

This poem describes Henry Morton Stanley's expedition to the kingdom of Buganda and his meeting with King Mutesa. Background for the poem is included in a headnote. In the early stanzas we learn of the hardships of the expedition—the heat of day, the chill of night, the sweaty bodies, and the loss of both animals and humans. As the expedition gets closer to its destination, "Hearts beat faster / Loads felt lighter" and thoughts turn to the welcome they will receive at Mutesa's court. When the expedition arrives, however, Stanley and his men are greeted in a subdued way. The Buganda community is unsure of what to expect. Then the gates are flung open and the tall black king grabs Stanley's hand and whispers "White man you are welcome." With that gesture "the West is let in" to the kingdom of Buganda.

GUIDELINES FOR DISCUSSION QUESTIONS

1. **Study the title of the poem and the headnote that precedes it. Who is the focus in stanza three, lines 23–26? Who is the focus in the last stanza, lines 55–60?**

   Henry Morton Stanley, the leader of the expedition, is the focus in stanza three. King Mutesa of Buganda is the focus in the last stanza.

2. **The obvious or surface meaning of line 6—"They bound for a kingdom"—is that the expedition was headed in the direction of King Mutesa's kingdom. Based on what you learned in the headnote of the poem, what further meaning might the poet imply by using the construction "bound for"?**

   The word *bound* can also mean "determined" or "resolved." The poet might be implying that the expedition was determined to acquire the kingdom.

3. **In the fifth stanza, the speaker reports that Stanley's party received a subdued welcome because "the country was not sure." What do you think the country was not sure of?**

They were not sure how to welcome the strangers. They had no way of knowing whether or not the expedition was a friendly one.

4. What is the literal meaning of the last line, "And the West is let in"? What is the symbolic significance of this line?

The literal meaning of the last line is that this expedition from the Western world has been let in to the Buganda community. The symbolic significance of the line is that the values of the Western world have been imposed on the Buganda community.

GUIDELINES FOR ASSESSING STUDENT WRITING

Have you ever had the desire to explore an unknown part of the world or at least a part of the world with which you are unfamiliar? If you were given the opportunity to go on an expedition, where would you go and what would you hope to accomplish? Write a short essay in which you explain what kind of expedition you would undertake, why you would choose such an expedition, and what you would hope to learn.

To help students think of places they might consider, direct attention to a world map. Point out places such as the upper regions of Canada, Greenland, South America, Africa, the Middle East, Russia, Asia, the Pacific Rim, and so on. Also ask students to think about how they would organize their expedition. Would they travel with a group, just a few friends, or alone? Would their goal be to study a culture, the habitat of some exotic animals, or the geography and history of a particular place? Assess students' essays on the clarity of their ideas and expression.

MABEL SEGUN

Poems

SUMMARY

In the poem "The Pigeon-Hole" the speaker wishes she could figure out who she is. Just when she thinks she knows, she has changed. She mentions a woman she knew who constantly worried about her delinquent child getting into trouble. She was in constant fear. If only she knew for certain. The speaker feels the same way. Her past, present, and future tug at her—sometimes with equal power. At those times she wishes for a pigeon-hole—a place where she would know for sure who she is.

In "Conflict" the speaker, probably speaking about the experiences of emerging black nations or emerging social classes, describes her people as "infants overblown"—in other words, adults but still infants in many ways. The speaker says her people are poised between two civilizations, between the past and the future. They long for something to happen to tip the balance, but there is no helping hand. They are temporarily caught in the middle and have no where to go.

GUIDELINES FOR DISCUSSION QUESTIONS

1. What is the meaning of *pigeon-hole* in line 1 of "The Pigeon-Hole"? What does the speaker say about herself in this stanza?

The dictionary definition of *pigeon-hole* that applies to this context is "to assign to a definite place in an orderly system." The speaker wishes that she knew exactly who she is but by the time she has figured it out she has already changed.

2. What does the speaker say about herself in the third stanza? What do you think "delinquent self" means in line 20?

She recognizes that she has three selves: an old, tested one; a present one; and a future one. All three have influence on her, which makes her long for a pigeon-hole—a single identity. *Delinquent* can mean "guilty of an offense or wrongdoing," but it can also mean "something that is past due." Perhaps the speaker is saying that she wonders what the self that she should be aiming for—her past-due self—would do if it were in control of her behavior. It is possible that the first meaning of *delinquent* is also intended. In this sense the speaker would be referring to her irresponsible self.

3. **Stanza 2 represents an interruption in the poem. Here the speaker talks about a woman she knows. Do you think this stanza adds anything to the poem, or does it detract from the poem as a whole? Explain your opinion.**

Some students may wonder why this apparent digression in stanza 2 was included. It seems to be about something completely different. Other students will notice that the two women's fears are identical. They both wait in fear for something to happen; they both wish they knew for certain what will happen. In this sense, the ideas in stanza 2 reinforce those in stanzas 1 and 3.

4. **Explain line 2 of "Conflict." What is an "infant overblown"?**

An infant overblown is a grown-up person—or a person still growing up—who still retains some of his or her infant self. Even though we have matured, all of us are influenced by behaviors and beliefs we had as children. Here it can also mean an adult who is experiencing a new situation and therefore is like an infant.

5. **This poem can be thought of as being a complaint from an emerging black nation or a complaint from an emerging social class. With this in mind, explain the first 8 lines.**

The speaker suggests that her people are poised between two ways of life, the past old one and a future new one. The speaker waits for something to happen and looks for a helping hand, but there is none.

6. **In line 10, what is "the middle way"?**

It is neither the old ways nor the new ways. It is an uncomfortable combination of both.

7. **In what ways are the ideas in this poem similar to those in "The Pigeon-Hole"?**

The speakers in both poems feel trapped in a state of flux. They both seek help, one a pigeon-hole, the other a helping hand. Both worry about the past and future. Both are concerned over how to act. They are looking for the right direction for their lives.

GUIDELINES FOR ASSESSING STUDENT WRITING

It is likely that in these two poems Mabel Segun's point of reference is her daily life in Nigeria and her political knowledge of the emerging nations of Africa, but the ideas in these poems also have universal applications. Do you ever find yourself being influenced by your past—your behavior and beliefs when you were younger? On the other hand, do you also find yourself thinking about the future and what it will bring? Write a short essay in which you assess your growth as an individual at this point in your life. Discuss to what extent you are still influenced by your past and what your worries about and hopes for the future are.

Students' essays on the above subject are likely to be quite varied. To get them thinking about this topic, ask them what they like most about their daily lives and how much of that represents a carryover from their younger years. Then ask them to think about the future. How do they envision their lives changing? What changes do they look forward to? What changes cause them to worry? Assess students' essays on the clarity of their ideas and expression.

LÉOPOLD SÉDAR SENGHOR

Poems

SUMMARY

In "Prayer to the Masks" the speaker addresses his tribal ancestors. He tells them that colonialism is dying and asks them to watch over his people as they help transform the new Africa—as they renew their dedication to their tribal heritage.

In "Night of Sine" a tribal couple rest after an evening of community activity. The speaker urges his wife to reflect on their ancestors—to listen to their voices—before they go to sleep.

In "Be Not Amazed" the speaker warns his wife not to be amazed if something should happen to him when he exchanges the peace of home for war drums. He hints that he may die. It is possible that the "beloved" Senghor is addressing this poem to is Africa itself.

DISCUSSION QUESTIONS

1. Note the title of "Prayer to the Masks." Who are the masks to whom this poem is addressed?

They are the ancestors of the speaker, the ancestors of tribal Africa. Clues to their identity are provided in lines 2, 5, 7, and 9.

2. What message does the speaker bring to the masks?

He announces that Africa of the empires (colonial Africa) is dying, and he asks that the ancestors fix their eyes on the people of Africa so that the people will be able to participate in the rebirth of Africa.

3. Explain the simile in lines 15-16.

In lines 15–16 the people of Africa (we) contribute to the rebirth of the world in the same way that leaven is needed to turn flour into bread. Note the secondary meaning of *leaven* in the footnote: "an element that produces an altering or transforming influence." The people will help transform Africa in the same way that leaven transforms flour.

4. In line 22, what do you think "we are the men of dance" means?

The speaker is referring to dance as a part of tribal ritual. He is identifying his people as tribal Africans.

5. Describing the peace of his tribal home in "Night of Sine," Senghor remembers earlier members of the tribe who, like himself, had wandered far. What situation is described in the first two stanzas of this poem?

A man and woman are resting in their hut after an evening of tribal activities. The bursts of laughter have grown sleepy; the storytellers are nodding their heads; the feet of the dancers grow heavy, as do the voices of the choruses; and the fire dies out.

6. Note line 16. What do you think "Like us, exiled" might be a reference to? (See footnote 3 and Senghor's biography for help.)

Elissa is a village in Guinea, which was once controlled by Portugal. On one level Senghor may be suggesting that the ancients were exiled from both Guinea and Senegal when the colonial powers took over. On another level he may be referring to his own long residence in France as a sort of exile.

7. In lines 5–6 and in the last stanza, what does the speaker recommend that he and his beloved do before falling asleep?

He suggests that they pay attention and respect to their tribal heritage, listening "to the beat of our dark blood," "to the deep pulse of Africa," to the voices of their ancestors, and to the living voice of their dead.

8. In "Be Not Amazed," why may the speaker's song grow dark?

The speaker warns his beloved that he may soon go to war.

9. What does the speaker predict might happen to him?

He predicts that by tomorrow his voice may be silent forever, that perhaps he will fall in battle—in other words, die.

10. Senghor's poetry often voices a nostalgia for an Africa that because of colonialism and changing cultures is rapidly disappearing. With this idea in mind, what other meaning can you find in the poem?

The speaker may be confiding that he needs to fight against colonialism in an effort to preserve the Africa of the ancient deities and that this effort may cost him his life. This poem was published in 1949, after Senghor's service in the French army. It is possible that his reference to war in this poem is a reference to World War II—the white man's war. In either event, the loss would be the same. By extension, it might be suggested that the "beloved" whom Senghor is addressing here is Africa itself, the Africa of his ancestors.

GUIDELINES FOR ASSESSING STUDENT WRITING

As one of the Negritude poets (see page xvii), Léopold Senghor believed strongly in rediscovering the cultural values of Africa. Reread "Prayer to the Masks," "Night of Sine," and "Be Not Amazed." Then write a short essay explaining how each of these poems deals with the theme of rediscovering the cultural values of Africa. Support your ideas with evidence from each poem.

Students should be able to find ample evidence in these three poems of the theme of rediscovering the cultural values of Africa. In "Prayer to the Masks" the prayer is addressed to the speaker's ancestors. He is asking for their help (presence) as his people attempt to rebuild Africa. He rejects the colonial world of marching and cannons and identifies his people as "men of dance," that is, men true to their tribal traditions. In "Night of Sine" the speaker urges his wife to listen to their ancestors, to the beat of their dark blood, to the deep pulse of Africa. He refers to his ancestors as "welcome spirits" in his hut and says that he wants to recall and repeat their living voice. In "Be Not Amazed" the speaker comforts his wife and prepares her for his possible death in battle. The battle he refers to may be a reference to World War II, the white man's war, or to a battle closer to home, perhaps against colonial powers. Either way, it is possible that the "beloved" whom Senghor is addressing in "Be Not Amazed" is Africa itself, the "black beauty" of his tribal ancestors. Assess students essays on the clarity of the ideas and their expression and on how well students support their ideas with evidence from the poems.

WOLE SOYINKA

Poems

SUMMARY

In "Fado Singer" the speaker addresses his comments to the fado singer, a singer of mournful folk songs. He tells the singer that he is profoundly affected by his music. His skin is pumiced by it. It reaches down to his hair roots. The torment in the music brings tears to his eyes. There is anguish and too much pain in it. In the last six lines the speaker longs to be free from the music's influence.

"Season" is a celebration of late summer when rust on the wilted corn plume means the corn is ripe. The speaker describes swallows weaving their way through the fields of corn stalks. The speaker and his fellow garnerers (farmers) await the rust on the tassels and what it promises—a bountiful harvest of ripe corn.

In "I Think It Rains" the speaker likens the falling of rain to some form of intellectual and perhaps spiritual renewal. I think it rains, the speaker says, so that tongues may become heavy with knowledge—in other words that people may learn something. Lines 5–8 offer a physical description of the sight of falling rain on the ashes of a fire raising up a cloud of ash dust. The speaker goes on to say that it must rain in order to open up the closures of the mind, which bind us in despair and sadness. Rain also sears (scorches, or perhaps exposes) our dark longings. In the last four lines, the speaker says that rain reeds (the thin lines of rain seen in a steady downpour) may yield (to the wind for example) but they are relentless, even baring crouching (half hidden) rocks close to the ground.

GUIDELINES FOR DISCUSSION QUESTIONS

1. **If the "I" in the poem is the speaker, who is the "you"? (Note especially lines 4 and 9–10.)**

   The "you" mentioned in the title is the fado singer.

2. **What is the effect of the singer's music on the speaker? Cite words and phrases from the poem to support your opinion.**

   The speaker is profoundly affected by the music. It has a painful hold on him, and he longs to be free from its influence (line 19). The music holds the "grief of gods" (line 5). The speaker is moved to tears (line 6). The music brings him to "the throne of anguish" (line 11). It brings with it "too much pain" (line 16).

3. What is the season celebrated in this poem? What words suggest this time of year?

The season is summer, probably late summer. Rust is ripeness, that is, the discoloration on the silk of an ear of corn or on the corn tassels indicates that the corn is ripe. The "garnerers" are getting ready to harvest the corn. The "wilted corn-plume" and "laden stalks" also help indicate the time of year.

4. In line 16, what is "the promise of the rust"?

It is the harvesting of the ripe corn.

5. In line 1 why does the speaker think it rains?

It rains so that tongues may become heavy with knowledge. This might be one way of saying that it rains so that we might learn something.

6. In line 9 why does the speaker say it must rain?

It must rain to open up closures in the mind that bind us in despair.

7. What are reeds? What might rain-reeds be?

Reeds are the straight stalks of any tall grasses. Rain-reeds might be the thin lines of rain one observes falling vertically during a downpour.

8. Do you think rain is being used symbolically in this poem? Explain.

Yes. it seems that the speaker is saying that certain things (rain) happen in life to teach us lessons, open our eyes, illuminate things around us.

GUIDELINES FOR ASSESSING STUDENT WRITING

For poet Wole Soyinka rain is a good thing, or it can lead to good things. What is your general reaction to rain? Do you view it as a nuisance? Does it make you feel sad? Do you consider it a necessary evil? Are there any times when rain makes you feel happy? Write one or two

paragraphs in which you describe your own reactions to rain. How many different reactions do you have? Be sure to explain the circumstances for each one.

Students should have little or no trouble finding something to say on this subject. Many will identify with the sadness or depression that rain brings, particularly when it spoils someone's plans for an outing of some kind. Some students will have difficulty understanding how rain can bring on happy feelings. For them, suggest the cooling effects of a sudden thunder shower on a stifling, humid summer afternoon, or the warm, cozy feeling of curling up inside with a good book on a damp, dreary spring afternoon. Remind students to include not only their reactions to rain but also the different kinds of circumstances that elicit those reactions.

EFUA T. SUTHERLAND

Edufa

SUMMARY

Prologue and Act One

The setting is Edufa's estate, both outer and inner courtyard. Edufa is a prominent businessman, popular in his community. In the Prologue, his sister Abena finishes collecting dew for her brother, a three-day effort to help him combat some unspecified problem. She wonders why he has shut the gates of the estate to keep out the community. His wife, Ampoma, is ill and could use the support of friends. Edufa tells Abena nothing, and she feels sad. In act one, scene 1, Edufa emerges from his bedroom, agitated. A chorus of women is nearby, and he fears they have come to sing a funeral dirge for his wife. He accuses Seguwa, an elderly resident of the estate, of revealing Ampoma's illness. She denies his charge but begs him to get help for his wife. He asks Seguwa to keep what she knows to herself. In scene 2 Ampoma appears and almost falls down. Edufa assures her that she will be okay by tomorrow. Ampoma fears she is dying and begs Edufa to take care of the children and not marry again. He agrees but assures her she will be okay. Then he laments that she should never have made that fateful promise, the first indication in the play that Ampoma has done something which is controlling her fate. In scene 3 Seguwa bitterly blames Edufa for Ampoma's troubles. In scene 4 Edufa's father Kankam tries to reason with his son. He reveals the tragic events that endanger Ampoma's life. Edufa had learned from a diviner that he was to die unless someone, in the presence of a potent charm, would agree to sacrifice his or her own life instead. Edufa obtained the charm and Ampoma innocently agreed to sacrifice her life, unaware that the hidden charm made her promise binding. Kankam begs Edufa to own up to his responsibilities in order to save his wife, but Edufa throws his father out after warning him not to reveal what he knows.

Act Two

In scene 1 the chorus of women come to Edufa's estate to drive evil away. Edufa welcomes them, and they perform their rite. Shortly after this, Edufa learns that Ampoma is better. In scene 2 Edufa's friend Senchi arrives for a visit. The chorus leaves after Senchi gets Edufa to promise that they can return for a party that night. Senchi then goes off to rest. Edufa's slave Sam returns from a trip to an oracle. He give Edufa three tasks to perform, including burning a charm, to break the spell on Ampoma. Edufa is elated that he now apparently has the means to save his wife.

Act Three
In scene 1 Edufa and Senchi have a serious talk before the party begins. Edufa discusses his postion as an important leader in the community. Senchi makes fun of himself as an irresponsible wandering troubadour. In scene 2 Edufa gives flowers to his sister to take to Ampoma, and Senchi sings a song of tribute to Ampoma. Ampoma informs her husband and Senchi that she will join them later. In scene 3 Senchi flirts with the chorus and performs for them. Ampoma appears and seems to be out of sorts. She almost falls down. Edufa proposes a toast to Ampoma. Ampoma expresses her love for Edufa by presenting him with a beautiful set of beads. Ampoma excuses herself, and as she leaves, she falls again. Seguwa breaks down, fearing the worst, and tells Senchi of her concerns. She then checks Ampoma's bedroom and discovers that Ampoma has died. Edufa comes out from the bedroom also, and Senchi and the chorus beg him to divulge what has happened. Slowly Edufa explains that Ampoma is dead and then, madness taking over, he runs off. Senchi is left by himself to mourn the tragic scene.

GUIDELINES FOR DISCUSSION QUESTIONS

1. **According to the classical definition of a tragic hero, the protagonist is a person better than ourselves who through some error in judgment, weakness of character, or twist of fate suffers crushing defeat or death. Explain how the character Edufa fits this definition.**

Edufa is a wealthy and highly respected businessman in his community. His error in judgment coupled with a twist of fate both occur before the play begins. Wanting security for himself, Edufa consulted a diviner who told him he was scheduled to die. However, by obtaining a powerful charm, Edufa could avert death if someone would sacrifice himself or herself in Edufa's place. Edufa foolishly obtains the charm, never considering that his precious wife Ampoma would be the one to agree to sacrifice herself. During the play Ampoma does become ill and Edufa tries everything in his power to prevent the inevitable, including obtaining more magical charms, but he cannot reverse what fate has set in place and Ampoma does die.

2. **Might Ampoma also fit the classical definition of a tragic hero? Explain your answer.**

Students will probably recognize that in some respects Ampoma does fit the definition. Certainly she more readily engages the sympathies of readers for her selfless behavior in the face of her husband's more obvious selfishness. And it is obvious that she is a victim of a cruel twist of fate, for which she dies. But it would be difficult to accuse her of any error in judgment and impossible to accuse her of a weakness of character. Her fateful promise was founded on pure, innocent love.

3. **From the very beginning of the play to the end, the fear of Ampoma's death hangs like a dark cloud over the proceedings. Does this fact make her eventual death more, or less, tragic— more, or less, painful to accept? Explain your opinion.**

Students might be tempted to assume that because the foreshadowing of Ampoma's death is so strong throughout the play, her actual death at the end would be anticlimatic or at least easier to take than otherwise might be thought. Don't be surprised, however, if students argue that her death is more tragic, more painful. Throughout the play, Ampoma's innocence and her devoted love for her husband are emphasized again and again. As a result, her death seems cruel and unfair. Even though it is ordained by fate, many students might confess that they were hoping some force would intervene to save Ampoma.

4. **Contrast Seguwa and Senchi. What purpose does each serve in the play?**

Seguwa seems to be the official voice of doom in the play. She serves as Edufa's voice of conscience. She constantly reminds him of his responsibility for the events that are happening and she repeats over and over her concerns for Ampoma and Ampoma's fate. When she is on stage, the anxiety level of the action increases. Senchi seems to stand for the forces of mirth and life. His joking with Edufa and with the chorus of women provides moments of comic relief in the otherwise serious play. Senchi is a comic figure who is not above making fun of himself. He looks for fun in life—sometimes at the expense of more responsible endeavors, but his intentions are good. He is a devoted friend to both Edufa and Ampoma, and when Ampoma dies at the end Senchi is left to say "Blank. I have ended up blank once again." Senchi's comic presence in the play makes the tragedy at the end even more compelling.

5. *Edufa* **is based on the Greek legend of Admetus and Alcestis, which is immortalized in Euripedes' play** *Alcestis*. **Find in your school library a plot summary of** *Alcestis* **(either in a book of**

famous literary plots or in an encyclopedia like *Encyclopaedia Britannica*). Read the plot summary and then explain the major difference between it and *Edufa*.

The plot lines are very similar. In the Greek legend, King Admetus is destined to die unless someone else dies in his place. His wife Alcestis makes the sacrifice. However Heracles fights death and saves Alcestis. King Admetus then persuades the gods to let both him and his wife live. In *Edufa*, of course, no one saves Ampoma. Senchi is the equivalent of the Heracles character, but as he says at the end, "I have ended up blank once again."

GUIDELINES FOR ASSESSING STUDENT WRITING

In the original Greek legend upon which *Edufa* is based, Alcestis, the equivalent of Ampoma, is rescued in the end and saved from death. Can you do the same for Ampoma? Can you figure out a way to come to her aid and bring a happy ending to *Edufa*? Create a new ending for *Edufa* in which some force for good—either an existing character in the play or a new one you add to the cast—rescues Ampoma from death. For the sake of simplicity, deal only with the events that happen near the end of the play—perhaps the last half of the last scene— and create your new ending in prose. If you would prefer the challenge of writing dramatic dialogue, you may do so, but it is not mandatory.

Encourage students to have fun with this writing assignment. Who will come to the fore to save Ampoma? Will Edufa find new moral courage and offer himself in Ampoma's place? Will the spirits be appeased and spare Edufa too? What powers for good might Senchi offer, or Seguwa, or Abena? What about Ampoma herself? Can her purity of love be her savior? Might someone from the outside—a new character—save the day? How might the chorus of women help introduce this new element to the plot? Students should enjoy working with the variety of possibilities for this assignment. Assess students' efforts on the basis of the creativity of their solutions and the clarity of their expression.

TSEGAYE GABRE-MEDHIN

Home-Coming Son

SUMMARY

The speaker in this poem addresses a "stranger" who is returning home. The speaker welcomes the stranger home and encourages the stranger to get "out of your foreign outfit" and "walk tall" and "walk proud" in the "motherland." The speaker concludes by encouraging the stranger (lost son) to reestablish his home roots. The speaker is probably addressing a native African who has spent a great deal of time outside Africa, perhaps in a western country.

GUIDELINES FOR DISCUSSION QUESTIONS

1. What color is emphasized in this poem? Find four places in the poem where the color is mentioned or alluded to? Why do you think the speaker emphasizes this color?

The color black is emphasized in the poem. It is mentioned in line 3 and line 15 and is alluded to in line 4 (dark side of the moon) and in line 35 (shine ebony). By emphasizing the color black, the speaker is drawing attention to the stranger's African roots.

2. Note the title "Home-Coming Son" and the three references in the poem to a "stranger." Who is coming home? Where is home? Where do you think the stranger has been?

An African is coming home to Africa. He has probably been out of the country a long time, long enough to become a stranger. Perhaps this poem is autobiographical. Tsegaye spent many years studying in the United States and Europe before he returned home to Ethiopia.

3. In the poem the speaker is addressing the stranger. What is the speaker trying to tell the stranger?

He welcomes the stranger home and wants him to shed his "foreign outfit" (perhaps the foreign ways he has learned) and reestablish his

African roots by embracing the spirits of his homeland. In other words, the speaker wants the stranger to reestablish his African identity.

GUIDELINES FOR ASSESSING STUDENT WRITING

Have you ever spent a relatively long period of time away from your home and friends? Perhaps you moved to another part of the country for a while. Perhaps you spent a year studying abroad or part of a summer at a camp. How did it feel to get back home? Were you happy? disoriented? Did you feel out-of-it for a time? Did you have to readjust? Write a few paragraphs in which you describe how it felt to be back home. If you haven't experienced such a situation, imagine what it would be like to leave home for a period of time and write about that. What do you take for granted at home? What would you miss most? What would you most enjoy about being away?

If students have trouble thinking of an appropriate situation to write about for the first option, take some time to brainstorm a few more possibilities—for example, returning home from a long hospitalization or after living with your relatives or after an extended vacation. Students who choose the second option should be encouraged to consider all aspects of their daily life. What would change if they moved away from home? What would remain the same? Would moving away be a positive or a negative experience? Regardless of which option students choose, assess their writing on the basis of clarity of description and creative use of sensory detail.

MATALA MUKADI TSHAKATUMBA

Message to Mputu Antoinette, Girl of the Bush, Friend of My Childhood

SUMMARY

"Message to Mputu Antoinette, Girl of the Bush, Friend of My Childhood" is a poem addressed to a beautiful black woman whom the author knew as a child. In addressing her directly as his "African sister" and describing her in terms of African plants and animals, he associates her closely with Africa itself. He warns her, and at the same time Africa, that though she is enchantingly beautiful, she is ignorant and has much to learn. The author ends on a hopeful note—that Africa will be "what together we make it."

GUIDELINES FOR DISCUSSION QUESTIONS

1. **Make a list of all of the nature imagery that you find in this poem. What do you think is the author's purpose in using it?**

   "Water," "spring," "sapodilla tree," "fruit," "gazelle," "thicket," "wood," "blue wave," "lianas," and "lokumé" are all examples of nature imagery found in the poem. There is also a reference to the Garden of Eden ("Edenic smile").
   Students should recognize that the poet uses nature imagery to express his delight in the enchanting beauty of the woman, but also to link her with Africa, which is also beautiful. Some perceptive students may also notice that the vegetative imagery (references to trees, vines, and fruit) connotes growth. The author uses it to show that Africa must grow to become "what together we make it."

2. **This poem is a typical example of the verse of the Negritude school (see page xvii). One common theme of this movement is that of Africans in exile. What details in the poem suggest that Tshakatumba is in exile?**

   The best clue that Tshakatumba is in exile is his mention of the cold that "benumbs" him. The author finds himself in a colder climate than what he is used to. Other, more subtle, clues are the fact that he is sending a "message" to someone who must now be far away. The reference to his childhood ("friend of my childhood") also suggests a distance—but one of time rather than space.

3. **For many of the Negritude poets, the black woman symbolizes Africa. How would you characterize the poet's attitude toward his childhood friend and the Africa she represents?**

The author clearly finds both his friend and Africa touchingly and enchantingly beautiful, and he says this directly (line 17). He uses nature imagery extensively to describe the beauty of both the friend and Africa. He is gently critical, however, in that he feels that the friend and Africa "do not know," "must learn," and "are ignorant." He is hopeful that both Mputu and Africa can be brought out of what he sees as the "half-light."

GUIDELINES FOR ASSESSING STUDENT WRITING

Tshakatumba makes good use of two poetic devices in this poem: parallelism and epithet. *Parallelism* is the repeated use of the same grammatical structure:
> you who do not know . . .
> you who must learn . . .
> you who are ignorant . . .

An *epithet* is an adjective or adjective phrase used to describe or characterize a person or thing:
> sister of the sapodilla tree . . .
> tireless gazelle . . .

Write a short poem to a friend of your childhood (or to anyone else who is important to you) focusing on that person's good qualities and the pleasant memories you have of your time together. Pattern your poem after Tshakatumba's by using parallelism and epithet.

This exercise is intended to help students familiarize themselves with two common poetic devices. Since the poem they write will be personal and unique to each student, the guidelines for its successful completion are fairly simple. Students should employ constructions that are in fact parallel. (Although Tshakatumba uses parallel construction to convey somewhat negative views, students will be providing positive ones.) The epithet(s) should be used to describe or characterize the person who is the focus of the poem. In order to encourage students to create fresh constructions and epithets, it may be helpful to conduct a brainstorming session in which students generate new examples before they begin writing their own poems.

AMOS TUTUOLA

Animal That Died But His Eyes Still Alive

SUMMARY

This story follows the travels of Adebisi, the African huntress, as she seeks to resolve the "three big troubles" of the jungle. She hopes to do this by driving away the pygmies (who detain hunters), killing dangerous animals with "light on eyes," and killing the dangerous boa constrictor.

As she travels through the jungle, she kills nearly all the wild animals in it. After a week she encounters a terrible beast as large as an elephant. The animal is remarkable for his eyes, which are large and shine with their own clear light. This "super-animal" is so fearsome that the animals he preys upon die of fright before he even reaches them.

The animal charges her, and she, realizing that it is impossible to kill the beast with one shot, quickly climbs a tree. The beast bites the tree until it falls, and the huntress jumps to another tree. The angry animal attacks the second tree, and the huntress shoots him. Enraged, he thrashes around and then charges the huntress. She defends herself with a cutlass and causes him to ram his horns into a tree stump. She then kills him with a poisonous cudgel.

She continues on her journey, killing animals and seeking the boa constrictor. When she travels back to the place where the "super-animal" was killed, she notices that although his flesh is rotting away, the light of his eyes is still alive. She then takes the head and fashions it into a kind of helmet. While wearing the helmet, she is like the animal was when he was alive. She uses the head as a light at night and wears it whenever she is hunting.

GUIDELINES FOR DISCUSSION QUESTIONS

1. **Early in the story, Adebisi explains that she must kill the dangerous animals who had "light on eyes." What do you think this phrase means?**

   There are various possible interpretations of this term. The "light on eyes" could refer to the reflective quality of the eyes of some animals, most notably cats. The reference might then be to large predators such as lions and leopards. The term may also have connections to evil spirits or mythical beasts.

2. **What is the purpose of Adebisi's quest in this story? In other words, what does she hope to achieve? Is she successful?**

Adebesi explains that she hopes to resolve three "big troubles" by driving the pygmies from the jungle and killing both the dangerous animals with "light on eyes" and the dangerous boa constrictor.

She is successful to a limited degree. By the end of the story, she has killed the wild animals so that there is no more fear of them. She is still seeking the boa when she comes upon the rotted remains of the "super-animal." When she wears the helmet she has fashioned from his head, she takes on the animal's power. Although her triumph over the "super-animal" was not part of her original quest, she views the head as a "very useful thing." The question of the pygmies is not addressed again in the story. (Note that students interested in ecological and conservation issues may have difficulty accepting her attitudes and actions.)

3. Both Tutuola's story and D. O. Fagunwa's "The Forest of the Lord" (p. 109) are fantastic tales about hunters and quests. How would you compare the tones of these two narratives?

The tone of Tutuola's story will probably strike most students as lighter and more playful than that of Fagunwa's.

GUIDELINES FOR ASSESSING STUDENT WRITING

At one time Tutuola's fellow Nigerians criticized him for using what they considered imperfect English. Try rewriting some of Tutuola's shorter paragraphs, this time using Standard English. What has been gained or lost by doing this? Which version do you prefer?

The Standard English versions should be simpler, easier to follow, and less ambiguous in some cases. Students may find, however, that their revisions of Tutuola's prose diminish the charming, energetic, and naïve quality of his narrator's voice.

Don't Pay Bad for Bad

SUMMARY

This tale describes the relationship of two best friends, Dola and Babi. Girlfriends since childhood, the young women even contrive to marry two brothers and live in the same household.

Soon after the wedding, Dola plants a kola-nut tree. She tends it carefully and comes to believe that it is inhabited by a benevolent spirit. After a few months, Babi notices that animals have started eating the leaves of the tree and stunting its growth. She gives the head of a large pitcher to Dola to put over the tree to protect it from the hungry animals.

The tree flourishes and produces crop after crop of high-quality kola nuts, which Dola sells, becoming a wealthy woman in the process. In a fit of jealousy, Babi demands that the head of the pitcher be returned to her unbroken. Since this is impossible now that the tree has grown, and believing that Babi only wants to destroy the tree, Dola appeals to a court of law. The judge orders the tree cut down and the pitcher returned to Babi.

Not long afterward Babi gives birth to a baby girl. Dola gives Babi a seamless brass ring as a present to put around the baby's neck. Ten years pass. On the girl's birthday, Dola comes to Babi and demands the ring back uncut. Since the girl's head is now larger than the ring, this is impossible to do without beheading the child. Despite Babi's pleadings, Dola insists. Again, the matter is brought before a judge. The judge rules that the child must be killed at the king's palace in the presence of the villagers to show that jealousy is bad. As the swordsman raises his sword to behead the girl, Dola stops him. She explains that her quarrel is with the mother, not the child, and that "if we continue to pay bad for bad, bad will never finish on earth." With this, Dola forgives Babi for killing the kola-nut tree, and the two remain good friends for the rest of their lives.

GUIDELINES FOR DISCUSSION QUESTIONS

1. Compare your ideas about the concepts of giving and friendship with those expressed in the story.

It is apparently an accepted fact in the story that a gift, even one freely given, can be recalled at the giver's request. (Note that Dola pleads to the judge that Babi really only wants to see the tree destroyed. Nevertheless, he rules that the gift must be returned.)

The two friends in the story like each other so well and value each other's company so much that they contrive to live their married lives in the same household. Babi offers her friend help (another function of friendship) in solving the problem when animals begin eating Dola's kola-nut tree. Despite the jealousy that surfaces and the ensuing two legal battles, the two women remain life-long friends.

Students will probably express the idea that a gift is truly a gift and cannot be reclaimed. They will offer a variety of positive traits that they feel are important in a friendship and may question whether any actual friendship could endure the events in this story.

2. As "Don't Pay Bad for Bad" approached its climax, were you fearful about the outcome? Did the resolution of the story satisfy you?

Most students probably do not expect the child to be beheaded. Most will also probably feel that the story effectively makes its moral point.

3. In a famous Old Testament story about the wisdom of King Solomon (see 1 Kings 3), two women both claim the same newborn child. Solomon offers to cut the child in half; horrified, the real mother surrenders her claim, whereupon Solomon awards her the infant. How is "Don't Pay Bad for Bad" like and unlike the biblical narrative?

In both the biblical narrative and in Tutuola's fable, an innocent child's life hinges on the outcome of a dispute; in the Old Testament story it is Solomon who engineers the solution; in Tutuola's fable it is not the judge, but one of the two disputants.

GUIDELINES FOR ASSESSING STUDENT WRITING

Imagine that you are a new judge in Dola and Babi's village, sent to replace the previous judge. The two friends have come to you with their dispute over the return of the brass ring that is now around the neck of Babi's young daughter. Knowing what you know about the details of this case, what would your decision be? Write an "opinion" explaining your thinking.

If students have participated in the class discussion before they write their opinions, they should have come to some general conclusions. If their opinion states that Dola should win the case, they will need to describe how the ring can be returned. (It is unlikely that students will order the sacrifice of the innocent child unless they plan to stop the execution at the last minute to make their point.) If their opinion states that Babi should win, they will need to explain why the social rule (of returning gifts on demand) does not apply in this case or should be broken, especially since Babi benefited from the law in the matter of the kola-nut tree. Some students may suggest various penalties or restitution levied against Babi, Dola, or both women.